International Papers in Political Economy

Series Editors
Philip Arestis
Department of Land Economy
University of Cambridge
Cambridge, UK

Malcolm Sawyer
University of Leeds
Leeds, UK

This series consists of an annual volume with a single theme. The objective of the IPPE is the publication of papers dealing with important topics within the broad framework of Political Economy.

The original series of *International Papers in Political Economy* started in 1993, until the new series began in 2005, and was published in the form of three issues a year with each issue containing a single extensive paper. Information on the old series and back copies can be obtained from the editors: Philip Arestis (pa267@cam.ac.uk) and Malcolm Sawyer (e-mail: mcs@lubs.leeds.ac.uk).

More information about this series at
http://www.palgrave.com/gp/series/14844

Philip Arestis • Malcolm Sawyer
Editors

Economic Policies for a Post-Neoliberal World

palgrave
macmillan

Editors
Philip Arestis
Department of Land Economy
University of Cambridge
Cambridge, UK

University of Basque Country UPV/EHU
Leioa, Spain

Malcolm Sawyer
University of Leeds, Leeds, UK

International Papers in Political Economy
ISBN 978-3-030-56734-7 ISBN 978-3-030-56735-4 (eBook)
https://doi.org/10.1007/978-3-030-56735-4

This Palgrave Macmillan imprint is published by the registered company Springer Nature Switzerland AG.
The registered company address is: Gewerbestrasse 11, 6330 Cham, Switzerland

Preface

This is the seventeenth volume of the series of *International Papers in Political Economy* (*IPPE*). This series consists of an annual volume with eight papers on a single theme. The objective of the *IPPE* is the publication of papers dealing with important topics within the broad framework of Political Economy.

The original series of *International Papers in Political Economy* started in 1993 until the new series began in 2005 and was published in the form of three issues a year with each issue containing a single extensive paper. Information on the old series and back copies can be obtained from the editors: Philip Arestis (e-mail: pa267@cam.ac.uk) and Malcolm Sawyer (e-mail: m.c.sawyer@lubs.leeds.ac.uk).

The theme of this seventeenth volume of eight papers is Economic Policies for a Post Neo-Liberal World. The papers in this volume were scheduled to be presented in late March 2020 at a one-day conference in Cambridge, UK (Downing College), organised by the Department of Land Economy, University of Cambridge, under the aegis of the Cambridge Trust for New Thinking in Economics. The papers were intended to be presented subsequently at the annual conference, entitled *Developments in Economic Theory and Policy*, held at the University of the Basque Country, Bilbao, Spain in June 2020. These conferences had to be cancelled as a consequence on restrictions on meetings and travel in response to the COVID-19 pandemic. We are grateful to the organisers of the Cambridge Trust for New Thinking in Economics and to the organisers of the *Developments in Economic Theory and Policy* conference series, for funding and help in the organisation of annual conferences over a number of years, which have enabled presentation of the relevant papers, and subsequently published in the *International Papers in Political Economy* series.

Cambridge, UK Philip Arestis
Leeds, UK Malcolm Sawyer

Contents

1 **Financial Stability: Still Unsettled for the Future** 1
Philip Arestis

2 **The Future of Capitalism in a Post-Neoliberal World** 43
Yiannis Kitromilides

3 **Moving People in a Post-Neoliberal Era** 85
Liliana Harding

4 **Productivity Slowdown and Inequality: Killing Two Birds with One Stone!** 133
Ahmad Seyf

5 **Environmental Policies to Save the Planet** 179
Richard Lewney

6 **Public Ownership in the Pursuit of Economic Democracy in a Post-Neoliberal Order** 225
Andrew Cumbers and Helen Traill

7 **Welfare as Freedom, the Human Economy, and Varieties of Capitalist State** 269
Louise Haagh

8 **Employment and Wage Policies in a Post-Neoliberal World** 345
Simon Deakin

Index 389

Notes on Contributors

Philip Arestis is Professor and University Director of Research, Cambridge Centre for Economics and Public Policy, Department of Land Economy, University of Cambridge, UK; Professor of Economics, Department of Applied Economics V, Universidad Del País Vasco, Spain; Distinguished Adjunct Professor of Economics, Department of Economics, University of Utah, USA; Research Associate, Levy Economics Institute, New York, USA; Visiting Professor, Leeds Business School, University of Leeds, UK; Professorial Research Associate, Department of Finance and Management Studies, School of Oriental and African Studies (SOAS), University of London, UK; and a visiting fellow, Centre for Globalization Research, Queen Mary College, University of London, UK. He served (2009–2010) as economics consultant on the Central Asia Regional Economic Cooperation (CAREC) programme, under the auspices of the Asian Development Bank (ADB). He was awarded the British Hispanic Foundation 'Queen Victoria Eugenia' award (2009–2010) and the 'homage' prize for his contribution to the spread of Keynesian Economics in Brazil by the Brazilian Keynesian Association (AKB), 15 August 2013. Also, he was honoured through the Thomas Divine Award of the Association for Social Economics (ASE). This award is presented annually to an Association member who over a lifetime has made important contributions to social economics and the social economy. The award was given at the annual meeting of the ASSA, Philadelphia,

USA, at their annual meeting of 4–6 January 2018. He served as Chief Academic Adviser to the UK Government Economic Service (GES) on Professional Developments in Economics (2005–2013). He has written widely in academic journals, and he is, and has been, on the editorial board of a number of economics journals.

Andrew Cumbers is Professor of Regional Political Economy at the University of Glasgow. He has previously worked at Universities of Durham, Middlesex and Aberdeen. He has held visits at Universities of Cologne and Frankfurt and the Leibniz Institute for Urban and Regional Planning in Berlin. He has written extensively on local and regional development and more recently on economic democracy and alternative economic strategies. He is principal investigator for 'Global Remunicipalisation and the post neo-liberal turn', funded by the European Research Council, and has been recipient of many research grants. He is editor in chief of the journal *Urban Studies* and has served on the editorial board of *Work, Employment and Society*. His 2012 book *Reclaiming Public Ownership: Making Space for Economic Democracy* won the Myrdal Prize from the European Association of Evolutionary Political Economy. His forthoming book *The Case for Economic Democracy* is scheduled for publication in 2020.

Simon Deakin is Professor of Law and Director of the Centre for Business Research at the University of Cambridge. Simon Deakin specialises in the study of labour, private and company law from an interdisciplinary and empirical perspective. His books include *The Law of the Labour Market: Industrialization, Employment and Legal Evolution* (2005, with Frank Wilkinson) and *Hedge Fund Activism in Japan: The Limits of Shareholder Primacy* (2012, with John Buchanan and Dominic Heesang Chai). He has recently been an investigator on ESRC-funded projects exploring the relationship between law and development, in the course of which he carried out fieldwork in China, Russia, South Africa and India. His projects include work funded by the Global Challenges Research Fund on the effects of conflict in terms of health in the Middle East and North Africa (MENA) region. He is also researching on the impact of digital technologies in labour markets and legal systems.

Louise Haagh is Professor in Politics at the University of York. Her work looks at problems relating to social and economic justice, the ethics and politics of development, comparative capitalism and welfare states, and human development ethics and governance. A particular interest is the link between institutions and well-being and in the formative role of motivational theories and statistical measurement in comparative public policy. Louise has designed and carried out surveys on institutions of representation and economic security and well-being in middle-income countries. More recently, her work centres on governing properties of comparative welfare state evolution, with a contemporary focus on Anglo-Liberal and Nordic states. She has acted as expert on economic security for a range of international organisations, including the World Bank, the Council of Europe, the World Health Organisation, and the Organisation of American States. She is chair of the Basic income Earth Network, a global educational charity based in the UK, a fellow of the Royal Society of Arts, and patron of the Citizens Basic Income Trust.

Liliana Harding is Senior Lecturer in Economics at the University of East Anglia School of Economics, UK; Convener of the East of England Migration Research Network; member of the Applied Econometrics and Finance research group, the Environment, Resources and Conflict research group, and the University of Sanctuary steering group; Economics Network Associate, UK; Guest Lecturer at the West University of Timisoara, Romania; Associate of East-European Center for Research in Economics and Business (ECREB). She was honorary consul of Romania in Scotland (2008–2010), board member of Grampian Racial Equality Council, and lecturer in Economics Robert Gordon University in Aberdeen. Postgraduate studies at the University of the West of England, the London School of Economics (Political Economy of Transition in Europe) and the University of Oxford (PPE). She has worked for the Directorate of Employment and Social Affairs – the European Commission, Brussels and the Regional Co-operation Partnership Banat-Romania, Nordrhein-Westfalen-Germany. Her work on the economics and political economy of migration and European emerging markets has been published. She is engaged with regional and urban development and the economics of the public arts and culture, as academic advisor for Timisoara European Capital of Culture 2021.

Yiannis Kitromilides is an associate member of the Cambridge Centre of Economic and Public Policy, Department of Land Economy, University of Cambridge. He has previously taught at the University of Greenwich, the University of Westminster, the University of Middlesex and the School of Oriental and African Studies, University of London. The focus of his teaching and his main research interests have been and still are in the areas of European Monetary Integration, Reform of Banking, Economics of Climate Change and the Political Economy of Economic Policy-making. He has written papers in journals, contributed to edited books and has authored books. His most recent publications include papers on the political economy of the austerity strategy, Greece and the Eurozone crisis, Technocracy and public policy-making, political economy aspects of 'Brexit' (his most recent published paper is on this aspect), and the EU and the UK after 'Brexit' from a Political economy dimension.

Richard Lewney is Chair of Cambridge Econometrics where he has worked since 1988, applying its macro-sectoral econometric models to policy issues. For the past four years, he has directed two major research projects for DG Energy to improve the methods of modelling the macroeconomic impacts of low-carbon policies. These have included a better treatment of the roles played by finance and innovation, of regional and income distribution impacts, and of the relevance of other megatrends to the low-carbon transition. Over 2017–18 he directed projects for the European Climate Foundation examining (i) the technological costs and economic impacts of alternative pathways to a net-zero GHG emissions European economy by 2050 and (ii) the economic impacts of decarbonising road freight and car transport. He has directed an assessment of the sectoral implications for jobs of meeting the 2020 energy and CO_2 targets and of policies designed to respond to these impacts (for DG Employment & Social Affairs). Also, a modelling analysis of the economic impact of the impact of environmental degradation to inform an assessment of the role that environmental risk factors could play in sovereign credit risk assessments (for the UNEP Finance Initiative).

Malcolm Sawyer is now Emeritus Professor of Economics, Leeds University Business School, University of Leeds, UK. He has been the principal investigator for the European Union-funded (8 million euros) five-year research project Financialisation, Economy, Society and Sustainable Development, involving 15 partner institutions across Europe and more widely (www.fessud.eu). He was the managing editor of *International Review of Applied Economics* for over three decades and has served on the editorial board of a range of journals and is editor of the series *New Directions in Modern Economics* published by Edward Elgar. He has written widely in the areas of post Keynesian and Kaleckian economics, fiscal and monetary policies, industrial economics and the UK and European economies. He has authored 12 books, the most recent being *Can the Euro be Saved?* (Polity Press, 2017). He has edited over 30 books including the annual series *International Papers in Political Economy* (with Philip Arestis). He has authored well over 100 papers in refereed journals and contributed chapters to over 100 books.

Ahmad Seyf is currently teaching at the Department of Economics at the New College of the Humanities. He has also taught at Staffordshire University and the University of Boston's London campus. His main research interests are International Business Economics, Globalisation and the Economic and Social History of the Middle East, and Economic Policies. He is a bilingual writer having written extensively on Iran, his country of birth. His recent publications include *The Economy of Iran Under Ahmadinejad*, H&S Media, 2012; *Crisis in Despotism*, Ameh Press, Tehran, 2014; *Capitalism and Democracy*, Mazmoon Book, Tehran 2016; *The Great Recession, an Iranian View*, Tehran; Mazmoon book, 2017; *The Global Financial Crisis, an Iranian View*, Tehran, Mazmoon book, 2017; *An Introduction to Political Economy at the Age of Globalisation*, Nashr Negah, Tehran, 2016; *The Political Economy of Iran from a Distance*, Nashr Kargadan, Tehran, 2017, and *On the Negation of Neoliberalism*, Tehran, Hezareh Sevvom, 2018.

Helen Traill is Research Associate in Urban Transitions in the Adam Smith Business School at the University of Glasgow. Dr Helen Traill's work spans sustainability transitions including work on the EU Horizon 2020-funded MPOWER project on municipal action for energy transitions and a recent Scottish Government- and EU-Social Innovation Fund project on the ethics of sustainability in areas of urban deprivation, which won a Scottish Knowledge Exchange Award in 2020. Dr Helen Traill holds a PhD from the London School of Economics and Political Science in Sociology, focused on community growing projects and their relation to urban land politics and practices of communality. Dr Helen Traill is an ECR committee member of the Royal Geographical Society's Food Geographies Working Group and attends meetings of the Glasgow Food Policy Partnership. Her research interests span community and belonging, the politics of land ownership, and the social life of sustainability.

List of Figures

Fig. 3.1	UK GDP growth and current account balance as a percentage of GDP. (Source: IMF and Office of National Statistics data; own elaboration)	91
Fig. 3.2	UK GDP growth against non-national inflows per 1000 population. (Source: Office of National Statistics/LTIM data and own elaboration)	93
Fig. 3.3	UK earnings dispersion* and net migration of non-nationals to the United Kingdom. (Data Sources: Atkinson et al. (2017), "The Chartbook of Economic Inequality" [Available at: https://www.chartbookofeconomicinequality.com/inequality-by-country/united-kingdom/]. Also, ONS/LTIM data and own elaboration. **Note*: The 90/50 dispersion of earnings measure used here represents earnings at the top decile relative to median earnings and has been compiled from the UK *Annual Survey of Hours and Earnings* records and ONS data updates.)	96
Fig. 3.4	UK immigration of non-nationals. (Source: Office for National Statistics/LTIM data and own elaboration)	124
Fig. 3.5	UK emigration of non-nationals. (Source: Office for National Statistics/LTIM data and own elaboration)	125
Fig. 3.6	Unemployment: gap between foreigners and natives in total labour (15–64 year olds). (Source: IPUMS-International	

[IOM data] Accessible at https://migrationdataportal.org/institute/ipums-international) 125
Fig. 3.7 Higher educated: gap between foreigners and natives in total labour (15–64 year olds) (%). (Source: IPUMS-International [IOM data] Accessible at https://migrationdataportal.org/institute/ipums-international) 126
Fig. 3.8 Over-qualified: gap between foreigners and natives in total labour (15–64 year olds) (%). (Source: IPUMS-International [IOM data] Accessible at https://migrationdataportal.org/institute/ipums-international) 126
Fig. 4.1 Real earnings and productivity, US, 1947–1975. (Source: Data extracted from Gordon (2017)) 154
Fig. 4.2 Real earnings and productivity, US, 1975–2011. (Source: Data extracted from Gordon (2017)) 155
Fig. 6.1 Ownership of share capital in UK's quoted companies 1963–2014. (Derived from Office for National Statistics, Ownership of UK quoted shares: https://www.ons.gov.uk) 230
Fig. 6.2 Privatisation proceeds ($ billion). (Data derived from Privatisation Barometer: www.privatizationbarometer.net) 230
Fig. 6.3 Labour's plan for a publicly owned energy network. (Source: Labour Party 2019, pp. 8–9: Bringing Energy Home) 255
Fig. 8.1 Shareholder protection in 30 countries, 1990 and 2013. (Source: Katelouzou & Siems, 2015) 361
Fig. 8.2 Shareholder protection in 30 countries, 1990–2013, scores for individual variables (see Table 8.1). (Source: Katelouzou & Siems, 2015) 362
Fig. 8.3 Employment protection trends in selected regions, 1970–2013. (Source: Adams et al., 2019) 366
Fig. 8.4 Employment protection trends in selected countries, 1970–2013 (China from 1986). (Source: Adams et al., 2019) 367

List of Graphs

Graph 7.1 PUBLIC REVENUE: Index of 1. Top marginal tax rate and multiple of average wage where set in. 2. Total tax revenue as % of GDP. 3. General Government Revenue in GDP
PUBLIC SPENDING ON HUMAN DEVELOPMENT: Index of 1. Public social expenditure as a percentage of GDP. 2. Training and job creation public expenditure in GDP. 3. Share of public expenditure on tertiary educational institutions. 4. Public/private education spending in GDP. 5. Public spending on family services in GDP (Sources and calculations see Table A.1 in Appendix.) 292

Graph 7.2 PUBLIC REVENUE: Index of 1. Top marginal tax rate and multiple of average wage where set in. 2. Total tax revenue as % of GDP. 3. General Government Revenue in GDP
PUBLIC SPENDING ON HUMAN DEVELOPMENT: Index of 1. Public social expenditure as a percentage of GDP. 2. Training and job creation public expenditure in GDP. 3. Share of public expenditure on tertiary educational institutions. 4. Public/private education spending in GDP. 5. Public spending on family services in GDP (Sources and calculations see Table A.1 in Appendix) 293

Graph 7.3 PROGRESSIVE PUBLIC FINANCE: Index of X and Y axes, Graph. 7.3
PUBLIC REVENUE: Index of 1. Top marginal tax rate and multiple of average wage where set in, 2007. 2. Total tax revenue as % of GDP, 2007. 3. General Government Revenue in GDP, 1007, and
PUBLIC SPENDING ON HUMAN DEVELOPMENT: Index of 1. Public social expenditure as a percentage of GDP. 2. Training and job creation public expenditure in GDP. 3. Share of public expenditure on tertiary educational institutions. 4. Public/private education spending in GDP. 5. Public spending on family services in GDP. EQUAL WELFARE: 1. Disposable income poverty rate, late 2000s, and trend. 2. Difference in inequality before and after taxes and transfers, mid 2000s. 3. Redistribution of cash transfers to lowest quintile, mid-2000s 4. Ratio of rich to poor. Mid-2000s, and trend. 5. Gini, late 2000s and trend. 6. Higher scores for lower private social expenditure, 2007, and trend. 7. The level and relative evenness of the value of public services at top and bottom of income quintiles (Sources and calculations see Table A.2 in Appendix) 295
Graph 7.4 X: SCHOOL EQUALITY Index of: 1. Public expenditure on education in GDP 2007, and trend. 2. Public expenditure on education in public expenditure, 2007, and trend. 3. Population that has attained upper secondary, 25–34 age cohort, 2007, and trend. 4. Public/private education spending in GDP, 2007, and rate of change. 5. Public/private ratio of students to teaching staff. 6. Lower scores for level of private household expenditure on education, 2007. 7. Students in publicly funded schools, 2007 and trend. 8. Unit of funding attained by public/private school students, 2007, and trend
Y: EMPLOYMENT STRUCTURE: Index of: 1. Education-employment return rate, females (lower secondary, and lower secondary to tertiary), 2008, and trend. 2. Education unemployment return rate, females, (lower secondary, and lower secondary to tertiary), 2008, and trend. 3. Relative education income return rates (lower

secondary as % of tertiary), 2007, and trend. 4. Higher scores for low earnings dispersion. 5. Incidence of long-term unemployment in total unemployment, females. 2009, and trend. 6. National unemployment rate, 2009, and trend. 7. Employment security index, ILO 2004)
(Sources and calculations see Tables A.3 and A.4 in Appendix) 298

Graph 7.5 Y axis: *WELFARE STATE INSTITUTIONS*: Index combining SCHOOL EQUALITY, composed of 1. Public expenditure on education in GDP 2000; 2. Public expenditure on education in public expenditure, 2000; 3. Population that has attained upper secondary, 25–34 age cohort, 2000; 3. Share of public expenditure on tertiary educational institutions, 2000; 4. Public/private education spending in GDP, 2000 Table A.5, columns 1–4—for 2000); and PUBLIC REVENUE, composed of 1. Top marginal tax rate and multiple of average wage where set in; 2. Total tax revenue as % of GDP; and 3. General Government Revenue in GDP; and PUBLIC SPENDING ON HUMAN DEVELOPMENT, composed of 1. Public social expenditure as a percentage of GDP; 2. Training and job creation public expenditure in GDP; 3. Share of public expenditure on tertiary educational institutions; 4. Public/private education spending in GDP; and 5. Public spending on family services in GDP, all 2000 (Table A.1, column 9 (1 & 2—for 2000) Combined, as given in Table A.6, column 7,e).

X Axis: *CONTROL OF TIME*: Index composed of 1. Average annual leisure hours 2. Males' share of part-time jobs in total male employment as a share of females' share of part-time jobs in female total employment; 3. Paid paternity, maternity and parental leave, months; 4. Task and time control and well-being at work (able to choose order of tasks, able to set work time, work gives feeling of work well done); 5. Employment security (share of job tenure over 10 years, lower scores for share of long-term unemployment in total) 55–59 age cohort with more than 5 years job tenure; and 6. Net cost of child-care fees, and

EMPLOYMENT STRUCTURE (pattern of employment returns to education), composed of: 1. Education-employment return rate, females (lower secondary, and lower secondary to tertiary), 2002; 2. Education unemployment return rate, females, (lower secondary, and lower secondary to tertiary), 2002; 3. Relative education income return rates (lower secondary as % of tertiary), 2000; 4. Higher scores for low earnings dispersion; and 5. Training and job-creation public spending in GDP. 2000. (Combined, as given in Table A.6, column 7,c) 301

Graph 7.6 Y axis: *WELFARE STATE INSTITUTIONS*: Index combining SCHOOL EQUALITY, composed of 1. Public expenditure on education in GDP 2007; 2. Public expenditure on education in public expenditure, 2007; 3. Population that has attained upper secondary, 25–34 age cohort. 2007; 3. Share of public expenditure on tertiary educational institutions, 2007; and, 4. Public/private education spending in GDP, 2007, and PUBLIC REVENUE: composed of 1. Top marginal tax rate and multiple of average wage where set in; 2. Total tax revenue as % of GDP; 3. General Government Revenue in GDP; and PUBLIC SPENDING ON HUMAN DEVELOPMENT composed of 1. Public social expenditure as a percentage of GDP; 2. Training and job creation public expenditure in GDP; 3. Share of public expenditure on tertiary educational institutions; 4. Public/private education spending in GDP; and, 5. Public spending on family services in GDP, all 2007 (Table A.1, column 9 (1 & 2—for 2007). Combined as given in Table A.6, column 7,f).

X Axis: *CONTROL OF TIME*: Index composed of 1. Average annual leisure hours; 2. Males' share of part-time jobs in total male employment as a share of females' share of part-time jobs in female total employment; 3. Paid paternity, maternity and parental leave, months; 4. Task and time control and well-being at work (able to choose order of tasks, able to set work time, work gives feeling of work well done; 5. Employment security (share of job tenure over 10 years, lower scores for share of long-term unemployment in total) 55–59 age cohort with more than 5 years job tenure, and, 6. Net cost of child-care fees; and EMPLOYMENT STRUCTURE (pattern of employment returns to education), composed of 1. Education-employment return rate, females (lower secondary, and lower secondary to tertiary), 2002; 2. Education unemployment return rate, females, (lower secondary, and lower secondary to tertiary), 2002; 3. Relative education income return rates (lower secondary as % of tertiary), 2000; 4. Higher scores for low earnings dispersion; and, 5. Training and job-creation public spending in GDP, 2000. (Combined, as given in Table A.6, column 7,d) 302

List of Tables

Table 5.1	Sources of economic value from ecosystem services	182
Table A.1	The welfare state, revenue and spending on human development: 2000, 2007	313
Table A.2	Direct and indirect sources of equal welfare, OECD	316
Table A.3	Education equality	320
Table A.4	Relative employment and income returns to education, females	324
Table A.5	Equality of education and employment returns, 1998–2002, 2007–8	328
Table A.6	Structure of employment and non-employment time, early to mid2000s, late 2000s	332
Table 8.1	Variables on shareholder protection: definition and coding algorithms	359
Table 8.2	Variables on employment protection: definition and coding algorithms	363

1

Financial Stability: Still Unsettled for the Future

Philip Arestis

1 Introduction

Following the Global Financial Crisis (GFC), a number of proposals emerged which support financial-stability policies. This is expected in view of 24 countries around the world that experienced banking crises. Weaknesses in regulatory architecture, a lack of proper control of the financial sector and undertaking of excessive risks, which were key causes of the GFC, are still evident. An important policy implication is that the focus on monetary policy to meet the single objective of inflation target, thereby macroeconomic and financial stability emerge, is insufficient (Arestis & González Martinez, 2015; Arestis, 2019b; also, IMF, 2009). Appropriate policies are needed. Especially so, as Cunliffe (2019b) argues, "the most important lesson we learned from the crisis is that financial

P. Arestis (✉)
Department of Land Economy, University of Cambridge, Cambridge, UK

University of Basque Country UPV/EHU, Leioa, Spain
e-mail: pa267@cam.ac.uk

P. Arestis, M. Sawyer (eds.), *Economic Policies for a Post-Neoliberal World*, International Papers in Political Economy, https://doi.org/10.1007/978-3-030-56735-4_1

stability is a necessary condition for macro-economic and monetary stability" (p. 14). Carney (2020) agrees, "Price stability clearly is not a guarantee for financial stability" (p. 2), and that coordination of monetary and financial stability is important. Indeed such coordination "is codified in the UK institutional set-up with independent monetary and financial policy committees that are required by remit to have regard of the actions of each other" (p. 22). The Bank of International Settlements (BIS, 2011) also confirms that price stability as a single target is not enough. What is needed is "a stability framework in which monetary, fiscal and prudential policy work together to build a robust and stable macroeconomic and financial system that will make the next crisis both less likely and less severe" (p. 3).

Fiscal policy is vital in both the short and the long run, and so is coordination with monetary and financial-stability policies, along with discretion in applying them. Especially so, and as Cunliffe (2019b) suggests, "financial stability depends in part on effective demand management" (p. 14). Financial stability should be the top priority of central banks' policies; the GFC events, and the coronavirus syndrome, testify to this important requirement. Financial stability, therefore, requires further investigation, the focus of this contribution.

Proposals and policies that aim at securing financial stability and avoid a similar crisis to GFC are in place, but still not fully implemented. Further complexities have emerged, which could produce serious problems. We proceed in Sect. 2 to discuss financial stability and the proposals following the GFC to account for it. Section 3 discusses further problems with financial stability. Section 4 focuses on required policies, and for the post-neoliberal era. Finally, Section 5 summarises and concludes.

2 Financial Stability and Post-GFC Proposals

Financial stability comprises of two regulation frameworks: microprudential (focusing on individual financial entities) and macroprudential (focusing on the entire financial system).[1] Our approach focuses on macroprudential financial stability.

The focus of financial stability should be on proper control of the financial sector so that it becomes socially and economically useful to the economy and to the productive sectors in particular. A well-functioning financial system should channel funds from surplus sectors to those with fund shortages. Banks, and other financial institutions, should serve the needs of their customers rather than targeting huge profits and excessive gains for shareholders. Proper monitoring and assessment of systemic risks, so that financial systems are robust, is an important part of financial stability. According to the Bank of England (2019; BoE hereafter), "Financial stability might sound confusing but it's just a way of describing the financial system when it's fulfilling its basic roles. With a stable financial system, the wheels of the economy keep turning, even when the conditions get difficult". Would macroprudential regulation have prevented the GFC? Aikman, Bridges, Kashyap, and Siegert (2019) suggest that "a macroprudential regime with a suitably strong mandate, coupled with powers to adjust financial system leverage and maturity/liquidity transformation and to limit household sector indebtedness, could have significantly ameliorated the macroeconomic fall-out from the collapse of the real estate bubble" (p. 127). Forbes (2019) suggests, "Macroprudential policy should improve the economy's ability to withstand shocks and allow the financial system to function effectively under adverse conditions" (p. 471)—see, also, BoE (2009) and IMF (2011).

We discuss next relevant proposals for macroprudential financial stability. We begin with the US Dodd-Frank Act.

[1] 'Macroprudential' was mentioned for the first time at the meeting of the Cooke Committee (28–29 June 1979), the forerunner to the Basel Committee (Clement, 2010, p. 59); never implemented prior to the GFC. Microprudential regulation has been around since 1979.

2.1 US Dodd-Frank Act

Dodd-Frank Act was law-signed on 21 July 2010. Relevant proposals include. Volcker Rule: eliminate proprietary investments to prohibit banks to use insured deposits to run own trading operations, and ownership of hedge funds.[2] Banks can hold 3% proprietary investments of their core capital. Size matters: no financial firm should become 'too big to fail'. The Act grants government the power to wind down failing financial institutions if they threaten the financial system. A new 'orderly liquidation' authority has the power to seize a failing 'systemically important' institution. An Office of Credit Ratings to be established to supervise credit rating agencies; 'shadow banking' and non-bank financial entities should also be regulated. However, and according to Tarullo (2019), "less attention has been paid to the risks of financial stability that may arise in the 'shadow banking' area". The shadow banking is still "outside the perimeter of prudentially regulated firms" (p. 70).

This Act is the most wide-ranging overhaul of US financial regulations since the 1930s. However, whether it would have prevented the GFC is an interesting question. Our response is in the negative in view of the non-separation of commercial and investment entities. Another problem relates to the 'Volker Rule'. This rule is one of the key provisions of the Act. Its aim is to prohibit banks from indulging in speculation. However, it could be that bank trading may shift to 'shadow banking', and thereby financial risks increase.

Criticisms of the Act emerged. The Financial Services Forum, which represents 18 top US banks, has argued that the proposed elimination of proprietary investments is too complicated and too costly to achieve. An additional argument is that such proposals put jobs at risk, damage the United States' competitiveness and threaten its growth. Also, tackling the 'too-big-to-fail' institutions should be through effective supervision, not as in the Act. Most frequent argument is that the Act is too complicated. Surely though, it is not as complicated as the collateralised debt obligations (CDOs), one of the main causes of GFC (Arestis, 2016).

[2] Hedge funds, lightly regulated, pool capital and invest it in a variety of assets.

The US President's criticisms focus on the repeal of Dodd-Frank Act. This is because the Act has prevented banks to provide sufficient credit. The President ordered a review of the Act in early February 2017, with a relevant report produced in June 2017 (see below). The House of Representatives voted, in early June 2017, to replace the Act with their own Financial Choice Act, whose focus is to repeal the Volcker Rule. The Senate proposed easing bank regulations, based on the argument that the economy is better without strict controls, and a split of banks would impair their ability to invest. Clearly, these criticisms aim at dismantling many of Dodd-Frank Act rules on the argument that freeing banks boosts growth.

The US Treasury released its report, 12 June 2017, on financial-regulations reform (Mnuchin & Phillips, 2017), which suggests that the current system of excessive financial regulations undermines the ability of banks to provide credit, thereby constraining economic growth. Since 2009, lending only rose by 25%, far less than in other recent recoveries. The report also claimed, "Dodd-Frank has increased the burden of regulatory compliance without adequate cost-benefit analysis and that Dodd-Frank has prolonged the moral hazard arising from regulations that could lead to taxpayer-funded bailouts" (p. 34). Although it did not reject the Act, it recommended its application with less rigour and greater consultation. In terms of the Volcker Rule, it proposed that it should only apply to very big banks engaged in large-scale operations.

The US Congress passed a bill, 22 May 2018, which exempts medium-sized banks from the stringent rules. Only banks with at least $250bn in assets are subject to strict Fed oversight, up from $50bn previously. It marks the biggest change of financial laws since the Dodd-Frank Act. The US Federal Reserve Board voted, 30 May 2018, to relax the limit of banks' ability to engage in proprietary trading, with the greatest relief for smaller banks. In effect, this proposal allows the combined commercial and investment banks to undertake riskier activities with insured bank deposits. If the Fed Board proposal went through, it would take it all back where it was initially. More recently, easing of the Volcker Rule has been undertaken for the financial services industry, which had been complaining that the Volcker Rule took too much of their time and money in view of it being complicated. Clearly, then, the Act is to be repealed. The US regulators ignore history, especially the causes of the GFC.

2.2 UK Vickers Report

The UK government appointed the Independent Commission on Banking in the summer of 2010 to consider whether a version of the US Dodd-Frank Act would be appropriate for the United Kingdom, and whether banks should be split into commercial and investment entities. The Commission (chaired by John Vickers) produced its final report in September 2011 (Independent Banking Commission, 2011), the Vickers Report. It recommends 'ring-fencing' banks' retail operations from their riskier investment activities. Each part of the ring-fenced bank is a separate legal entity with its own board. The ring-fencing applies to the largest UK banks that have more than £25bn deposits. The UK Prudential Regulation Authority (PRA)[3] has the regulator role in relation to the ring-fenced banks. The Vickers Report thereby aims to protect retail-banking activities from losses incurred in investment-banking operations and to prevent taxpayer bailouts of 'too-big-to-fail' banks. The reform came into force on 1 January 2019.

Proudman (2018) suggested that had ring-fencing been in place prior to GFC, it would have reduced the likelihood of government support. However, there are problems with the Vickers Report. The main problem of ring-fencing is that banks may be encouraged to take greater risk within the ring-fencing activities, such as mortgages, corporate and other type of assets. This is so since such activities would be more likely to be bailed out. No wonder the UK Parliamentary Banking Commission

[3] There are three UK financial regulation committees. The Prudential Regulation Authority (PRA), which is part of the Bank of England (BoE) and is responsible for the supervision and regulation of banks, building societies, credit unions, insurers and major investment firms, at the level of individual institutions. There is also the Financial Conduct Authority (FCA), which regulates the financial services industry. It is accountable directly to Treasury and Parliament. The Financial Policy Committee (FPC) is an official committee of the BoE, with its focus on macroeconomic financial issues, and is responsible for managing the financial sector, with its primary objective to deliver financial stability. It cooperates and coordinates with the PRA and FCA. The PRA and FPC are co-located with the Monetary Policy Committee, at the BoE. They enjoy overlapping membership, and the Governor of the BoE chairs these committees.

proposed a review of this rule so that a full separation of the whole industry is undertaken if the ring-fence is not followed properly. Another problem is Vickers' (2016) argument that the BoE did not adopt the recommendation that banks should ring-fence extra capital equivalent to 3% of their risk-weighted assets (RWA). The BoE suggested that 1.0% should be sufficient. There are problems with the UK Vickers Report and doubts whether it has been implemented properly.

2.3 The European Commission's Liikanen Report

The European Union (EU)-Commission committee, headed by Erkki Liikanen, the Finnish Central Bank Governor, made a ring-fence proposal in 2012. The committee suggested ring-fencing banks' trading business from their retail activities, opposite to the Vickers Report. The report's objective is to contain "banking group's incentives and ability to take excessive risks with insured deposits" and to "prevent the coverage of losses incurred in the trading entity by the funds of the deposit bank, and hence limit the liability of taxpayer and the deposit insurance system" (Liikanen Report, 2012). The Liikanen Report has been criticised in that governments in a crisis may still bail out banks, even ring-fenced ones. Companies may turn away from bank loans to capital markets, thereby disrupting the flow of corporate bank funding. Ring-fencing trading assets would limit the liquidity of corporate bond trading, making this form of financing more expensive. In October 2017 the European Commission withdrew its proposal. The main reason was lack of progress, and in view of the objectives of the proposal, which had already been accounted by other regulations. It is not clear though, how other regulations had accounted for the relevant objectives.

2.4 The IMF Proposal

This proposal (Claessens, Keen, & Pazarbasioglu, 2010) includes high capital and liquid-asset requirements, along with legal regimes that provide orderly resolution of failing institutions. An important complement to these regulatory reforms is to tax the financial sector. The International Monetary Fund (IMF) bank tax proposals, for the G20 finance ministers' consideration, rely heavily on the need for a global approach. They are designed to ensure that financial institutions bear the direct costs of crises and future bailouts would be funded by banks. The taxes comprise of: (i) the 'Financial Stability Contribution' (FSC) tax, which would require banks and other financial institutions to pay a levy, initially at a flat rate. This would be adjusted to reflect risk so that financial-sector activities that pose a greater risk would pay a higher rate. At a later stage, (ii) a Financial Activity Tax (FAT) is proposed, which is a tax on the sum total of profits and remunerations paid by financial institutions. The sum would be a kind of Value-Added Tax (VAT), from which financial institutions are currently exempted. So that imposing such a tax would make the tax treatment of the financial sector similar to other sectors. This would deter the financial sector from being too large on purely tax reasons. It would also contain the tendency of the financial sector for excessive risk-taking.

Required international agreement did not emerge in view of disagreements among the G20 members. Objections to this proposal were raised by Australia, Brazil, Canada and Japan, the countries least affected by the GFC. The central banks of these countries argued that taxing banks would reduce their capital, thereby making them more, not less, vulnerable to financial crises. No doubt, relevant banks argued, taxing liabilities and transactions to stave off future financial crises carried their own problems. The main objection was that the financial sector would not be able to provide what is required by their customers; requiring banks to hold more capital could actually result in banks providing less lending than otherwise. Such rules might create a new credit crunch. Countries resisted reform, on weak grounds, but with powerful lobbying.

2.5 The Basel III/Basel IV Package

The 27-member countries of the International 'Basel Committee on Banking Supervision' (BCBS) of the Bank for International Settlements with the Group of Central Bank Governors and Heads of Supervision, at their meeting on 12 September 2010 and at the 2011 G20 meeting in Paris, reached a relevant agreement. The 'Basel III Package' (2010) is concerned with bank capital and liquidity standards. The ruling, phased in from January 2013 with full implementation by January 2019, requires banks to hold equity requirements to 9.5% of their risk-weighted assets (RWA)[4] and liquidity standards, with banks required to meet a 3% leverage ratio.

The new capital ratios were lower than they should be and introduced by 2019. This long phase-in period was a concession to small banks, especially in Germany. These small banks struggled with the new rules because of undercapitalisation. In addition, no relevant regulations were provided in the case of banks migrating to the 'shadow banking' sector and to other lightly supervised non-bank financial-services companies. Another problem concerns the definition of capital ratio, defined in relation to RWA, not to total assets. An implication of this is that toxic leverage is highly probable. When the RWA is a small proportion of total assets, the exposure of the banking sector to risk would be high. The IMF (2012) in its 2012 Global Financial Stability Report argued that Basel III rules raised the incentive to develop new products to circumvent the framework. This is so because big banking groups are in a better position to absorb the costs of relevant regulations. Big banking groups would become even more prominent, thereby making the relevant markets even more concentrated. This framework would push riskier activity into less regulated parts of the financial system. The most serious problem of Basel III is that the group failed to achieve agreement on the RWAs. The countries could not agree at their meetings of 28–29 November 2016 and 7–8 January 2017 on the definition of RWAs.

In December 2017, the BCBS published a package of reforms referred to as 'Basel IV'. Its principal feature is the way banks calculate their RWAs. The BCBS proposes that a calculation of a bank's RWAs, using internal models, should not fall below 72.5% of the calculation using standardised models. This lower limit is an 'output floor'. When computing RWAs based on internal models, input parameters must not fall

[4] 'Risk-weighted assets' are calculated by risk coefficients, based on credit ratings. The higher the risk of an asset, the higher the relevant coefficient.

below certain minimum levels, called the 'input floors'. The BCBS proposes a nine-year implementation timetable, along with a five-year 'phase-in' period to commence on 1 January 2022, with full implementation from 1 January 2027. An interesting question is whether Basel IV would be implemented properly and timely.

Financial-stability committees have been set up; two examples make the point. The Financial- Stability Oversight Council, established as part of the US Dodd-Frank Act. However, the problem is that this Council "in its current form does not have sufficient powers to ensure financial stability in the face of credit boom" (Aikman, Bridges, et al. 2019, p. 124). The FPC in the United Kingdom, and according to Aikman et al. (op. cit.), "is the most muscular macroprudential regulator in the world" (p. 126). Whether the FPC could have helped to account for the GFC is an interesting question. Aikman, Bridges, et al. (2019) suggest that the FPC is probably the only regime sufficiently equipped to help avoid another similar crisis to the GFC. However, "a similar regime in a rerun of the crisis would still have required political backing to widen the perimeter of regulation to capture loosely regulated nonbank financial institutions and then to act aggressively!" (p. 127).

Proper measures to increase stability in the financial sector have been bypassed. The financial sector that caused the GFC looks unaltered. What is required is a complete institutional separation of retail banking from investment banking; whether such a proposal would emerge is an interesting question.

3 Further Financial-Stability Problems

Our financial-stability discussion demonstrates that since the Dodd-Frank Act, the banking reforms remain a work in progress. After the GFC, though, central banks in advanced countries intervened and managed to save their banking sectors from collapse. Very low interest rates, along with quantitative easing (QE, namely, "large-scale purchases of financial assets", Bernanke, 2020, p. 94) and forward guidance (FG, namely, "explicit communication of central bank's outlook and policy plans", Bernanke, op. cit., p. 944), have been pursued. Furthermore, fiscal policies introduced after the June 2009 G20 countries' meeting, avoided another Great Depression. However, at the June 2010 G20 countries' meeting, 'fiscal sustainability' was abandoned and 'fiscal consolidation' was suggested. Fiscal policies were abandoned when austerity policies were introduced in 2010. Monetary policies did not work. The IMF (2018b, footnote 17) reported that aggregate banking credit growth to the private sector declined in a number of countries. In a sample of 47 countries for which relevant data existed, credit to the private sector declined from the pre-crisis period (2000–07) to the post-crisis period (2010–15) in 27 countries. Goodhart (2015) suggested that although financial support did help initially after the GFC, subsequent monetary policy was not effective in terms of restoring robust recovery. Bank lending to the private sector did not increase as had been expected.

3.1 Potential Financial Instability

Financial-instability problems have emerged. While banks have been saved, risk has shifted to the shadow-banking sector. Shadow banking has grown to 13% of total financial assets, according to the Financial Stability Board (FSB).[5] The IMF (2018b) agrees with the European Central Bank (ECB) ex-President's suggestion that 42% of the region's entire financial system is actually shadow banking, expressing relevant concerns about the risks to the financial system, which could produce "globally systemic risks" (IMF, op. cit., p. 69, and p. 73). The US subprime mortgages and CDOs are back in fashion. The *Financial Times* (28 May 2019) reported that in Q1 of 2019, subprime mortgages accounted for 77% of total loans, backing $16.5bn of CDOs. China's shadow banking has expanded substantially; in 2019, shadow banking in China surged, in view of regulators supporting it to enhance growth. Not only is shadow banking not regulated, but is also poorly equipped to weather financial shocks. If the past helps to predict the future, these developments could potentially produce dangers of a similar type as those that caused the GFC.

[5] Available at: https://www.crowdfundinsider.com/2017/05/100601-financial-stability-board-publishes-report-shadow-banking/

Another problem is with the yield-curve[6] flattening, and reversal of the yield curve occurred. Not only had the flattening and reversal of the yield curve emerged before the GFC, but also in the case of the past seven recessions (Haltom, Wissuchek, & Wolman, 2018). Inversion of the yield curve has historically been a predictor of economic recessions, with a lag. On 4 December 2018, the difference between two- and ten-year US Treasury yields dropped to single digits for the first time since the GFC. The *Financial Times* (5 April, 2019) reported that there was 'yield curve inversion' in the United States on 22 March 2019, when the interest rate on ten-year bonds fell below two-year bonds—and that happened for the first time since August 2007. Such an inversion, as the *IMF Blog* (2 July 2019) suggests, "is a gauge of investors' confidence in the economy and signals doubts about future growth". It may also mean that such US yield-curve inversion emerged from the Fed's QE and its holdings of a significant share of long-term bonds. Reversal of the yield curve is especially acute for the banking sector in view of its normal lending over a long period at higher rates than it pays on short-term deposits. Such an outcome dampens the willingness of banks to lend, constraining credit to the private sector and thereby hurting growth. However, in view of signs of positive US growth at that time lifted the yield curve back to a positive territory.

On 14 August 2019, and in view of worries about the global economy slowing, due to the US/China trade tensions, the gap between the two- and ten-year US yields dropped below zero. Inversion of the yield curve that produces serious problems might take longer than previously because growth was slowing, not collapsing. In the middle of October 2019, however, flattening of the yield curve emerged in the United States, after the previous inversion, in view of the reduction of the Fed-funds rate. In early April 2020, due to the spread of coronavirus, worries and urgent rally to the safety of the 'heaven' government assets, the ten-year US Treasury yield decreased to 0.58%, causing a further gap in the treasuries,

[6] The yield curve depicts the difference between the yields on government short-term and long-term bonds. A normal yield curve slopes upwards, with long-term government bonds bearing higher interest rates than short-term ones. When the two yields move closer to each other, the yield curve becomes flatter. When the short-term yields become higher than the long-term ones, the yield curve is inverted.

with further flattening of the yield curve emerging. Similar experiences were evident in other countries.

Flattening of the yield curve might occur even if the risk of recession increased (Haltom et al., 2018). This could be because lower long-term interest rates, QE activities and FG indicate to the markets that future expansion of the level of economic activity would emerge, in which case the markets expect no recession to occur. Still, a flattening yield curve is a sign of a forthcoming recession, and especially an inverted yield curve indicates that a crisis of the GFC type may occur. In fact the New York Fed's own probability model indicated that the yield-curve-derived recession probability was near to a 30% chance of recession over the next 12 months (*Financial Times*, 5 July 2019). Policymakers should be aware of this possibility, and proper policies should be undertaken. The Fed-funds rate reduction, the China-US trade agreement (see Note 9) and fears over the spread of the coronavirus have caused the yield curve to flatten more recently, May 2020, with the ten-year Treasury-bill rate reduced to 0.6% (and the two-year Treasury-bill rate to 0.13%). In early 2020, the relevant rate of interest was 2.87% in China, negative in Germany and Japan, below 1% in the United Kingdom and below 2% in Spain (*Financial Times*, 6 January 2020).

The excessive debt of the GFC has become worse. According to the International Finance Institute (IFI), in 2018, it was 70%, more than when the Lehman Brothers collapsed in September 2008 (Bases, 2018). Bases (op. cit.) reports that the increase in the global debt-to-GDP ratio in 2018 was 318%; in 2019 (Q3) it reached an all-time high of over 322%. The global non-financial corporate debt rose to 92% of GDP in 2019 from 84% in 2009 (IFI, reported in *The Economist*, 14 March 2020). The New York Fed (2018) suggests, in the case of the United States, "total household debt increased by $219 billion (1.6%) to $13.51 trillion in the third quarter of 2018. It was the 17th consecutive quarter increase and the total is now $837 billion higher than the previous peak of $12.68 trillion in the third quarter of 2008". In 2019 (Q2), the US corporate debt was 74% of GDP and the government debt over 100% of GDP. The IMF (2018b), reports, "Banks have increased their capital and liquidity buffers since the crisis, but they remain exposed to highly indebted companies, households, and sovereigns; to their holdings of opaque and illiquid assets" (pp. ix–x). The IMF (2020b) predicts total debt-to-GDP ratios above 120% by 2021 in view of the coronavirus syndrome.

The BoE (2018) reports that the UK household debt-to-income ratio has decreased since the GFC. It amounted to 125% of household income (excluding student loans), lower than the 144% in 2008, but it remains high by historical standards. Moreover, "while total corporate indebtedness remains below pre-crisis levels, leverage of UK companies outside the commercial real estate (CRE) sector has increased to a level that is now above its pre-crisis level" (p. 43), and "[a] high level of debt can pose risks by increasing potential losses to lenders. It can also increase the likelihood of sharp cuts in consumption, especially by high indebted households, which may amplify a downturn and, in turn, the risk of losses to lenders on all forms of lending" (p. 38). All this is partly due to QE and low interest rates. When financial tightening emerges, reducing debt is uncertain. The IMF (2019b) suggests, "In advanced economies, corporate debt and financial risk-taking have increased. The creditworthiness of borrowers has deteriorated. So-called leveraged loans to highly indebted borrowers continue to be of particular concern". Further explanations of the excessive debt are inequality, low wages and poor productivity. Debt has also increased in emerging countries, especially in China. Private debt in China, excluding the financial sector, "has risen from 115% in 2008 to 200% of GDP" (Cunliffe, 2019a, p. 10).

Another problem is the $1.3tn leveraged-loans global market, loans granted to indebted companies "with a high credit-risk profile" (Pedraz, 2019, p. 1). More recently, not only are 'shadow banks' involved in providing leveraged loans but they have replaced the traditional banking sector as the primary providers of these loans. The IMF (2018b, chapter 1) suggests that leveraged loans may be approaching a threatening level, especially so since 85% of all leveraged loans are 'covenant-lite'. These are loans issued with insufficient restrictions on the borrowers and lesser protections for the lenders. The leveraged-loans magnitude is getting dangerously large and invites comparisons with the pre-GFC subprime-mortgage boom. The BIS (2018) suggests that leverage loans have "doubled in size since the Great Financial Crisis" (p. 10). Moreover, as Pedraz (2019) notes, "Following the financial crisis and in a low interest rate environment, many institutional investors have found that leveraged loans are an opportunity to earn higher yields" (p. 1). However, if leveraged loans cannot be repaid, their impact on the economy could be as serious as the GFC subprime mortgages.

A number of central banks have raised concerns about the size of leveraged loans, in that their global size is larger and growing as fast as the US subprime mortgages since 2006. Leveraged loans are to companies whose debt is more than four times their earnings, before interest and tax deductions. Borrowers face fewer restrictions in terms of posting collateral payments. Lenders have less protection, thereby facing greater risk. The United States and Europe (especially Spain; Pedraz, 2019, p. 8) have experienced a growing share of leveraged loans. The Fed Open Market Committee, at its September 2018 meeting, sent a warning for the first time that leveraged loans are a potential risk to financial stability. The BIS in September 2018, the IMF in October 2018 and the BoE in late 2019 expressed similar concerns and warnings. Another development that adds to these concerns has emerged. This is the worsening of the credit standards of the leveraged loans, especially in the United States (Adrian, Natalucci, & Piontek, 2018). Even fewer restrictions are placed on the borrowers and lesser protection for the lenders. In an economic downturn, holders of leveraged loans are at a high risk of default.

The United States leads the $1.3tn of deals in the global market of leveraged loans; they are $1.1tn according to the credit rating agency Standard & Poor's. These are collateralised loan obligations (CLOs) and held by asset managers.[7] Investor demand comes from packaging loans into CLOs and slicing them into different tranches of risk. The Fed's estimate for slower growth may very well decrease the demand for CLOs. A recession would force selling CLOs, thereby flooding the market. This would not create a banking crisis, since it is institutional investors, rather than banks, that are mostly the creditors.[8] Mnuchin and Phillips (2017)

[7]The majority of CLOs are held by non-banks, such as insurance companies, pension funds and other similar companies. An amount of around $750bn in CLOs is now outstanding globally. One third is held by banks in the United States, Europe and Japan (where banks hold a significant number of US and European CLOs); the rest is held by non-banks.

[8]There is a difference between CLOs and CDOs. CDOs are based on mortgages, thereby housing, and are, therefore, vulnerable to common shocks. The CLOs spread across investors and are diversified; not all investors are likely to become vulnerable to a common shock.

state: "For companies that do not have an investment-grade credit rating, and therefore have limited access to the public capital markets, leveraged loans play a significant role in supporting their business growth and increasing returns to investors" (p. 102). According to the BoE (2018), if the US $1.1tn stock of loans is calculated more widely than the Standard & Poor's leveraged-loans index, the amount of leveraged loans is much greater. A broader definition includes institutional loans outside the above index, which produces an estimated stock of leveraged loans of $2.2tn. This compares with the stock of US subprime mortgages in 2006 of $1.1tn (numbers as in the BoE, op. cit., p. 47). The US highly leveraged loan deals account for about half of new corporate debt; these deals emerge when debt is more than five times the relevant earnings (before allowing for interest, tax and depreciation). Not surprisingly, the Fed's second Financial Stability Report (7 May 2019) expresses serious concerns in terms of the high magnitude of leveraged loans.

The BoE (2018) suggested that UK leveraged loans grew rapidly. They reached a high level of £38bn in 2017, with an additional £30bn issued by October 2018. Drawing parallels with the growth of subprime mortgages prior to the GFC, the BoE (op. cit.) noted, "The scale, growth and deterioration of underwriting standards of leveraged lending in recent years share similar trends with the USA subprime-mortgage market before the crisis. But there are also important differences between these markets, which matter for the ultimate risks to UK financial stability" (p. 43). The UK leveraged loans are 20% of corporate borrowing—as the Deputy Governor for Financial Stability told a parliamentary select committee on 17 October 2018—and around half of it, issued by banks, is packaged and sold through CLOs. The BoE (2018) confirmed, "CLOs are held mainly by non-bank investors, although international banks are estimated to hold around a third of the outstanding stock, mainly the less risky tranches. UK banks, in contrast, only have small holdings of CLOs and their domestic corporate lending has not shifted materially towards higher-risk borrowers" (p. 42). Mutual funds have become major buyers of these instruments. Since the underwriting standards have declined, owners of CLOs and leveraged loans are at an increasing risk of loss (BoE, op. cit.). Europe's share of leveraged loans and CLOs is smaller but growing.

The IMF (2018b, chapter 1) suggests that leveraged loans are a potential source of financial instability, since the global leveraged-loans market is larger than the US subprime mortgage market of 2007. When monetary policy normalisation emerges, especially under high debt levels, turbulence seems likely. Also since the coronavirus continues to spread, serious financial sector fragilities could trigger a debt crisis—especially so in Minsky's (1986, 1992) view that debt causes financial instability. Indeed, and in view of the coronavirus syndrome, central banks and governments have initiated unprecedented monetary and fiscal policies to support their economies. Relevant details follow below.

4 Required Policies for Financial Stability

4.1 Current and Future State of Economies

Economic growth has been anaemic since the GFC and inflation below its target. However, at the beginning of 2019, the global economy began to perform better due to fiscal policies in the United States and China; that did not last for long in view of the tariff war between the United States and China.[9] Weak factory output in China emerged in early 2019,

[9] The US-China tariff war poses serious risks to the global economy. Trade tensions emerged in view of the US President's decision to increase the tariffs on Chinese imports from 10% to 25% on $200bn initially, and later a 25% tariffs on additional $325bn imports (10 May 2019). China responded by imposing tariffs on $60bn of US imports, at 25%. The US President responded by imposing 10% tariffs on $300bn of Chinese products to take effect in September 2019, subsequently postponed for mid-December 2019. China responded by announcing new tariffs on $75bn of US products. The United States added tariffs of 15% on $112bn of Chinese imports on 1 September. Existing tariffs on $250bn of Chinese imports increased to 30% from 25% on 1 October 2019, and the US President called on US companies to shut down their operations in China. However, due to negotiations on 11 October, China suspended tariffs for a year on certain imports from the United States, while the United States postponed tariff increases scheduled for 15 October 2019. The truce, though, did not account for the levies imposed previously. Negotiations continued. The IMF (2019a) suggested that trade tensions affected negatively emerging and advanced economies. China's growth was affected negatively by the trade tensions. Failure of the talks would have serious negative effects not just on China but also on financial markets and the global economy. The United States would also be at risk in terms of the escalation of trade tensions. Additional imposition of tariffs would produce drop in the US growth sharply and more so than in China and the Euro Area (ECB, 2019). However, a 'Phase 1' trade deal between them was signed on 15 January 2020. This deal involves a gradual reduction of tariffs, in view of the fact that signifi-

with exports declining. China's large current account surplus declined, reducing China's purchases of global financial assets, especially the US ones. Not only did that escalation affect China, but it also had effects on the US economy. The IMF (2018b) suggested, "The recent rise in trade tensions has so far mostly affected sectors directly exposed to the announced trade measures. However, further rounds of trade measures and countermeasures could lead to a broader tightening of financial conditions, with negative implications for the global economy and financial stability" (p. 35). Great uncertainty is very much around in view of coronavirus throughout the world. The IMF (2020c) suggests that global growth is expected to turn negative at -4.9% in 2020 (and 5.4% in 2021). All this depends on how long and serious the coronavirus syndrome evolves into. In China, due to coronavirus, industrial output already contracted in 2020 (Q1) at the fastest rate ever, and unemployment reached its highest ever rate (*Financial Times*, 17 March 2020). China's central bank has responded by launching a $79bn stimulus to help the business sector. In addition, the central bank reduced banks' reserve requirements, which would provide an additional $78.8bn to enable banks to lend to companies (*Financial Times*, 14 March 2020). Similar problems emerged, and the authorities of other countries, as reported below, have undertaken relevant policies. Georgieva (2020) suggests that the global outlook for the 2020 growth is negative, and possible recession as bad (if not worse) as that of the GFC would emerge. Fiscal, monetary and financial-stability policies are very important under these circumstances, and have been implemented.

No recovery is expected in the Euro Area. GDP was 1.2% in 2019, and -10.2% growth is expected for 2020 (and 6% in 2021; IMF, 2020c). Unemployment is high at 7.4% (May 2020; reported in *The Economist*,

---

cant tariffs were not removed until a more comprehensive agreement could be reached. Imposition of tariffs may emerge in view of the fact that both countries reserve the relevant right if the other party does not adhere to its commitments. The current tension between China and the United States with regard to the coronavirus syndrome threatens the 'Phase 1' trade deal between them; actually, tensions have worsened. China and the EU agreed to reach a deal on China opening its market to foreign investors, which was a 'breakthrough' in the relations between China and the EU (*Financial Times*, 10 April 2019). China stated that "strong Europe helps international stability and benefits Beijing" (*Financial Times*, 21 March 2019). A trade deal between the EU and the United States is also expected (*Financial Times*, 23 January 2020).

18 July 2020). The service sector has been affected by the deterioration in the export-driven manufacturing (*Financial Times*, 23 November 2019). In addition, due to coronavirus, consumer confidence is lowest since the GFC (*Financial Times*, 23 April 2020). Unemployment is even higher in some countries; for example, and in May 2020 (*The Economist*, 18 July 2020), it was 14.5% in Spain, 7.8% in Italy, 8.1% in France and 15.5% in Greece (April 2020). In terms of GDP growth, it is not promising. Some examples of 2019 are as follows: Austria 1.5%, France 1.2%, Germany 0.6%, Greece 2.2%, Italy 0.3% and Spain 2.0% (*The Economist*, 28 March 2020).[10] Monetary policy has not been effective,[11] and fiscal policy cannot be used in the Euro Area in view of the 'fiscal compact' dogma that fiscal policy should not be employed (see, e.g., Arestis, 2017, 2019a); at the end of March 2020, however, it was announced that the Euro Area balanced budget rules were suspended. The ECB, in view of the coronavirus pandemic, and on 19 March 2020, launched an emergency €750bn package (called the Pandemic Emergency Programme, PEPP), in addition to the €120bn announced on 12 March 2020. All this is to purchase government and private sector debt until the end of 2020.[12] In addition, the rate of interest on TLTROs (targeted

[10] Spain's 2019 growth, due to lower labour costs, improved Spain's competitiveness and helped its exports increase. Healthier banks and an increase in aggregate demand due to expansionary government measures in the 2018 budget helped the economy. Further economic recovery has a long way to go, especially so in view of the high 14.5% unemployment rate (May 2020). The exports of Germany, which dominate the Euro Area and depend on global trade, are 50% of GDP. Global trade uncertainty is a serious concern for Germany and the Euro Area. Germany's GDP growth is the lowest over the last six years (*Financial Times*, 16 January 2020), and its banks are the least profitable in the Euro Area (*Financial Times*, 8 April 2020). Germany's economy is expected to shrink by 10% in the three months leading to June 2020 (*Financial Times*, 4 April 2020).

[11] Monetary policy in the Euro Area has not been effective, especially in the case of the low-cost loans stimulus (known as 'targeted longer-term refinancing operations', TLTRO). It has not been effective in view of poor loan demand for business and consumer credit, due to uncertainty in economic activity and high debts. Inflation rate was 1.2% in 2019 (*The Economist*, 28 March 2020), the lowest since 2016 and below the ECB's target inflation rate.

[12] Germany's constitutional court, on 5 May 2020, threatened to block fresh QE that would include German bonds, because the ECB would thereby exceed its mandate. This is against the EU treaty in terms of the ECB independence; also, it puts unnecessary pressure on the ECB, especially under the current situation, when relevant policies are urgently needed. The ECB President's response was that note of this situation was taken, but the bank would remain committed to undertake what would be necessary to achieve the inflation target.

longer-term refinancing operations; see note 11) was reduced to 0.75%.[13] Also, and on 30 April 2020, the ECB reduced the rate at which the banks borrow money from the ECB to -1%.

The Fed, at its meeting of 19 December 2018, went away from relevant pressure from the US President and increased its federal funds' rate of interest to 2.25%–2.50%. However, it signalled a slower pace of interest rate increases in 2019 and a more data-dependent interest rate path. There was a drop in US long-term bond yields, which caused a flattening of the yield curve and inversion of the yield curve as noted above. The Fed, however, decreased its rate in July 2019 (2%–2.25%), in September 2019 (1.75%–2%), in October 2019 (1.5%–1.75%) and in March 2020 twice (1.00%–1.25%; 0.00%–0.25%), accompanied by a $700bn package for government bonds and corporate debt purchases, along with the removal of reserve requirements for the smaller financial institutions. In addition, liquidity operations and funding were introduced, including a new repo facility for major foreign central banks. The March 2020 decreases of the Fed's interest rate and the rest of stimulus were in view of the coronavirus syndrome. The IMF (2020c) suggests growth for 2020 to be -8% (and 4.5% for 2021). The US unemployment increased to 11.1% (*The Economist*, 18 July 2020), a rate not seen since the Second World War—it was actually only 10% during the latest recession. The Fed also signalled that it was prepared for further monetary policy easing if necessary. A further flattening of the yield curve thereby emerged. In terms of fiscal policy, the US House of Representatives and the Senate approved at the end of March 2020 a $2.2tr stimulus package to limit the impact of the coronavirus epidemic.

In the United Kingdom, the BoE's Monetary Policy Committee, at its meetings on 7 November 2019, 19 December 2019 and 30 January 2020, kept its interest rate unchanged at 0.75% and made no change to its QE. The United Kingdom faces the problem of leaving the EU and under what conditions, which creates serious uncertainty. In the global mini-boom of 2017 and 2018, nearly all advanced countries experienced

[13] The ECB, along with heads of national central banks, proposes the creation of a 'bad bank' to remove toxic debt, left over from the GFC and from the coronavirus syndrome (*Financial Times*, 20 April 2020).

faster growth with the exception of the United Kingdom—in view of the possible leaving of the United Kingdom from the EU. On this point, Carney (2019b) suggested that the UK economy contracted in Q2 of 2019. Stagnation occurred in Q3 and Q4. Investment kept falling since 2018, and although it recovered slightly in 2019 (Q1), business surveys suggested that the underlying trend was still negative (Broadbent, 2019b). It is interesting, though, that employment in the United Kingdom remained robust despite the problems just mentioned. Unemployment at 3.9% (as in December 2019; *The Economist*, 18 April 2020) was the lowest rate since 1974. With fewer workers from the EU, businesses in the United Kingdom sought new sources for labour successfully. The Office of National Statistics (2020) confirmed that such sources were majorly women, who accounted for 80% of the increase in employment. This is a record number of women in work. Although the labour market is strong, a clearer picture of weak investment spending, manufacturing production and exports emerged. The fear in the United Kingdom is that the economy not only deteriorated in 2019 (a growth rate of 1.4% is the worst annual performance since the GFC), but will also deteriorate in 2020 in view of the United Kingdom leaving the EU (Brexit), and especially due to the coronavirus syndrome. In terms of the latter, BoE (2020) expects a 14% annual contraction of GDP in 2020, and 9% unemployment (would be higher without the government's job retention schemes)—worst economic performance since 1709 (IMF's, 2020c, prediction is -10.2%, and 6.3% for 2021). The BoE study (Bloom et al., 2019) showed that the UK investment was reduced by 11% since 2016, and productivity of firms decreased by 2% to 5%; this is all mainly due to high Brexit uncertainty (NIESR, 2019). The BoE, on 11 March 2020, reduced its rate of interest to 0.25%, and on 19 March 2020 to 0.1%, and relaunched its QE stimulus in terms of purchase of government and corporate bonds (£200bn in total). In addition, a new Term Funding Scheme, introduced on 10 April 2020, to complement other programmes, especially for small- and medium-sized enterprises (TFSME). The UK government, at the same time, introduced significant fiscal stimulus (it amounts to £60bn). Both expansionary monetary and fiscal policies were due to coronavirus threats. The Treasury and the BoE agreed (early April 2020) for the former to use its account at the latter on a 'temporary and short-term basis'; relevant drawings should be paid before the end of the year. This 'ways-and-means' facility was also used in 2008.

The economic prospects of the other world economies have deteriorated. Figures, and as in *The Economist* (28 March 2020), show that the US economy expanded at an annual rate of 2.3% in 2019, below the 3.4% growth of Q3 of 2018. The US slowdown was due to the end of the temporary tax cuts introduced in late 2017. However, despite the tax cuts, the long-awaited expansion in capital expenditure did not materialise—the US business investment actually stalled. This could be in view of that fact that US corporate profits were not promising.[14] China's growth rate in Q4 of 2018 was 6.1%, low in relation to its previous growth rates (it was 6.6% in 2018). However, government spending on infrastructure in China enhanced the level of economic activity. China recorded a 6.4% economic growth rate in Q1 (2019), only 6.1% in Q2 and Q3 (2019), and 6% in Q4 (2019) mainly due to the trade war and infrastructure investment downturn. The government's growth target was at 6.0%–6.5% for 2019; actually it was 6.1% (*The Economist*, 28 March 2020), which was below China's normal annual growth rate and the lowest since 1992 when the National Bureau of Statistics began calculating series of GDP data. The question is whether domestic demand in the near future will offset the turmoil of the trade war, and of the coronavirus impact (IMF, 2020c, expects a 1% growth rate in 2020, and 8.2 in 2021).[15] However, China's GDP plunged 6.8% (2020, Q1, year-on-year), first drop since 1992, when quarterly data began to be published (China National Bureau of Statistics, 17 April 2020). The 18 economies of the Euro Area grew at 1.2% in 2019. Euro Area inflation was 1.2 in 2019 (*The Economist*, 28 March 2020), below the ECB inflation target.[16]

[14] Slowdown in other sectors in the United States emerged. Residential investment has been shrinking in the United States since early 2018. Employment in the housing sector has fallen since March 2019. Manufacturing activity has also faltered, with manufacturing output having fallen by 15% by August 2019 since December 2018 (*The Economist*, 31 August 2019).

[15] China's central bank deputy director of its Research Bureau made a recent statement to suggest that no QE or significant reduction in interest rates would be undertaken. Instead, fiscal policy and economic restructuring, along with coordination of fiscal and monetary policies, is planned.

[16] The ECB is the only central bank that, in addition to its inflation target, has a 'reference value' for the M3 money supply. This is 4.5%, and deviations from this reference value would 'signal risks to price stability'. This target has proved unstable and so the ECB focuses less on the M3.

Further economic problems have already emerged in view of the coronavirus syndrome, as mentioned above.

In 2016 and 2017, the global economy had the highest growth in six years (3.8%). Since early 2018, the global economy has lost its momentum, and continued so in 2019. The IMF (2020a) suggests that the estimated global growth is expected to increase from 2.9% in 2019 to 3.3% in 2020 and 3.4% in 2021. This is a revision of 0.1% lower for 2019 and 2020, and 0.2% for 2021, in relation to the October IMF report (2009) and the World Economic Outlook (WEO). The recent coronavirus epidemic tends to depress global growth further. More recently, the IMF (2020c) expects recession to emerge, with a -4.9% growth rate in 2020, and 5.4% in 2021. Clearly, and as argued below, coordination of economic, fiscal, financial-stability and monetary policies is needed to achieve healthy growth rates. This is a requirement for all economies, but especially for the Euro Area, where fiscal policy is not an option in view of the 'fiscal compact' (although some relaxation has been introduced, as noted above) and there exists no centralised fiscal policy. The Euro Area has a great deal of room for fiscal stimulus in view of its very low aggregate deficit; it was 0.6% of GDP in 2018, and still is very low. The Euro Area countries, though, could easily coordinate budgetary loosening, which would help to avoid a Euro Area stagnation. The ECB ex-President Mario Draqui suggested, in an interview with the *Financial Times* (30 September 2019), that fiscal stimulus was necessary in addition to loose monetary policy, along with a serious commitment to a Euro Area fiscal union. Moreover, in his final speech, he suggested that monetary policy would achieve its objectives faster if aligned with fiscal policy (*Financial Times*, 29 October 2019; see, also Lagarde, 2019b). The G20 promised at its meeting on 26 March 2020 to inject more than $5tr into the global economy to tackle the coronavirus syndrome.

Further problems are evident. Despite the Fed's recent interest rate reductions, the quality of leveraged loans and CLOs has declined. The covenant-lite of late-2019 issues account for more than 80% of total issues in the United States, and 90% in the Euro Area (Lloyd, 2019). The ex-Fed Governor Janet Yellen suggested (*Financial Times*, 15 December 2018) that relevant 'standards were deteriorating', thereby weakening financial stability. The prolonged period of low interest rates and QE, since the GFC, has made companies rely heavily on cheap, and high-risk, debt. Another problem is with credit rating agencies, which contributed significantly to the emergence of the GFC (Arestis, 2016). Reform of them is needed, especially so in terms of the conflict of interest of their operations. Issuers, not investors, pay credit rating agencies for the ratings; the larger credit rating agencies receive most of their revenues from the issuers they rate. These fees were enhancing their revenues and profits substantially during the boom, thereby creating a serious case of 'conflict of interest', which was reinforcing their contribution to the GFC. Relevant reforms should be changing the way of their remuneration. Abolishing these agencies given their unacceptable performance in over-rating, which contributed to the GFC, is another potential reform. Some further proposals include what the Chancellor of Germany and the President of France proposed, 'a clampdown on credit rate agencies'. In addition, the BoE and the ECB have signalled a clear break away from credit rating agencies. These proposals are a way forward, if implemented.

There is also the concern that in the long period of QE and very low interest rates, financial intermediaries have extended too much credit to risky borrowers of the corporate sector. In addition, the riskiness of credit allocation to households is worrying in that indebtedness of lower-income vulnerable households has increased significantly (IMF, 2018a, p. 73). This potentially could produce financial instability; it is thereby important that "[p]olicymakers and supervisors should pay close attention to its evolution" (IMF, op. cit., p. 72). The corporate credit to GDP ratio is around its historical highs in developed and emerging economies. There is also the possibility that the increased credit was allocated to risky firms, thereby threatening financial stability (IMF, 2018a, chapter 2). This is consistent with Minsky's (1986, 1992) 'Financial Instability Hypothesis', namely the endogenous generation of financial fragility in the system. In good times, the financial sector forms unrealistic optimistic expectations, thereby extending credit to risky firms, enabling them to increase their leverage excessively. The IMF (2018a) study examines this possibility to conclude, "An increase in the riskiness of credit allocation signals heightened downside risks to GDP growth and a higher probability of banking crises and banking sector stress, over and above the previously documented signals provided by credit growth. Thus, a riskier allocation of corporate credit is an independent source of financial vulnerability" (p. 57).

Giroud and Mueller (2018) examine empirically for the period 1976–2011, across regions in the United States, the impact of increases in firms' borrowing. They conclude that in the case of a single region, firms' borrowing increases the growth of regional employment in the short run, but declines in the medium run. Across regions, with higher leverage, stronger growth is evident in the short run, but also stronger decline in the medium run. According to Cunliffe (2019a), "it is the growth rate of debt rather than its actual level that is the leading indicator of financial crises. The BoE (2018) study, based on 130 downturns in 26 advanced economies since the 1970s, suggests that a rapid build-up of debt is the best early warning indicator of a recession" (p. 6). Moreover, "[t]he actual level of debt matters rather in determining the depth, as opposed to the probability, of the crisis. So we need to look at the growth rate as well as the level" (p. 6). Household leverage growth produces similar results. The IMF (2018a, chapter 2) study provides empirical evidence that supports these propositions. Clearly, "crisis is inherent to capitalist finance", the main contribution of Minsky (1986, 1992), as Kregel (2018, p. 4) suggests, and supported both theoretically and empirically. Policies to contain financial fragility are thereby paramount.

There have been recent monetary policy attempts by central banks around the globe, in the form of QE and near-zero interest rates, to stimulate their economies. However, the global economic picture is gloomy, especially so in the economies of the United States, the United Kingdom, the Euro Area and China, which do not look much promising, as argued above. Further policies become vital. The IMF (2019c) is clear on this point: "While we expect to see a pickup next year, trade tensions, geopolitical risks, and political uncertainties are among the challenges. So we agree we need to act promptly to protect the expansion … Fiscal policy, for example, should remain flexible and growth-friendly, rebuild buffers, and strike the right chord between debt sustainability and supporting demand … We will also need to tackle financial stability risks … with all the available tools, including macroprudential tools". Also and according to the Brookings Institution think-tank and the Financial Times Tracking Index for the Global Economy Recovery (*Financial Times*, 8 April, 2019), the global economy entered a 'synchronised slowdown', which would not be easy to reverse in 2019–20. The IMF expects global GDP to continue its downward decline in 2019–20 at the slowest rate since 2010 (*The Economist*, 6 July 2019). Indeed, Christine Lagarde has suggested many times, as, for example, at the G20 Leaders' Summit on 29 June 2019, that the global economy is increasingly unsettled, especially so in view of trade tariffs. Economic policies are desperately needed, especially so fiscal policies on top of monetary policies. Also closing the gender gap would boost GDP significantly (see, also, Lagarde, 2019b)—not forgetting financial-stability policies. Relevant policies, and in terms of the coronavirus syndrome, should also be seriously taken on board currently.

4.2 Required Financial-Stability Policies

The above suggestions on required economic policies are relevant, and in view of the current economic situation worldwide. The expected IMF (2020c) 2020 world economic growth rate of -4.9% (and positive at 5.4% in 2021), in view of increasing global economic uncertainty and the coronavirus syndrome, is not good news.[17] Furthermore, and as the ex-Governor of the BoE argued, despite the introduction of a number of relevant changes since the GFC, problems still exist in terms of the financial sector (Carney, 2018). The most serious problem according to Carney (op. cit.) was and still is that the changes and innovations since the GFC "did not deliver lasting macroeconomic stability" (p. 3). Carney (2018) further suggested that Minsky (1986, 1992) was right on this issue. The Financial Instability Hypothesis of Minsky (1986, 1992) suggests endogenous generation of financial fragility in the system. In good times, the financial sector forms unrealistic and optimistic expectations, extending credit to risky firms, thereby enabling them to increase their leverage excessively. 'Markets always clear' is not right. Markets cannot regulate, as the authorities had argued prior to the GFC. In addition, "[t]he crisis showed that if left unattended, markets can be prone to excess and abuse" (Carney, 2018, p. 5), especially so in the case of the financial markets.

[17] Global economic uncertainty is at its highest, according to the Policy Uncertainty Geopolitical Risk Index (*The Economist*, 23 November 2019).

Consequently, markets need proper macroprudential regulation. The financial sector should have sufficient capital to absorb losses of a future crisis. Central banks in a number of countries have introduced liquidity stress tests to account for such possibility, but this is not enough. Carney (2019a) proposes that a new BoE is needed to "create an environment for a more resilient, effective and efficient financial system" (p. 3); financial stability is one of the priorities of such proposals. Advanced economies need more economic policies, especially so since lower growth calls for major investment initiatives. Easy financial conditions have left a legacy of debt—household and corporate in particular. Increases in interest rates could have serious effects. Inequality is another factor, which carries the seeds of future disruptions unless growth can become more inclusive. Above all and in view of the coronavirus syndrome, new policies are vitally necessary, and have been introduced, as noted above.

The GFC forced changes in the global financial regulatory systems. The IMF (2018b, chapter 2) report discusses the failings of the financial sector before the GFC and the progress on relevant reforms since the crisis. The main conclusion is that progress has been achieved on this score since the GFC. 'Capital and liquidity accords', macroprudential tools and supervision, especially of large banks, have become more intensive. The IMF (2018b, chapter 2) reports the case of some countries where 'systemic oversight authorities' have been introduced to account for macroprudential activities. In the United Kingdom, for example, and as Cunliffe's (2019a) financial-stability discussion suggests, "[t]he BoE tests the core UK banking system annually against a stress scenario to ensure it has the resilience to absorb the losses that would arise from a very severe but plausible set of domestic, global and market shocks" (p. 3).

However, the IMF (2018b) study concludes that "macroprudential authorities in many jurisdictions still lack powers and tools. This is an area that needs to be addressed" (p. 71). Edge and Liang (2019) evaluate the relevant macroprudential policies of the 2018 Financial Stability Committees (FSCs), in 58 economies around the globe (28 advanced economies and 30 emerging and developing economies), along with their interaction with central banks. Only 11 countries had FSCs and macroprudential policies. Edge and Liang (op. cit.) report that over that period, "no countries created a new single regulatory agency with sole authority for macroprudential policies" (p. 2). Edge and Liang (2019) also provide relevant empirical evidence, employing cluster analysis (dividing the FSCs into clusters) to conclude that only one-quarter of FSCs have provided relevant and appropriate tools to implement the macroprudential policies (11, which are mostly small countries, of the 58 countries examined have no FSCs). Their central banks are given macroprudential authority. Central banks, however, "are not especially able to undertake macroprudential actions when FSCs are not set up to do so" (Edge and Liang, op. cit., p. 1). Still central banks should be involved in view of their macroeconomic forecasting and in implementing counter-cyclical monetary policy. In terms of whether FSCs have strong tools, Edge and Liang (2019) conclude that very few have hard tools. The frequency of changes for most tools 'is very limited', which implies that relevant tools "are not used in a time-varying way to address cyclical vulnerabilities" (Edge and Liang, op. cit., pp. 15–16).

An important tool of financial stability is the so-called counter-cyclical capital buffer (CCyB). It is an amount of capital financial institutions should set aside to avoid breaching their minimum capital requirements, and should also be required to hold more capital during upturns (in addition to institutions' capital requirements) and reduce it to absorb losses in bad times, so as to ensure that credit is available during a crisis. The CCyB's higher bank capital increases the loss-absorbing capacity of the banking system; it also increases the resilience of the financial system, thereby reducing the likelihood of a financial crisis. Forbes (2019) suggests, "The CCyB is a macroprudential tool that has widespread academic and policy support and a well-defined framework. It could cushion economies against booms as well as busts. Although many countries have a framework in place to use the CCyB, as of 2017 only about six countries have tightened it at all. None have tightened it or varied it as aggressively as suggested by basic calculations on its optimal use" (p. 473).[18] The CCyB should also be applied to non-bank financial institutions, especially to shadow banking in view of its enormous expansion recently, as shown above. The CCyB policy should not be merged with monetary

[18] The FPC of the BoE decided that the appropriate setting of the CCyB should be "in the region of 1% in standard risk environment" (Kohn, 2019).

policy because it would easily lead to inadequate attention being paid to financial-stability risks (Taylor, 2019). Furthermore, and as Aikman, Giese, Kapadia, and McLeay (2019) suggest, the CCyB and monetary policy should be coordinated to minimise the overall loss function of the central bank, which comprises of both financial-stability and monetary policy objectives. Cappelletti, Margues, Varasso, Budrys, and Peeters (2019) examine empirically the impact of higher bank capital buffers in the Euro Area and conclude that they have a positive effect in terms of reducing banks' risk-taking and a temporary decrease in credit supply. The *Financial Times* (6 April 2020), and according to own calculations, reported that central banks around the word freed around $599bn of the CCyB for lenders to help them in view of the coronavirus pandemic. In addition, and in a number of countries, banks have been advised to reduce dividends in order to conserve capital to absorb losses.

King's (2016) proposal 'pawnbroker for all seasons' is also relevant. Banks should pay yearly a compulsory insurance premium so that in a crisis, they can access funds from the central bank. A liquidity coverage ratio (LCR), a portion of high-quality assets (cash and short-term government debt), can be used in a crisis. Actually, in many countries recently, financial authorities have eased banks' LCR, including foreign exchange requirements; they also eased banks' reserve requirements. Targeted leveraged ratios (total debts/total assets, which restricts banks to exceed a minimum ratio) and limits on foreign currency loans, when financial risks emerge, are further measures. These measures would increase the banking sector's resilience to systemic risks. An important requirement for banks is to account for the riskiness of their assets, and hold more capital in the case of high-risk assets. In terms of the borrower-targeted instruments, loan-to-value ratios (enforcing cap on new loans) and debt-to-income ratios (constraining household indebtedness by imposing a limit) are also important. In terms of the CCyB, Broadbent (2019a) suggests, "The aim is to ensure that, in the event of a downturn and losses on their books, banks don't make it worse by actively cutting back on lending" (p. 17). Moreover, "[k]ey priorities include completing implementation of the leverage ratio and of frameworks for the cross-border resolution of banks and for insurer solvency. Macroprudenial authorities must also have an adequate toolkit with which to contain systemic risks. Existing progress in challenging areas such as bank compensation practices and use of credit rating agencies must be built upon, but new thinking may also be needed. Financial sector reform efforts must continue to be coordinated internationally" (p. 56).[19] Stress tests are of course important to identify emerging threats to financial stability. The focus should be on identifying whether banks, and other financial institutions, could manage large losses that might arise from financial crises (BoE, 2013). On 20 March 2020, and in view of the coronavirus, stress tests in the United Kingdom were cancelled for eight major banks and building societies. The BoE also reduced the CCyB to 0% from 1%; also banks' capital and liquidity buffers would be reduced as necessary.[20]

Nuno (2018) discusses possible central bank digital currency (CBDC)[21] and analyses its possible implications for monetary policy and financial stability (see, also, BIS, 2019). Nuno (2018) suggests that central banks have already considered this possibility. According to the BIS (2019), of the 63 central banks approached in a relevant survey, including emerging and developed economies, 70% responded to say that they are either currently working or will be engaged with CBDC. There are of course similarities and differences between CBDCs and the banknotes and bank reserves of the central banks. CBDC would be a deposit at the central bank by households and firms, and considered as legal tender by the government. This clarifies the difference and similarity with deposits of banks with central banks and currency. Clearly, significant effects on the transmission of monetary policy would emerge, and central banks would have greater control over the financial conditions in the economy. However,

[19] Another possible new financial stability policy is what the Fed Chairman suggested at the press conference following the Fed's monetary policy meeting (29 January 2020). Control of the yield curve is the relevant suggestion (see, also, Bernanke, 2020). This policy would require the central bank to intervene in the bond market to keep yields on target, in the same way as it intervenes to set its base rate.

[20] In the Euro Area, Eurobonds could emerge as safe assets to serve as an anchor of financial stability. They would also signal the determination of the authorities to overcome the coronavirus crisis.

[21] Digital currencies are private digital means (credit cards, payments such as mobile ones) and technological innovations of what is called 'cryptocurrencies' (Nuno, 2018)—cryptocurrencies have raised concerns by financial authorities, in view of their operations without institutional backing and the fact that they are borderless. In the United Kingdom, the FCA regulates crypto assets, and recently, it investigated companies in view of concerns about growing relevant risks (*Financial Times*, 31 December 2018).

financial stability might be severely affected in a financial crisis. Central bank money could be viewed safer than bank deposits, and holders could proceed to withdraw their funds from banks and deposit them in CBDC accounts, thereby exasperating the financial crisis.

Our suggestion of institutional separation of retail banking from investment banking is a way forward; this should deliver a more stable financial entity, and avoid the high risk-taking of the combined banking. In addition, control of non-bank financial institutions is urgently required. Policymakers should develop and deploy new tools, with appropriate coordination between them. This is vital to contain another crisis. Our suggestion on relevant policies is that, in addition to financial-stability policies, fiscal and monetary policies are also required. Most important is proper coordination of the three policies, with a focus on financial stability (see, also, Arestis 2016, 2018, 2019a, 2019b).[22] Coordination should help fiscal, monetary and financial-stability policymakers to be aware of each other's policy objectives and policy decisions. The more predictable their policy is, the easier it is to successfully achieve their objectives in a coordinated way. Such coordination should enable central banks to deliver properly, since they would have the backing of political authorities. Combes, Debrum, Minea, and Tabsoba (2018) argue that their theoretical analysis and empirics, utilising a large panel of 140 advanced and developing countries, and using 'a two-step system GMM dynamic panel estimator', imply that "central bank independence and fiscal policy rules in the light of post-GFC conditions … could … benefit from internalising the likely interdependence between these institutional arrangements" (p. 2782). Clearly, Combes et al.'s (2018) findings point to potential benefits of reforming macroeconomic frameworks in a coordinated manner, so that coordinated monetary and fiscal policies contribute to macroeconomic stability. Coordination of fiscal and monetary policies is suggested in the *IMF Blog* under the coronavirus syndrome; also "continuous international coordination will be essential to

[22] The current IMF Managing Director, speaking to the *Financial Times* (9 October 2019), suggested that the global economy is in 'a synchronised slowdown', in view of monetary policy being constrained. Fiscal response to the slowdown is required.

support vulnerable countries, to restore market confidence, and to contain financial stability risks" (Adrian & Natalucci, 2020).

Central bank independence is a relevant problem. Angeriz, Arestis, and McCombie (2008) conclude that a marginal effect of such independence is in evidence in terms of its impact on inflation, inflation persistence and containment of inflationary expectations. Moreover, and since the GFC, the inability to achieve the targeted inflation rate and the 2019 economic downturn severely question central bank independence. Sharp (2019) suggests that the independence of the BoE is overstated. This is so because it is the Parliament that has delegated the relevant authority to the BoE; and operates, "within the constraints of laws passed by Parliament. The Bank is transparent and is subject to layers of oversight, for example all members of policy committees are appointed by the Government" (p. 3). Sharp (op. cit.) also suggests, "Given potential threats to the constrained central bank independence which I fear might emerge, I believe greater clarity supporting the legitimacy of the separate policy committee is merited" (p. 7).

Central bank independence is weakening. The Euro Area and the United States are two examples. The US President has initiated unprecedented open interventions to the Fed's decision-making, thereby undermining Fed's independence. Moreover, the President threatened firing the Fed Chair, and proposed nominations for the Fed's Board of Governors Committee who would be willing to support the President's political aims. However, the President failed to install his loyalists on the Board. Jordan and Luther (2019) suggest that the Fed "is less independent than most other central banks" (p. 2), and that the Fed's operating regime "has increased the appointment power of the President and improved the bargaining power of the Congress" (p. 2).

In the Euro Area, a relevant example is the disagreement between the ECB and the national regulators (including the relevant governments) over the question of who should supervise clearinghouses. A deal has been reached between national governments and the European Parliament, whereby the European Securities and Markets Authority is given the power to monitor clearinghouses' risk management. The ECB officials have categorically suggested that such deal violates the ability of the ECB to conduct its independent monetary policy. There is also the argument that in some Euro Area countries, like Spain and Greece, public trust on the ECB is very low. This is so since the ECB is thought to be partly responsible for the austerity imposed in these countries. Mario Draqui, the ex-President of the ECB, at the annual 2019 meeting of the IMF, said that he was 'very worried about central bank independence'.

It is indeed important that coordination of fiscal policy[23] with monetary and financial-stability policy is paramount, as previous and current experiences clearly support such coordination. Ryan-Collins and van Lerven (2018) examine fiscal and monetary policy coordination in the twentieth century, focusing in particular over the period 1930s–70s, and provide examples when central banks and Ministers of Finance/Economics cooperated closely. They conclude that the number of cases examined clearly support fiscal and monetary policy coordination (see, also, Eggertsson, 2006, for relevant and supportive empirical evidence). In addition, over the long period since the GFC, the case of the inability to achieve the inflation targets of the central banks in most advanced countries is relevant. Economies require more help from the fiscal side. Coordination of fiscal, monetary and financial-stability policies becomes paramount, as argued in this contribution—especially so in view of the QE and near-zero interest rates, with central banks needing new monetary policy tools—and of enormous significance for the post-neoliberal world.

The BoE's Monetary Policy Committee, after its meeting on 26 March 2020, suggested that coronavirus forces are causing business to close and consumer spending to reduce. These developments produce a recession. Financial stability becomes relevant under such circumstances, whereby central banks should take measures to reduce the cost of borrowing, improve cash flows and support consumers' and companies' spending. Fiscal policy is also relevant along with monetary policy; well as coordination of both with financial stability. Bernanke (2020) discusses the costs of QE and FG guidance to conclude that the most serious cost is financial instability. Consequently, monetary policymakers should take it seriously and undertake macroprudential policies properly coordinated with monetary and fiscal policies.

---

[23] The cost of servicing the debt, especially of developed countries, is the lowest currently over the last four decades. Fiscal authorities should and could use relevant fiscal policies to stimulate their economies.

5 Summary and Conclusions

We have discussed in this contribution financial stability, which had not been addressed prior to the GFC, and still requires further investigation. We have reviewed a number of relevant proposals, and concluded that, in effect, none of them is in place to avoid another financial crisis of the GFC type. More relevant policy action is urgently required—especially so in view of what Lagarde (2018) suggested at the G20 leaders' meeting in Argentina, "We have had a good stretch of solid growth by historical standards, but now we are facing a period where significant risks are materialising and darker clouds are looming". Lagarde (op. cit.) also argued, "More broadly, financial sector risks require action, including by avoiding a rollback of post-crisis advances to financial sector regulation".[24] In addition, Lagarde (2019a) suggested that "we need stronger international cooperation"[25] and countries "need to avoid self-inflicted wounds, including tariffs and other trade barriers". Progress has been evident, but since the GFC, the reform agenda has not been completed (see also, IMF, 2018b, chapter 2) and international cooperation does not seem to become stronger.

It follows from our analysis that the main operation of any central bank should be financial stability and coordination with monetary and fiscal policies. This clearly follows from the events leading to the GFC, which testify to this important requirement. A relevant committee within the central bank would be required to undertake such a role. With the objective of financial stability, such committee of the central bank should seek to influence the credit and lending policies of the full range of financial institutions, along with supervisory intensity. Prevention of a future crisis is incomplete. Obviously then, financial-stability policies along with monetary and fiscal policies, all of them properly coordinated, are an important economic policy dimension to be introduced, especially after neoliberalism.

---

[24] The financial sector, however, and according to Mark Carney (*The Economist*, 18 April 2020), has enough capital, a lesson learnt from the GFC experience.

[25] A relevant example is the IMF and the World Bank joint announcement (IMF Press Release, No. 20/161, 15 April 2020) that their suggestion for a debt relief to 25 of the world's poorest countries, worth $214m, was accepted by the G20 Finance Ministers' meeting.

In view of the coronavirus syndrome, central banks and governments around the world have initiated monetary and fiscal policies, as well as the IMF and World Bank in terms of their own policies, in a way that suggests global capitalism is changing. The 'New Consensus Macroeconomics' unthinkable policies (Arestis & González Martinez, 2015) have been transformed into essential ones. The idea that good governments are small ones and that markets are always in a position to respond to any economic problems seems now to be a serious challenge. Central banks and governments have also worked closely to protect their economies from the coronavirus syndrome. Neoliberalism may be ending.

References

Adrian, T., & Natalucci, F. (2020, April 14). COVID-19 Crisis Poses Threat to Financial Stability. *IMF Blog*. Available at: https://blogs.imf.org/2020/04/14/covid-19-crisis-poses-threat-to-financial-stability/?utm_medium=email&utm_source=govdelivery

Adrian, T., Natalucci, F., & Piontek, T. (2018, November 15). Sounding the Alarm on Leveraged Lending. *IMF Blog*. Available at: https://blogs.imf.org/2018/11/15/sounding-the-alarm-on-leveraged-lending/#more-25017

Aikman, D., Bridges, J., Kashyap, A., & Siegert, C. (2019). Would Macroprudential Regulation Have Prevented the Last Crisis? *Journal of Economic Perspectives, 33*(1), 107–130.

Aikman, D., Giese, J., Kapadia, S., & McLeay, M. (2019, May). *Targeting Financial Stability: Macroprudential or Monetary Policy?* (ECB Working Paper Series, No. 2278).

Angeriz, A., Arestis, P., & McCombie, J. (2008). *Does Central Bank Independence Affect Inflation Persistence and Volatility?* (CCEPP Working Paper). Cambridge Centre for Economic and Public Policy, Department of Land Economy, University of Cambridge.

Arestis, P. (2016). Main and Contributory Causes of the Recent Financial Crisis and Economic Policy Implications. In P. Arestis & M. C. Sawyer (Eds.), *Emerging Economies During and After the Great Recession*, Annual Edition of *International Papers in Political Economy*. London: Palgrave Macmillan.

Arestis, P. (2017). Monetary Policy Since the Global Financial Crisis. In P. Arestis & M. C. Sawyer (Eds.), *Economic Policies Since the Global Financial Crisis*,

Annual Edition of *International Papers in Political Economy*. Houndmills, Basingstoke: Palgrave Macmillan.
Arestis, P. (2018). Importance of Tackling Income Inequality and Relevant Economic Policies. In P. Arestis and M. C. Sawyer (eds.), *Inequality: Trends, Causes, Consequences, Relevant Economic Policies*, Annual Edition of *International Papers in Political Economy*. London: Palgrave Macmillan.
Arestis, P. (2019a). The Past and Future of the Euro. *Revista de Economia Critica, 27*(2), 6–15.
Arestis, P. (2019b). Critique of the New Consensus Macroeconomics and Proposal for a More Keynesian Macroeconomic Model. In P. Arestis & M. C. Sawyer (Eds.), *Frontiers of Heterodox Macroeconomics*, Annual Edition of *International Papers in Political Economy*. London: Palgrave Macmillan.
Arestis, P., & González Martinez, A. R. (2015). The Absence of Environmental Issues in the New Consensus Macroeconomics Is Only One of Numerous Criticisms. In P. Arestis and M. Sawyer (Eds.), *Finance and the Macroeconomics of Environmental Policies*. Annual Edition of *International Papers in Political Economy*, Houndmills, Basingstoke: Palgrave Macmillan.
Basel III Package. (2010). *Basel III: International Regulatory Framework for Banks*. Basel Committee on Banking Supervision. Available at: https://www.bis.org/bcbs/basel3.htm
Bases, D. (2018). *Global Debt Load at a Record $247 Trillion in Q1-IIF*. Available at: https://www.reuters.com/article/global-debt-iif/global-debt-load-at-a-record-247-trillion-in-q1-iif-idUSL1N1U51A2
Bernanke, B. (2020). The New Tools of Monetary Policy. *American Economic Review, 110*(4), 943–983.
BIS (Bank of International Settlements). (2011, December). *Fiscal Policy and Its Implications for Monetary and Financial Stability* (BIS Papers, No. 59). Basel, Switzerland: Bank for International Settlements. Available at: http://ssrn.com/abstract=2002654
BIS (Bank of International Settlements). (2018, September). International Banking and Financial Market Developments. *BIS Quarterly Review, 2018*, 1–90.
BIS (Bank of International Settlements). (2019, January). *Proceeding with Caution – A Survey on Central Bank Digital Currency* (BIS Papers, No. 101). Basel, Switzerland: Bank for International Settlements. Available at: https://www.bis.org/publ/bppdf/bispap101.pdf
Bloom, N., Bunn, P., Chen, S., Mizen, P., Smietanka, P., & Thwaites, G. (2019, August). *The Impact of Brexit on UK Firms* (BoE Staff Working Paper No. 818).

BoE. (2009, November 24). *The Role of Macroprudential Policy* (Discussion Paper). Available at: https://www.bankofengland.co.uk/paper/2009/the-role-of-macroprudential-policy

BoE. (2013, October 1). *A Framework for Stress Testing the UK Banking System* (Discussion Paper). Available at: https://www.bankofengland.co.uk/news/2013/october/framework-for-stress-testing-the-uk-banking-system

BoE. (2018, November). *Financial Stability Report* (Issue No. 44). Available at: https://www.bankofengland.co.uk/-/media/boe/files/financial-stability-report/2018/november-2018.pdf

BoE. (2019). *What Is Financial Stability?* Available at: https://www.bankofengland.co.uk/knowledgebank/what-is-financial-stability

BoE. (2020). Monetary Policy Report, Monetary Policy Committee, 07 May 2020. Available at: https://www.bbc.com/news/amp/business-52566030

Broadbent, B. (2019a, January 23). *Debt Dynamics*. Speech Given at the London Business School. Available at: https://www.bankofengland.co.uk/speeches

Broadbent, B. (2019b, May 20). *Investment and Uncertainty: The Value of Waiting for News*. Speech Given at Imperial College Business School, London. Available at: https://www.bankofengland.co.uk/publications/Pages/speeches/default.aspx

Cappelletti, G., Margues, A. P. Varasso, P., Budrys, Z., & Peeters, J. (2019). *Impact of Higher Capital Buffers on Banks' Lending and Risk Taking: Evidence from the Euro Area Experiments*. (ECB Working Paper No. 2292).

Carney, M. (2018, October 19). *True Finance – Ten Years After the Financial Crisis*. Speech Given at the Economic Club of New York. Available at: https://www.bankofengland.co.uk/news/speeches

Carney, M. (2019a, April 29). *A Platform for Innovation*. Speech Given at 'Remarks at Innovate Finance Global Summit', London. Available at: https://www.bankofengland.co.uk/news/speeches

Carney, M. (2019b, August 23). *The Growing Challenges for Monetary Policy in the Current International and Monetary and Financial System*. Speech Given at the Jackson Hole Symposium 2019. Available at: https://www.bankofengland.co.uk/news/speeches

Carney, M. (2020, January 9). *A Framework for All Seasons?* Speech Given at the BoE Workshop on *The Future of Inflation Targeting*. Available at: https://www.bankofengland.co.uk/news/speeches

Claessens, S., Keen, M., & Pazarbasioglu, C. (2010, September). *Financial Sector Taxation: The IMF's Report to the G-20 and Background Material*. The IMF's Report to the G-20 and Background Material. International Monetary

Fund. Available at: https://www.imf.org/external/np/seminars/eng/2010/paris/pdf/090110.pdf

Clement, P. (2010). The Term 'Macroprudential': Origins and Evolution. *BIS Quarterly Review, 2010*(March), 59–67.

Combes, J. L., Debrum, X., Minea, A., & Tabsoba, R. (2018). Inflation Targeting, Fiscal Rules and Policy Mix: Cross Effects and Interactions. *Economic Journal, 128*(615), 2755–2784.

Cunliffe, J. (2019a, May 7). *Financial Stability Post Brexit: Risks from Global Debt.* Speech Given at CFO Agenda, London. Available at: https://www.bankofengland.co.uk/speeches

Cunliffe, J. (2019b, October 14). *Financial Stability and Low for Long.* Speech Given at the Society of Professional Economists Annual Conference, London. Available at: https://www.bankofengland.co.uk/news/speeches

ECB. (2019). The Economic Implications of Rising Protectionism: A Euro Area and Global Perspective. *ECB Economic Bulletin, Issue 3/2019.* Available at: https://www.ecb.europa.eu/pub/economic-bulletin/articles/2019/html/ecb.ebart201903_01~e589a502e5.en.html#toc1

Edge, R. M., & Liang, N. J. (2019). *New Financial Stability Governance Structures and Central Banks.* Finance and Economics Discussion Series 2019-019. Washington, DC: Board of Governors of the Federal Reserve System. Available at: https://doi.org/10.17016/FEDS.2019.019

Eggertsson, G. B. (2006). *Fiscal Multipliers and Policy Coordination* (Federal Reserve Bank of New York Staff Reports, No. 241). New York: Federal Reserve Bank of New York.

Forbes, K. J. (2019). Macroprudential Policy: What We've Learned, Don't Know, and Need to Do. *AEA Papers and Proceedings, 109*, 470–475.

Georgieva, K. (2020, March). *Statement Following a G20 Ministerial Call on the Coronavirus Emergency* (IMF Press Release No. 20/98). Available at: https://www.imf.org/en/News/Articles/2020/03/23/pr2098-imf-managing-director-statement-following-a-g20-ministerial-call-on-the-coronavirus-emergency?cid=em-COM-123-41300

Giroud, X., & Mueller, H. M. (2018). *Firm Leverage and Regional Business Cycles* (Working Paper 25325). Cambridge, MA: National Bureau of Economic Research. Available at: http://www.nber.org/papers/w25325

Goodhart, C. (2015). Why Monetary Policy Has Been Comparatively Ineffective? *The Manchester School, 89*(4, Supplement), 20–29.

Haltom, R., Wissuchek, E., & Wolman, A. J. (2018, December). *Have Yield Curve Inversions Become More Likely?* (Economic Brief, pp. 1–5). Federal Reserve of Richmond.

IMF. (2009, October). *World Economic Outlook – Sustaining Recovery.* Washington, DC: International Monetary Fund. Available at: http://www.imf.org/external/pubs/ft/weo/2009/02/index.htm

IMF. (2011). *Macroprudential Policy: An Organizing Framework.* Washington, DC: International Monetary Fund. Available at: https://www.imf.org/external/np/pp/eng/2011/031411.pdf

IMF. (2012, April). *Global Financial Stability Report: The Quest for Lasting Stability.* World Economic and Financial Surveys, Monetary and Capital Markets Department. Washington, DC: International Monetary Fund.

IMF. (2018a, April). *The Riskiness of Credit Allocation: A Source of Financial Vulnerability?* Global Financial Stability Report. Washington, DC: International Monetary Fund.

IMF. (2018b, October). *A Decade After the Global Financial Crisis: Are We Safer?* Global Financial Stability Report. Washington, DC: International Monetary Fund.

IMF. (2019a, April). *Full Report and Executive Summary.* World Economic Outlook: Growth Slowdown, Precarious Recovery. Washington, DC: International Monetary Fund.

IMF. (2019b). *Global Financial Stability Report.* Transcript of the Press Conference of April 2019. Washington, DC: International Monetary Fund.

IMF. (2019c, April 13). *IMFC Press Conference.* Washington, DC: International Monetary Fund. Available at: https://www.imf.org/en/News/Articles/2019/04/13/tr041319-transcript-imfc-press-conference?cid=em-COM-123-38657

IMF. (2020a, January). *An Update of the Key WEO Projections.* World Economic Outlook: Update. Washington, DC: International Monetary Fund.

IMF. (2020b, May 4). *World Economic Outlook Reports.* World Economic Outlook. Washington, DC: International Monetary Fund.

IMF. (2020c, June 24). *World Economic Outlook Update.* World Economic Outlook. Washington, DC: International Monetary Fund.

Independent Banking Commission. (2011). *Independent Commission on Banking: Final Report.* Department of Business, Innovation Skills and Treasury. Available at: https://webarchive.nationalarchives.gov.uk/20120827143059/http://bankingcommission.independent.gov.uk/

Jordan, J. L., & Luther, W. J. (2019). *Central Bank Independence and the Federal Reserve's New Operating Regime* (AIER Sound Money Project Working Paper, No. 2019-07). Available at: https://ssrn.com/abstract=3313068

King, M. (2016). *The End of Alchemy: Money, Banking and the Future of the Global Economy*. London: Little Brown.

Kohn, D. (2019, May 15). *How Can the Objective of Macroprudential Policy Be Operationalised, Given the High Uncertainty About the State of the Financial System?* Speech Given at the Joint Bundesbank-ECB Spring Conference 2029, Frankfurt. Available at: https://www.bankofengland.co.uk/publications/Pages/speeches/default.aspx

Kregel, J. (2018). *Preventing the Last Crisis: Minsky's Forgotten Lessons Ten Years After Lehman* (Policy Note, No. 5). Levy Economics Institute of Bard College.

Lagarde, C. (2018, November). G20: Step Up to Boost Inclusive Growth. *IMF Blog*. Available at: https://ar-ar.facebook.com/pg/christinelagarde/posts/?ref=page_internal

Lagarde, C. (2019a, April 11). *Opening Remarks for Spring Meetings Press Conference*. International Monetary Fund. Available at: https://www.imf.org/en/News/Articles/2019/04/11/sp-md-opening-remarks-for-spring-meetings-press-conference

Lagarde, C. (2019b, November 22). *The Future of the Euro Area Economy*. Speech at the European Banking Congress, Frankfurt. Available at: https://www.eurasiareview.com/22112019-lagarde-the-future-of-the-euro-area-economy-speech/

Liikanen Report. (2012, October). *Report of the European Commission's High-Level Expert Group on Bank Structural Reform*. Available at: https://en.wikipedia.org/wiki/Liikanen_report

Lloyd, C. (2019). *Leveraged Loans–History Rhyming?* Available at: https://www.bbntimes.com/en/global-economy/leveraged-loans-history-rhyming

Minsky, H. P. (1986). *Stabilising an Unstable Economy*. New Haven, CT: Yale University Press.

Minsky, H. P. (1992, May). *The Financial Instability Hypothesis* (The Jerome Levy Economics Institute Working Paper No. 74).

Mnuchin, S. T., & Phillips, C. S. (2017). *A Financial System That Creates Economic Opportunities Banks and Credit Unions*. Report to President Donald J. Trump Executive Order 13772 on Core Principles for Regulating the United States Financial System, USA Department of the Treasury.

National Institute of Economic and Social Research (NIESR). (2019). The UK Economy: Forecast Summary. *National Institute Economic Review, 249*(3, August), F44–F54.

Nuno, G. (2018) Monetary Policy Implications of Central-Bank Issued Digital Currency. *Economic Bulletin 3/2018*, Banco de Espana, Spain.

Office of National Statistics. (2020). Employment in the UK: Estimates of Employment, Unemployment and Economic Inactivity for the UK. Available at: https://www.ons.gov.uk/employmentandlabourmarket/peopleinwork/employmentandemployeetypes/bulletins/employmentintheuk/latest

Pedraz, C. G. (2019). Leveraged Loans: Definition and Market Development. *Economic Bulletin, No. 4*, Banco de Espana. Available at: https://ssrn.com/abstract=3473739

Proudman, J. (2018, November 26). *From Construction to Maintenance: Patrolling the Ring-Fence*. Speech Given at the Cass Business School, London. Available at: https://www.bankofengland.co.uk/news/speeches

Ryan-Collins, J., & van Lerven, F. (2018), *Bringing the Helicopter to Ground: A Historical Review of Fiscal-Monetary Coordination to Support Economic Growth in the 20th Century* (UCL Institute for Innovation and Public Purpose (IIPP) Working Paper Series 2018-08). Available at: https://www.ucl.ac.uk/bartlett/public-purpose/wp2018-08

Sharp, R. (2019, March 19). *Central Bank Independence as a Prerequisite for Financial Stability*. Speech Given at the Cass Business School London. Available at: https://www.bankofengland.co.uk/news/speeches

Tarullo, D. K. (2019). Financial Regulation: Still Unsettled a Decade After the Crisis. *Journal of Economic Perspectives, 33*(1), 61–80.

Taylor, M. (2019). *Overcoming Macroprudential Inertia: an Ambush and the Votes that Never Were*. Speech Given at the 5th Annual Macroprudential Conference, Frankfurt, Germany, 21 June 2019. Available at: https://www.bankofengland.co.uk/news/speeches

Vickers, J. (2016, April). *The Systemic Risk Buffer for UK Banks: A Response to the BoE's Consultation Paper* (LSE Financial Markets Group Paper Series, Special Paper 244).

2

The Future of Capitalism in a Post-Neoliberal World

Yiannis Kitromilides

1 Introduction

Debates about the future of capitalism are not new. It is a theme that has been continuously discussed since Karl Marx's famous nineteenth-century prognosis that the capitalist system would eventually collapse under the pressure of its own internal contradictions. Towards the end of the twentieth century, however, it was Soviet-style communism, the economic system that for seventy years was presented to the world as an alternative to capitalism that collapsed. Capitalism now 'rules the world' and it has become the sole remaining mode of production throughout the globe. In today's world, unlike the previous Cold War era, there is no competition between two alternative economic systems but simply a clash between two different varieties of the same system (Milanovic, 2019).

The 'victory' of capitalism over communism and the end of the Cold War was, of course, supposed to signal the 'end of history' (Fukuyama,

Y. Kitromilides (✉)
Cambridge Centre of Economic and Public Policy, Department of Land Economy, University of Cambridge, Cambridge, UK

P. Arestis, M. Sawyer (eds.), *Economic Policies for a Post-Neoliberal World*, International Papers in Political Economy, https://doi.org/10.1007/978-3-030-56735-4_2

1969). It was also supposed to finally put an end to speculation about the future of capitalism since with regard to the system of political and economic organisation the world has reached its final destination. This clearly did not happen, and the debate about the future of capitalism continues unabated with some important new elements.

One such major new element is that the contemporary critiques of capitalism and the various concerns expressed about its future are not confined solely to the 'usual suspects' of Marxist and other left-wing critics of capitalism. A great deal of the various concerns about the way capitalism is currently operating are expressed by critics who are on the whole sympathetic to capitalism. One of the most remarkable and memorable statements in this regard was that of Ray Dalio (2019), the billionaire founder of Bridgewater Associates, one of the world's largest hedge funds, who stated that although he was a capitalist even he thought that capitalism was broken. Dalio (op. cit.) believes that capitalism, as currently operating in the USA, is an economic system in urgent need of reform. This is primarily because of the spectacular increase in inequality which has now reached pre-1929 levels and which makes the system not only unfair but also unproductive.

According to Dalio (2019), capitalism in order to survive must improve the incomes as well as the opportunities of the middle classes or the bottom 60% of citizens. In similar vein and equally astonishing, the *Business Roundtable*, an association of CEOs of the US leading companies, released a new statement on the *Purpose of a Corporation.*[1] The statement was signed by 181 CEOs of US corporations *committing* to lead their companies for the benefit of all stakeholders—customers, employees, suppliers and communities, as well as shareholders. If such a commitment is seriously implemented, maximising shareholder value would no longer be the primary aim of corporate America.

There is an assumption implicit in this commitment in favour of stakeholder capitalism, that shareholder capitalism has been responsible not only for the rise of inequality and the increase in uncertainty and insecurity among the middle classes, but also for the many adverse environmental consequences including the most serious environmental crisis,

[1] Available at: https://opportunity.businessroundtable.org/ourcommitment/

the threat of irreversible climate change. 'Stakeholder capitalism' is supposed to take these developments seriously into account.

The threat of catastrophic climate change forms another, perhaps the most important, new element in the overall concern about the future of capitalism. If capitalism is responsible for catastrophic climate change the debate concerning its future is less about the prospect of the 'end of history' and more about the apocalyptic prospect of the 'end of the world'! The future of capitalism and the future of the world, therefore, seem to be closely inter-connected.

The way that these concerns about the future of capitalism can be addressed and translated into policies depends crucially on the operation of the political system. There are, however, equally serious concerns that not only the economic system but also the political system of contemporary capitalism is also malfunctioning. The corrosive influence of money in politics is one serious concern. The emergence at a global scale of the political phenomenon of 'populism' is another. Both are posing a serious threat to the established political order of liberal democratic politics. A 'broken capitalism' at the level of the economy combined with a 'broken capitalism' at the political level is, of course, a profoundly serious matter.

'Capitalism is broken' and 'Capitalism is not working', therefore, have become not merely the slogans of left-wing demonstrators and anti-capitalism agitators but headlines in mainstream media. The central question posed by this type of 'internal' critique of capitalism is how capitalism can be re-set or repaired and *not* how capitalism can be replaced by an alternative economic and political system. The latter question debated within the Marxist and socialist tradition, concerning the long-term viability of capitalism although significant and important, will not be considered in this contribution.[2]

If, however, capitalism is to be re-set and repaired so must the policies and the theories underpinning these policies must be re-set and repaired or replaced. Neoliberalism is the economic creed that sustained and maintained, mainly US type of capitalism, for the past forty years. As a concept neoliberalism is widely used in public debate but without a single generally accepted definition. It is very often associated with

[2] See, for example, Mason (2016).

support of policies of liberalisation of trade and international capital movements, limiting the power of trade unions, privatisation of state-owned enterprises, cuts in direct taxation and public spending and maintaining fiscal discipline in public finances by avoiding deficit spending. In this contribution we will use the term neoliberalism to indicate a general support for these policies and also a manifestation of an excessive faith in markets and a powerful mistrust of government involvement in the economy. Post-neoliberalism will involve a shift away from the beliefs and policy commitments of neoliberalism.

In dealing with the rising discontent with capitalism, therefore, the construction of a post-neoliberal alternative model of capitalism is necessary. The aim of this contribution, therefore, is to examine this vision of a post-neoliberal world and consider the future of capitalism when stripped of its 'neoliberal' foundations. Can the various concerns identified by the various contemporary critics of capitalism, in particular the threat of climate change, be dealt with simply by abandoning neoliberalism and neoliberal economic policies? Anthropogenic climate change pre-existed the advent of neoliberalism in the 1970s and the widespread adoption of neoliberal economic policies. How would a post-neoliberal world cope with the climate change challenge?

This contribution will proceed as follows: Section 2 examines the basic elements of 'neoliberal' capitalism and briefly reviews the ascendancy, spread and policy dominance of the 'neoliberal' paradigm. Section 3 discusses briefly the so-called end of history debate and evaluates the impact the collapse of communism had on the spread of 'neoliberalism'. With communism vanquished was the world converging towards a single political and economic model? Section 4 considers the various critiques of neoliberal capitalism and asks whether the era of neoliberal hegemony is coming to an end. Section 5 concentrates on one critical global policy challenge that emerged during the neoliberal era which has not been adequately dealt with within the existing global policymaking framework: the threat posed by irreversible climate change. Section 6 deals with the political economy aspects of designing appropriate policies to tackle the climate change challenge. Section 7 considers the debate about the future of capitalism in the context of the outbreak of the COVID-19 pandemic and examines the likely consequences of the crisis for neoliberal capitalism. Section 8 summarises and concludes.

2 The Emergence Spread and Dominance of 'Neoliberalism'

It is important to distinguish between neoliberalism as a *concept* and neoliberalism as an *economic system* that has embraced and adopted the particular philosophy and policies of neoliberalism. In this section, we will examine neoliberalism both as a concept and as an economic system that has adopted and implemented neoliberal policies. It is, of course, entirely possible that capitalism can operate well without adopting neoliberal policies.

The term neoliberalism has a long intellectual history going back to the nineteenth century, although the first use of the term can be traced to the so-called Walter Lippman colloquium held in Paris in 1938 and attended by a number of intellectuals, including Ludwig von Mises and Friedrich Hayek. The motivation for the colloquium was the concern about the future of classical liberalism perceived to be under threat from developments like Roosevelt's New Deal in the USA and other manifestations of 'collectivism' like Soviet communism (Iber, 2018). Both von Mises and Hayek witnessed such developments in their native Austria with the establishment of democratic socialism in so-called Red Vienna between 1918 and 1934 (Slobodian, 2018). Equally disconcerting for Hayek when teaching at the London School of Economics in the 1930s were the ideas of John Maynard Keynes who was advocating an expanded and active role for government in the management of aggregate demand in the economy. It was in 1947, however, that neoliberalism became an organised intellectual force with the founding of the Mont Pelerin Society. A short history of the society and its aims is provided by the society's website that states:

> After World War II, in 1947, when many of the values of Western civilization were imperilled, 36 scholars, mostly economists, with some historians and philosophers, were invited by Professor Friedrich Hayek to meet at Mont Pelerin, near Montreux, Switzerland, to discuss the state and the possible fate of liberalism (in its classical sense) in thinking and practice. The group described itself as the Mont Pelerin Society, after the place of the first meeting. It emphasised that it did not intend to create an orthodoxy, to

> form or align itself with any political party or parties, or to conduct propaganda. Its sole objective was to facilitate an exchange of ideas between like-minded scholars in the hope of strengthening the principles and practice of a free society and to study the workings, virtues, and defects of market-oriented economic systems. (p. 1)[3]

Among the thirty-six scholars invited by Hayek to Mont Pelerin (Keynes, his arch-rival and nemesis had died the previous year) were the philosopher Sir Karl Popper and the economists Milton Friedman and George Stigler of the University of Chicago, which along with the University of Virginia, were subsequently to become the academic centres and philosophical bastions of neoliberal economics.

Although the origins of neoliberalism can be traced back to the middle of the twentieth century, it was not until the 1970s that it begun to have an impact in academia as well as the policymaking environment. Until then the dominant paradigm in post-World War II economics and economic policymaking was a form of social democracy that envisaged a much greater role for government intervention in managing and regulating the market economy and, in the case of northern Europe, greater acceptance of public ownership and the welfare state. The so-called stagflation crisis of capitalism in the 1970s was attributed to the application of these policies that pushed unemployment below its 'natural' level, empowering trade unions thus causing inflation and destroying incentives with high redistributive taxes.

If Hayek was the 'grandfather' of neoliberalism, Milton Friedman was undoubtedly the 'father' of neoliberalism. As Monbiot (2016) points out:

> But in the 1970s, when Keynesian policies began to fall apart, and economic crises struck on both sides of the Atlantic, neoliberal ideas began to enter the mainstream. As Friedman remarked, 'when the time came that you had to change … there was an alternative ready there to be picked up'…After Margaret Thatcher and Ronald Reagan took power, the rest of the package soon followed: massive tax cuts for the rich, the crushing of trade unions, deregulation, privatisation, outsourcing and competition in public services. Through the IMF, the World Bank, the Maastricht treaty

[3] Available at: https://www.montpelerin.org/about-mps/

> and the World Trade Organisation, neoliberal policies were imposed – often without democratic consent – on much of the world. Most remarkable was its adoption among parties that once belonged to the left: Labour and the Democrats, for example. (p. 3)

It is fair, however, to point out that what Monbiot describes, as the Keynesian policies that 'fell apart' in the 1970s, were not, as many Post-Keynesian economists would argue, very 'Keynesian'. As already mentioned above, the theoretical framework upon which most of the 'failed' policies of the 1970s were based on was the neoclassical synthesis that, although accepting a much more active interventionist role for government in the economy, it retained many of the elements of neoclassical economics that Keynes had criticised in his work. The 'ready-made' alternative that Friedman and neoliberalism offered was the weakening and diminution of the Keynesian element in the post-war neoclassical synthesis, namely the expanded size and active role of the public sector in the economy.

According to this narrative, neoliberalism was offering not only a way out of the 'impasse' created by Keynesianism and the interventionist state but also a promise that a 'free' market economy liberated from the shackles of 'big government' will unleash the creative potential of capitalism, providing growth and prosperity for all. The philosophy of neoliberalism, therefore, is based, as stated above, on an excessive faith in 'free' markets and an inherent mistrust of governments and government intervention in the economy.

3 Neoliberalism and the Collapse of Communism

The fall of the Berlin wall on 9 November 1989 is often viewed as marking the end of communism as a rival economic system to capitalism. Although communism as practiced in the Soviet Union and the so-called satellite states of Eastern Europe collapsed, it is important to recognise that the process of abandoning the centrally planned economy as an economic model had already begun well before the fall of the Berlin wall and the actual collapse of the Soviet Union in 1991. In China, the other major communist country in the world, after the death of Chairman Mao the new political leadership of the communist party in power decided on the progressive introduction of market mechanisms into the Chinese economy. Also, in the Soviet Union the policies of *Perestroika* and *Glasnost* were introduced by President Michail Gorbachev in order to achieve the necessary reforms that would transform the economic *and* the political system of Soviet communism in the same direction of a market economy. There were, however, fundamental differences in the approach of how the transition from communism to capitalism was to take place. In the Chinese model of transition to a market economy, the effort was concentrated purely on reforming the economic system without reforming the authoritarian political system. In the Soviet Union, Gorbachev's vision was to achieve both political and economic transformation through *Glasnost* and *Perestroika.* (Gorbachev, 2017). A debate in the Soviet Union intensified in 1988 on the appropriate strategy of reform. The debate was on whether the reform effort should be directed, as in China, solely towards reforming the economy without altering the political system or, as Gorbachev was advocating, whether both should be reformed at the same time (Nove, 1989). As is well documented the debate initiated by Gorbachev was inconclusive and in 1991 Gorbachev was ousted from power and the Soviet Union disintegrated in a chaotic way.

For some, the collapse of Soviet-style communism in Europe and the gradual transformation of China into a market economy had signalled the end of so-called Cold War, which was the result of the existence of two nuclear super-powers, the US and the USSR, that had competing economic systems. That was no longer the case and Fukuyama (1969) went a step further and declared not only the end of the Cold War but also the 'end of history': "What we may be witnessing is not just the end of the Cold War, or the passing of a particular period of post-war history, but the end of history as such: that is, the end point of mankind's ideological evolution and the universalization of Western liberal democracy as the final form of human government" (1969, p. 1).

A detailed examination of Fukuyama's (1969) 'non-Marxist' Hegelianism is beyond the scope of this contribution. Of course, thirty years after it was first announced there appears to be an end neither to the

Cold War, transformed as a conflict between NATO and Russia, nor to the 'end of history' debate. The ideological significance of the introduction of this concept, however, cannot be exaggerated. While the communist world was abandoning communism in favour of markets, the capitalist world was being reshaped into a 'neoliberal' form of capitalism. The 'universalised' form of Western liberal democracy that was supposed to be the final form of human government was, of course, 'neoliberal' capitalism. It was the system adopted and the policies implemented by Ronald Reagan in the US and Margaret Thatcher in the UK in the 1980s and beyond.

4 The Era of 'Neoliberal' Hegemony. Is It Coming to an End?

The message from the 'end of history' debate was loud and clear. There was no need or scope for ideological disputes in the world because such disputes have been resolved by the triumph of capitalism over communism and 'neoliberalism' over 'Keynesianism'. In a *post- ideological* world, the task ahead was to construct and maintain a 'neoliberal' world economic order in which individuals operating in competitive markets and liberated from 'collectivism' will achieve growth and prosperity for all.

For Hayek and Friedman, the long journey that begun in Mont Pelerin in 1947 received a major push forward by the elections of Margaret Thatcher in the UK in 1979 and Ronald Reagan in the USA in 1980. The conversion of Reagan, which begun much earlier as governor of California, and Thatcher to the neoliberal cause was, of course, a pivotal factor in the ascendancy and spread of the doctrine. The fall of communism and the disappearance of the centrally planned economy as an actual economic system provided an additional reinforcement to the claim that there was *no alternative* to free markets as an economic system. It was in fact the icing on the cake that established and solidified the hegemonic status of neoliberalism in both theory and practice. It is ironic, as Monbiot (2016) points out, that a doctrine promising choice and freedom should have been promoted with the famous TINA slogan that There Is No Alternative.

According to Sitaraman (2019), during the forty years of its hegemony, neoliberalism in both the USA and the UK went through four different phases. In the first phase it gained traction, in the second phase it achieved consolidation, in the third phase it was embraced by the opposition and in the fourth post-2008 phase neoliberalism began to unravel.

In the first phase under the political leadership of both Reagan and Thatcher neoliberalism was rich in rhetoric but fell short of the grand vision of reducing 'big government' despite the privatisation programmes and the attacks on organised labour. As Sitaraman (2019) points out "early leaders were not as ideologically bold as later mythmakers think" (p. 3). In the second phase neoliberalism persisted beyond the founding personalities and both Bush and Major who succeeded the early leaders normalised and consolidated neoliberalism to such an extent that during the third phase the other side adopted it. Under Clinton and Blair, the philosophy of neoliberalism was extended to the financial sector. Clinton abolished the 1933 Glass-Steagall Act and Blair left Thatcher's 'Big Bang' liberal reforms of the City of London, as well as the privatisation and trade union 'reforms', intact. This pushed neoliberalism to its fourth stage, the period from the 2008 Great Crash to the present date. This, according to Sitaraman (2019), is the stage of "collapse, irrelevance, and a wandering search for the future" (p. 4). With the world in crisis, neoliberalism, although still the dominant theoretical and policymaking paradigm, has no viable solutions to pressing problems facing the world today. "As an answer to the problems of deregulation, privatization, liberalization, and austerity, it offers more of the same" (Sitaraman, 2019, p. 4). By offering 'more of the same', however, neoliberalism has provoked, as mentioned in the introduction of this contribution, critical reactions from critics who although are on the whole sympathetic to market capitalism, they nevertheless put forward a variety of proposals on how to fix or 're-set' a 'broken' capitalism system which invariably involve departures from the neoliberal agenda. A common theme running through most of these critiques is that a change is necessary not in order to overthrow but rather in order to *save* capitalism (Wolf, 2019).

There are several areas in which critics insist that neoliberal capitalism, mainly in its Anglo-Saxon variant, is in urgent need of reform. Pearlstein (2020) distinguishes three such areas in which three fundamental and inter-related ideas of the neoliberal agenda—supply-side economics, maximising shareholder value and 'trickle-down' economics—need re-examination.

Supply-side economics is based on the belief that a reduction in the size and scope of government in the economy will increase economic efficiency and therefore the supply of goods and services produced by the economy. This reduction in 'big government' is achieved through cutting taxes, deregulation of both product and financial markets, privatisation of public enterprises and limiting the ability of the state to run fiscal deficits and accumulating debt.

The idea that maximisation of shareholder value must be the sole objective pursued by corporate business was first articulated by Friedman (1962, 1970) who insisted that any other objective such as 'social responsibility' or 'stakeholder interests' was tantamount to "preaching pure and unadulterated socialism" (p. 1). It was not until 1997, however, that the doctrine of shareholder primacy received official endorsement by the Business Roundtable, representing America's largest corporations. In its statement on corporate responsibility, it formally accepted that the principal objective of a business enterprise is to generate economic returns to its owners, the same doctrine having previously received legal enforcement by the decision of the Delaware Court of Chancery in 1986 that directors of a cosmetics company had to put the interest of shareholders first. According to this doctrine, without adhering strictly to profit maximisationtaking tough actions such as cutting costs, laying off workers, closing down less profitable parts, raising prices when necessary—corporations cannot survive the fierce competition of global markets.

'Trickle-down economics' is based on the claim that increased inequality of income and wealth does not matter because the greater prosperity generated by the operation of the inherently inegalitarian market system has the effect of lifting everybody out of abject poverty and therefore resentment for those who are rewarded 'unequally' by the market economy is simply based on the 'politics of envy'.

Pearlstein (2020) maintains that these three ideas "have become a morally corrupting and self-defeating dogma that threatens the future of American capitalism. Almost everything distasteful about it can be traced back to these flawed ideas" (p. 18). Pearlstein (2020) launches a savage attack on the 'free market ideologues' who pushed these ideas to such extremes never envisaged by those who originally proposed them. First, 'mindless animosity towards all regulation' has provided a rationale for handing over control of regulation to those who are supposed to be regulated, effectively 'putting the foxes in charge of the chicken coop'. Second, 'supply-side tax fantasies' has resulted in many Republican politicians genuinely believing that jobs can be created, and wages for the struggling working classes increased by lavishing trillion dollars tax relief on the wealthy. Third, the 'single-minded' pursuit of shareholder value maximisation has provided corporate executives with a pretext for "bamboozling customers, squeezing employees, evading taxes, and engaging in endless rounds of unproductive mergers and acquisitions…even defrauding shareholders themselves" (Pearlstein, 2020, p. 8). The recent conversion and commitment of the Business Roundtable, mentioned in the introduction above, to the concept of stakeholder capitalism was described by Stiglitz (2019) as 'too good to be true'. It is a somewhat belated realisation that due to the presence of important externalities such as climate change and environmental pollution as well as the inherent short-sightedness of market signals resulting in insufficient investments in the workforce and communities, maximising shareholder value does not necessarily result in the maximisation of social welfare (Grossman & Stiglitz, 1980). Gillian Tett (2019) adds that this 'conversion', if genuine, might be a reflection of the fact that ignoring stakeholder interests can actually impair the value of assets owned by corporations. A commitment to the long-term interest of stakeholders may be a smart move motivated by self-interest. It may provide those corporations adopting the stakeholder principle with a competitive advantage, by avoiding regulatory pressures and avoiding a backlash among consumers, especially young ones, employees and ethical investors.

Finally, the third pillar of the neoliberal ideology often summarised by the phrase 'greed is good' has also been severely criticised. Pearlstein (2020) points out that the proposition that the huge and glaring inequalities resulting from the policies of neoliberal capitalism during the last forty years are *morally* acceptable because the system raises the standard of living of everybody is now increasingly questioned. Not only for many citizens are living standards falling, not rising, but even for those whose living standards are rising Pearlstein (2020) claims that the capitalism they experience, "feels more and more like a corrupt and corrupting system" (p. 8).

Criticism of neoliberalism has also come from an unexpected quarter. In 2016 the International Monetary Fund (IMF) who, along with the World Bank, was instrumental in the spread of neoliberal policies throughout the globe joined the growing number of critics of some aspects of neoliberalism. Although there is indeed 'much to cheer' in the neoliberal agenda because by promoting global free trade and transfer of technology through expanded foreign direct investment millions of people throughout the world have been lifted out of abject poverty, in two specific policy areas, neoliberalism has been 'oversold' (Ostry, Loungani, & Furceri, 2016). These are the policies of removing restrictions on cross-border movement of capital, also known as capital account liberalisation and the policies of fiscal consolidation or 'austerity' which are policies aiming at reducing fiscal deficits and overall public indebtedness. In assessing the effects of these policies, the authors conclude that the benefits of financial openness and fiscal consolidation have been 'overplayed' while the costs of both policies 'underappreciated' (Ostry et al., 2016).

According to the critics examined so far, capitalism needs re-setting because of the effects of implementing neoliberal policies. Philippon (2019), however, argues that the problem with US capitalism is in fact the non-implementation of one of the most fundamental principles and policies of neoliberalism: the maintenance of competition. The dynamism and superior efficiency of capitalism relies on what Schumpeter, Hayek and Friedman preached—the presence of strong competitive forces. Yet Philippon (2019) concludes that

> American markets, once a model for the world, are giving up on healthy competition. Sector after economic sector is more concentrated than it was twenty years ago, dominated by fewer and bigger players who lobby politicians aggressively to protect and expand their profit margins. Across the country, this drives up prices while driving down investment, productivity, growth, and wages, resulting in more inequality. Meanwhile, Europe-long dismissed for competitive sclerosis and weak antitrust-is beating America at its own game. (p. 1)

The neoliberal promise of free-market capitalism had been transformed into what Martin Wolf (2019) calls an unacceptable form of 'rigged' or 'rentier' capitalism, an economic system in which market and political power allows a few privileged individuals and businesses to extract rent from the rest of society. The concentration of wealth and power in the hands of a few privileged rentiers is depriving capitalism of its most dynamic element: capitalists! This is a situation that Erixon and Weigel (2018) describe as a capitalist system without capitalist. They conclude that "With all that circulation of credit and cash, large nonfinancial enterprises have increasingly come to operate as savings institutions that make money by simply lending their capital at rates that are higher than the cost of the capital they borrow" (p. 8).

Neoliberalism dominated economic theory and policy at least since the 1980s. After the Global Financial Crisis (GFC) of 2007 and the Great Recession of 2008, apart from a brief period in 2009, business-as-usual resumed, although by 2019 dissatisfaction with neoliberal policies grew and criticism of neoliberalism and concern about its future direction became more pronounced and the calls for reform more persistent. In this section two sets of criticism of neoliberalism have been examined. One set is concerned with the failures of *applying* the basic planks of neoliberalism—supply-side economics, maximisation of shareholder value and 'trickle-down' economics. While another concentrates on the *failure to apply* the fundamental basis of neoliberalism—the maintenance of free-competitive markets. Both sets of critics agree that capitalism is in need of reform and re-setting. Not everybody agrees, however, that such a re-set button exists and if it does it can be pressed by the plutocrats that have 'captured' the media and the political system.

As Roos (2019) points out "By opposing the 'bad' capitalism of the unproductive rentier to the 'good' capitalism of productive enterprise, however, the conventional liberal narrative overlooks the fact that the two are inextricably entwined… the idea that capitalism's reset button – if such a thing could be said to exist – might be safely pressed from the boardroom is not supported by the lessons of history" (p. 2).

Growing inequality of both income and wealth and the existential threat posed by anthropogenic climate change are the two major unresolved global policy issues of our time that were closely associated with the neoliberal era. While growing inequality of income and wealth was primarily the result of deliberate neoliberal policy choices such as the huge reduction in progressive taxation in the US (Saez & Zucman, 2019), the climate change threat was the culmination of a process that started with the industrial revolution and continued throughout the twentieth century to the present day. However, since the 1980s to the present day, it was estimated by CICERO, the Centre for International Climate Research in Norway,[4] that the level of carbon dioxide emissions increased dramatically, accounting for half the total human emissions since 1870. Explanations about the nature and underlying causes of inequality have been extensively dealt with elsewhere (see, e.g. Arestis & Sawyer, 2018). In the next section, we concentrate mainly on the nature, underlying causes and policy failures of the global climate change challenge. Is it a coincidence that the dramatic increase in CO_2 emissions coincided with the neoliberal era?

5 The Nature, Underlying Causes and Policy Response to the Climate Change Challenge

The level of public awareness of the problem of global warming gained prominence and was brought under the spotlight when the Intergovernmental Panel on Climate Change (IPCC) was set up by the UN in late 1988. In the same year James Hansen leading a group of eminent climate scientists of the National Aeronautics and Space Administration told a Congressional committee that the observed trend towards global warming was not a natural variation but was caused by a build-up of carbon dioxide and other artificial gases in the atmosphere. As early as 1988 therefore scientists have been sounding alarm bells and warning that timely interventions could slow down the rate of change in global warming substantially thus giving the world time to develop mechanisms so that the cost to society and the damage to ecosystems can

---

[4] Available at: https://cicero.oslo.no/en/about/

be minimised. Ignoring the problem and hope for the best would spell disaster. Scientists, informed politicians and concerned citizens have been giving similar warning ever since. Despite these warnings, emissions continued to rise.

The threat of climate change is a public policy issue that has two distinctive characteristics. First, by its very nature, its causes and consequences transcend national boundaries and therefore the resolution of the problem requires concerted global action. Second, in attempting to tackle the threat of climate change, perhaps more than any other policy issue, a balancing act is required involving issues of inter-generational as well as geographical conflicts of interests and equity. Moreover, the predicted catastrophic consequences on the planet of failing to tackle this problem are of such enormity and extent that, once the scientific case on which such predictions are based is accepted, it is impossible not to regard this as the number one policy problem facing the world. Potentially, of course, the same is true of a number of other environmental problems such as ozone depletion and combating global pandemics. Many of the arguments presented in this contribution, therefore, could be pertinent in dealing with other global policy challenges.

Climate change is a natural phenomenon, which could be caused and aided by humans and studied by natural scientists specialising primarily in the discipline of climatology. There is a virtually unanimous scientific consensus embodied in the various IPCC reports concerning the causes, consequences and possible remedies to the threat posed by catastrophic climate change. According to this scientific consensus climate change is taking place and the causes are human-made. Climate change is nothing new in the history of our planet but in the past such episodes had natural causes or explanations, for example, large volcanic eruptions or variations in solar output. In many scientific models of climate change the current trend is towards rising global temperatures. This trend however cannot be accounted for by natural causes and therefore an alternative explanation is given as to the cause of global warming, namely the increased concentration in the earth's atmosphere of predominantly, but not exclusively, CO_2 emissions which results from the human activity of burning fossil fuels. Greenhouse gases occur naturally and are essential to the survival of humans and millions of other living things, by keeping some of the sun's warmth from reflecting back into space and making Earth liveable. But after more than a century and a half of industrialisation, deforestation and large-scale agriculture, quantities of greenhouse gases in the atmosphere have risen to record levels not seen in three million years. As populations, economies and standards of living grow, so does the cumulative level of greenhouse gas (GHG) emissions.

According to the UN, there is some basic well-established scientific knowledge concerning the concentration of greenhouse gases (GHGs) in the earth's atmosphere. Since the industrial revolution, the concentration has been rising steadily and so have mean global temperatures. The most abundant GHG, accounting for about two-thirds of GHGs, carbon dioxide (CO_2), is largely the product of burning fossil fuels.

In 2013 the IPCC in its Fifth Assessment Report clearly concluded that climate change is real and caused mainly by human activities. The Fifth Assessment Report provided a comprehensive assessment of sea-level rise as well as estimates of cumulative CO_2 emissions since pre-industrial times. The report also provided a CO_2 budget for future emissions to limit warming to less than 2 °C. In October 2018, the IPCC issued a special report on the impacts of global warming of 1.5 °C, finding that limiting global warming to 1.5 °C would require rapid, far-reaching and unprecedented changes in all aspects of society.

The report finds that limiting global warming to 1.5 °C would require 'rapid and far-reaching' transitions in land, energy, industry, buildings, transport and cities. Global net human-caused emissions of carbon dioxide (CO_2) would need to fall by about 45% from 2010 levels by 2030, reaching 'net zero' around 2050. This means that any remaining emissions would need to be balanced by removing CO_2 from the air.

In 2015 in Paris, Parties to the United Nations Framework Convention on Climate Change (UNFCCC) reached a landmark agreement to combat climate change and to accelerate and intensify the actions and investments needed for a sustainable low-carbon future. The Paris Agreement's central aim is to strengthen the global response to the threat of climate change by keeping the global temperature rise this century well below 2 °C above pre-industrial levels and to pursue efforts to limit the temperature increase even further to 1.5 °C.

On 23 September 2019, Secretary-General António Guterres convened a Climate Summit to bring world leaders of governments, the private sector and civil society together to support the multilateral process and to increase and accelerate climate action and ambition. He named Luis Alfonso de Alba, a former Mexican diplomat, as his Special Envoy to lead preparations. The Summit focused on key sectors where action can make the most difference—heavy industry, nature-based solutions, cities, energy, resilience and climate finance. World leaders reported on what they are doing and what more they intend to do when they convene in 2020 for the UN climate conference, where commitments will be renewed and may be increased. In closing the Climate Action Summit, the Secretary-General congratulated the participants for delivering a boost in momentum, co-operation and ambition but reminded them that there is still a long way to go and that more concrete plans and more ambition is needed.

The Paris Agreement central aim is to strengthen the global response to the threat of climate change by keeping a global temperature rise this century well below 2 °C above pre-industrial levels and to pursue efforts to limit the temperature increase even further to 1.5 °C. The Paris Agreement is indeed a landmark international treaty signed by 195 nations and represents a significant move, after nearly twenty years of negotiations, towards a global response to the threat of climate change.

The agreement, however, was criticised because of the lack of a mandatory scheme and an adequate enforcement mechanism. James Hansen, the NASA climate scientist whose testimony to the US Congress in 1988, as mentioned above, alerted the world to the dangers of global warming, described the Paris Agreement soon after was reached in 2015 as worthless and no action, just promises.[5]

The aims of the Paris Agreement will be fulfilled by means of a series of Nationally Determined Commitments (NDC) the achievement of which is not a legally binding obligation on the country undertaking the commitment. Although the agreement provides a robust 'advanced transparency framework', which enables participants to know and monitor

[5] Available at: https://www.theguardian.com/environment/2015/dec/12/james-hansen-climate-change-paris-talks-fraud/

what everybody is doing. An analysis by the Climate Action Tracker, a consortium of research institutions, concluded that the NDCs, if fully implemented, could result in warming of 3 °C, far below the 1.5 target.[6]

Current commitments made by national governments under the Paris Agreement fall far short of what is required—taken together, they would still condemn the world to an estimated temperature rise of more than 3 °C by the end of the century. According to the UN's latest 'emissions gap' report, published a few days before the start of this year's talks, countries must reduce their greenhouse gases by about 7.6% a year for the next ten years, to stay within the 1.5 °C limit.

The Paris Agreement also provides for a global stocktake every five years to assess the collective progress towards achieving the purpose of the Agreement and to inform further individual actions by Parties. The now postponed Glasgow summit of December 2020 was supposed to fulfil this purpose. After thirty years of negotiation the world produced just one agreement to hold temperatures to a limit that is too high, and we are not even remotely on track to honour that agreement.[7]

Science provides the information and the facts, which can be used to formulate policy. World political leaders are urged both by the scientific community and the UN to show more ambition and more commitment to the cause of preventing climate change in setting national targets and in formulating national policies.

Why are national political leaders failing to respond adequately to these pleas for more urgent and ambitious commitments? According to Nordhaus (2020) the answer is simple and straightforward, and it is derived from the basic economic theory regarding the properties of public goods. When goods are non-rival and non-excludable there is a strong inducement for 'free-riding' behaviour. In order to overcome the 'free-rider' problem *within a nation state*, legal compulsion, either in the form of taxation or rules and regulations, is necessary in order to force 'free-riders' to participate towards the effort of providing the public good. The Paris accord, however, which is the international agreement currently in

[6] Available at: https://climateactiontracker.org/documents/507/CAT_2018-12-11_Briefing_WarmingProjectionsGlobalUpdate_Dec2018.pdf/

[7] Available at: https://www.theguardian.com/news/2019/dec/02/climate-crisis-what-is-cop-and-can-it-save-the-world/

place whose aim is to prevent global warming and climate change, is a voluntary agreement. The absence of an enforcement mechanism induces 'free-riding' behaviour on the part of nation states which in turn undermines the international agreement. Nordhaus (2020) concludes that "nations can overcome the syndrome of free-riding in international climate agreements if they adopt the club model and include penalties for nations that do not participate. Otherwise, the global effort to curb climate change is sure to fail" (p. 1).

Nordhaus (op. cit.) assumes that nation states behave in exactly the same way as individual consumers and citizens when faced with the problem of public good provision. Why pay for a good or a service when once produced it is impossible to be excluded from consuming the benefits of a public good? What is missing from this analysis, however, is an explicit *political* model. What is the *political mechanism* that produces the free-riding behaviour by the nation states that signed the Paris accord?

6 The Political Economy of Global Policymaking

Public policymaking is part of the political process. Sovereign nation states can formulate and implement policies on climate change which ultimately involves imposing restrictions and limits on emissions of greenhouse gases. These policies will involve significant behavioural changes on the part of citizens within the political jurisdiction of the nation state as well as monetary costs. The Paris Agreement was signed by 195 nation states with a variety of political systems and methods of engagement of citizens in the process of political decision-making. The question that needs to be explored is to what extent the inadequate national commitments to climate change targets is a true reflection of the wishes of citizens within the signatory nation states?

In a political system of liberal democracy and representative government politicians are accountable to voters through periodic elections. The G7 countries of Canada, France, Germany, Italy, Japan, UK and US are all, more or less and for the present, democratic countries with a working system of representative government. China, the world's largest emitter of CO_2 gases, was initially considered to be a developing country and therefore was outside the Kyoto protocol and was not under a requirement to reduce emissions. China is now a signatory to the Paris Agreement but without a political system of representative government. Of the six top emitters of CO_2 gases US, China, EU, Russia, Japan and India, only China does not have, at least formally, a system of representative government.

An extremely basic and highly simplified version of the workings of the political and policymaking system of representative democracy can be described as follows: voters elect politicians who act as their representatives in formulating policies. The politicians once in power want to be re-elected and consequently aim at delivering policies that are broadly in line with the wishes of the majority of voters. Of course, the influence of voters on policymaking must not be overestimated. There are many powerful interests that exert pressure on politicians to pursue policies that promotes their special interests. For instance, powerful interests in the fossil fuel industries may exert undue influence on government policy. Moreover, politicians may manipulate the electors through various methods into believing that they are promoting *their* interest, instead of that of powerful groups.

Nevertheless, it is assumed that on the whole a democratic system ensures that not many genuinely democratically elected governments can survive for a long time if they persistently pursue many very seriously unpopular policies. In addition to periodic elections, the presence in the system of liberal institutions (civil liberties, freedom of thought and expression, free press, media, etc.) ensures, within limits, that politicians cannot easily suppress, hide or manipulate information in order to pursue vastly unpopular policies. This is in a very simplified form how a liberal, pluralist democracy is supposed to work.

The fact that some policies are popular does not, of course, always mean that they are enlightened policies. Abolition of the death penalty, easing immigration controls, improving race relations and protecting minority rights are not always popular policies. Although politicians would naturally like to support popular policies, in order to ensure their election or re-election into office, it is not uncommon for politicians to take the lead on certain issues and introduce and persevere with initially unpopular policies. In doing so they run the risk of losing ground to opportunistic populist rivals who oppose the policy for the purpose of gaining political advantage. However, despite the obvious risks, political consensus, or common understanding not to engage in party political competition on certain issues does emerge from time to time although with the emergence of populism such a consensus is in danger of disappearing.

There is no effective system in place of effective global policymaking despite the UN institutions created in the post-1945 period. Global co-operative agreements, of course, do emerge from time to even on environmental issues such as the problem of ozone depletion, but not on vital problems like nuclear disarmament, pandemic prevention and climate change, although it is clear that these issues cannot be tackled by a single country in isolation. It is equally clear that for international action to be successful an effective system of global governance must be established which goes beyond the ad hoc arrangements, which may produce isolated successful outcomes, like the well-known success of the G20 meeting in preventing a global depression in 2009. As long as the US, the world's largest economy and one of the largest emitters of greenhouse gases both in absolute and per capita terms, remains outside international agreements, it is difficult to envisage how an effective system of global climate change policy can be established.

So far a very 'technocratic' picture, much favoured by economists, of policymaking has been presented as a rational process of identifying a problem, setting objectives and seeking the best means of achieving given ends. The choice of ends or objectives is a political matter; the choice of means or instruments a technical one. Actual policymaking is a far messier, pragmatic affair both in the way ends are chosen as well as in the choice of means. Politicians in making their policy choices are subjected to many influences not least, as we assumed above, the wishes of individual voters. But how individual voters approach the policy problem of climate change?

At this point it is necessary to make an assumption, which economists in general and neoliberal economists in particular have been making since the time of Adam Smith about individuals in society and their primary motivation. Conventional economic theory assumes that the primary motivation of individuals in society is self-interest. Furthermore, the pursuit of self-interest, as Smith famously proclaimed in the invisible hand theory, has beneficial effects for society as a whole. Appealing to individuals' self-love can promote the common good far more effectively than appealing, as Smith puts it, to their humanity or altruism. The self-seeking individual instead of being viewed with suspicion and mistrust has been transformed by the invisible hand theory into, as Galbraith (1987) puts, a 'public benefactor'. It is, of course, well known that Smith makes a contradictory claim in *The Theory of Moral Sentiments.*

It was recognised then and considerably more now that there are significant exceptions to this general rule that self-interested individuals operating in perfectly competitive markets can produce a socially optimal result. When there is market failure as it is the case when public goods and externalities are present self-seeking behaviour by individuals does not promote the collective good. In almost all of these cases self-seeking behaviour not only does not promote the collective interest, but it fails to advance even narrow self-interest.

There is, therefore, a clear and well-established link between the workings of capitalism and climate change. This link is generally understood in mainstream economics in terms of the theory of externalities and market failure. The workings of 'free' competitive markets do not always result in an optimal allocation of resources. According to this theory, in a limited number of circumstances, a decentralised market economy cannot deal effectively with market failure and various types of 'externalities' without government intervention. Lord Stern (2006) in the *Stern Review* describes climate change as "the greatest example of market failure we have ever seen" (p. 1).

The theory of market failure, however, has been developed and applied almost exclusively in dealing with market failure issues within a nation state. Climate change is, of course, a *global* market failure requiring a *global* policy response. Government intervention by a single nation state, however well designed and executed, would not be adequate to prevent catastrophic climate change. Can a global co-ordinated policymaking response be achieved in time and what is the road map for achieving this goal? The *political economy* of climate change policy, therefore, is as significant as the *science* of climate change policy.

It has to be acknowledged that the division of opinion on the critical issue of climate change is far more complex than the conventional split between those critics who are pro and those who are against capitalism as an economic system. There are divisions and disagreements about the significance of this challenge and how to deal with it which transcend conventional left-right divisions. There are divisions between advanced industrial and developing and emerging economies as well as division between young and old citizens, mainly, in advanced countries. There are also divisions, admittedly now at a diminishing scale, and also mainly in advanced countries, between those who accept and those who *deny* the validity of the scientific consensus among climate scientists about the severity and urgency of the challenge.

Market failure is, of course, very pertinent to the debate on climate change policy. The various instances of market failure cases have been variously described as 'the tragedy of the commons', 'the prisoner's dilemma' or 'the free-rider problem'. A commonly owned resource, the earth's atmosphere, is over-utilised with disastrous consequences for all. There are many other well-known cases of over-utilisation and destruction of commonly owned resources—fisheries, forests and mines. Preventing the destruction of a communally owned resource is a public good, which is defined as a good whose benefits are non-rival and non-excludable. If global warming is prevented the benefits are enjoyed by everybody and those who have not contributed towards the costs cannot be excluded from consuming them. Even when individuals realise the consequences of their action there is no de-centralised mechanism of reversing the process, although Ostrom (1990) has demonstrated empirically that voluntary collective action does take place overcoming the 'tragedy of the commons' problem under certain conditions.

Returning to the question of what the reaction of a rational self- seeking individual to the threat of global warming would be, it is tempting to conclude that self-interest would dictate that cutting down on personal emissions would be a rational response. This would require radical changes in behaviour that would have the effect of reducing the individual's environmental 'fingerprint' such as reducing the demand for goods and services that produce emissions for example air travel, using the car or home heating.

Such a course of action of course will be rejected by *homo economicus* because the individual incurs personal costs without the prospect of any future benefits. Unless millions of other individuals act in the same way, and casual introspection will lead to the conclusion that they will not, there is no point in acting in isolation. *Homo economicus* is not interested in setting examples. If global warming is going to take place anyway why incur the costs?

Economists do not regard this situation, however, as an entirely lost cause. The invisible hand of the market might fail but the 'visible' hand of the government can come to the rescue. Many rational individuals would be prepared to incur the personal costs of protecting a communal resource if they can be assured that others would be forced to act in the same way. What individuals fail to do when acting alone the government can do collectively on their behalf by enacting and enforcing appropriate policies and laws. There are many examples of government policies, at the national level, which succeeded in protecting communal resources (clean air acts in London and elsewhere) but also many cases of failures (ecological disasters from abandoned mines in the US).

The crucial question that needs to be considered next is whether rational self-seeking individuals would behave in similar fashion in the political sphere. Would individual citizens *vote* for policies to prevent global warming from taking place even if it involves significant personal costs?

The answer seems deceptively simple. It is rational and also in one's self-interested to vote for a policy that would prevent climate change. Given the assumptions we made above about the effects of global warming costs will always be small in relation to the benefits. Therefore, voters would tend to vote for those policies that promise to prevent global warming at minimum cost to the individual voter. Even with less pessimistic assumptions, risk-averse individuals might like to vote for the policies as insurance in case the pessimists are correct, provided the insurance costs are not too high. There are, however, important qualifications to this conclusion which basically arise from two uncertainties.

First, voters must have confidence that the policy would be effectively implemented and the desired reduction in emissions will be achieved. Otherwise, global warming would take place anyway in which case they would be incurring costs now without any future benefits. This means that a national policy would have a greater chance of being supported by voters if it is part of a well-co-ordinated and effectively policed global policy. Why, for instance, would a citizen of a country like the UK, which is responsible for only 2% of global emissions, be interested in a national climate change policy without an effective international agreement? Any uncertainty about the intentions and actions of other countries about curbing emissions would undermine confidence in the possibility of arresting global warming and, therefore, making national climate change policy which requires personal sacrifices very unpopular.

The second uncertainty relates to what economists call the problem of time preference and inter-temporal choice. Economic theory assumes that individuals have positive time preference, that is, they prefer current consumption to future consumption perhaps, as Pigou (1920) speculated, in an exaggerated way. Individuals will sacrifice current consumption to avoid a future disaster but if some voters of a certain age feel that, they may not be around to enjoy the benefits of their current sacrifices, that is, the saving of the planet, would they still vote for such policies? Democracies by definition take into account only the wishes and preferences of the current generation since future generations do not have a vote. Some voters may not wish to bear the costs of policies whose benefits will be enjoyed by future, possibly wealthier and in possession of superior technologies generation. The other side of the coin is that not preventing global warming in order to save current costs is transferring these and even higher costs to future generations. There is of course ample evidence to suggest that many voters even if they may not be alive to enjoy the future benefits, they are, nevertheless, prepared to sacrifice personal interest for the benefit of their children. It is debateable if they would be ready to incur with the same enthusiasm current costs for the benefit of their grandchildren or great grandchildren.

Many younger voters, such as the young global climate activist Greta Thunberg, do have, unlike some of the 'selfish' older generation, a great deal of interest in ensuring that policy action is taken now to prevent catastrophic future climate change. Not all young voters, however, have a vote while some may have the vote but also have what Pigou (1920) called 'defective telescopic faculties'—looking at the future from the wrong end of the telescope thus heavily discounting the future. The irrational 'myopia' of the young often acts to the detriment of their own interest, such as making inadequate provisions for old age pensions. Democratic politics, therefore, might still fail future generations if a disproportionate number of 'selfish' older voters combine with a number of 'myopic' younger ones to vote against climate change policies which involve high personal costs such as loss of jobs and livelihood or radical lifestyle changes.

So far two arguments have been advanced as to why national climate change policy is likely to be unpopular with voters and consequently, as long as national politicians are engaged in policy competition, they would all offer similar policies which ultimately do not involve radical behavioural changes or personal sacrifices. A democratic system of representative government combined with the assumptions of orthodox economic theory about human motivation produces a pessimistic scenario of impotent public policymaking in the face of momentous dangers.

Voters can be induced to change their hostility towards climate change policies if measures are taken to remove the two uncertainties mentioned above that act as an inducement to voters not to take the climate change threat more seriously. First, there is the 'free-rider' problem and second, the problem of inter-generational conflict between old and young voters and the conflicts between those whose livelihoods will be destroyed by the tough new policies and those who will not be affected so much, both within nation states and between nations.

The establishment of a more effective system of international co-operation and co-ordination of policies, perhaps through a reformed UN or through the creation of a 'Climate Club' along the lines suggested by Nordhaus (2020) by removing the 'free-rider' problem, is undoubtedly a *necessary* condition for a wider popular support for climate change policies, but it is by no means sufficient. The second factor, however, will continue to act as deterrent to greater popular support and acceptance of tougher climate change targets even in the absence of a 'free-rider' problem. Natural science warns that unless the world takes urgent action now, irreversible global warming is imminent. Social science, including Political Science and Economics, on the other hand, points out to another danger: the world does not currently possess the policymaking capacity of preventing global warming and preserving democracy.

In an important book examining how and why past societies have collapsed, Jared Diamond (2005) gives a fascinating account of the process whereby some past and some present societies committed ecological suicide—undermining themselves by destroying their environment. Are there any similarities between those past collapses, such as the ecological collapse in Easter Islands due to deforestation, and the situation the world faces today with regard to climate change?

In the introduction of this contribution the question was posed whether it was coincidental that the gigantic increase in global CO_2 emissions occurred during the neoliberal era? It is of course no great secret that neoliberal ideology is not generally in favour of massive government intervention in the free-market economy but a massive global government intervention to deal with a massive global market failure is essential. The current impotence of international climate change policy, however, cannot be attributed entirely to the inherent hostility of neoliberal ideology towards government interventions in the market economy. The current impasse in the implementation of international climate change policy has more to do with some aspects of the political economy of climate change policy discussed in this section and the way democratic politics and policymaking works rather than the ideological obstacles posed by neoliberalism. Nevertheless, a shift away from neoliberalism and the adoption of some reforms like stakeholder capitalism and massive public investment in Green New Deals can result in greater public support for effective climate change actions and elevate climate change to the top of the political agenda. The next section examines this question of whether and how attitudes towards government intervention in general, and in climate change policy in particular, might change as a result of the coronavirus pandemic crisis.

7 Neoliberalism in the Aftermath of the Crisis Caused by the COVID-19 Pandemic

Neoliberalism not only failed to foresee and prevent the catastrophic Great Crash of 2007–2008, but it had also failed in the aftermath of the crisis to learn the lessons and address adequately the important policy failures that led to the crisis (see, e.g., Arestis, 2020). The situation in the discipline of economics in 2019 when Lord King (2019) issued a warning that the world economy was 'sleepwalking' into another Great Crash was not too dissimilar to that of the 1930s in which, following the Wall Street crash and the Great Depression, there was a huge gap between the conclusions of mainstream economic theory and economic reality. Unlike the 1930s, however, during which new thinking and questioning of the prevailing orthodoxy produced the Keynesian revolution in economics, no comparable new thinking or challenge to neoliberal capitalism has taken place following the Great Financial Crisis of 2007–8. As Skidelsky (2020) points out the brief 'exhumation' of Keynes in 2009 did not represent a permanent shift away from neoliberalism. Once the co-ordinated global fiscal expansion agreed by the G-20 countries in the historic 2009 London meeting had the desired effect, by 2010 'business-as-usual' was resumed and interventionist policies were quickly abandoned in favour of policies of fiscal austerity aimed at reducing the size and role of government in the economy.

By the beginning of 2020, however, the need for greater role of government intervention in the economy in the form of fiscal policy has never been greater. The prospect of another Great Crash similar to the GFC of 2007 and the Great Recession of 2008 was real. In August 2019, the yield curve between two-year and ten-year notes in the US was inverted for the first time since 2007. Since yield curve inversions usually precede recessions the question of how well equipped the prevailing dominant neoliberal economic policy framework was in dealing with another serious global recession was very pertinent.

Such speculation, however, concerning the timing as well as the adequacy of the likely policy response to another Great Crash has been rendered redundant by the arrival of the COVID-19 Pandemic, which triggered a simultaneous supply and demand shock of 'unprecedented severity'. As De Grauwe (2020) explains the twin supply and demand shocks are likely to trigger many 'domino effects' whereby companies that suffer a sudden and unexpected fall in income will quickly face financial difficulties, which may affect banks and other institutions that have lent money to these companies which will also experience financial difficulties and so on. Sudden and massive economic shocks often can lead to banking crises except that in the current crisis, unlike the previous Great Recession of 2008, the initial shock did not originate in the financial sector and then spill over into the real economy. The shocks emerged from the real economy due to the imposed lockdowns to fight the pandemic, which spread to the rest of the economy including financial markets.

As Elliot (2020) points out: "Instead of production being scaled up, it is being scaled back…This is not 1940, with factories working round the clock. It's more like a neutron-bomb attack that targets the people but leaves the buildings unscathed" (p. 1). In other words, the pandemic is a 'supply shock' and not by origin a 'demand shock' though there are demand consequences.

Similarly, Eichengreen (2020) explains

> The problem today, however, is a sudden stop in production, which monetary policy can do little to offset. Fed chair Jerome Powell cannot reopen factories shuttered by quarantine, whatever Donald Trump may think. Likewise, monetary policy will not get shoppers back to the malls or travellers back onto airplanes, insofar as their concerns centre on safety, not cost. Rate cuts cannot hurt, given that inflation, already subdued, is headed downward; but not much real economic stimulus should be expected of them. The same is true, unfortunately, of fiscal policy. (p. 1)

At the time of writing, therefore, the speculation is no longer about what policy changes are necessary to prevent another Great Crash, but rather about what kind of economic, social and political future is to be expected *after* the economic crash caused by the coronavirus pandemic. Is global capitalism about to experience a radical transformation because of the coronavirus pandemic or is it the case that 'business as usual' would be the most likely outcome after the crisis? Inevitably several intermediate scenarios are also discussed. In the rest of this chapter we will briefly consider some of these scenarios.

It is important, in examining these scenarios, to avoid 'selective perception' and 'confirmation bias'. As Rodrik (2020) points out "we are likely to see in the COVID-19 debacle an affirmation of our own worldview. And we may perceive incipient signs of a future economic and political order we have long wished for" (p. 1). In examining these scenarios, therefore, it is essential to avoid wishful thinking. It is important to maintain a clear distinction between a scenario that is desirable and one that is likely to happen or between *prescription* of how neoliberal capitalism should change and a *prediction* of how it will change in response to the crisis.

As far as prediction is concerned the various scenarios fall into three broad categories. One category sees the crisis as a temporary phenomenon during which exceptional measures involving massive and unprecedented interventions of the state in the economy need to be employed to deal with an exceptional crisis. These measures, however, although necessary are essentially temporary in nature and will be reversed as soon as the crisis ends. The neoliberal *status quo* will not be disturbed once the crisis is over. As was the case in 2008 'business-as-usual' in policymaking will resume once recovery begins.

Another category includes those who expect that the world following the pandemic is unlikely to be radically different from the one that preceded it and that the crisis may simply accelerate tendencies for change already present before the crisis. In other words, the pandemic may turn out to be less of a watershed in global politics and economics than many expect. As Rodrik (2020) puts it "Rather than putting the world on a significantly different trajectory, it is likely to intensify and entrench already-existing trends" (p. 1).

Finally, a third category includes those who expect something positive can come out of this crisis. The crisis can become a catalyst for the long overdue re-setting and a radical policy shift in global capitalism away from the neoliberal policy paradigm and towards a post-neoliberal world. As stated above, neoliberalism is based on a combined belief in the power of 'free' markets and the impotence of governments and government interventions in the economy. The crisis caused by the COVID-19 pandemic has demonstrated the exact opposite—the *impotence* of markets and the power, and the *necessity* of government intervention in dealing with the crisis. Some, therefore, expect that such a 'paradigm shift' will be inevitable after the crisis.

At the time of writing there is no clear indication which scenario within these three categories will prevail. Victor Gaspar, the director of the Fiscal Affairs Department of the IMF, reported on 15 April 2020 "So far, countries have taken fiscal actions amounting to about $8 trillion to contain the pandemic and its damage to the economy… But in times of emergency, the implication for policymakers is do whatever it takes but make sure to keep the receipts" (p. 2).[8]

One prediction that is safe to make, therefore, is that after the crisis the rise, although possibly not the level, in public indebtedness will be unprecedented in peacetime. The 'whatever-it-takes' approach to public spending during the pandemic crisis would result in 'war-time' levels of public indebtedness after the crisis. The only uncertainty is about how large the increase in public indebtedness would be. Predictably the familiar debate—not so familiar of course during war time—about the so called burden of public debt and how the huge increase in debt would be reduced begun almost immediately.

Wyplosz (2020)[9] is in no doubt that large debts are a 'burden' and that they must be rolled back and reduced once the crisis is over. Large public debts are a 'burden' because taxes must be raised to serve interest and reimburse the debt, ignoring, of course, the fact that public debts in sovereign countries are an asset of the public and interest on the debt forms part of private income. According to Wyplosz (2020) large debts are also 'dangerous'. "The lenders keep worrying whether they will ever be paid back. They stay put and, then all of a sudden, they panic as a herd when a few of them are seen selling their stakes" (Wyplosz, op. cit., p. 1).

[8] Available at: https://blogs.imf.org/2020/04/15/fiscal-policies-to-contain-the-damage-from-covid-19/?utm_medium=email&utm_source=govdelivery/

[9] Available at: https://www.charleswyplosz.info/2020-4-22-covid-19-the-long-run/

There are several ways of reducing public indebtedness. Wyplosz (2020) discusses four such methods. First, there is the method known as fiscal consolidation or 'austerity'. This solution involves increasing taxes, cutting spending or a combination of both in order to achieve a budget surplus, which can be used to reduce public indebtedness. A particular version of this solution involves attempting to achieve a fiscal surplus through cutting public spending rather than increasing taxes. This approach is based on the theory of 'expansionary fiscal contraction' or 'expansionary austerity' developed by Alessina, Favero, and Giavazzi (2019). This was of course the method favoured by the IMF, the World Bank and other creditors dealing with a sovereign debt crisis as was the case with the recent eurozone crisis.

Second, the debt to GDP ratio will, of course, decline with nominal growth of GDP but also, public indebtedness can be reduced by allowing inflation to erode the value of the public (and also private) debt. This can be achieved quickly through Weimar Republic-type of hyperinflation (which, of course, is extremely disruptive) or slowly as was the case with post World War II debts.

The third method of reducing public debt is financial repression. Inflation would not achieve the desired debt reduction if interest rates are allowed to rise proportionately, with a lag, of course, as the interest rate on bonds is fixed at the time of sale. If, however, the monetary authorities maintain interest rates below inflation financial repression combined with inflation would over a period of years reduce public indebtedness.

Finally, public debt can be partially or totally eliminated through the ultimate weapon of default or debt restructuring. This is a weapon of last resort which, of course, is not a solution that is necessary to use in countries that have sovereign control over their currency.

Wyplosz (2020) concludes: "In the end, the public debt problem will become a painful thorn. No solution is easy, and most are painful. And yet, something will have to be done if we want to avoid highly disruptive financial crises" (p. 2). Similar conclusions are reached in a series of article by the *Economist* (2020).

It should be pointed out that even those who express concerns about the likely painful consequences from debt accumulation after the crisis are *not* in any way suggesting that this is the time to worry about the legacy of public debt. But should we be concerned about public indebtedness even *after* the crisis and if so how quickly should any measures to reduce indebtedness be taken? There is an inevitable feeling of *Déjà vu*.

During the 2007–2008 crisis any concerns and reservations about deficit spending and public indebtedness were set aside in order to save the banking system and stimulate the global economy experiencing the worst recession since the 1930s. As soon as an anaemic recovery begun in 2010 the lessons of co-ordinated fiscal expansion were forgotten, and policies of deficit reduction and fiscal consolidation were adopted by country after country in Europe and North America. The media were full of stories about 'bond vigilantes' and the likelihood of sovereign defaults and bankruptcies while academia was discussing the prospect of economic collapse if countries were to allow the debt to GDP ratio to rise above 80% (Reinhart & Rogoff, 2009). Deficit spending was considered acceptable in order to deal with an *exceptional* emergency but there was no choice but to return to 'normality' quickly by eliminating deficits through savage austerity.

In 2010 when policies of austerity and deficit reduction were adopted, the 'conventional wisdom' of neoliberal economics was, and still is, that persistent budget deficits and 'excessive' public debt accumulation will lead to economic disaster. 'Ending up like Greece' is now a universal expression used to describe what happens to countries that mis-manage their public finances and accumulate too much debt irrespective of whether they belong to a malfunctioning monetary union like the eurozone or not.

On the subject of public indebtedness, the conventional narrative is that governments, like households and firms, must live 'within their means'. The government's 'means' are the taxes they collect from their citizens. When governments spend beyond their means the result is a budget deficit which, like deficits in household or firm budgets, is financed by borrowing. Persistent budget deficits in either public or private sectors result in an accumulation of debt. This, in itself, is not necessarily a bad thing. Both the private and the public sectors can accumulate debts either to invest or to smooth out consumption over time provided they do so in a *sustainable* manner. Fiscal irresponsibility and unsustainable public finances, therefore, can spell disaster for a country in exactly the same way as for firms and individual households. What exactly is wrong with this mainstream narrative and policy prescription that governments 'should live within their means'?

Keynes in a much-quoted passage from the preface to the *General Theory* talks about the difficulty most of us experience, not so much in accepting new ideas but "in escaping from the old ones, which ramify…. into every corner of our minds" (p. viii). One such 'old' idea which has proved difficult to escape from is the widely held view both among academic economists and the general public that government expenditure is *constrained* by government revenue.

A rejection of this idea forms the basis of Modern Monetary Theory (MMT) that was developed over the past twenty-five years by a number of 'heterodox' economists (Mitchell, Wray, & Watts, 2019). Governments do not need to collect taxes in order to finance public spending; nor do they need to borrow money. Governments can just 'print' the money they need for their spending priorities. But is this not a recipe for 'ending up like Greece' and 'calling in the bailiffs' or even worse ending up like the Weimar Republic or Zimbabwe? The answer, according to MMT, is no. Countries that are *in control of their own currency* cannot go bankrupt because governments can never run out of money; and most developed economies are not like the Weimar Republic or Zimbabwe or Venezuela.

If government revenue is *not* a constraint on government spending what limits the printing and spending of money by governments? The limit according to MMT is reached when the economy achieves full employment. Any further increase in spending will cause inflation. Ultimately it is the objective of preventing inflation, not the availability of government revenue, that sets a limit to government expenditure. MMT, therefore, is not to be confused with the naive belief in the existence of a Magic Money Tree! It is simply an alternative way of thinking about government budgeting in which we are asked to escape from the 'old idea', deeply engrained in our minds (and those of the architects of the monetary union in Europe and the Fiscal Compact), that public spending levels should be determined in relation to government revenues (no revenue, no spending) and that public borrowing or printing money to finance public spending should be avoided—an 'old idea' that Japan appears to have forgotten and failed to put into practice over the last two decades!

It is, of course, worth escaping from 'old ideas' only if it can be shown that these ideas merit escaping from. The MMT ideas challenging the orthodox view of public debt are not new—they go back at least to J.M. Keynes (1936) and Abba Lerner (1943), but have recently received renewed attention because of the interest shown towards these ideas by US politicians on the left like Bernie Saunders and Alexandria Ocasio-Cortez. It should be pointed out that MMT is not only rejected by mainstream economists as 'nonsense' (Rogoff, 2019) but even economists sympathetic to Keynesianism (Krugman, 2019) have expressed doubts about its validity as well as many post-Keynesian and heterodox economists (Palley, 2019; Sawyer, 2019).

A full appraisal of MMT, however, is out of place here. Nevertheless the 'whatever-it-takes approach' and actual policy response in many advanced economies to the crisis caused by the coronavirus pandemic sparked off renewed interest in MMT from more conventional sections of the media as well as academia. In 2020 the 'we are all MMTers now' has replaced the 'we are all Keynesians' claim of 2009! This provoked a reaction from Nersisyan and Wray (2020), who explain that what many commentators and pundits present as MMT is in fact a misrepresentation of MMT which is *not* "merely a blueprint for turning on the printing press". MMT is simply a *description* of

> how a government that issues its own currency actually spends, taxes, and sells bonds as a matter of course. In doing so, the theory demonstrates that a government like that of the US does not, in fact, face financial constraints… MMT's proponents have always maintained that government spending is limited only by available economic capacity. (p. 2)

In fact, as Nersisyan and Wray (op. cit.) emphasise if there is an MMT element in all the gigantic spending bills and rescue measures announced during the pandemic crisis is that these measures are not 'paid for' either through increased taxes or cuts in spending elsewhere. According to MMT the spending bills will be paid as always by the Central Bank.

Is this not a monetary finance of fiscal deficits? Turner (2020) confirms that this is in fact the case. "Almost certainly, central banks will end up providing monetary finance to fund fiscal deficits. The only question is whether they should make that explicit" (p. 1). Vlieghe (2020) reaches an almost identical conclusion. "If we were the central bank of the Weimar Republic or Zimbabwe, the mechanical transactions on our balance sheet would be similar to what is actually happening in the UK right now" (p. 14). The policies adopted during the pandemic crisis therefore confirm the *description* of the budgetary process provided by MMT. As Turner (2020) points out, however, "There is no doubt that monetary finance is technically feasible and that wise fiscal and monetary authorities could choose just the 'right' amount. The crucial issue is whether politicians can be trusted to be wise" (p. 1).

At the time of writing there is no way of knowing what the actual impact of this recognition of the *descriptive* relevance of MMT on the actual conduct of monetary and fiscal policy. No doubt there will be powerful and persistent arguments presented that such policies work in an emergency and that once the crisis is over fiscal austerity is necessary in order to pay down the debt. On the other hand, there may be arguments pointing in the other direction. As Cassidy (2020) writes,

> If, in extremis, the Fed can buy trillions of dollars' worth of Treasury bonds, mortgage bonds, corporate bonds, and municipal bonds—and if it can also issue credit directly to corporations and universities—then why can't it exploit its unique ability to create money on a more regular basis for other purposes, such as financing green investments or sending money to needy individuals. (p. 5)

In other words, if it becomes so clear and obvious that a massive government intervention in the economy financed by the Central Bank can *deal* with a crisis once it occurred, could not the same principles and policies be employed to *prevent* a crisis from occurring such as the threat of catastrophic climate change which require the right types of investments? Could the 'affordability' narrative with regard to public spending alter fundamentally as a result of the experience of government policies during the pandemic crisis?

8 Summary and Conclusions

At the beginning of 2020, there was a real prospect that after four decades of dominance of both economic theory and policy, the neoliberal era was coming to an end. The idea that neoliberal policies were not only largely responsible for the GFC and the Great Recession of 2008, but also that they were dangerously inadequate in dealing with another global economic collapse, was gaining momentum and credence. This contribution discussed several such warnings about the need to fix a 'broken capitalism'. During the forty years of dominant neoliberal policies the world became more unequal, more economically unstable and closer to ecological collapse despite the Paris accord of 2015.

At the beginning of 2020 both Donald Trump and Boris Johnson, the leaders of the first and fifth largest economies in the world, were very bullish about the economic prospects for their respective countries and the economic philosophy underpinning these prospects. Trump continued to claim that his policy of 'America first' has and will make America great again, while Johnson, who got 'Brexit done' on 31 January 2020, insisted that 'Global Britain' will, by following neoliberal policies, make Britain economically great again. A few months later both leaders along with the rest of the world discovered that 'big government' was the *only game in town*. The question that only time can answer is whether this sudden discovery of 'big government' is, as was the case in 2009, a temporary aberration, to be abandoned as soon as the emergency is over, as was the case in 2010 or it would have a more permanent impact on government policy and the appropriate balance between the private and public sectors of a capitalist economy.

There are some hopeful signs that the experience shared by billions of individuals throughout the globe, of how governments are having to deal with a global crisis, may have a positive effect on the way the climate change policy issue is perceived. This is because climate change policy as argued in this contribution requires both 'big government' in the form of public investments in a 'Green New Deal' and the setting up of global institutions for global co-operation, co-ordination and enforcement of climate change policies.

The shock of the pandemic experience may not entirely remove the huge obstacle of lack of effective global co-operation, but it might help make the problem less intractable. If the twin elements of government commitments to public investments combined with global co-operation were present the coronavirus pandemic crisis could have been prevented. The crisis has, therefore, shaken two of the most fundamental premises of neoliberalism. First, 'Big government' is not—as neoliberal dogma maintains—part of the problem but in a post-neoliberal world, it is part of the solution. If in an emergency tax revenue is *not* a constraint on government spending could government spending be utilised to *prevent* an ecological crisis or reduce the gross inequalities of income and wealth? Second, *there is*, despite Margaret Thatcher's claims to the contrary, such a thing as 'society'. *Homo economicus* can learn important lessons. A society consisting of a collection of individuals motivated purely by self-interest would be unable to deal with a pandemic or an ecological crisis.

In the aftermath of the crisis it is possible to see what Rodrik (2020) calls the 'slow death of neo-liberalism'. If the unthinkable but preventable pandemic could happen once could this experience change social and political attitudes towards an even greater but preventable catastrophe-climate change? What may be said with some confidence is that the chances of a neoliberal world emerging after the crisis unscathed, as it did after the previous crisis, have been greatly diminished.

References

Alessina, A., Favero, C., & Giavazzi, F. (2019). *Austerity: When It Works and When It Doesn't.* Princeton, NJ: Princeton University Press.

Arestis, P., & Sawyer, M. (Eds.). (2018). *Inequality, Trends, Causes, Consequences, Relevant Policies, Annual Edition of International Papers in Political Economy.* London: Palgrave Macmillan.

Arestis, P. & Sawyer, M. (Eds.). (2020). *Economic Policies in a Post Neo- Liberal World. Annual Edition of International Papers in Political Economy*. London: Palgrave Macmillan.

Cassidy, J. (2020, April 28). The Man with the US Economy (and Trump's Re-election Chances) in His Hands. *The New Yorker*.

Dalio, R. (2019). Why and How Capitalism Needs to Be Reformed. *Linkedin Blog*. Available at: https://www.linkedin.com/pulse/why-how-capitalism-needs-reformed-parts-1-2-ray-dalio/

DeGrauwe, P. (2020, March 18). The ECB Must Finance Covid-19 Deficits. *Project Syndicate*.

Diamond, J. (2005). *Collapse. How Societies Choose to Fail or Survive*. London: Penguin Books.

Economist. (2020, April 23). *After the Disease the Debt*.

Eichengreen, B. (2020, April 13). Donald Trump Is Wrong, the Economic Hit of the Coronavirus Will Last for Years. *The Guardian*.

Elliot, E. (2020, March 22). The coronavirus crisis may lead to a new way of thinking. *The Guardian*.

Erixon, F., & Weigel, B. (2018). *Capitalism Without Capitalists*. Available at: https://americanaffairsjournal.org/2017/08/capitalism-without-capitalists/

Friedman, M. (1962). *Capitalism and Freedom*. Chicago: Chicago University Press.

Friedman, M. (1970). *The Social Responsibility of Business Is to Increase Its Profits*. Available at: https://web.archive.org/web/20060207060807/, https://www.colorado.edu/studentgroups/libertarians/issues/friedman-soc-resp-business.html/

Fukuyama, F. (1969). The End of History? *The National Interest*, Summer 1989.

Galbraith, J. K. (1987). *A History of Economics. The Past as the Present*. London: Penguin Books.

Gorbachev, M. (2017). *The New Russia*. Cambridge, UK: Polity Press.

Grossman, S., & Stiglitz, J. (1980). On the Impossibility of Informationally Efficient Markets. *American Economic Review, 70*(3), 393–402.

Iber, P. (2018). *Worlds Apart. How Neoliberalism Shapes the Global Economy and Limits the Power of Democracy*. Available at: https://newrepublic.com/article/147810/worlds-apart-neoliberalism-shapes-global-economy/

Keynes, J. M. (1936). *The General Theory of Employment, Interest and Money*. London: Macmillan.

King, M. (2019, October 19). The World Turned Upside Down: Economic Policy in Turbulent Times. *The Per Jacobsson Lecture,* Washington, DC. Available at: file:///C:/Users/User/Downloads/per-jacobsson-lecture-2019.pdf/

Krugman, P. (2019, February 25). Running on MMT (Wonkfish). *New York Times*.

Lerner, A. (1943). Functional Finance and the Federal Debt. *Social Research, 10*(1), 38–51.
Mason, P. (2016). *Post-Capitalism: A Guide to Our Future*. London: Penguin.
Milanovic, B. (2019). *Capitalism Alone. The Future of the System that Rules the World*. London: The Belknap Press of Harvard University Press.
Mitchell, W., Wray, L., & Watts, M. (2019). *Macroeconomics*. London: Red Globe Press.
Monbiot, G. (2016). *Neoliberalism-the Ideology at the Root of All Our Problems*. Available at: https://www.theguardian.com/books/2016/apr/15/neoliberalism-ideology-problem-george-monbiot/
Nersisyan, Y., & Wray, L. (2020, April 20). The Myth of Helicopter Money. *Project Syndicate*.
Nordhaus, W. (2020, May/June). The Climate Club. How to Fix a Failing Global Effort. *Project Syndicate*.
Nove, A. (1989). *Glasnost in Action-Cultural Renaissance in Russia*. Boston: Unwin Hyman.
Ostrom, E. (1990). *Governing the Commons. The Evolution of Institutions for Collective Action*. Cambridge, UK: Cambridge University Press.
Ostry, J., Loungani, P., & Furceri, D. (2016). *Neoliberalism: Oversold?* Available at: https://www.imf.org/external/pubs/ft/fandd/2016/06/ostry.htm/
Palley, T. (2019). *What's Wrong With MMT. A Critical Primer*. Available at: https://thomaspalley.com/?p=1738
Pearlstein, S. (2020). *Moral Capitalism. Why Fairness Won't Make Us Poorer*. New York: St Martins Griffin.
Philippon, T. (2019). *The Great Reversal: How America Gave Up on Free Markets*. Cambridge, MA: Harvard University Press.
Pigou, A. C. (1920). *The Economics of Welfare*. London: Palgrave Macmillan.
Reinhart, C., & Rogoff, K. (2009). *This Time Is Different. Eight Centuries of Financial Folly*. Princeton, NJ: Princeton University Press.
Rodrik, D. (2020, April 6). Will Covid-19 Remake the World? *Project Syndicate*.
Rogoff, K. (2019, March 4). Modern Monetary Nonsense. *Project Syndicate*.
Roos, J. (2019, September 20). Rentier Capitalism Does Not Come With a Reset Button. *New Statesman*. Available at: https://www.newstatesman.com/politics/economy/2019/09/rentier-capitalism-does-not-come-reset-button/
Saez, E., & Zucman, G. (2019). *The Triumph of Injustice*. New York: W.W. Norton &Company, Inc.
Sawyer, M. (2019). *Modern Monetary Theory. Is Any Value Added?* Available at: http://www.paecon.net/PAEReview/issue89/Sawyer89.pdf/

Sitaraman, G. (2019). *The Collapse of Neoliberalism*. Available at: https://newrepublic.com/article/155970/collapse-neoliberalism/

Skidelsky, R. (2020, March 7). *Interview with Project Syndicate*. Available at: https://www.project-syndicate.org/onpoint/ps-say-more-robert-skidelsky?barrier=accesspaylog/

Slobodian, Q. (2018). *Globalist. The End of Empire and the Birth of Neoliberalism*. Cambridge, MA: Harvard University Press.

Stern, N. (2006). *The Economics of Climate Change. The Stern Review*. Cambridge, UK: Cambridge University Press.

Stiglitz, J. (2019, August 27). Is Stakeholder Capitalism Really Back? *Project Syndicate*.

Tett, G. (2019, September 6). Does Capitalism Need Saving from Itself? *Financial Times*.

Turner, A. (2020, April 20). Money Finance Is Here. *Project Syndicate*.

Vlieghe, G. (2020). *Monetary Policy and the Bank of England's Balance Sheet*. Available at: https://www.bankofengland.co.uk/speech/2020/gertjan-vlieghe-speech-monetary-policy-and-the-boes-balance-sheet/

Wolf, M. (2019, December 4). How to Reform Today's Rigged Capitalism. *Financial Times*.

Wyplosz, C. (2020). *The Long Run Cost of Covid-19*. Available at: https://www.charleswyplosz.info/2020-4-22-covid-19-the-long-run/

3

Moving People in a Post-Neoliberal Era

Liliana Harding

1 Introduction

The appeal of neoliberalism lies in its proffered defence of freedom and choice, and in as much as that is what it can deliver, it is not easy to argue against it. Yet what a neoliberal theoretical framework has come to mean over the last four decades, and the way in which it has informed economic relations and daily lives, might need more scrutiny.

I propose a re-evaluation of the fundamental freedoms that this framework is purporting to offer, with an underlying expectation that the mobility of capital and international movement of workers would allow for widespread benefits in their interplay with local markets. Yet, what these freedoms really mean can be understood with reference to the relationship of governments with markets and their implications for members of society that they are arguing to protect. As such, welfare

L. Harding (✉)
School of Economics, University of East Anglia, Norwich, UK
e-mail: liliana.harding@uea.ac.uk

P. Arestis, M. Sawyer (eds.), *Economic Policies for a Post-Neoliberal World*, International Papers in Political Economy, https://doi.org/10.1007/978-3-030-56735-4_3

implications of both capital and labour mobility must be considered more closely.

In the same way as financial liberalisation needs supervision and a regulatory framework while keeping the liberalisation of capital movements, the mobility of people in an international context is far from just a free choice of migration for work. Regulations and restrictions represent the norm rather than an exceptional feature in global mobility, especially when this refers to the mobility of labour. As such, both the analysis of what affects economic migration and of its ultimate impact must be qualified in a policy perspective, along with a societal response function in mind. I shall underline these dimensions in the discussion of this chapter, departing from the principle of free movement of factors that would underlie the neoliberal paradigm.

An initial portrayal of the effects of capital and labour mobility across national borders will be considered—by linking both factors' inflows with business cycle fluctuations and GDP growth and drawing on UK data as an example. Then, the effect of labour mobility on individuals within the economy is captured, linking labour inflows with measures of inequality of income or earnings. I shall consider next the extent to which free choice and free movement really apply to labour mobility and, second, how they can be reinterpreted in various circumstances. The premise of the discussion is that labour mobility represents a qualified type of freedom, and a restricted choice reserved for selected categories of skills and workers.

I shall thus offer an overview of how global labour mobility can be better understood as a selective process with instances of mobility under preferential agreements—as in the recent example of gradual liberalisation of movement in the European Union (EU). Finally, I propose to offer the latter a closer attention and reconsider the mechanisms at play both when 'free movement of labour' is emerging as a negotiated process and when it is re-evaluated, based on outcomes for the economies and societies where it is taking place.

This chapter is structured as follows. It begins first with an attempt to position migration beyond the unconstrained choice suggested by the term 'free movement'. Next, I illustrate the impact of factors that flow across borders in terms of economic growth—with the latter being the main objective in an economy informed by the neoliberal framework; a subsection then illustrates how earnings inequality evolves along capital versus labour mobility. The next sections question the specific implications of migration on public welfare, with an overview of the roles played by public preferences, community and network considerations, as well as policy choices and migration effects on revenues and public services. I also consider the governance of international labour mobility along the lines of preferential agreements and a gradual liberalisation in Europe. Finally, I summarise and conclude.

2 Neoliberalism and 'Free Movement'

While there is no consensus on what exactly neoliberalism really stands for, the term made an early appearance in the economic literature with an 1898 article by Charles Gide in *The Economic Journal*, and advocates the pursuit of free competition above all else in market economies (Birch, 2017). This is also the main framework of economic theory and has informed economic policies of capitalist countries, around the world, since the beginning of the 1980s. As part of the package, that is as well the point in time when the role of states has been diverted away from welfare provision and towards the support of markets and the 'freedom to pursue individual choices'. Perhaps not surprising in this sense, inequality, which had been on a clear downward trend until the late 1970s in advanced economies, has levelled off and then seen a sustained rise in more recent times. At the same time, some freedoms were progressing rapidly at the level of the global market, such as the free of movement of capital, while other freedoms materialised more slowly, including the movement of workers across borders.

Before questioning the consequences of the market promoting free choices through free movement, the first thing I propose to consider is the authenticity of agency for individuals faced with their own mobility as workers. As Wrenn (2015) observes, a lack of authentic agency for individuals allows for the principles and rhetoric of neoliberalism to diverge from the reality in which it operates. This proposition can be re-evaluated with reference to the principle of free movement of workers, by questioning the way in which restrictions for some individuals are enacted in the name of protecting the privileges of others. Striving for freedom of movement for labour in a global economy, while at the same time protecting the economic well-being of a localised workforce, suffers from the internal contradiction of global versus selective freedom. To make it a win-win situation, the rules of this interplay need to be both transparent and carefully designed, to give everyone an equal playing field and promote co-operation of otherwise unequal participants.

> Otherwise, a discrepancy of interests persists. Local populations feel threatened by unfair competition from lower paid migrants arriving in their local markets. At the same time, international migrants face barriers to entry in these local markets. Such barriers ultimately under-price migrants' labour and their skills, and the competitive threat to locals becomes real where foreign labour has limited options to work abroad.

Last, but not least, there are as well barriers to exit, with individuals remaining trapped in economies offering them poor prospects and with little choice to move themselves.

The rhetoric of liberalisation towards a free market that benefits all is also breaking down in the face of cultural or social preferences to preserve separate identities along with the migrants' own freedom to move across borders. Even where quantifiable effects of immigration are insignificant or positive for the local economy, some sections of the population in host societies can lose out from higher labour market competition, or simply prefer limitations to others' access to their local market. In fact, there is little evidence of restrictions to cross-border mobility being asked for by incumbents based on negative economic effects from immigration in local labour markets. For example, going out from responses collected in 21 countries by the European Social Survey, Card, Dustmann, and Preston (2012) find that socio-cultural concerns are up to five times more important in shaping attitudes towards immigration than any economic concerns. Essentially, individuals prefer to live and settle in communities which emulate their own characteristics.

This is the case for both settled and mobile individuals—as attested by a large literature emphasising the role of social networks and their significance in the choice of migrants' destinations (see, e.g., Bauer, Epstein, &

Gang, 2009; Chiswick & Miller, 2002). Yet, the chance for free movement to be beneficial for everyone also depends on differences and complementarities between incumbents and new arrivals. There might be little point to add an equal type of worker if the objective of a local group is to increase its marginal output—a process which according to marginal productivity theory requires the addition of complementary workers. It is the case though that 'compositional amenities' matter more to individuals than the freedom to interact with an uncertain—even if potentially better—alternative community that is changed by inward migration of workers from a variety of international origins.

3 Factor Mobility, the Economy and Inequality

Economic growth in itself is the main objective on the neoliberal agenda, and whether this has been achieved through the liberalisation of factor mobility merits scrutiny, too. Here I reflect on the role of factor mobility for macroeconomic performance, first going out from an expectation of positive effects on the economy from free competition of factors. The relevant discussion draws initially on findings in the literature regarding the effects of both international capital and labour mobility on economic growth, and presents trends for the United Kingdom over a longer period of time. Then, noting that the business cycle itself can influence both capital and migrant flows, we will illustrate recent developments associated with the Global Financial Crisis (GFC) for both capital and migrant flows in the United Kingdom. In a second step I question the association of factor mobility with income inequality for the United Kingdom, and map the association of migration and earnings dispersion. The direction of the effect between earnings inequality and migrant flows is thereby reconsidered over the last 60 years.

Freedom of movement of capital had been accepted as a destabilising factor for the economy, both before and after World War II, and hence global flows of capital were restrained until the 1980s. Yet, from the last decades of the twentieth century global capital flows have been encouraged by a neoliberal norm and promoted by most major economies and institutions, from the IMF to the OECD. In turn, free labour mobility remained the privilege of a few, with individuals moving frequently around the world as intra-company mobile workers or under the specific provisions of trade agreements discussed in Sect. 9.

3.1 Capital Flows, Migration and Growth

Reinhart (2020) gives an overview of capital flows[1] from a long-term perspective, noting the way in which these are linked to the risk of defaults or disruptions to trade over time. Sudden stops are notable during the 1930s, with a similar effect in 2020 with the COVID-19 pandemic and a comparatively less sharp decline in capital flows during the 2008–2009 GFC. A note of caution is thereby needed when observing net capital flows. Central banks play a major role in modern times and intervene by changing reserves to 'lean against the wind' (Reinhart, op. cit.)—thereby obscuring the different responses to global factors of the private sector and the government, as reflected in current account balances.

A recent IMF paper (Bluedorn, Duttagupta, Guajardo, & Topalova, 2013) provides a breakdown of capital flows for sets of countries around the world, noting the volatility in both developed and emerging markets, and for all types of flows-whether we are looking at equity or debt flows. Bluedorn, Duttagupta, Guajardo, and Topalova (op. cit.) thus note that '[f]or advanced economies, both gross inflows and outflows rise during good times, thereby offsetting the effects on net flows. A similar pattern is also observed for emerging and other developing economies, but the size of the correlation with GDP is much stronger for gross inflows, implying that net capital flows track mostly the behaviour of foreign investors' (p. 22). In this context a difference between advanced and emerging markets is given by the more balanced inflows and outflows captured in the net flows of advanced economies. That ultimately lowers the volatility of their total net inflows, despite higher volatility of various components.

Eichengreen (2002) reflects on the evidence linking capital flows and growth in the economic literature and finds no indication that capital account openness and growth go together. This is sometimes challenged

---

[1] A current account deficit is equal in size with a capital outflow. That is, capital flows are measured historically by the absolute value of current account balances (Eichengreen, 2002).

and attributed to the length of the period under consideration in various studies (Eichengreen, op. cit.). As the lack of evidence of a positive impact on economic performance challenges the neoliberal stance expecting capital flows liberalisation to benefit growth, I reconsider below the data linking capital flows and GDP growth in the case of the UK.

Figure 3.1 captures capital flows based on current account balances. While the indicator is affected by some of the issues associated with aggregation discussed above in relation to the current account balances, the indicator is still capturing the high volatility associated with capital flows. As suggested by the literature, there is also clear indication here of net capital inflows following a strong downward trend at the time of crisis. For example, the 4% drop in GDP during the 2008–2009 GFC in Fig. 3.1 is accompanied by a decrease of a similar 4% in the net capital inflow (represented here as a percentage of GDP). In this case, the financial crisis is the main trigger in the capital flow drop and the downward

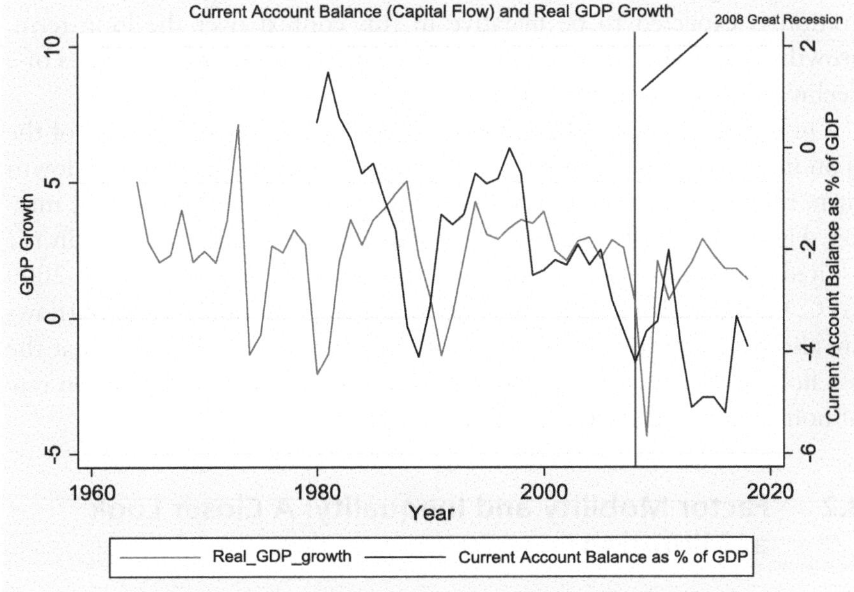

Fig. 3.1 UK GDP growth and current account balance as a percentage of GDP. (Source: IMF and Office of National Statistics data; own elaboration)

business cycle. On the other hand, there is no indication that the economy would be particularly boosted by the capital inflows increasing during good times, when investment opportunities are better.

Then, perhaps surprisingly, given the frequent public debate on migration rather than capital movements, the economic literature on the link between migration and economic growth is rather scarce, and clearly thinner than the analysis on financial globalisation and its impact. Borjas (2019) attempts to disentangle the inconclusive empirical findings of the existing literature regarding the effect of migration on economic growth. Drawing on the Solow canonical model he notes that based on a one-time supply shock to the economy with immigration, a higher level of output is expected. After an initial drop in per-capita income in the host country, the economy is modelled to return to a steady-state per-capita income—as capital and labour returns readjust towards a constant capital-to-labour ratio. Yet, where migration represents a permanent shock, the economy will experience a negative per-capita income effect over the long term. I would further add that as the wage effect of immigration is expected to be negative in this context over the long term, growth should also be expected to slow down—under the pressures of a declining wage share of income.

On the other hand, while migrant flows are following the trend of the economic cycle, and immigration declines as a consequence of a downturn, migration can act as a buffer for the economy and the labour market. Figure 3.2 illustrates how the net migration of non-nationals in the United Kingdom was falling, for example, during the 2008–2009 GFC. Comparative data for non-nationals' migrant inflows and outflows are also provided in the Figs. 3.4 and 3.5, and further illustrate that the net flow of non-nationals is driven primarily by a strong emigration rate of non-nationals during the GFC.

3.2 Factor Mobility and Inequality: A Closer Look at Migration

While increasing volatility and the incidence of financial crisis, the globalisation of capital flows, along with the financialisation of the economy,

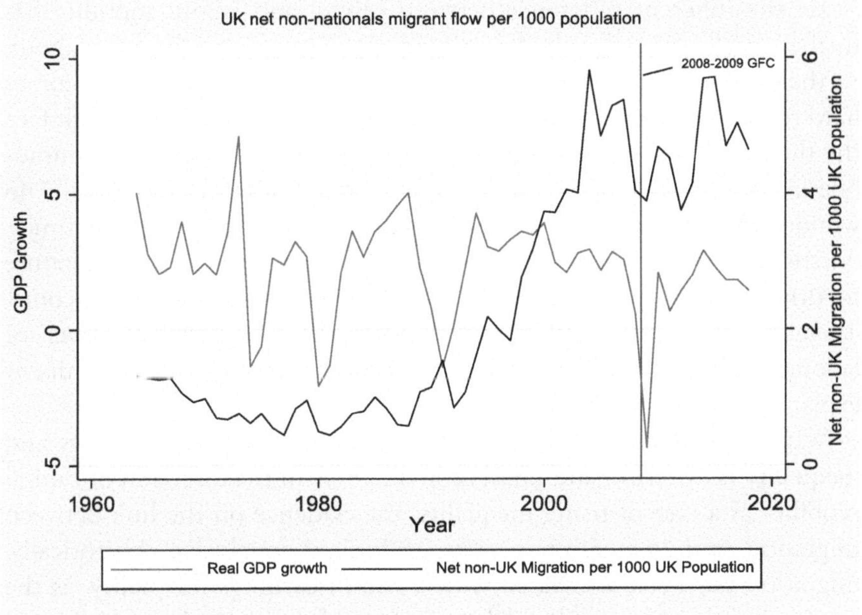

Fig. 3.2 UK GDP growth against non-national inflows per 1000 population. (Source: Office of National Statistics/LTIM data and own elaboration)

can worsen income inequality. Sawyer (2018) notes that previous to the easing of capital controls from the 1970s, economies around the world had experienced a long period of low-income inequality between 1945 and 1973. Subsequent to capital market liberalisation, a large number of empirical studies reviewed found that the financial sector is able to extract economic rents and generate large wage premia, with top earnings in the financial sector rising sharply and driving inequality.

In this context, Tridico (2018) looks at financialisation, along with factors such as labour flexibility or the reduction in social spending by governments in the OECD, to explain the rise in inequality. Thereby, flexibility implies weaker social protection and is shown to be a further driver of income inequality. In order to link capital and labour market liberalisation at this point, I note that flexibility has been indicated by employers as the main reason for preferring foreign workers in the United Kingdom (see Rolfe, 2017).

Yet the inherent difference between capital and labour mobility has further implications for the bargaining capacity of capital versus labour. As the former can threaten to leave a jurisdiction at any point, it becomes hard to tax. In turn, labour and in particular unskilled workers both face the threat of outsourcing of their production and are themselves immobile in the face of high taxation. Rodrik (2017) notes that it is thus no wonder that the labour share of income has declined in recent times. Arestis (2018) further documents a set of factors found in the literature to drive inequality along the falling share of wages in total income. Thereby both globalisation and the decreased bargaining power of labour—and in particular of unskilled workers—remain a prominent explanation of higher inequality.

While the literature on the link between global financial flows and inequality is extensive and points convincingly in the direction of capital mobility as a case of rising inequality, the evidence on the link between migration and inequality is once again less conclusive. Historically, migration has been associated with a rise in earnings inequality, as the relative supply of low-skilled labour increased significantly in traditional migrants' destinations, such as the United States. Yet, when large international flows of labour have been associated with large flows of capital in the same direction, the impact of migration on income inequality is limited (see Hatton & Williamson, 2005).

Wadsworth, Dhingra, Ottaviano, and Van Reenen (2016) have mapped the evolution of hourly wages in the United Kingdom for the top-, median- and bottom-decile income earners in the UK population against EU immigration. They note that there is no correlation of the strong upward trend in immigration to the United Kingdom following the post-2004 expansion of the EU and wages. Moreover, it appears that wages in the lowest decile are growing fastest in the years immediately following EU enlargement for the United Kingdom. In contrast, and based on a different sample, Dustmann, Frattini, and Preston (2013) find a slight increase for upper wages in the United Kingdom as a consequence of immigration and an effect of depressed wages below the 20% percentile of the wage distribution.

Similarly, a widely cited study by Card (2009) on migration and inequality in the United States highlights the strong substitution effect between the native population with below high school education and recent migrants. Yet, the most significant negative effects on wages are found amongst the lowest-skilled and within migrant communities themselves. The overall wage effects of immigration remain insignificant for the population as a whole.

I follow next Hatton and Williamson's approach (2005) to look at longer trends in migration, as associated with income inequality. I thereby use an inequality indicator for the United Kingdom compiled in Atkinson, Hasell, Morelli, and Roser (2017) and analyse the gap in earnings between the top 10% of earners and the median earners in the United Kingdom. Figure 3.3 illustrates the trends in this indicator under the 90/50 earnings dispersion schedule, which is set against trends in the immigration of foreign workers to the United Kingdom for the same period. The migration indicator captures a net inflow of non-UK nationals since 1960 and has been calculated here as a rate per 1000 UK population, based on long-term immigration statistics (LTIM) available through the ONS. The expectation is that migration increases the scarcity of the top earners relative to the median worker, rather than concentrating on the low-skilled. This aligns better with the UK immigrants' skill composition, which resembles more strongly the native population—rather than migration being biased towards the unskilled, as is the case for the United States.

Based on the data in Fig. 3.3 I find that the correlation between the 90/50 earnings dispersion measure and our migration indicator is in fact at a relatively high level of 0.8895 for the period as a whole. Yet, for a selection of years after the EU enlargement in 2004, that correlation becomes negative at -0.3408, a result that aligns with the more recent studies cited in this section. I also used a VAR regression specification with one lag to test for the link between migration and earnings dispersion and obtained a small positive yet highly statistically significant correlation coefficient for the two indicators.

A Granger causality test further reveals that it is a rising wage dispersion which causes higher net migration of non-nationals in subsequent years, rather than migration causing the wage dispersion to rise. That result

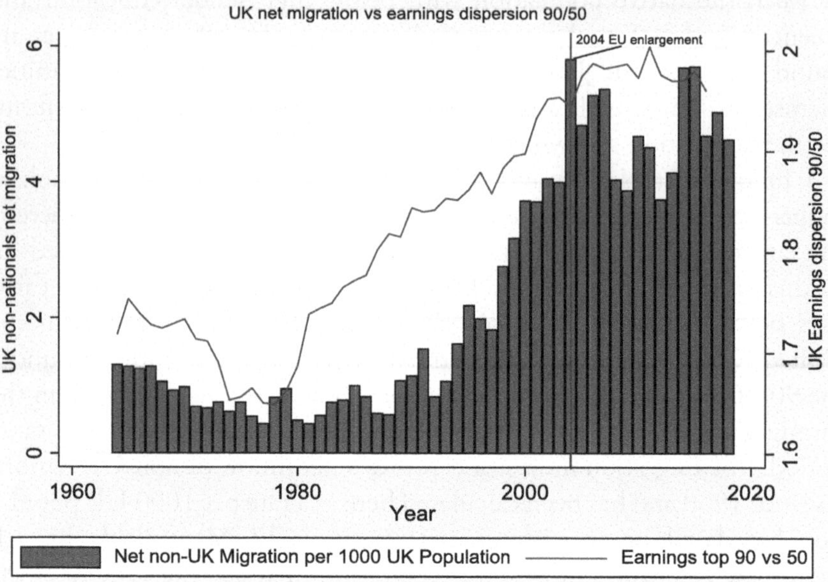

Fig. 3.3 UK earnings dispersion* and net migration of non-nationals to the United Kingdom. (Data Sources: Atkinson et al. (2017), "The Chartbook of Economic Inequality" [Available at: https://www.chartbookofeconomicinequality.com/inequality-by-country/united-kingdom/]. Also, ONS/LTIM data and own elaboration. **Note*: The 90/50 dispersion of earnings measure used here represents earnings at the top decile relative to median earnings and has been compiled from the UK *Annual Survey of Hours and Earnings* records and ONS data updates.)

is consistent with a positive self-selection of migrants[2] in our sample. It can also be explained by the proportion of skilled migrants with higher education in the United Kingdom, which according to Clark, Drinkwater, and Robinson (2014, p. 13) reached by 2011 a 36%, 37% and 39.9% for UK migrants arriving from post-2004 EU members, older EU members or non-EU member states, respectively. In view of these results, we might experience the situation where higher earnings opportunities at the top of the distribution attract migrants to the United Kingdom, rather than immigration causing inequality and a fall in earnings at the bottom or medium of the distribution.

[2] See, for example, Borjas (1994) for a discussion of the self-selection theory of migrants.

While there are other reasons for the growing earnings dispersion beyond migration, and technological change or the retrenchment of the welfare state have quite a lot to account for growing inequality in the United Kingdom, the two indicators trend together, and probably reinforce an already strong advantage of the top earners. Under a laissez-fair approach the neoliberal framework is not offering tools for directly addressing these underlying causes of inequality in earnings in the United Kingdom. Hence, while restricting labour mobility, which is already low compared to capital mobility, there is certainly scope for redistribution from the highest to the lowest earners, and for that matter, from capital to labour, which is losing its fair share of income.

4 Free Movement of People Between State and Markets

International migration is one of the widely debated issues of present times and offers a subject of study to a variety of disciplines. In practical terms, it involves people crossing borders and then, temporarily or permanently, settling abroad. Additionally, the purpose of individuals' stay in a foreign country allows for the distinction between various categories of migrants. Some people move abroad for political reasons, fleeing repressive regimes at home and seeking refuge in a safe destination. Others just try to evade a natural catastrophe in the country of origin or migrate to join family members. The countries of destination generally accept such migrants on humanitarian considerations. The integration in societies of destination is not always easy, and governments intervene with various policies. Intervention can include the ascription of the right to work for foreigners residing legally abroad, but refugees and those migrating for family reunification are primarily regarded as individuals whose human rights are to be safeguarded. No consideration is given to their labour market characteristics when entering the country of destination and labour market integration can be very slow.

On the other hand, while some economic migrants are accepted without restrictions in labour markets abroad, others are seen as a threat to employment opportunities for the national workforce—based on the assumption of a substitution effect shaped within a neoliberal framework. Thus, despite migrants' reasonable quest to seek improvement in living conditions through their own hard work, they often become illegal workers by virtue of destination countries' restrictions to their formal labour market integration. The freedom of foreigners to seek employment abroad is broadly governed by criteria of nationality and, sometimes, by the occupational and skill characteristics of workers. Moreover, the more similar the country of origin to that of destination and the higher the skills of migrants, the more freedom they are usually granted to seek employment abroad.

The wide debate around the topic of migration suggests that it addresses various interests, which often contradict each other. People seek employment abroad according to their own decisions and perceptions of benefitting. The main driver of labour migrants in a neoliberal market perspective is to improve individual standards of living. Migration thus primarily benefits mobile workers who choose to move for better income prospects for themselves and their families. Yet, often the option to move is not what migrants would prefer in a first instance. Instead, they are pushed into migration by poor working conditions in their home countries. As Delgado Wise (2015) argues, most migrants are in this sense 'forced migrants', even where they are not directly displaced by unemployment, or conflict or environmental concerns. Labour mobility is often driven by the lack of provision of decent working conditions, including a lack of opportunities that allow for the full use of skills in home economies. Migrants' skills are hence wasted in destinations where they are forced to seek irregular employment, or employment below their educational standards.

In a neoliberal framework, for the country of destination, an increased supply of workers implies lower costs of labour. Thus, employers welcome foreign workers, especially if the latter have advanced skills in short supply to perform the jobs on offer in local markets. Beyond some highly skilled professions—and as the 2020 pandemic has especially uncovered—shortages can be associated with a variety of key sectors, from agriculture to nursing and caring industries. While foreign workers in these sectors are welcome, they often obscure an underlying 'brain drain'-cum-social waste process affecting migrants and their home economies. The young and able foreign workforce in these sectors are deserting a vulnerable population in poorer economies, with children and senior citizens left to fend for themselves in migrants' countries of origin. Delgado Wise (2015, p. 11) labels this as a 'transfer of a demographic dividend'—and that remains unaccounted for in most economics textbooks.

Foreign labour is also welcome by selective migration policies, in particular where migrants are employed in high-profile occupations or in large corporations—as intra-company transferees. There is an implicit assumption that such 'skilled migrants' benefit local labour markets through their higher productivity and tax contributions. Yet, while their migration proceeds in line with the idea of freedom of mobility being beneficial to all, intra-company mobile workers are employed in occupations with earnings premia that are replicating the power of the corporations transferring them—including companies in the financial sector. The liberalisation framework is thus focussed on a selected few, well-earning internationally mobile individuals, working frequently outside the sphere of activities with direct positive social impact. Yet, this mobility is promoted as a positive, 'skill-based' mobility by the free movement model of neoliberalism. There is a fallacy as well in equating highly skilled individuals to high-earning individuals, as in the example of the proposals for a new skill-based immigration policy in the United Kingdom (Home Office, 2018). Therein, skill has been, at least initially, defined by an individual's ability to earn over £30,000 per annum. Yet, most higher-earning occupations exclude care workers or teachers, who need to be redefined in order to allow for any immigration to continue in these sectors[3] (see as well Rolfe, Runge, & Hudson-Sharp, 2019).

On the other hand, nationals in countries of immigration often expect negative effects from increased competition in their local labour markets. Indeed, where migrants substitute nationals, the latter are expected to lose out from immigration, while capital captures all the benefits of

[3] Later on, a variable threshold has been proposed for the new policy. This acknowledges lower pay in education, research or the health sector, which often fill their specific skill shortages through immigration.

higher returns with cheaper labour. Native workers in immigration countries are thus motivated to support a restrictive migration regime, especially towards foreigners seen as potential substitutes to themselves—unless redistribution occurs to compensate them for their losses. While this might be a first-best solution, with higher taxation of capital allowing for compensation for native workers, it rarely if at all has been enacted. One reason for this is arguably the fact that capital itself is footloose, while native workers are less mobile, carrying both the threat from international mobile workers' competition and the burden of local taxation. Equally, while it is often those on the lowest side of the income distribution who are estimated to lose most from immigration (Dustmann et al., 2013), a clear group in need for compensation is difficult to identify.

As governments are directly involved in the process of migration, states necessarily become the next group of actors to observe. The framework of analysis must depart from a neoliberal perspective understanding states as primarily a defender of their associated markets. Governments thereby aim to protect the interests of their countries' citizens, and arguably of those who are most vulnerable with free movement—that is, immobile native workers in direct competition with internationally mobile capital and labour. We can understand in this context the exceptional framework established in Europe, where the EU acts beyond national interests, and with the main goal of protecting the single market and 'free movement' of workers as a supra-national principle. Inside the present EU, mobility of labour between member states is indeed promoted as a desirable mechanism towards a more efficient allocation of labour. In contrast, international migrants from outside the EU are generally accepted as a threat to the Union's labour market, and their mobility remains highly restricted—with the role of the EU governments and the European Commission changing once again, away from market facilitator to a guardian of boundaries and the potential welfare of citizens within Europe.

A typology of the economic literature on international migration, which tackles the issues considered relevant in our discussion, addresses the link between economic research and policymaking itself. As highlighted by Borjas (1994), research mainly focusses on the effects of migration on developed economies, and revolves around three broad questions: 'How do immigrants perform in the host country's economy?', 'What impact do immigrants have on the employment opportunities of natives?', and 'Which immigration policy benefits the host country?'

Beside economic factors, the set of determinants to migration and its structure go well beyond the individual choices of potentially mobile individuals, and that is where analysis needs to leave the strict boundaries typical to a neoliberal space. Any discussion of migration and its effects must consider social networks and public attitudes to migration, but also necessarily migration policies and governance structures that shape labour mobility. The role of such factors that go beyond individual choices to migrate, and the wider effects of mobility of labour for an economy and society are the primary focus of analysis in the rest of this chapter.

5 The Economics of Migration Networks

An additional value of information for the decision to migrate to an uncertain environment is given by the network theory of migration. There is a growing economic literature looking into the chain behaviour of migrants and the responses of migrant communities to additional migration (e.g. Bauer et al., 2009; Bauer, Epstein, & Gang, 2002; Epstein, 2002; Lazear, 1998). Moreover, various sociological projects analyse the role of social networks in the perpetuation of migration to particular destinations (see Massey et al., 1993 for a review of existing approaches).

The predominant economic approach to migrant networks estimates these by the size of the migrant population from a given origin in a particular destination. It is commonly understood that migrant networks are extensively used by immigrants for the acquisition of information about the destination country, as well as for the provision of help with accommodation and job search on arrival in a new environment.

Migrants settled in ethnic communities abroad make use of the strong social network within migrant enclaves to get moral support, ethnic specific goods, as well as jobs—especially when their foreign-language proficiency is poor. In sum, it can be argued that additional migrants create a positive externality for other migrants, by increasing the wealth of social interaction and support in their community. However, while networks abroad initially attract new immigrants, as the migrant network gets too large, it also becomes less attractive (see Bauer et al., 2009).

An explanation is the fact that 'strong social ties', inside an enclave, isolate a community from the rest of the society, by reducing the 'weak links' with the latter. Loose social networks with the entire host society would translate in more trade and more widespread positive externalities from networking for the migrant community (Gurak & Caces, 1992). Additionally, a crowding effect sets in if an immigrant community is increasing, as more and more individuals compete for a limited number of jobs in the existing enclaves, and their wage levels are consequently brought down. In this sense Bauer et al. (2002) model an inverted U-shaped network effect of the increased migrant community, taking into account the benefits of social interaction, and the negative externality of oversized communities. Following Epstein (2002), they observe a second type of externality as well, derived from the estimation of previous migrants' incentives to move to a particular destination.

New migrants seek to reduce the uncertainty surrounding their destination choice, and resume to what is labelled as 'herd behaviour'. This means that migrants consider the attraction of a given location to earlier emigrants from the same origin as a signal of unobserved benefits at destination, beyond any present private signals that a destination is desirable. Such an effect cumulates with the expected benefits from their community ties, once migration has occurred, and causes the positive network effect to expand beyond the maximum social benefit derived from socialisation in a destination community.

6 Migration Preferences and Political Economy Considerations

A complementary approach to community concerns shaping migrants' incentives to move and stay abroad is the analysis of individual preferences of natives in the host countries with respect to migrant workers. This approach allows for a differentiation of attitudes to migration in countries of destination, depending on individual characteristics of natives, such as their own skill level (e.g. Scheve & Slaughter, 2001). Preferences are further linked to macroeconomic considerations and assume that unskilled natives are most negatively affected by immigration. Scheve and Slaughter (op. cit.) find that natives' skills are significantly and positively correlated with a positive attitude towards immigration. Unexpectedly however, people in high immigration areas do not have a stronger correlation between skills and immigration policy preference, despite the potential of being (at least in the short term) disproportionally and negatively affected by immigration. This has been attributed to the strong positive link between the immigrant status and general liberal preferences. Such preferences have been further replicated in recent studies on the attitudes to migration and the vote for Brexit. Thereby, areas in the United Kingdom with a higher share of immigrants had a more positive attitude to migration, all else being equal (see Becker, Fetzer, & Novy, 2017).

For the elucidation of the link between public perceptions and migration flows, an additional approach is useful, as summarised under the political economy framework. Hillman (1993) reminds us that the neoliberal framework generally ignores the influences of politics, religion or ethnic and cultural characteristics on individual preferences, and ultimately on migration policy. Nevertheless, decision-makers see the need to design a policy which considers voters' cultural preferences, and cannot ignore such factors. An earlier study by Hollifield (1992) applied the political-economic model to an empirical analysis of migration in France. The analysis attempted to test to what extent foreign employment in a country is a joint outcome of market conditions (Market), the debate among political groups (Group) and state policy (Policy). Unsurprisingly, Hollifield (op. cit.) finds that apart from market conditions, both group politics and state policy concerning migration very much contributed to the fall in the number of foreign workers in France before 1990. Moreover, state policy appeared as the strongest factor reducing migration rates to France in the short term, rather than specific economic conditions.

It is often assumed by academics and in public discussions that immigrants diminish the average skill of labour in a given country, as workers coming from poorer areas of the world are less skilled than natives. Beyond migrants' similarity or dissimilarity to the population of the country of destination, immigrants are then treated as more or less able to increase the productivity level in the host economy. Yet Card et al. (2012) demonstrate, on the basis of the European Social Survey data, that attitudes to migration are shaped primarily by preferences for compositional amenities, going beyond economic considerations. Thereby, skill or productivity itself does not feature in such preferences, but rather cultural preferences.

Earlier work by Gang, Rivera-Batiz, and Yun (2002) also constructed a multivariate analysis including factors quantifying the attitudes towards foreigners in the EU. The study used the 1988 and 1997 Eurobarometer survey data to account for public attitudes towards immigrants in Europe, and essentially estimated the determinants of a person's likelihood to have a negative attitude to foreigners. Their model relies on a set of individual socio-economic characteristics and on indicators describing the social environment and behavioural characteristics of respondents. Attitudes are regressed on a set of explanatory variables accounting for the respondent's labour market status, education, work experience, number of children in the household, foreigners in the neighbourhood, racial bias and the gender of the household head. The results of Gang, Rivera-Batiz and Yun (op. cit.) point to a rising negative attitude between 1988 and 1997, whereby labour market competition with migrants explains just a small percentage of this attitude and racial bias represents the strongest determinant to anti-foreigner sentiments.

Thus, unemployed individuals, who are affected by adverse conditions in the labour market, do not in general identify immigration as one of the factors contributing to their precarious status. Yet, being retired has a significant impact, in the form of negative opinions about immigration. On the other hand, a relevant factor shaping attitudes towards immigrants appears to be the variable 'children'. If there are children in the household, a person has a more positive attitude to immigrants. Educational attainment for a respondent was previously shown to deter negative attitudes towards foreigners (e.g. Scheve & Slaughter, 1999). However, according to Gang et al. (2002), that appears to become less significant to the formation of attitudes towards foreigners over time, in Europe. In sum, when linked with the economic status of different individuals, negative attitudes to immigrants generally reflect concerns with social amenities or status rather than a significant threat to labour market opportunities.

The 'compositional amenities' referred to in this section emphasise an inclination towards individuals with similar characteristics to our own, including when it comes to immigration preferences expressed by natives. Yet, to increase productivity in the local economy, a selective immigration policy[4] should attract complementary workers to the local labour force, which often means *different* types of workers and with different skills from the native population. Rolfe, Runge, and Hudson-Sharp (2019) emphasise in this sense the need to reconcile apparently contrasting public and employer or policy preferences when it comes to immigration. Once the expected contribution of foreign workers is more carefully evaluated and understood, public preferences align much better with the profile of complementary workers, rather than simply asking from foreigners to be 'more skilled' or more similar to natives.

7 From Locational Choice to Welfare Effects of Migration

While the traditional literature often explores how taxation determines migrant flows (e.g. Simula & Trannoy, 2010) I would consider here the reverse effect, and look at the implications of migration on government tax inputs. I consider per-capita tax revenue as a source of government income benefitting the average individual, with immigration typically adding to the working-age population rather than displacing native workers. It can thereby mitigate the burden of increasing dependency ratios and allows for higher per-capita tax revenues.

The design of taxation systems needs to consider the possibility of individuals voting with their feet where mobility is allowed between national tax jurisdictions (Mirrlees, 1982). In the real international context, restricted movement of people across borders means that locals often have little choice but to accept the national tax regime—unlike capital,

[4] See for the United Kingdom the White Paper proposal for a new 'skill-based' migration policy (Home Office, 2018).

which easily crosses borders to avoid higher taxation. Yet, economic integration as in the case of the EU single market allows for the relevance of tax competition to translate to the supranational level). Net migration can thus result from emigration of the native population shopping for the most advantageous tax regime (Simula & Trannoy, 2010), as well as being the result of immigration responding to tax incentives. We would ultimately expect lower taxes with mobile labour, due to increased competition between alternative locations. Such effects are to be quantified empirically, as lower tax rates can induce higher tax collection, with an ambiguous outcome for tax revenues.

A related part of the existing literature has as primary interest the impact of international openness on national budgetary revenues. The opening of borders can arguably increase the vulnerability of sections of the native population due to increased competition from abroad, a process which calls for a larger state and public budgets. Yet Dreher (2006) shows that the evidence is inconclusive in terms of what effect we can expect on the final tax revenue from globalisation. The literature, nevertheless, generally relates economic openness with flows of goods and capital mobility, rather than labour migration. Openness relying on capital flows can be interpreted, in this context, as a means to increase the level of international investment and with potential to raise capital taxation.

On the other hand, international mobility of people is most frequently scrutinised for its potential to raise fiscal transfers. The literature on the welfare effect of migration thus considers the significance of net transfer payments to foreign nationals residing within a tax jurisdiction. The related research question asks, to what extent migrants are attracted by 'welfare magnets'. Under this perspective, the migrant flow can be geared by the prospect to withdraw resources from the destination country's welfare system.

The evidence in this direction is mixed. Borjas (1999) shows, for example, that in the United States more generous states, in terms of access to welfare, tend to be more attractive locations for foreign nationals. Other studies focussing more widely on the OECD (e.g. Belot & Ederveen, 2012) find no evidence of the attractiveness of more generous welfare systems to migrants. There are also differences in the estimated outcomes of migration on welfare payments in the short and in the long term.

Unskilled migrants in particular are considered to impose a cost on natives if they withdraw more benefits, compared to their tax contributions. Equally, sometimes the displacement of the local population in areas of immigration can reverse the positive contributions of migration, including tax revenues. However, non-nationals often represent a significant contribution to the skilled workforce, with positive consequences to productivity, economic activity and tax revenues (see, e.g., Hunt, 2004 and/or Bhagwati & Hanson, 2009). Razin, Sadka, and Swagel (2002) further argue that tax rates in host economies decline with unskilled migration—as the native population is trying to avoid transfers that benefit unskilled migrants. Based on this reasoning, where migrants are skilled, they contribute more in tax and we should perhaps expect increased support for higher tax rates at the local level in the presence of a selective, skilled migration.

Empirical evidence from around the world (e.g. Boeri, Hanson, & McCormick, 2002; Gaston & Rajaguru, 2013; Vargas-Silva, 2013) further indicates that there are differences between countries in terms of net transfers to migrants. Rowthorn (2008) surveyed various channels by which migration generates a fiscal impact, differentiating for the demographic characteristics of migrants, their length of stay abroad, as well as the mechanisms by which immigration interacts with natives' mobility and the general provision of public goods. The resulting net fiscal impact of migration on developed economies was estimated in the range of ±1% of GDP.

Dustmann, Frattini, and Halls (2010) first assessed the fiscal impact of recent migrants to the United Kingdom and showed that after controlling for individual characteristics, migrants have a 13% lower propensity to access benefits compared to similar natives. Dustmann and Frattini (2014) looked into detailed areas of public spending and the net fiscal impact on each of these by UK population categories depending on their origins. After controlling for age and gender, European Economic Area (EEA) migrants in the United Kingdom appear to have the lowest rates of benefit claims and social housing access—as compared to both natives and non-EEA migrants.

8 A Choice Between Free Movement of People and Public Services

Overall, preferences over migration restrictions are shaped, according to Hatton (2017), by the immigrant stock and the share of social benefits in GDP in various countries. Where the two are higher, locals oppose migration more strongly. On the other hand, concerns with access to social welfare have increased where the recent Great Recession hit hardest, and negative feelings about immigration followed suit. That is irrespective of the fact that migrants have often themselves carried the highest adjustment burden of an economic crisis (Hatton, 2016).[5] They are again amongst the first to lose jobs and labour market prospects with the onset of the 2020 emergency crisis. Borjas and Cassidy (2020) document for the United States that migrants' job-finding rates are lower and job losses are higher than for natives during the pandemic.

Thus, in periods of economic stagnation, when pull factors for cross-border mobility are subsiding, and inflows are quickly adjusting downwards, immigration rates become insignificant. Yet public debate surrounding immigration can get paradoxically more acrimonious in these circumstances, as individual insecurity is rising. Whether it is during such uncertain times, or more generally over the economic cycle, a question deserving scrutiny in welfare states is the potential dilution of available public funds per capita with increased migration. I consider next the way in which immigration is interacting more generally with public finances.

The overall cost of providing public services for a population expanding through migration should indeed increase where the local and immigrant populations have equal rights of access—which is, however, not the case (see, for example, residence requirements for housing benefits). Neoclassical economics calculations would convey that it is the marginal social cost of the provision of such goods as set against the extra benefit or revenue generated from taxing additional workers that governs decisions to provide extra public services. In reality, it is ultimately the

[5] See as well Fig. 3.6, with the unemployment gap between foreigners and native workers clearly showing the disadvantage of migrants during the Great Recession of 2008–2009.

willingness to provide such extra services that makes public services accessible to all.

As the neoliberal framework refocusses decision-making on government efforts towards the promotion of markets, rather than the direct provision of public goods, that is where the adequate allocation to social welfare is breaking down. A constant stock of public goods that ignores an expanding labour force or population simply induces lower accessibility of public services for each individual in an otherwise expanding market, while potentially shifting the blame on migrants.

On the other hand, as migrants are a significant group of workers in a variety of industries, they support budgetary revenues, through tax and other types of contributions. Labour migrants' typical working-age profiles also make them good candidates for paying more into taxation than what they withdraw in health or welfare spending. They tend to be younger than the average population, and temporary migrants—as they often are in the case of intra-European mobility—return to their country of origin before reaching pensionable age. On the other hand, non-natives' access to welfare is often restricted by explicit clauses of 'no access to public funds' or limited entitlement to public services. In instances where migrants have an informal status in the host economy, this further disqualifies them from the constitutional rights available to the average citizen. As such, the aggregate impact of migration on both tax revenue and spending becomes an empirical question.

9 Freedom of Movement of Workers: An Annex to Free Trade[6]

Most international trade today is taking place under the governance of regional and bilateral free trade agreements, increasingly including beyond the liberalisation of movement of goods provisions facilitating trade in services. The latter have been supported within the WTO (World Trade Organisation) framework of the GATS (General Agreement on

[6] Parts of this section have been included in an earlier contribution by the author for 'The Conversation' (Harding, 2018)

Trade in Services) and make provisions for the movement of natural persons. The GATS refers to the physical mobility of people under Mode 4 of services liberalisation, focussing on two broad categories of individuals. These are key employees transferred abroad on an intra-company basis, such as managers and technical staff, and business visitors or, increasingly, independent foreign professionals in specific sectors. The stay of international visitors is generally restricted in time, with extensions being permitted in some instances. However, most movements of people remain restricted to short-term visitors, and do not allow for gainful employment in the host country. It is telling that only 1%–2% of all trade is accounted for through Mode 4 natural-person mobility in the GATS framework.

The WTO recorded 304 RTAs (regional trade agreements) in force by June 2020, with half of these including specific provisions on free movement of services. Thereby, some 40 agreements include exemptions that extend preferences to people mobility. However, the model liberalising labour mobility is far more complex than this simple number of relaxations to restrictions suggests. It is certainly not a regime of free movement of people per se, and in most cases, it involves restrictions of time over which mobility can be exerted, as well as labour market access limitation, extra requirements for citizens of partner countries, restricted sectors and areas in which natural persons can be active across borders, and so on.

It is true, however, that more advanced economic integration projects include statements underlying the desirability of freedom of movement of people as a long-term objective and are linked to ambitions of completing common markets. I detail such a process of liberalisation in the next part of this chapter. However, the reality of migration liberalisation is much less prevalent than suggested within the statements of bilateral or regional trade agreements. There are various barriers to the implementation of freedom of movement, not least determined by the complexity of free movement of people with social rights, as opposed to the free movement of goods and services. Furthermore, even where provisions for free movement exist, administrative barriers and difficulties in enforcement of such freedoms are making the reality of mobility of people less straightforward than a simple opening of borders would suggest. And as both

Brexit and the pandemic have demonstrated, free movement can be reversed, even in free trade areas which have seemingly achieved complete market integration, and with freedom of movement of labour on their statutes.

With respect to administrative arrangements concerning movement of labour under various regional or bilateral agreements, these include: full visa exemptions, temporary visa exemptions, visa exemption for specific activities or agreements without specific instruments regarding entry rights or visa-free travel. Here are some examples. For full visa exemptions, the best example is the EU, specifically providing for free movement of member states citizens in its territory, as well as extending this to a 'European citizenship'. Yet even here there is a specific link between free movement and economic activity, with an expectation that mobile individuals are gaining employment within three months of arrival in a different member state. Another agreement with full mobility and no restrictions to the period of residence or specific categories of workers is the Nordic Common Labour Market in Europe.

Then, there is the Common Market of the South (MERCOSUR). Under its 'Agreement on

Residence for State Party nationals' it envisages to grant all MERCOSUR citizens an automatic visa and the freedom to live and work in another member state. Note, however, that this has not been fully approved. Instead, a visa exemption applies to artists, scientists, sports people, journalists, specialised professions and technicians for up to 90 days.

Examples where mobility is restricted to certain categories of individuals can be found with the United States–Mexico–Canada Agreement and NAFTA, upon which the former is based. In NAFTA there are temporary arrangements for the mobility of business visitors, traders and investors, intra-company transferees or professionals, with different requirements applying to Canadian or Mexican citizens in the United States. This agreement includes as such a professional visa and is aimed specifically for economic purposes, related to intra-company mobility and professionals' mobility or the highly skilled on a temporary basis.

The EU-Canada Comprehensive and Economic Trade Agreement (CETA), which has also served as a reference in the Brexit process, is also cited to have a 'liberal regime' in terms of the mobility it allows between trade partners. Yet this is once again an example where freedom of movement is linked to business services and professionals, while also envisaging a platform promoting the mutual recognition of qualifications. The stated objective of the Agreement under its Chapter 10 is to allow for people mobility to 'facilitate trade in services and investment by allowing temporary entry and stay to natural persons for business purposes and by ensuring transparency in the process', rather than freedom of movement or migration in itself.

Finally, with respect to the level of labour market access, RTAs can also offer different levels of mobility liberalisation, with the final emphasis lying on 'trade' rather than free movement of people. Ultimately, free movement in this context is to be understood as instrumental for facilitating trade in goods, services or investment rather than an end in itself. Based on Nita et al. (2017), four broad approaches are distinguished in liberalising people mobility in RTAs. The options include:

- Regional organisations or agreements offering full mobility of labour.
- Regional arrangements granting access to their labour markets only for selected categories of workers.
- Regional arrangements granting labour market access only to temporary service providers on a temporary basis.
- Regional arrangements restricted to the protection of migrant workers' rights.

In this context, what trade agreements should emphasise is 'decent work' for migrants, which in itself can further reduce migration and social dumping, as emphasised by Rodrik (2017) and supported by Rolfe et al.'s (2019) observation of a preference to include migration into 'trade agreements'. Furthermore, a 'right not to emigrate' should be supported by all countries, based on decent standards in home economies and with free movement implying that people would exert migration as an option, rather than seeing it as a necessity (Delgado Wise, 2015). The next section documents how free movement of people can evolve in practice, going out from an original set of bilateral agreements between countries or regional blocs. While this allows for the mobility of people to be liberalised in a fully integrated market, sustainability of free movement depends not just on the legal framework, but also on the way in which free movement is being perceived and accepted in society.

10 Free Movement of People: A European Case Study

10.1 Free Movement of People and Free Movement of Workers

A point that needs clarification from the beginning is that while some international agreements allow people to move freely between partner countries, they do not imply that once people seek employment or settlement abroad, they will benefit from a similar freedom. In today's EU, freedom of movement of people co-exists with freedom of movement of labour. The freedom of movement envisaged by the Treaty of Rome had the objective of creating optimum conditions for economic welfare augmentation in the single market as a whole. As such, freedom of movement in the EU does not imply the automatic freedom of establishment for citizens of one EU country in another member state, or equal entitlements to public goods and social protection. Should any EU citizen wish to settle outside her country of origin *and* benefit from equal rights, that intention is necessarily connected with her engagement in an economic activity abroad.

In other words, even EU citizens wanting to move to another member state for a longer time must look for employment at their destination. They must be successful in their search for work within a period of three months after arrival in the host country. Otherwise, the right of establishment abroad is written off, and access to social security can be curtailed. Exceptions exist, as is the case where a working migrant has a family with whom they move. Family members have the right to establishment in the EU state to which the worker moves, independent of their economic status.

Apart from this, each EU member state still applies separate regulations for non-EU nationals. Hence, non-EU citizens established in a member state and who, also, have the right to work there are not automatically permitted to seek employment somewhere else in the EU. As the International Labour Organization (ILO) has indicated in this context, such distinctions between workers result in further economic marginalisation of different categories of EU labour, including migrant origins (Vandamme, 2000).

10.2 Extending Freedom of Movement

Free mobility of labour has progressed in Europe within the EU, with liberalisation towards third countries only occurring in a limited number of situations. Complete liberalisation implies that workers enjoy full freedom of movement and equal treatment in employment with incumbents in the reference labour market; priority in employment for nationals remains an exception, such as in the case of the exercise of official authority (e.g. government offices).

First, there have been a series of bilateral agreements, introduced between the EU or its member states and non-EU members. These allow for limited mobility of workers across national borders of pairs of countries. Freedom to move is conditional on international workers fulfilling a set of strict criteria, permitting EU entry for specific categories of workers, from selected national origins. Under bilateral arrangements, restrictions still impede international labour migration of most nationals of the parties endorsing such agreements. A first example was the arrangements between the original EU member states and South European countries, or between EU members and Yugoslavia or Turkey. These were initiated in the 1950s and 1960s, when Northern Europe faced a labour shortage in its booming manufacturing industries. The selective freedom of movement in these cases had run in accordance with the demand for labour in earlier EU members.

Yet, full freedom of movement can be achieved inside an economic union or even beyond its borders. For example, non-EU EEA countries benefit from full freedom of movement of their workers even without becoming members of the EU, such as Norway. This is also the case with non-EEA countries such as Switzerland, relying instead on a set of bilateral agreements and allowing for free movement.

10.3 How Free Movement Shifted East

The neoliberal, free-choice human capital model of migration was applied for example by Michael Burda (1995) to address relevant aspects of East-West European migration in the early days of European Union eastward expansion. Burda (op. cit.) thereby introduced the classical investment approach to economic migration and, additionally, looked at possible effects of uncertainty on individual decisions to move abroad. The study thus tried to explain why, despite large emigration predictions from Central and Eastern European Countries (CEECs), such mobility did not materialise before the EU enlargement of 2004—but largely failed to acknowledge the role of persistent regulatory restrictions to labour mobility.

One major reason Burda identifies is migrants' imperfect information concerning potential destinations, as well the positive evolution of general living conditions in migrants' origin. Uncertainty thus can offset the expected arbitrage behaviour of individuals seeking to bridge the very large income disparities between Eastern and Western Europe, and migration can remain low where improved living standards are envisaged at home. While this can certainly be true, such a framework essentially ignores the limitation of migration choices and the policy framework gradually liberalising mobility, which resulted in much larger East-West mobility flows than predicted by economists. For example, the original model of Dustmann, Casanova, Fertig, Preston, and Schmidt (2003) predicted a net migration from new member states of under 15,000 for the United Kingdom upon enlargement in 2004, whereas the real numbers were in the range of hundreds of thousands.

In fact, many studies at that time investigated the extent to which East-West migration impacted on labour markets in EU member states, following the transition to a market economy. Their aim was to predict how an inflow of labour from the East would affect incumbent EU member states upon the CEECs' accession to the European Community, based on pre-enlargement observations of migration choices (e.g. Brücker, 2000). Surely, though, we can go a step back and reverse the question, asking how the option of exerting freedom of movement was influenced by the liberalisation process in the first instance. In its interplay with the endeavour to protect local labour markets in incumbent EU member states, the policy framework was guiding migration decisions way more strongly than individual choices. Thus, besides any economic decisions made by migrants, until very recently, the governance of the migration flow has been a crucial element in determining the number of foreign workers, or whether legal migration across borders occurred at all.

I will give below a detailed account on how the mobility of people between Eastern and Western Europe has evolved during CEECs' accession to the EU. It would also exemplify how the decision to migrate is not a simple matter of exerting market-driven free movement, but rather a consequence of policy gradually changing direction over time. Bilateral agreements liberalising the movement of people were the main instrument governing migration of CEECs nationals in Europe for many years. Equally, it is conceivable that Brexit would call once again for bilateral arrangements between the United Kingdom and the EU in the near future. As such, East-West bilateral agreements on people mobility merit to be revisited, beyond relegating once again the question of free movement to the appendix of a new preferential trade agreement. Next, the characteristics of bilateral East-West mobility arrangements leading to what is today free movement of workers in Europe will be scrutinised. This would allow us to reflect on the scope of bilateral agreements where free movement of people is not a given, and even if goods or capitals keep moving freely.

11 Bilateral Agreements for Labour Mobility

Bilateral agreements on migrant labour originate from decisions of states to accept a limited number of foreign workers, conditional on the requirements of labour markets in the country of destination. In most cases, the right to migrate under these agreements is given for work in selected sectors, often requiring unskilled employees to fill in shortages in local labour markets. Examples in this direction are most seasonal and contract work arrangements, specifically designed for agriculture, construction work or care services—some of which have only recently been relabelled as 'key services' under the pressures of the coronavirus pandemic.

Even though such bilateral agreements do not fall within the realm of EU provisions, they have been encouraged in Europe under the so-called Europe Agreements and can be viewed as a step towards the full freedom of movement for workers from CEECs in Europe. The agreements were initiated by individual EU member states and will be treated here as a form of 'partial liberalisation' of migration. The labour flows addressed in bilateral agreements fall under five broad categories: guest workers' arrangements, project-tied work agreements, seasonal work, border commuting for work and 'au-pair' arrangements.

Guest workers' (trainee) agreements with CEECs had the stated objective to let foreign workers acquire vocational education and to improve their language skills in an EU country where they could be employed for up to one year. Usually a low immigration quota is allowed for under this type of agreement. It ranged from only 50 persons in the 1991–1992 agreement between Belgium and Poland to some 2000 placements of Hungarian workers in Germany during the 1990s (Profazi, 1998).

Seasonal workers are employed in economic sectors with high fluctuations in activity. The number of workers employed under such schemes ranged from some 2700 Polish workers in France by 1998 to a 204,000 Polish seasonal workers' scheme in Germany in the same year.

Project-tied work was conducted under similar provisions as those applying for 'key personnel' migrating with a company opening branches abroad. The difference is that under project-tied work agreements, employees of the foreign company do not have to be managers, or to possess 'uncommon knowledge'. In addition, the company itself does not settle abroad, but works as a sub-contractor on behalf of a host country company.

Project-tied work was also limited in time and in quantity, by quota provisions. Quotas ranged from an insignificant number in the case of the Finnish-Estonian agreement (Werner, 1996) to a level of around 23,000 Polish employees in Germany with 1997 as a reference year (Garnier, 2001).

Border commuters worked under bilateral agreements in old EU regions neighbouring the CEECs. These were concentrated at the

German-Czech and German-Polish frontiers. This type of employment is restricted to the case where local workers were not available in the EU border region. The number of border commuters was not always easily determined, but some 1500 Poles and 6000 Czechs had been estimated to commute to Germany in 1996 (Hönekopp, 1997).

Finally, the United Kingdom had initiated *'au pair' agreements* for young CEEC citizens (European Commission, 2001). It allowed CEEC nationals to seek employment in the United Kingdom for a limited time, and for this very specific job. The United Kingdom also considered to extend to East Europeans the working holiday visas usually reserved to young people from New Zealand and Australia, which is conceivable to happen in the Brexit transition period once more.

In terms of the period of employment, guest workers' schemes usually limited the stay of CEEC workers in the EU to up to one year. Project-tied employment also restricted the stay, to the length of the project undertaken by CEEC workers. Border commuting required actual residence in the CEECs. Seasonal work is for three to nine months, and 'au pair' (along with nursing) contract work could be for up to a few years.

It can be said that what all bilateral agreements have in common is to allow for a limited number of foreign workers to be employed in local markets, where shortages, business interests or seasonal conditions require labour. At the same time, they restrict the stay of individual workers abroad, typically to less than a year.

It can be inferred that the majority of legal workers under bilateral agreements return to their home country after a year abroad, thus relegating free movement to a temporary migration flow, rather than the permanent migration usually observed by the economic migration literature, typically focussed on the United States. It also means that the foreign workers abroad each year differ from foreign employees in the previous year, with little accumulation of local social capital—albeit the number of new arrivals may depend on earlier migrants, by virtue of the operation of social networks.

As some bilateral agreements are regulating cross-border commuting, it can be argued that bilateral agreements between states within and outside a European free mobility area are simply a reflection of the geographical proximity of two countries. That was also true between the EU and CEECs in the case of guest workers' conventions, for example, between Sweden and Finland and the neighbouring Baltic states, or between Bulgaria and Greece. Even the UK 'au pair' agreements operated selectively with the most advanced CEEC reformers, such as the Czech Republic, Slovenia, Hungary and Slovakia, meaning that bilateral agreements are more likely between countries at similar development.

There were however a few exceptions from these 'rules' in the case of the East-West opening to mobility. For example, Germany, while bordering a small number of CEECs, had bilateral agreements with all CEECs, not just with those in its immediate proximity. Furthermore, bilateral agreements in the context of East-West mobility could be treated as an expression of the EU government's preference to extend freedom of movement rather than protect specific local markets in Europe.

The policy objectives safeguarded by a system of bilateral agreements are still not to be confused with the public preferences for immigration in the EU. In Germany, for example, people were sceptical about the benefit of immigration or enlargement, despite the various bilateral agreements initiated by the government, and along with the early 'visibility' of immigrants from CEECs in this country. On the other hand, in Nordic countries, both the public and the government supported enlargement towards the Baltic states. Thereby, bilateral agreements could have reflected early on the general support of integration and free movement across the region.

Despite the frequent renegotiation of the terms of bilateral agreements indicating the consideration of local labour market conditions in migrant-receiving countries, there is some continuity in the operation of bilateral agreements. The EU member states that initiated such agreements in the past—usually in the beginning of transition in Eastern Europe—maintained the agreements with CEECs throughout the period of transition and ultimately during the process of EU accession. What fluctuated across years is mainly the number of CEECs workers, for which each bilateral agreement provided for some freedom of movement, thus governing a large share of the number of migrants observed in the East-West mobility flows before EU enlargement.

Germany was the main signatory of bilateral agreements with CEECs, and it is worth to look more attentively at the numbers of workers from Eastern Europe employed under different types of bilateral agreements in this destination. The number of CEEC nationals working there varied with the upper limits set yearly by the quotas decided by the German government, even though the limits probably reflect as well the underlying labour market conditions in this country which can encourage or deter migration.

Additionally, the number of contracts employing CEEC nationals in a year and the full time worked in each year by CEEC nationals also varied before EU accession. In 1999, for example, the number of seasonal and contract workers was three times higher than the actual full-time workers equivalent for that year. That reflects the temporary nature of employment of many mobile CEEC workers in the EU and the high frequency of contracts below one year. This has further implications on the access to and provision of public services not only according to the number of immigrants but also with respect to the lower security of jobs encouraged for a migrant workforce.

Under bilateral agreements there were clearly very high numbers of seasonal workers relative to any other category of migrants recorded in the EU. Over time, all other types of bilateral agreements but seasonal work have sent a decreasing number of workers to the EU. As a direct consequence, the yearly full-time equivalent of foreign employment from CEECs under bilateral agreements had stagnated, or even decreased, before EU enlargement and relative to the beginning of transition in Eastern Europe. Moreover, as quotas determine the upper boundaries to the number of mobile workers on a yearly basis, quotas might not be completely filled in any given year. Yet labour migration proceeded outside bilateral agreements, often based on informal networks abroad and showing the limitation of this type of governance structure for cross-border mobility. Moreover, in Germany, where large numbers of CEEC workers have been legally employed under bilateral agreements in the recent past, trade unions ultimately opposed the practice of contract work. The flexibility of such forms of employment extended to foreign workers can ultimately undermine conditions for the local workforce, rather than protecting the natives' position and employment conditions.

Any consideration of redrawing free movement on the principles allowed for by bilateral agreements, as the United Kingdom is about to do as its transition period of free mobility with the EU is expiring, must take into account the temporary nature of the flows that the agreements encourage and new implications for communities and social networks. Such effects go beyond the simple impact on public coffers. Along with the legal framework governing temporary work versus unrestricted mobility, the motives of people taking up temporary employment across borders can differ from the motives behind long-term migration. New barriers to mobility might also imply supply constraints, as in the recent pandemic, where, against all odds, the United Kingdom and other parts of the EU are seeking to import workers in essential sectors relying on foreign workers.

Finally, looking at how EU countries designed bilateral agreements with CEECs before the latter's assimilation into the single market, it appears that the 'selection' of CEECs migrants' occupation was largely attributed to the related migration policy and was less a reflection of the migrants' skills. Migrants' selection into jobs, rather than being the subject of their self-selection, as allowed for in a neoliberal framework with free movement, replicates the patterns of bilateral agreements. The latter required temporary workers, in seasonal jobs, and often led to a downgrading of migrants' skills on arrival in EU destinations, which also explains part of the 'over-qualification' observed in CEEC workers' employment in Europe. As such, any 'skill bias' in the immigration policy, as currently advocated by the United Kingdom, might operate along the lines of bilateral arrangements in the recent past of European mobility. However, the occupational mix and labour market outcomes in that case were not necessary along the lines of skilled jobs for foreign workers and increased security for unskilled local workers—in spite of the arrival of relatively well-skilled migrants.

In contrast to the typical low-skill occupations observed for East-West migrants, studies across Europe suggested early on that 12%–14% of CEEC immigrants were highly qualified (Morawska, 2000). In the United Kingdom, and by 2011, the percentage for highly educated migrants from CEECs was recorded to be as high as 36% (Clark, Drinkwater, & Robinson (op. cit.). Where the over-qualification[7] inci-

[7] Over-qualification represents the situation where an individual is employed in an occupation requiring a lower level of education than their own highest qualification.

dent with occupational downgrading is perpetuating amongst migrant labour (see as well Biagi, Grubanov, & Mazza, 2019 and Figs. 3.6 and 3.7), it puts pressure on local unskilled workers, who cannot possibly compete for the same jobs as higher-skilled migrants. Hence, a vicious circle of destitution and potential feelings of unfairness come to dominate the views on migration amongst local, non-mobile workers where they initially appear more supportive of a positive selection of migrants' skills.

Where official movements of people are limited, they also co-exist with informal markets, thereby allowing for the operation of unregulated supply and demand mechanisms to perpetuate. In the East-West migration context, many CEEC nationals, for example, found employment in the informal labour markets of the EU during the regime of bilateral agreements. The jobs available in the informal sector of the economy are generally unskilled, and the arrival of relatively better-skilled migrants in such informal markets created pressures in the local labour markets for the native unskilled. I would argue that selective but restrictive migration policies focussed on attracting skilled foreigners can produce an indirect pressure on the low-skilled by encouraging unfair informal labour market competition between migrants and the local unskilled hoping for good jobs (see as well Wilpert, 1998). This can ultimately defeat the intention of policy to protect vulnerable local workers. As such, I agree as well with the propositions made by Peters (2019), whereby abuses of workers' rights related to immigration emanate from migrants' own precarious status, preventing them to complain about employers and about any mistreatment. Indeed, making low-skilled immigrants' conditions of work more secure improves everyone's labour market conditions.

12 Summary and Conclusions

To summarise, and then conclude, it can be argued that both capital and labour mobility appear to be supported, in principle, by the neoliberal framework governing our economies. Yet, the reality at present translates into largely unrestricted capital flows taking advantage of opportunities when conditions are good in global markets or retreating when the going gets tough and causing strong fluctuations and vulnerability for economies around the world. On the other hand, migration, while involving large numbers of people crossing borders, remains relatively modest as a proportion of all workers and of most host countries' total population. At the same time, neither the large flows of global capital nor migrant flows, restricted and selective as the latter might be, have proven to bring any significant contribution to economic growth.

Moreover, the distributional consequences of factors' mobility are often ignored, as the welfare state has retreated where markets are promoted by governments around the world. In addition, evidence is showing that inequality of income is rising in the face of financial globalisation, strongly driven by the ability to extract rents by the highest earners, especially in the financial sector. While migrant workers might be motivated themselves to chase these highest incomes, they often fall behind while offering their labour for a lower premium. Then, once the cover of their own flexibility is lifted, they remain exposed in economic downturns, and benefit from only limited social and community protection.

Overall, limited mobility of workers relative to capital deprives labour of its bargaining power, while capital is able to avoid both risks and taxes. Still, policy is moving first towards more restrictions to the freedom of movement of people, as with the example of the United Kingdom's proposed new 'skilled migration system'. This is no guarantee for the protection of the more vulnerable workers anywhere, and potentially leaves unskilled local labour even further behind, as they are themselves immobile in the face of poor funding towards public services or higher taxes to cover for a shrinking number of workers.

As this chapter has shown, migration is governed by a system of preferential agreements, and is mostly presented as an addendum to free trade. As such, without further clauses in bilateral agreements that support decent working conditions, both at home and in the countries of destination, we might just see the export of poor practices along with cheaper goods across our borders. Finally, while bilateral agreements govern the mobility of people between states, an agreement between each state and its own people is probably more urgent to give everyone a better chance at decent work and earnings.

Appendix

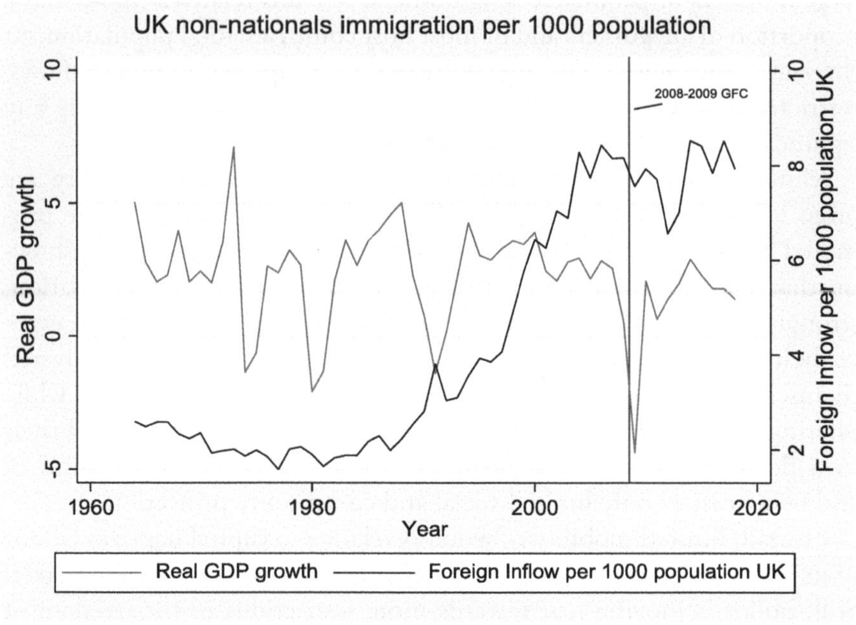

Fig. 3.4 UK immigration of non-nationals. (Source: Office for National Statistics/LTIM data and own elaboration)

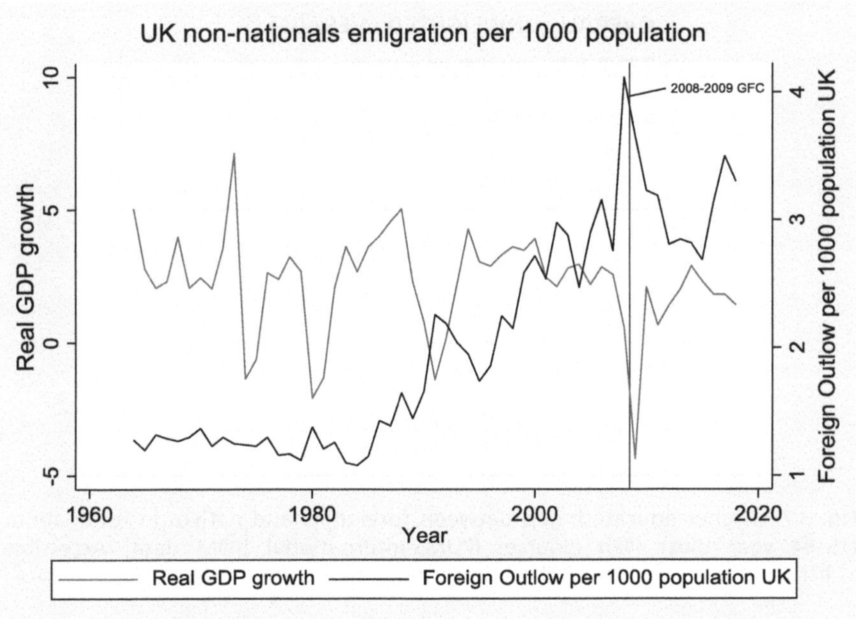

Fig. 3.5 UK emigration of non-nationals. (Source: Office for National Statistics/ LTIM data and own elaboration)

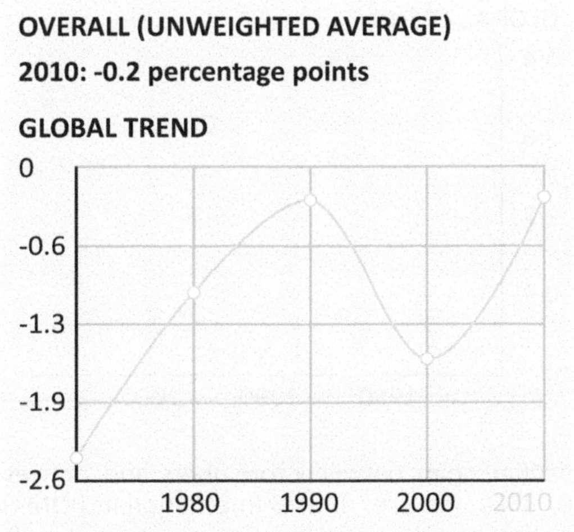

Fig. 3.6 Unemployment: gap between foreigners and natives in total labour (15–64 year olds). (Source: IPUMS-International [IOM data] Accessible at https://migrationdataportal.org/institute/ipums-international)

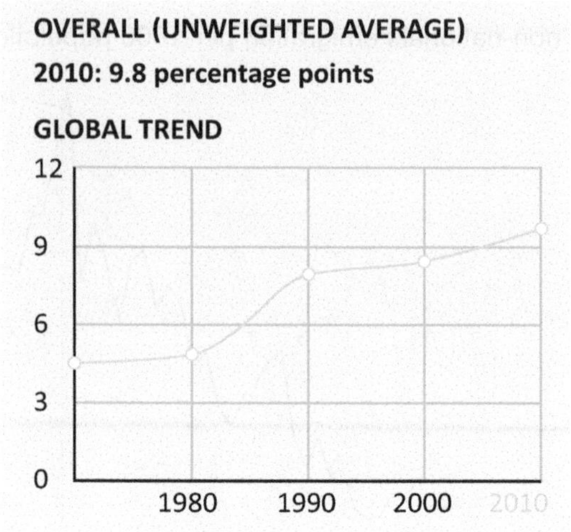

Fig. 3.7 Higher educated: gap between foreigners and natives in total labour (15–64 year olds) (%). (Source: IPUMS-International [IOM data] Accessible at https://migrationdataportal.org/institute/ipums-international)

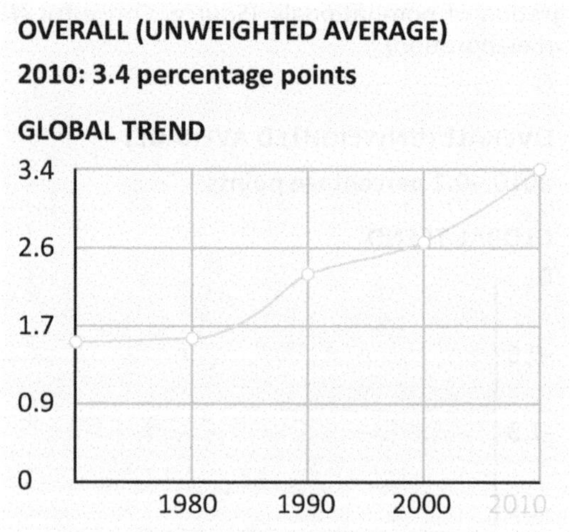

Fig. 3.8 Over-qualified: gap between foreigners and natives in total labour (15–64 year olds) (%). (Source: IPUMS-International [IOM data] Accessible at https://migrationdataportal.org/institute/ipums-international)

References

Arestis, P. (2018). Importance of Tackling Income Inequality and Relevant Economic Policies. In P. Arestis & M. Sawyer (Eds.), *Inequality. Trends, Causes, Consequences, Relevant Policies, International Papers in Political Economy*. Cham: Palgrave Macmillan.

Atkinson, H., Morelli, & Roser. (2017). The Chartbook of Economic Inequality. Available at: https://www.chartbookofeconomicinequality.com

Bauer, T., Epstein, G., & Gang, I. N. (2002). *Herd Effects of Migration Networks? The Location Choice of Mexican Immigrants in the US* (IZA Discussion Paper No. 551). Available at: http://ftp.iza.org/dp551.pdf

Bauer, T., Epstein, G., & Gang, I. N. (2009). What Are Migration Networks? Measuring Ethnic Linkages Among Migrants. *International Journal of Manpower, 30*(1–2), 56–69.

Becker, S. O., Fetzer, T., & Novy, D. (2017). Who Voted for Brexit? A Comprehensive District-Level Analysis. *Economic Policy, 32*(92), 601–650.

Belot, M., & Ederveen, S. (2012). Cultural Barriers in Migration Between OECD Countries. *Journal of Population Economics, 25*, 1077–1105.

Bhagwati, J. N., & Hanson, G. H. (2009). *Skilled Immigration Today: Prospects, Problems, and Policies*. Oxford, UK/New York: Oxford University Press.

Biagi, F., Grubanov, S., & Mazza, J. (2019). *Over-Education of Migrants? Evidence from the EU*. EC: Ispra, JRC115881.

Birch, K. (2017). *A Research Agenda for Neoliberalism*. Cheltenham, UK: Edward Elgar Publishing.

Bluedorn, J., Duttagupta, R., Guajardo, J., & Topalova, P. (2013). *Capital Flows Are Fickle – Anytime, Anywhere* (IMF Working Paper). International Monetary Fund. Available at: https://doi-org.uea.idm.oclc.org/10.5089/9781484389041.001

Boeri, T., Hanson, G. H., & McCormick, B. (2002). *Immigration Policy and the Welfare System: A Report for the Fondazione Rodolfo Debenedetti*. Oxford, UK: Oxford University Press.

Borjas, G. J. (1994). The Economics of Immigration. *Journal of Economic Literature, XXXII*(December), 1667–1717.

Borjas, G. J. (1999). Immigration and Welfare Magnets. *Journal of Labor Economics, 17*, 607–637.

Borjas, G. J. (2019, May). *Immigration and Economic Growth* (NBER Working Paper No. w25836). Available at http://www.nber.org/papers/w25836

Borjas, G. J., & Cassidy, H. (2020). *The Adverse Effect of the COVID-19 Labor Market Shock on Immigrant Employment* (IZA Discussion Paper No. 13277). Available at: http://ftp.iza.org/dp13277.pdf

Brücker, H. (2000). *The Impact of Eastern Enlargement on Employment and Labour Markets in EU Member States.* A Study for the European Commission. Available at: http://europa.eu.int/comm/dgs/employment_social/key_en.htm

Burda, M. C. (1995). Migration and the Option Value of Waiting. *The Economic and Social Review, 27*(1), 1–19.

Card, D. (2009). Immigration and Inequality. *American Economic Review, 99*(2), 1–21.

Card, D., Dustmann, C., & Preston, I. (2012). Immigration, Wages, and Compositional Amenities. *Journal of the European Economic Association, 10*(1), 78–119. https://doi.org/10.1111/j.1542-4774.2011.01051.x.

Chiswick, B. R., & Miller, P. W. (2002). *Do Enclaves Matter in Migrants Adjustment?* (IZA Discussion Paper No. 449). Available at: https://www.iza.org/publications/dp/449/do-enclaves-matter-in-immigrant-adjustment

Clark, K., Drinkwater, S., & Robinson, C. (2014). *Migration, Economic Crisis and Adjustment in the UK.* (IZA Discussion Paper No. 8401). Available at: http://ftp.iza.org/dp8410.pdf.

Delgado Wise, R. (2015). Migration and Labour Under Neoliberal Globalization: Key Issues and Challenges. In C.-U. Scherup, R. Munck, B. Likic-Brboric, & A. Neergaard (Eds.), *Migration, Precarity, and Global Governance: Challenges and Opportunities for Labour.* https://doi.org/10.1093/acprof:oso/9780198728863.001.0001.

Dreher, A. (2006). The Influence of Globalization on Taxes and Social Policy: An Empirical Analysis for OECD Countries. *European Journal of Political Economy, 22*, 179–201.

Dustmann, C., Casanova, M., Fertig, M., Preston, I. P., & Schmidt, C. M. (2003). *The Impact of EU Enlargement on Migration Flows* (Home Office Report 25/03). London.

Dustmann, C., & Frattini, T. (2014). The Fiscal Effects of Immigration to the UK. *The Economic Journal, 124*, F593–F643. https://doi.org/10.1111/ecoj.12181.

Dustmann, C., Frattini, T., & Halls, C. (2010). Assessing the Fiscal Costs and Benefits of A8 Migration to the UK. *Fiscal Studies, 31*, 1–41.

Dustmann, C., Frattini, T., & Preston, I. (2013). The Effect of Immigration Along the Distribution of Wages. *Review of Economic Studies, 80*(1), 145–173.

Eichengreen, B. (2002). *Capital Flows and Crises.* The MIT Press. Available at: https://doi.org/10.7551/mitpress/1731.001.0001

Epstein, G. S. (2002). *Informational Cascades and Decision to Migrate* (IZA Discussion Paper, No. 445). Available at: http://ftp.iza.org/dp445.pdf

European Commission. (2001, March 6). *The Free Movement of Workers in the Context of Enlargement*. Information Note.

Gang, I. N., Rivera-Batiz, F. L., & Yun, M.-S. (2002). *Economic Strain, Ethnic Concentration and Attitudes Towards Foreigners in the European Union* (IZA Discussion Paper No. 578). Available at: http://ftp.iza.org/dp578.pdf

Garnier, P. (2001). Foreign Workers from Central and Eastern European Countries in Some OECD European Countries: Status and Social Protection. In *Migration Policies and EU Enlargement. The Case of Central and Eastern Europe*. Paris: OECD.

Gaston, N., & Rajaguru, G. (2013). International Migration and the Welfare State Revisited. *European Journal of Political Economy, 29*, 90–101.

Gide, C. (1898). Has Co-operation Introduced a New Principle into Economics? *The Economic Journal, 8*(32), 490–511.

Gurak, D. T., & Caces, F. (1992). Migration Networks and the Shaping of Migration Systems. In M. Kritz, L. Lim, & H. Zlotnik (Eds.), *International Migration Systems: A Global Approach*. Oxford, UK: Clarendon Press.

Harding, L. (2018, October 2). *How the Special Migration Rules in Free Trade Deals Work*. Available at: https://theconversation.com/how-the-special-migration-rules-in-free-trade-deals-work-103709

Hatton, T. J. (2016). Refugees, Asylum Seekers, and Policy in OECD Countries. *American Economic Review, 106*(5), 441–445.

Hatton, T. J. (2017). Refugees and Asylum Seekers, the Crisis in Europe and the Future of Policy. *Economic Policy, 32*(91), 447–496.

Hatton, T. J., & Williamson, J. G. (2005). *Global Migration and the World Economy. Two Centuries of Policy and Performance*. London/Cambridge, MA: MIT Press.

Hillman, A. E. (1993). The Political Economy of Migration Policy. In Siebert, H. (1993). *Migration: A challenge for Europe*, J.C.B. Mohr (Paul Siebeck): Tübingen.

Hollifield, J. S. (1992). *Immigrants, Markets, and States. The Political Economy of Postwar Europe*. Cambridge, MA/London: Harvard University Press.

Home Office. (2018). *The UK's Future Skills-Based Immigration System* (White Paper). London: HMSO. Available at: https://www.gov.uk/government/publications/the-uks-future-skills-based-immigration-system

Hönekopp, E. (1997). *Labour Migration from Central and Eastern Europe – Old and New Trends* (IAB Topics, No. 23). Nürnberg: IAB.

Hunt, J. (2004). Are Migrants More Skilled than Non-Migrants? Repeat, Return, and Same-Employer Migrants. *Canadian Journal of Economics, 37*, 830–849.

Lazear, E. (1998). *Diversity and Immigration* (NBER Working Paper 6535). Available at: http://www.nber.org/papers/w6535

Massey, D., Arango, J., Hugo, G., Kouaouci, A., Pellegrino, A., & Taylor, J. E. (1993). Theories of International Migration. *Population and Development Review, 19*, 431–466.

Mirrlees, J. A. (1982). Migration and Optimal Income Taxes. *Journal of Public Economics, 18*, 319–341.

Morawska, E. (2000). *Transnational Migration in the Enlarged European Union: A Perspective from East Central Europe* (Robert Schuman Centre Working Paper No. 2000/19). Florence: European University Institute.

Nita, S., Pécoud, A., De Lombaerde, P., Neyts, K., Gartland, J., & De Guchteneire, P. (2017). *Migration, Free Movement and Regional Integration.* Paris/Brugge, Belgium: UNESCO/UNU-CRIS.

Peters, M. A. (2019). Economics After Neoliberalism. Instead of Implementing Trade Restrictions, We Should Welcome More Low-Skill Immigration. *Boston Review*, (Summer Issue). Available at: https://bostonreview.net/forum/economics-after-neoliberalism/margaret-e-peters-trade-restrictions-wont-work

Profazi, M., (1998). *From Legal Barriers to Obstacles to Transnational Mobility: Bilateral Agreements and Free Movement of Persons.* Part of the Report Prepared for DGV, the European Commission on The Impact of Migration, Berlin (Unpublished).

Razin, A., Sadka, E., & Swagel, P. (2002). Tax Burden and Migration: A Political Economy Theory and Evidence. *Journal of Public Economics, 85*, 167–190.

Reinhart, C. (2020, May 28). Capital Flow Cycles: A Long Global View. *Economica- Philips Lecture* podcast, Thursday. LSE (London). Available at: http://www.lse.ac.uk/lse-player?id=4894

Rodrik, D. (2017). The Trouble with Globalization. *The Milken Institute Review*, Fourth Quarter. Available at: https://drodrik.scholar.harvard.edu/files/dani-rodrik/files/rebalancing_globalization_october_2017.pdf

Rolfe, H. (2017). It's All About the Flex: Preference, Flexibility and Power in the Employment of EU Migrants in Low-Skilled Sectors. *Social Policy and Society, 16*(4), 623–634. https://doi.org/10.1017/S1474746417000240.

Rolfe, H., Runge, J., & Hudson-Sharp, N. (2019). Immigration Policy from Post-War to Post-Brexit: How New Immigration Policy Can Reconcile Public

Attitudes and Employer Preferences. *National Institute Economic Review, 248*(1), R5–R16.

Rowthorn, R. (2008). The Fiscal Impact of Immigration on the Advanced Economies. *Oxford Review of Economic Policy, 24*, 560–580.

Sawyer, M. (2018). Financialisation, Financial Crisis and Inequality. In P. Arestis & M. Sawyer (Eds.), *Inequality. Trends, Causes, Consequences, Relevant Policies, International Papers in Political Economy*. Cham: Palgrave Macmillan.

Scheve, K.F., & Slaughter M. J. (1999). Labour market Competition and individual preferences over immigration policy. NBER Working Paper 6946. Available at http://www.nber.org/papers/w6946.

Scheve, K. F., & Slaughter, M. J. (2001). What Determines Individual Trade-Policy Preferences? *Journal of International Economics, 54*(2), 267–292.

Simula, L., & Trannoy, A. (2010). Optimal Income Tax under the Threat of Migration by Top-Income Earners. *Journal of Public Economics, 94*, 163–173.

Tridico, P. (2018). The Determinants of Income Inequality in OECD Countries. *Cambridge Journal of Economics, 42*(4), 1009–1042. https://doi.org/10.1093/cje/bex069.

Vandamme, F. (2000). Labour Mobility Within the European Union: Findings, Stakes and Prospects. *International Labour Review, 139*(4), 437–455.

Vargas-Silva, C. (2013). The Fiscal Impact of Immigration in the UK. *Migration Observatory Briefing*. February ed. COMPAS, University of Oxford, Oxford, UK.

Wadsworth, J., Dhingra, S., Ottaviano, G., & Van Reenen, J. (2016). *Brexit and the Impact of Immigration on the UK* (CEP Brexit Analysis No. 5). London: Centre for Economic Performance. Available at: http://cep.lse.ac.uk/pubs/download/brexit05.pdf

Werner, H. (1996). *Befristete Zuwanderung von ausländischen Arbeitnehmern. Dargestellt unter besonderer Berücksichtigung der Ost-West Wanderung* (IAB Mitteilung 1/96). Nürnberg: IAB.

Wilpert, C. (1998). Migration and Informal Work in the New Berlin: New Forms of Work or New Sources of Labour? *Journal of Ethnic and Migration Studies, 24*(2), 269–294.

Wrenn, M. V. (2015). Agency and Neoliberalism. *Cambridge Journal of Economics, 39*(5), 1231–1243. Available at: doi-org.uea.idm.oclc.org/10.1093/cje/beu047

4

Productivity Slowdown and Inequality: Killing Two Birds with One Stone!

Ahmad Seyf

1 Introduction

Between 1970 and 2018, UK's real GDP increased from £713.9 billion to £2061.5 billion (inflation adjusted), a rise of nearly threefold.[1] During these years, UK labour productivity has also more than doubled,[2] and yet, during the same period, labour share of national income declined by more than 5%.[3] On the other hand the share of the top 1% increased from about 7% in 1970, to 14.5% in 2013.[4] Likewise, the share of the top 10% of the national income has increased too. Is this because the top 1% or 10% are the most productive members of the UK economy, and

[1] https://www.ons.gov.uk/economy/grossdomesticproductgdp/timeseries/abmi/bb

[2] https://www.ons.gov.uk/employmentandlabourmarket/peopleinwork/labourproductivity/timeseries/lzvb/prdy

[3] https://www.oecd.org/g20/topics/employment-and-social-policy/The-Labour-Share-in-G20--Economies.pdf

[4] https://wid.world/country/united-kingdom/

A. Seyf (✉)
The New College of the Humanities, London, UK

P. Arestis, M. Sawyer (eds.), *Economic Policies for a Post-Neoliberal World*, International Papers in Political Economy, https://doi.org/10.1007/978-3-030-56735-4_4

have become even more productive, or is there a much more complex set of factors in action, producing this outcome?

More than ten years on from the start of the global financial crisis (GFC) the global economic context remains challenging, with economic growth still below its historical trends in advanced capitalist economies and continuing to slow in emerging markets. Two further issues are concerning too. We witness also a worrying slowdown in productivity growth, which predates the GFC and has intensified since then. If productivity growth is not revived, expected growth rate would be low, and there would be less incentive for firms to invest in the future. It could be argued that we are effectively dealing with a vicious circle of sluggish productivity growth, perpetuating low real earnings growth, leading to below the trend rate of economic growth via its impact on weak aggregate demand. A related issue is that this decline in productivity growth has coincided with a rising or at best persistently high inequality of income, wealth and well-being in general. Are these two interconnected with essentially shared drivers and conjointly underpinning mechanisms? We would argue in this contribution that these developments are linked and tend to reproduce and reinforce one another. The slowdown in productivity growth is primarily caused by weakness in investment in productive capital, including Research and Development (R&D). Conventionally productivity and equality are viewed as competing objectives in economic policy debate (Okun, 1975). At the same time, there is ample evidence that higher inequality hurts long-term growth. Hence it becomes doubly important to find ways to revitalize productivity growth and simultaneously policy instruments should be in place ensuring that productivity growth is reflected in real earnings growth. Reviving the growth of real earnings would enhance aggregate demand and positively influence the growth rate. It is equally important to ensure that growth is environmentally sustainable too. Extra aggregate demand that would be generated would be primarily financed by higher earnings linked with higher productivity and thus tend to be sustainable. Given the common causes of productivity growth slowdown and growing inequality—weak investment and depressed aggregate demand—it follows that efforts to boost productivity and enhance equity would be positively interconnected. Introducing policies to ensure inclusiveness and environmental sustainability would tackle potential conflicts that might emerge between productivity growth and equality, and further, the higher growth would not clash with environmental or human boundaries.

The structure of this contribution is as follows: Section 2 offers a relevant literature review, giving an outline of the evolution of productivity and inequality in the last four decades. We would also discuss the weak investment and examine some of the factors contributing to the current depressed state of investment. Section 3 would focus on productivity and factors affecting its growth. Section 4 discusses the link between inequality and the slowdown in productivity growth and brings these findings together and offers some policy recommendations. Finally, this chapter ends with a summary and conclusions.

2 Literature Review

Economic theory and history testify that productivity growth is the main driver of rising living standards. On the other hand, in view of stagnant and ageing population in the advanced capitalist economies, reviving productivity growth becomes even more significant in assisting these economies to grow and to prosper. Bell and Dervis (2019, p. xix) pointed out that "between 1950 and 2000, the share of world's population that is sixty or older increased slightly, from 8% to 10%, and is projected to more than double between 2000 and 2050, from 10% to 21%". Additionally, "though some developing countries, like India, currently have a large and growing workforce of younger people, the pace of population ageing in the developing world is substantially faster than has occurred in developed countries in the past" (Foda, 2019, p. 47). Potentially, in economies facing an ageing and stagnant population, it is possible that immigration from more populous regions could help. However, in most of these countries, US and UK in particular, the current political climate is not conducive to taking such measures. It is probable that in post-Brexit UK, labour mobility may be constrained, and with this potential development, reviving productivity growth assumes a far bigger significance. Contrary to a greater need for higher productivity growth the added problem here is that global productivity growth is slowing down and Jones (2017, p. 313) points out that the slowdown is global in nature. While the decline began much earlier (Baily & Montalbano, 2016, p. 4), in the US productivity growth has declined sharply since 2004 (McKinsey Institute, 2017). Szezepanski (2018) points out that the process of the slowdown in the growth of labour productivity—output per hour—in major capitalist economies started in the 1960s, and the growth "decelerated further after the financial crisis to reach the present historic low" (p. 3). Dolphin and Hatfield (2015, p. 3) argue that in relation to productivity the UK has two problems.

- There is a productivity gap—output per hour—between 23 and 32% between the UK and comparable countries such as Germany, the Netherlands and France.
- There is a productivity gap of 17% between the UK's current level of productivity and what it would have been if it had continued to increase at the average rate for the 25 years up to 2007.

Dolphin and Hatfield (2015) went on to add that for the period between 1971 and 2007, productivity fell in just three calendar years, 1974, 1984 and 1989. But in the post GFC crisis years, and more specifically between 2007 and 2013, productivity has fallen in four further years, 2008, 2009, 2012 and 2013 and for 2014, its growth was only 0.2% (ibid. p. 5).

Haldane (2017, 2018) and Taylor and Omer (2018) examining the situation in the UK, and in the USA respectively, came up with a dualism hypothesis that in both of these economies we have stagnant sectors, namely, low productivity sectors, and frontier or dynamic sectors where productivity growth rate is among the highest in the world. Taylor and Omer (2018) add that the share of employment in the laggard sectors in the US rose from 47% in 1990 to 60% in 2016. Likewise, for the UK, Roland (2018) points out that 60% of all private sector employment is in Small and medium-sized enterprises (SMEs) and further they "collectively account for 73% of all net private sector job creation in the UK between 2010 and 2017" (p. 4). HM Government (2017, pp. 19–20) appreciates the fact that UK is experiencing some of its highest ever employment levels but, "if the long tail of lower productivity persists, it will hold back UK growth, wages and living standards". Haldane (2018) having outlined the importance of productivity growth points out that "since 2008, productivity in the UK has essentially flat-lined" (p. 4). In his view, this is a "lost decade" for which there is no end in sight. While there is some commonality and the situation in other advanced economies is similar but "in the UK, the problem is a big one by any historical standard" (ibid., p. 2). Dolphin and Hatfield (2015, p. 14) point out that labour productivity in the UK actually fell by 0.7% between 2007 and 2014. On a sectoral basis, they reckon that manufacturing in the UK is 27% less productive than in France and 33% less productive than in Germany (ibid., p. 3). It is probably because of this fall that The Advisory Conciliation and Arbitration Service (ACAS) (2015, p. 2) believes that between 2007 and 2013, the UK's relative performance against the rest of the G7 deteriorated from 9 percentage points behind the average to 19 percentage points behind the average.

Haldane (2018) seems to argue that the main problem is technological diffusion, that is, while a small number of firms in the UK are among the best in the world, there is a long tail of laggards. In addition to two productivity gaps, Haldane (2018) introduces a third gap which exists between the top and bottom performing companies and this gap in the UK is larger than in similar economies. Schneider (2018) shares the dualism hypothesis with others, but in his view, slower growth in productivity is almost entirely driven by more productive firms in the economy. He goes further and suggests that "indeed, the lower section of the distribution grew faster, post-crisis, than they did before", whereas "the slowdown in growth after the crisis is isolated to the top quartile, whereas the third quartile grew at about the same rate as it did pre-crisis, and the quantiles below the median tended to grow more than before" (pp. 10–11). Furman and Orszag (2018) studying the situation in the USA make a similar claim and point out that one of our findings is puzzling, in that "most of the decline in investment comes from the leading firms in an industry" (p. 7). Centre for Cities (2018) accepts the existence of a long tail in productivity distribution in the UK, but mainly focuses on some structural issues relating to this tail. The main point made in this context concerns the fact that most firms in the long tail are local business services which "are both low productivity and have limited scope for growth" (ibid., p. 1). It is argued here that the gap between frontier firms and laggards has widened since the recession, and this study adds a new dimension to the productivity puzzle in the UK. This new dimension is a regional dimension of productivity distribution in the UK, and looking at Greater South East and the rest of the UK, it is suggested that this gap also widened since the recession (Centre for Cities, 2018, p. 10). Given these characteristics, Centre for Cities (ibid.) argues that to tackle productivity problem and to improve productivity, there should be a sharper focus on improving the productivity of companies involved in exporting. Given the regional dimension of productivity distribution in the UK, performance of exporters across the country should be assessed with the aim of how to improve it. The point raised in this study, about the limit imposed on productivity growth on some activities in the service sector, is supported by the fact that between 1990 and 2017 in sectors producing computers, electrical equipment and information and communication productivity more than doubled during this period. For the same period the productivity in chemicals and pharmaceutical industries tripled whereas it increased by just 2% in accommodation and food services, and in fact, declined in arts, entertainment and recreation services during the same period (ibid., p. 3).

The Trade Union Congress (TUC) (2015) rejects the idea that we face a productivity puzzle in the UK, and adds "it is simply a failure to see the economic consequences of austerity and the need to promote growth, earnings and employment" (p. 21). It is argued here rather than falling real wages and impaired economic growth being due to poor productivity, poor productivity has been caused by austerity via its negative impact on aggregate demand. In the past, when there was a recession, insufficient demand would be manifested as higher levels of job losses, but this time, the price of labour, real wages, adjusted to accommodate lower economic growth and inadequate aggregate demand that had been generated. Tily (2017) offers a longer view of productivity problem in the UK, while accepting that the GFC has amplified pre-crisis trends, argues that the fall in productivity growth can be dated back to long before the GFC, at least to the 1970s. Given the long-term nature of the problem, dealing with just what has happened since the crisis would not be enough to tackle this prolonged slow growth of productivity, and hence, some serious reassessment is needed. In his examination of the productivity puzzle in the UK, Oulton (2018, p. 34) argues that "rapid rates of immigration in conjunction with rates of growth of export demand in the aftermath of the Great Recession can explain the UK productivity puzzle". In his view, "our flexible labour market…makes us very receptive to immigration" whereas "in much of the rest of the EU labour markets are less flexible" (ibid., p. 3). Lower demand for exports, combined with growth of labour supply, would lead to capital shallowing, that is, decreasing capital per worker, which would lead to low productivity growth. It is clear that to address this problem, investment should be revived, and this according to Oulton (ibid.) could only be done by a rise in demand for exports. In view of the elevated uncertainty about the future of the Brexit, it is unlikely that this issue could be settled soon, but Oulton (2018) is clear, "so 'just ending austerity' in the UK will not do the trick" (p. 32). Tenreyro (2018) defines the UK's productivity puzzle as a situation in which its productivity "has fallen well below its pre-crisis trend" (p. 3). Two factors are discussed, persistently, weak investment and elevated uncertainty. Barnett, Batten, Chiu, Franklin, and Sebastia-Barriel (2014, p. 114) point out that since the GFC, labour productivity growth in the UK "has been exceptionally weak" and try to explain this shortcoming by tackling a number of questions:

- How much of the weakness has been due to "cyclical explanations related to demand conditions"?
- How much has been due to "more persistent causes related to the financial crisis"?

Two further issues should be considered in this regard. Reduced investment in both physical and intangible capital and, equally important, impaired resource allocation from low- to high-productive uses should be examined.

Haldane (2018) pointed out that UK productivity is running 20% below its level in view of the fact that it has continued its pre-crisis trend.

Related to slowdown in productivity growth, some researchers pointed out that this may be linked with weak investment (Banerjee, Kearns, & Lombardi, 2015; Foda, 2019; Ramsden, 2018; Tenreyro, 2018). We examine this link below, but why there may be an investment gap, between the historical trend and the actual rate, is not easy to explain. Jones and Philippon (2016, p. 4) studying the situation in the USA, point out that despite very low interest rates, there has been very weak corporate investment and add that the average ratio of net investment to net operating surplus, which stood at 32% between 1970 and 1999, has fallen to 20.5% for the period between 2000 and 2015. They argue that corporate investment in the US is less than what is expected based on profitability and financial market conditions. The main culprit here is decreased competition in the goods markets, which leads to insufficient willingness to invest, which in turn drives the slow recovery of the US economy. They also consider the growth of short-termism in decision making and find strong support for this and inadequate competition as the mean drivers of weak investment. Jones and Philippon (op. cit.) suggest variables capturing the impact of competition and governance "explain about 80% of the aggregate underinvestment relative to Q" (ibid., p. 46).[5] Gutierrez and Philippon (2017, p. 37) examining the same issue arrive at the same conclusion; declining competition and greater market concentration is responsible for weak investment and this process started in the early 2000s. Greater market concentration and a much reduced risk of market entry (Barclays, 2019; Bell & Tomlinson, 2018; Corfe & Gicheva, 2017; DeLoecker, Eechhout, & Unger, 2019; Sablik & Trachter, 2019) work as an effective disincentive reducing investment and the urge for innovation. Bussiere, Ferrara, and Miloxvich (2015, p. 38) find that expected demand is by far the most important driver, while elevated uncertainty and, to a much lesser degree, capital costs, have played a role too. From their perspective, boosting aggregate demand would be sufficient to fill the investment gap. Banerjee, Kearns, and Lombardi, (2015) argue that weak investment can be explained by elevated uncertainty about the future state of the economy and expected profits play a key role here. The initial collapse of investment in 2008, they argue, was due to the contraction in aggregate demand, a point confirmed by the IMF (2015). In their view, given the very low interest rates and widely accessible capital market financing, it is a puzzle that

[5] Tobin Q is the ratio between the market value of the firm and the book value of the firm.

investment remains rather weak. Banerjee et al. (2015) argue that there is a mismatch between favourable financial conditions and investment opportunities. Firms with best opportunities do not have sufficient internal funds or easy access to external funding, and those that do, do not face attractive opportunities. Uncertainty about the future and especially about the future demand plays a key role here. Those firms not sure about future demand are not keen to invest in physical capital. In the US as in other major capitalist economies, debt could be issued at very favourable terms, but many firms use this source of funding not for investment but to buybacks their own shares. Banerjee et al. (2015) conclude that lack of funding does not seem to explain weak investment in these economies and make an important point that "future, rather than current, profits drive investment" (p. 71), and the elevated uncertainty about this is responsible for the current depressed state of investment.

On the investment gap itself, IMF (2015) pointed out that, "private fixed investment in advanced economies contracted sharply during the global financial crisis- by an average of 25%- and there has been little recovery since" (p. 111). In addition to policy uncertainty, overall weakness of economic activity and financial constraints are suggested to be the causes of this depressed situation. Further "addressing the general weakness in economic activity is crucial for restoring growth in private investment" (ibid. p. 111). Dottling, Gutierrez, and Philippon (2017) confirmed the weakness of private fixed investment but argued "that the reasons are cyclical in Europe and structural in the US". In the US, the weakness started around 2000 and "the gap is driven by industries where competition has decreased over time" (p. 129). Another structural factor in the US is decreased anti-trust enforcement (IMF, 2015, p. 129). Relating to the UK, ACAS (2015) offered a depressing narrative and pointed out that lower wage and lower productivity sectors account for a higher share of the GDP and added that faced with unprecedented uncertainty, firms held back productivity enhancing investment programmes, a decision helped by cheap and plentiful labour.

Kose, Ohnsorge, Ye, and Islamaj (2017) focused on weak investment in emerging markets and developing economies and showed that since 2010, it slowed sharply. Part of the explanation for the situation in these economies is the spill-over of the secular stagnation in the advanced economies and a reduction in global foreign direct investment (UNCTAD, 2018, p. 2).

It is true that the GFC has seriously affected investment (Alexander & Eberly, 2016), but weak investment in the UK has a much longer history. Gieve (2006, p. 4) pointed out that in 2005, "business spending on investment in the UK was at its lowest relative to whole economy income since 1965". An attempt to fill the existing gap between the historical trends and the actual investment must include an examination of factors causing the slow growth in the period leading to the GFC. In addition to a secular fall in profitability in major capitalist economies since the 1960s (Roberts, 2016, 2019) inadequate competition and greater market concentration (Jones & Philippon, 2016; Qureshi, 2017) are the main culprits affecting investment decisions. As inadequate investment affected dissemination of new technologies, hence innovation, it generated much lower growth (Bahar & Foda, 2019). The issue of insufficient competition will not go away on its own accord or by any magical forces in the market. New technologies changed the rules of the game in relation to competition in the market. We now face significant market concentration, and in most capitalist economies we have effectively witnessed a dual economy in operation (Andrews, Criscuolo, & Gal, 2016; Haldane, 2018; Oulton, 2018; Qureshi, 2017). Yang (2018) depicting the death of the main street in the US economy, gives details of the enormous growth of e-commerce and adds "Amazon now controls 43% of total e-commerce in the United States" (p. 33). Google, Amazon and Facebook take more than 60% of global advertising revenue (IPPR, 2018, p. 60). Generally speaking, it looks as if a consensus is emerging. In most of these economies, we face:

- Frontier or superstar firms, relatively a small number of firms—around 5%—dominant in the market, taking a disproportionate market share, while making super profits. They have excessive market power enabling them to raise prices without losing many customers. At least part of the market power and concentration originate from the digital technology, which produces products with extensive network effects, that is, a product becomes more desirable the more people use it. Over and above these features, the cost structure of software platforms and

online services is such that they act as barriers to entry, relatively high fixed costs with nominal marginal costs, not costly to expand—when installed.
- Non-frontier—laggard—firms, less productive firms filling the long tail of the productivity distribution.

Some researchers add a subset of zombie firms among the laggard which complicates the situation further. There is a growing gap in productivity growth of these groups of firms (Andrews et al., 2016; OECD, 2017). Accepting this dichotomy opens up a new possibility towards understanding the problem, that is, the problem may not be the technology itself, but rather its lack of diffusion and consequently, one should focus on looking at factors preventing greater diffusion of these new ideas across firms. Following this line, Haldane (2018) proposed that what is needed is a "diffusion infrastructure" (p. 2) to improve the diffusion process.

These frontier firms enjoy a much higher productivity growth, and keep widening the gap between themselves and the second group of firms, that is, the laggards. By contrast, the laggard firms enjoy a much lower productivity growth and hence, in this narrative, the productivity problem is reduced to a problem of diffusion.

Having said this, it should not be overlooked that combined with inadequate competition, there is a much-reduced market entry too. As to market concentration, Mitchell (2016, pp. 9–10) examining the situation in the US found that "Just two companies make seventy% of our beer; one company processes more than one-third of U.S. milk; and four companies slaughter and process over eighty% of U.S. beef. In finance, the share of banking assets held by megabanks rose from seventeen% in 1995 to fifty-nine% today". In this environment, Mitchell (ibid. p. 10) adds "starting a new entrepreneurial venture appears to have become harder than ever" and "the number of start-ups launched each year fell by nearly half between 1978 and 2011" and " the precipitous drop since 2006 is both noteworthy and disturbing".

In a sense, a much-reduced competition seems to be a main driver of US and UK's current productivity problem. The channels in operation are via reduced investment in tangible inputs, physical and human capital and intangible inputs, or what is usually referred to as knowledge-based capital. Furthermore, as a potential outcome of inadequate investment, there would be lower within firms' productivity growth, resulting from inadequate innovation and adoption and diffusion of new technologies. On the other hand, inadequate competition would also affect productivity growth by reducing across firms' reallocation of resources, that is, from less productive to more productive firms (Bahar & Foda, 2019; Bell & Dervis, 2019).

In this contribution, we would argue that most of the problems discussed above are caused by insufficient productive investment in the economy. We argue for an investment-led growth instead of the model used in the last four decades, that is, a debt-led consumption. To achieve this aim, an active-state is needed, that is, the state should intervene in the markets not only to correct market failures, but to shape markets and to influence the outcomes. Debt-led expansion is especially worrisome because debt has not been used to fund technological innovation that promotes long-term economic growth supported by growing productivity. Instead it has been used to maintain high levels of spending—not supported by their earnings—or to buy existing assets, such as real estates and share buybacks. The outcomes had been the creation of financial bubbles, waiting to burst, as in 2001 and 2007. Further clarification is needed here. This investment-led growth has to be a green growth, and attempts to revive productivity growth should be complemented by monetary as well as fiscal measures to reduce inequality needed to make the economy sustainable.

3 Productivity Puzzle

There is a consensus that while for a variety of reasons, a much faster productivity growth is needed, productivity growth slowed down in most economies. While there may be differences in details, this trend is generally referred to as productivity puzzle or riddle (Askenazy & Erhel, 2015; Calligaris, Del Gatto, Hassan, Ottaviano, & Schivardi, 2015; Elstner, Feld, & Schmidt, 2018; Goldin, Koutroumpis, Lafond, Rochowicz, & Winkler, 2019; Haldane, 2017; Szczepanski, 2018). McGowan, Andrews, and Millot (2017) examined productivity performance in The Organisation for Economic Cooperation and Development OECD countries and found that in addition to frontier and laggard firms, there is also a subset of zombie firms in operation. They found that the prevalence of and resources sunk in these firms rose since the mid-2000s. Tracey (2019, p. 1) defines zombie firms as those who receive subsidized bank loans, loans with repayment holidays and ever-greening by extending further credits to a troubled borrower, and adds that in 2014, around 10% of all firms in the EU were in this category. KPMG (2019, p. 2) defining a zombie firm as a business which is unable to cover its debt servicing costs from current profits over an extended period claims that between 8 and 14% of listed UK companies are zombie firms. In view of low productivity of these firms Tracey (2019, p. 1) shows that this kind of lending would have a depressing impact on aggregate output, investment and total factor productivity. The depressing impact intensifies as the continued survival of these firms suppresses the process of creative destruction, preventing reallocation of resources from low- to high-productivity firms. Subsidized lending to these firms constrains lending to more productive firms, and negatively impacts productive investment in the economy, the argument goes. The main providers of loans to zombie firms are weakly capitalized or distressed banks who extend new loans at below-market interest rates to assist their impaired borrowers with the liquidity necessary to meet payments on other outstanding loans. The justification for doing this appears to be that distressed banks endeavor to roll over bad loans instead of writing them off, hoping that the respective borrowers would eventually regain solvency (Acharya, Eisert, Eufinger, & Hirsch, 2019). Tracey (2019, p. 37) concludes that zombie firms would not harm non-zombie firms in the economy, a conclusion not shared by other researchers in this field (Gouveia & Osterhold, 2018).

For Guouveia and Osterhold (2018) zombie firms are non-viable firms, effectively on some kind of life support machine. Given the unviability of these firms, they drag down aggregate productivity. Furthermore, via market congestion, distort competition prevents the mechanism of creative destruction to function. In contrast to Tracey (2019), Gouveia and Osterhold (2018) find evidence that non-zombie firms would be harmed by the activities of zombie firms. McGowan et al. (2017)

studying the situation in the OECD countries confirmed the negative impact of zombie firms on non-zombie firms and taking the period of 2003 to 2013, found that higher share of industry capital sank in these firms contributed to lower investment, reduced employment growth and less productivity enhancing capital reallocation in these economies.

In a market economy, it is expected that competitive market forces would compel poorly performing firms to either improve their efficiency or exit the market. It is true that the operation of creative destruction would impose social costs linked with structural adjustment and would also have implications for public finance. The exit of these firms and greater unemployment that it generates reduces government's tax income while at the same time increases its expenditure to finance increased unemployment. In the years since the GFC, it seems as if the emergence and growth of zombie firms have been the outcome of policy choices. While there may be different reasons for these policies, measures, such as loose monetary policy, have helped this process.

Over and above the long tail of the laggard firms that lowers aggregate productivity in the economy, this subset of zombie firms intensifies this downward pressure by widening dispersion in productivity performance across firms. The overall channel via which zombie firms damage the economy is by enhancing misallocation of resources (Calligaris et al. 2015).

Finally, many researchers blame declining business dynamism, a process helped by the existence of zombie firms, as a major contributor to lower investment, hence lower productivity growth (Barkai, 2016; Furman & Orszag, 2018; Qureshi, 2017). It is pointed out that due to market congestion, start-up rate is down in many economies (McGowan, Andrews, & Millot, 2017, p. 8) and as a result of this combination of factors, unproductive firms that would typically exit in a competitive environment are surviving, and this would lower average productivity growth in the economy and could potentially crowd out growth opportunities for more productive firms (McGowan et al., 2017).

While the situation may be worse in the UK, similar situations arise in other advanced economies, such as the USA (McKinsey Global Institute, 2017), Germany (Elstner et al., 2018) and France (Askenazy & Erhel, 2015). If Tomorrow's Company (2018) suggestion is to be believed, namely that "since the financial crisis, UK productivity has been static in absolute terms and falling relative to other countries" (p. 8); adding that in 2007, British average productivity—output per worker—was 9% below the OECD average, and by 2015, the gap had widened to 18%. The situation regarding productivity per hour of work was even worse, and was 35% below Germany and 30% below that of the US (ibid., p. 8, see also Sisson, 2014, p. 2).

One factor that goes some way in explaining this situation is the prolonged use of unconventional monetary policy (Albrizio, Conesa, Dlugosch, & Timiliotis, 2019). The use of exceptionally very low interest rates for a long time has led to a situation where cleansing effect of recession may have been muted and consequently many unproductive or zombie firms continue to survive. So long as low interest rates continue, this is likely to continue. In short, as a result of recession, output fell but for a variety of reasons the number of workers did not fall as much, hence labour productivity collapsed. Depressed investment did not help the situation either. In view of reduced investment, there was also capital shallowing, that is, capital-labour ratio fell too (Pessoa & Van Reenen, 2013). Institute of Directors (2018) pointed out that the long tail was mainly caused by slow adoption of existing best management and technology. In their view, reasons for weak investment were higher uncertainty, weak overall economic growth and the spare capacity that were built up over the past decade. It was also stated that the gap became larger (ibid., p. 6) and if effective policies could be used to remove the gap, the UK's GDP would rise by £270 billion a year. The key driver of productivity growth would be investment in management and technology (ibid., p. 7). To Goldin et al. (2019), the productivity growth slowdown could be attributed to reduced investment and growing gap between frontier and laggard firms. Sisson (2014) offers a more serious narrative of the problem and states "although a very live issue, poor productivity has dogged the UK for decades. There is a measure of consensus that the condition is deep-seated and path dependent, reflecting corporate governance arrangements and a financial system that encourage 'short-termism' and consequently a lack of investment in people as well as technology" (p. 1). Considering the unconventional monetary policy, it was supposed to help investment, but it did not and, it is even possible that via prolonging the life of zombie firms, it may have harmed investment further.

Stagnant real wage rate could be a powerful incentive to persuade firms to substitute labour for capital, in turn, leading to deeper capital shallowing, hence, further slowdown of productivity growth. Barnett, Chiu, et al. (2014) offered two sets of hypotheses to explain the slowdown by a mixture of cyclical factors, caused by the fall in aggregate demand, and more persistent causes that could be linked with the GFC.

The first hypothesis is based on the idea that the slowdown is temporary, and as soon as the overall economic conditions improves, and aggregate demand picks up, this declining trend could be reversed. We do not share this optimistic assessment of a serious problem. In the meantime, though, and in view of the prevailing elevated uncertainty, firms may decide to hold on to their employees to avoid the costs of staff adjustment and safeguard their skills for the time that aggregate demand recovers. While it is not directly stated as such, on the basis of this hypothesis, productivity puzzle in the UK seems to be a transitory phenomenon, not related to any structural factors. Taking this point further, secular stagnation in the economy has effectively created this surplus productive capacity within firms. We would argue that employment growth that the UK economy experienced in the last few years clearly refutes this cyclical explanation of productivity slowdown. We are not dealing with labour hoarding as suggested by some researchers, but increasingly a larger number of workers are involved in the production process. We consider this as the beginning of a regressive structural transformation of the UK economy. Let us add here, as Coulter (2016) puts it, "at the end of 2014 employment was at its highest ever level, at 31 million, a rate of 73.2 per cent and more than 1 million above the pre-crisis peak in 2008" (p. 197) suggesting that firms were unable to meet their demand with existing levels of staffing, including those who should have been laid off, but were not—that is, refuting the labour hoarding hypothesis.

As to the structural hypothesis, this is linked with the aftermath of the GFC and its impact on the productive capacity in the economy. It is argued that following the GFC, impaired access to credit and elevated uncertainty about the overall macroeconomic environments may have negatively affected companies' willingness to invest and undertake long-term commitments. Inadequate investment, combined with the growth in employment as indicated above, led to capital shallowing, that is, capital per worker declined. The credit crunch that followed the GFC may have added extra pressure to hold back investment. Once again, we would argue that we should not overlook the role that declining real wages may have played in this process (see Blundell, Crawford, & Jin, 2013). In the previous four decades, declining union density in the UK had supressed the growth of real wages, and increased its flexibility. It allows employing workers on contracts that offer flexibility for the employer, at the expense of pay and certainty for the employee. Taking these changes into consideration, Martin and Rowthorn (2012) suggest that lower real wages may have in fact encouraged firms to create low-productivity, low-paid jobs in the service sector. To support this view further Barnett, Batten, et al. (2014, p. 120) pointed out that between 2008 (Q1) and 2013 (Q4) real wages fell by 5 percentage points. On the issue of declining real wage rates in the UK, Disney, Jin, and Miller (2013) wrote that " In 2012 (Q1), four-and-a-half years after the recession, the average real wage was 0.7% below the level in 2008 (Q1) and about 10% below its historical trend" (p. 68). In their assessment while some decline may be explained by mismeasurement of productivity, the bulk of the decline seems to be linked with strategic decision making. Reduced investment in physical and intangible investment and impaired resource allocation lead to an unusually high survival rates for unproductive firms. We accept that in addition to investment and technological progress, another factor that affects productivity growth is reallocation of resources across firms, that is, reallocation from low- to high-productive firms. It is argued here that anything harming this process will have a detrimental impact of productivity growth.

Qureshi and Dervis (2019) offer a different take on the productivity puzzle. They argue that in the past two decades, technology has been booming with an unprecedented depth and speed, and yet productivity growth slowed down in advanced economies and in many emerging economies too. They refer to digital innovation, sophisticated computer systems and cell phones and growing applications of robotics and artificial intelligence in industry and services. This said, despite very low borrowing costs and high corporate profits, investment, especially fixed capital formation, has been persistently weak (see also Disney, Jin, & Miller, 2013). We would suggest two factors to explain this situation.

First, in most advanced economies there is less competition and insufficient dynamism in the operation of the markets, adversely affecting firms' motivation for productivity enhancing investment.

Second, in running a typical capitalist firm, a managerial model of the firm has been replaced by a finance model of the firm. According to Lazonick (2014) up to the late 1970s, the basic principles of corporate resource allocation were based on the idea of "retain-and-reinvest". The main aim of the firm under this system was to produce goods and services most efficiently to maximize profits. To achieve this, corporations would retain their earnings and reinvest them to enhance their productive capabilities. Business strategies and investment decisions were devised with the specific aim of increasing value creation, leading to more revenue and bigger market share. Given this longer view, cooperation and sharing the benefits were essential to ensure the sustainability of the strategy. Areas of investment were chosen to achieve this objective, that is, workers' skills, technology, and research and development (Mazzucato, 2018, p. 176). The end result of 'retain-and-reinvest' was clear, the size of the national economic pie was bigger, enjoying the higher growth rate and even if a bigger share was going to capital, there would still be a larger share going to labour. From the late 1970s, 'retain-and-reinvest' has been replaced by 'downsize-and-distribute' allocation strategy. The main aim of the corporation changed to maximizing shareholders' value and the vehicle to achieve this is downsize and distribute. Influenced by the Chicago School economists, a superior corporate performance had been defined as ever higher quarterly earnings per share. With this new approach, the aim has been to downsize the labour force and distribute earnings to financial interests. This new corporate strategy relied heavily on the notion of Principal-Agent theory. Agents, the managers, are charged with prime aim of serving the interests of the principals, the shareholders, with the sole aim of maximizing their value. From then on, short-term objectives dictate business strategy and investment. It is clear here that productive investment would suffer and what becomes significant will be 'value-extraction' rather than 'value-creation'. Tomorrow's Company (2018) discusses the issue of weak investment in the UK at length and offers possible ways out of this gridlock. It is appreciated that there is a serious investment problem in the UK, and while the Brexit vote of 2016 and the subsequent political chaos that followed did not help, this problem has roots, which are far deeper than June 2016. While different terms are used, the report confirms that the main culprit is a finance model of the firm. Tomorrow's Company (2018) refers to this as "an increasingly anti-investment culture in UK corporate boardrooms" (p. 5) and adds "short-term anti-investment culture and general risk aversion has developed in the boardroom over the past decade, compounded by the role and motivation of many asset managers" (ibid., p. 6). What is referred to as an "anti-investment culture" is in fact a manifestation of a shift to maximize shareholders' value. In 2015, 82% of annual total compensation of the 500 highest paid executives in the US was based on stock options and stock rewards (Lazonick, 2016, p. 5). It is not surprising that these top executives would leave no stone unturned to boost the share price by whatever means, including buyback. It is in this context that we learn that from 2003 through 2012, the top 500 corporations in the US dispensed 54% of their earnings buying back their own shares and another 37% was paid in dividends, thus leaving little for productive investment or higher payment for workers (Lazonick, 2014, p. 2). In a recent article, Lazonick, Tulum, Hopkins, Sakine, and Jacobson (2019, p. 1) point out that the US corporations continue on the same line. They also add that between 2009 and 2018, the 466 companies in the S&P 500 Index that were publicly listed spent $4.00 trillion on buybacks, that is, 52% of profits, and paid $3.1 trillion, another 40% of profits on dividend. Hence, there would be just 8% of the profits for investment and any pay rise to people who work in these corporations. The same transformation has taken place in the UK too. For the UK, it is reported that "the proportion of internal cash flow spent on dividends or buybacks has increased from 10% in the 1970s to around 60% today" (Tomorrow's Company, 2018, p. 13).

On the face of it, when the economy is nearly at full employment, a condition should usually stimulate plenty of new opportunities for investment, but this kind of investment simply has not been happening in recent years. Why British corporations, like their US counterparts, prefer share buybacks and higher dividend pay-outs as the key mechanisms by which share price is effectively manipulated? We would argue that this is happening at the expense of an alternative strategy of investing in the long-term value creation.

If the last decade is considered, there is no doubt that some of the measures taken, such as quantitative easing, and prolonged low interest rates, failed to stimulate public and private investment. The underlying reason for this failure is that the causes of weak investment were not shortage of investible fund or tighter credit conditions. Two important problems that should be resolved in order to tackle the problem of weak investment are:

- The preference of short-term shareholder returns over long-term investment should be reversed.
- Appropriate measures should be taken to ensure that financial markets would recycle dividends into productive new investment.

4 Inequality and Productivity

Over and above of what has been discussed so far, we argue in this contribution that slow growth of productivity in the main capitalist economies has an institutional dimension too. In the past four decades, we have witnessed a gradual weakening of labour market institutions, namely trade unionism, in these economies. One outcome of this institutional change has been the de-coupling of real earnings and productivity growth. While this may manifest itself as stagnant or even declining wages, we argue that this de-coupling may have also contributed to slower productivity growth. Focusing on the UK, Sumner and Blond (2018, p. 2) point out that very high employment level in the UK is combined with one of the lowest levels of productivity in the OECD with a long tail of low-productivity, low-skilled jobs. This is partly due to the fact that government has effectively become the 'trade union' of first and last resort for some workers, deciding the standards of living for many workers at the very low scale of wage via its policy of 'living wages'. Any improvement in minimum wages would be welcomed, but if the current secular stagnation is to be tackled, there should be non-governmental institutions whose main function would be to upgrade the skills and wages of workers in the UK. It is also clear that in view of rising inequality, UK's economic growth in the past four decades was an exclusive growth. This situation has not changed in the last few years despite growth in employment and fall in unemployment. UK's public policy has been based on actively discouraging trade unionism and encouraging labour market flexibility, which despite all the flawed promises, led to a low-productivity, low-wage economy, a recipe for disaster especially under the extra competitive pressure of globalization.

Examining the impact of economic institutions on income distribution, Levy and Temin (2007) postulate that in the early years after the Second World War in the USA the economic discourse was dominated by trade unions. In addition, a negotiating framework set in the Treaty of Detroit,[6] progressive taxation and a high national minimum wage all devised to have a "shared prosperity" by fairly distributing the gains from economic growth. Wage adjustment to productivity gains became recognized as necessary and fair. It is perhaps because of this arrangement that during 1948–1973 the average productivity of labour, output per hour, in the US increased by 96.7%, and during the same period, average real wage has also risen by 91.3% (Bivens & Blair, 2017, p. 9). By contrast, during the time that labour market institutions were weakened, Levy and Temin (2007, p. 1) report that in the 25 years between 1980 and 2005, business sector productivity increased by 71% and median weekly earnings of full-time workers rose only by 14%; nearly four-fifths of the growth in productivity did not benefit workers. Two conclusions are straightforward. First, in the second period with weaker labour unions, productivity growth declined by nearly 30% compared with the first period. Second, higher productivity creates higher revenue and when the average worker's earning is not raised by this increase, clearly elsewhere in the distribution, there would be a bigger-than-productivity-rise jump in earnings. Figure 4.1 shows the relationship between real earnings and productivity in the US between 1947 and 1975 and Fig. 4.2 demonstrates clearly the breakdown of the link between the two after 1975.

[6] For the main points of this treaty, see https://en.wikipedia.org/wiki/Reuther%27s_Treaty_of_Detroit

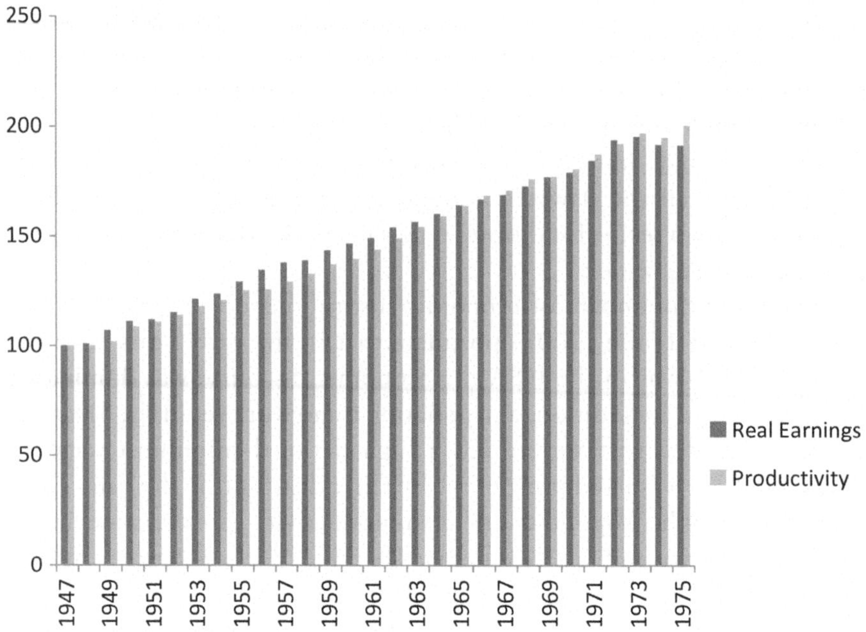

Fig. 4.1 Real earnings and productivity, US, 1947–1975. (Source: Data extracted from Gordon (2017))

The breaking of the link between wage growth and productivity growth has been present in other major capitalist economies too. Uguccioni, Sharpe, and Murray (2016) writing on Canada confirmed that between 1976 and 2014 median real hourly earnings grew by only 0.09%, compared to labour productivity growth of 1.12% per year during the same period. It is to be noted while the middle groups of workers did not benefit much from the productivity growth, the situation with the top earners and the poorest paid workers was different, and their earnings, especially at the top of the income distribution grew in line with average growth rate of productivity (ibid. p. 15). A similar analysis was conducted for the USA (Bivens & Mishel, 2015). Their results are similar and for the period 1973–2014 labour productivity grew by 72.2% but during this period the average earnings increased by only 42.5%; nearly 30% of the productivity growth was not reflected in earnings. Interestingly the wages of the top 1% grew 167%, far more than the average growth in

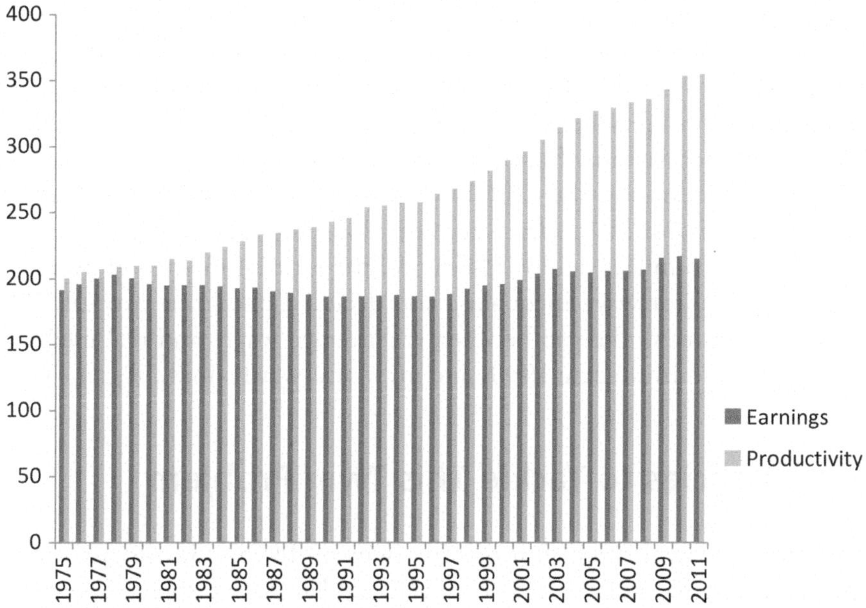

Fig. 4.2 Real earnings and productivity, US, 1975–2011. (Source: Data extracted from Gordon (2017))

productivity between 1973 and 2013 and their share of total wages nearly doubled, from 6.8% in 1973 to 13.2% in 2013 (ibid., p. 13). For the UK, Pessoa and Van Reenen (2013, p. 10) stated that between 1972 and 2010, average productivity grew by 114%, but the growth of real wages was only 72%, once again 42% of productivity growth had no impact on earnings. In the US, the share of income of the top 1% exceeded 20%, higher than it has been for a century and is the same as it was in 1928. While in the UK the share of the top 1% is lower, but it still rose from 6% in 1979 to 15% by the eve of the Great Recession (ibid., p. 12).

Gregg, Machin, and Fernandez-Salgado (2014, pp. 2–4) focused on the declining real wage rate in the UK and commented that since 2008, real weekly wages have fallen by around 8% and offered three drivers for this fall. Unemployment, low wages and low business investment and de-coupling of wage growth from productivity growth. Business investment fell by 14% from 2008 to 2009 and most of the growth of productivity went to top 1% and 2% of wage earners (ibid., p. 4). In relation to wages and productivity, they point out that from around 2003, average wages started to lag behind productivity, but the median wages de-coupling from productivity started from around the mid-1990s (ibid. pp. 17–19). Schwellnus, Kappeler, and Pionnier (2017, pp. 5–6) examined this issue among the OECD countries and looked at the period between 1995 and 2014. They confirm declining labour share in two-thirds of the countries, and furthermore, the ratio of median to average wages, a proxy for wage inequality, also declined in all but two OECD member countries. The gap between real average wages and real median wages appeared in the late 1990s and grew afterwards (ibid., Fig. 4.1).

5 Policies to Tackle This Twin Problem

We offer a general discussion on this twin problem, and discuss some specific economic policies that could be used to tackle these problems, that is, slow productivity growth and rising inequality.

As discussed, the so-called productivity puzzle is a very complex and serious problem and should be tackled at various levels. With some qualification, we accept the dualism hypothesis pertaining to the existence of frontier or superstar firms versus laggard firms with vastly different productivity and productivity growth. In the long tail, there is also a subset of zombie firms who are effectively on a life support machine. To see the two sides of the productivity problem, let us note that average productivity growth has fallen by half in advanced economies, from just 2% annually between 1990 and 2004 to about 1% between 2004 and 2016. Frontier firms' productivity grew at 3% a year between 2001 and 2013, compared with 0.5% annual growth for all other firms (Bell & Dervis, 2019, p. x). The main factor causing all these unfavourable outcomes is inadequate investment that predates the GFC but intensified by it (IMF, 2015; Jones & Philippon, 2016). As to the current depressed state of investment, two sets of factors have been discussed.

- A change in the governance, that is, a change in the way that a typical capitalist firm is organized and managed. This in turn led to the growth

of short-termism in decision making, and hence, long-term productive investment has been adversely affected.
- The second factor that may have contributed to bring about the growth of short-termism in decision making is a secular fall in profitability in major capitalist economies (Maito, 2014, p. 10) that convinced the owners of capital that it was not profitable enough to invest in heaps of new technologies to replace labour (Roberts, 2019).

Responding to this declining trend in the post-crisis years, companies have preferred to keep their labour force and if needs be employ new workers on more precarious contracts. There is ample evidence confirming this trend (ACAS, 2015; Barnett, Batten, et al., 2014; Barnett, Chiu, et al., 2014; Dolphin & Hatfield, 2015).

The share of investment in the productive value creating sector in these economies declined because of the increase in investment in less productive labour and sectors. To put it differently, while there has been a secular fall in fixed asset investment in these economies, speculation in fictitious capital, buying and selling shares and bonds have been booming, manifesting itself in the current financial bubble in share prices that cannot be explained by the historical low growth rate or depressed state of productivity. We would argue that inter alia, falling profitability in productive investment, made investment in financial assets more attractive as it provides quicker returns.

As indicated earlier, the use of unconventional monetary policy, especially quantitative easing and low interest rates, while helping fictitious capital via financial bubbles, harmed the prospect of productive investment further. It is to be noted here that despite the recent stock market booms in many capitalist economies, the profitability of productive investment continues to stay low and along with it, low investment growth and poor productivity growth continue. In response to GFC, jobs were lost in all sectors, but, most job losses were concentrated in the productive industries and amongst full-time workers and the young. When the recovery began there has been an increase in insecure work, including temporary employees, self-employment and part-time workers that replaced full-time and permanent jobs lost in the recession (Dolphin & Hatfield, 2015, p. 24). Ellis (2016) pointed out that in the UK, the total number of jobs in manufacturing slumped by 385,500 in the previous seven years. Furthermore, attention should be drawn to other aspects of the changes that took place. TUC (2017, p. 9) pointed out that since 2011 levels of insecure work have risen by more than 600.000, that is, 27%, to 3.2 million. The number of people with zero-hours contracts increased from 70.000 in 2006 to 810.000 in 2016. In 2016, nearly 4.8 million people were self-employed, up from 3.8 million in 2006.1.7 million self-employed people earn below the level of government's national living wage. The Office for National Statistics (ONS) (2019)[7] data shows that in the start of 2006, 7,227,000 million people worked part-time, 620.000 of them, because they could not find full-time jobs in the economy. Towards the end of 2019, the total number of people working part-time went up to 8.389.000 people, a rise of 16% and 918.000 people, a rise of 48% were those who could not find a full-time job. Self-employment is likely to be less productive and likewise, part-time workers would not do enough productive work and zero-hour contract workers would not accumulate sufficient human capital to enhance their productivity.

One major problem that should be tackled is the demand for and supply of skills in the UK. Levels of employer demand for skills are low, and investment in continuing vocational training per employee in the UK is half the EU average and further, in real terms, declined by 13.6% between 2007 and 2015 (IPPR, 2017, p. 4). To address this problem, we argue for greater investment in education and training to fill this gap. In addition to reducing income inequality, there are other outcomes that matter for the well-being of the citizens, such as employment prospect, job satisfaction, health and educational outcomes and social cohesion. These objectives could not be achieved unless we reverse the twin trends of slowing productivity and growing inequality. Conventionally productivity growth and greater equity were often seen in terms of a trade-off, but recent research has refuted the proposal of a trade-off between the two (Berg, 2013; Okun, 1975; Qureshi, 2017). Policy makers should appreciate that technology has altered the economic setting and the rules of

[7] https://www.ons.gov.uk/employmentandlabourmarket/peopleinwork/employmentandemployeetypes/datasets/fulltimeparttimeandtemporaryworkersseasonallyadjustedemp01sa

competition between firms have changed too. There have been other changes too. The nature of work has not remained unaffected. As indicated above, demand for skills did not stay static. In relation to skills, public policy in the UK in the last few decades failed because it focused on the supply of skills at the expense of overlooking demand for skills. Both sides of skills problem should be considered. Many employers in the UK do not invest enough in training, and many do not use the skills of their workforce effectively. Institute for Public Policy Research (IPPR) (2018, p. 102) estimates that fully one-third of adult employees in the UK are over-qualified for their jobs. Another area that requires urgent and effective attention is how to invigorate competition. Policy makers should introduce adequate and effective rules and regulations to prevent abuse of market power in a digital age. In view of the operation of superstar firms, this consideration assumes further significance. There is a strong argument to review and re-examine rules and regulations of merger and acquisition to ensure that the impact on efficiency and competition, that is, on market structure, is equally considered in each and every case of merger and acquisition. Furthermore, given the persistent rise in merger and acquisition in the last few decades and subsequent growth of market concentration (Gutierrez & Philippon, 2017, p. 37; Jones & Philippon, 2016, p. 1; Autor, Dorn, Katz, Patterson, & Van Reenen, 2017; Barkai, 2016; Corfe & Gicheva, 2017; Bell & Tomlinson, 2018) the enforcement of anti-trust rules deserve special attention. Blonigen and Pierce (2016) examining the situation in the US confirm that "we find that M&As significantly increase mark-ups on average, but no statistically significant average effect on productivity" (p. 3). Andrews et al. (2016) argue that there has been a structural change in the global economy, and mention digitalization as a case in point and add that there has been a slowdown in the diffusion process. Furthermore, the rate of new business formation has been on a declining trend and the rate at which firms exit the market has also slowed (Qureshi, 2017, p. 9). In addition to entry and exit, unequal access to capital may be a contributing factor to slow growth too, as unequal access to capital for small but highly productive firms prevents them from growing. If needs be, anti-trust laws and competition policies should undergo a thorough overhaul to make them relevant for the digital age. It is important to consider that new technologies produced two anti-competitive outcomes.

- Winner takes most dynamics.
- Quasi-natural monopolies.

Super-star firms do what is natural to their position in the market place, that is, erect a variety of barriers to entry to maintain and even strengthen their dominant position. Qureshi (2017) points out that there is a growing gap in productivity growth of superstar firms and the rest, and accepting this dichotomy, leans towards the idea that the problem may not be the technology, but rather its lack of diffusion. Consequently, one needs to look into factors preventing greater diffusion of these new ideas across firms. It is here that restoring competition would become a top priority for policy makers in these economies. Qureshi (2017, p. 9) adds that in industries less exposed to competitive pressures, technological diffusion is weaker, productivity gap between firms are wider and aggregate productivity growth is lower.

In the UK, since 2008 wage growth has been exceptionally weak whereas employment growth has been unusually strong. While quantity of jobs is important, equally significant is quality of jobs created, and this should be looked into very closely. To improve the quality of jobs, the role of education and training should be reassessed. If training and retraining were available, it would enhance productivity via more human capital. Nevertheless, we maintain that this could not be done effectively and efficiently on an individual basis. This brings us to argue for institutional reforms in the labour market. To ensure the sustainability of this programme and to advance the interest of UK industry and economy at the same time, the active public policy that discourages trade unions should be reversed. It is important that every effort be made to develop shared objectives around growth, shared prosperity and improved productivity. Working together is necessary so that the energy and skills of people could be harnessed to secure better quality work, which is the basic requirement of higher productivity. It is true that new technology is important, and that a better machine will enhance productivity, but in a largely service-based economy, like the UK, the quality and willingness of human labour to ensure that the productivity jigsaw puzzle is successfully completed is essential. This requires the highest possible level of engagement by employees to drive up productivity. Whatever the dimensions of the UK's productivity puzzle, it is a collective problem, affecting everyone, and the sooner the importance of a collective voice and collective effort to resolve it is appreciated, the better. The world has changed and we are aware that globalization and technological transformations changed the way the economies work. Our argument for the reform of the labour market institutions relies heavily on the fact that the alternative model that has been used in the last four decades has been a total failure. It failed to create higher growth and it did not improve productivity, nor did it achieve sharing the proceeds of growth. We argue that the UK is faced with a clear choice, would we strive to have a high-engagement, high-productivity service-based economy or do we continue with what we have done in the last four decades and end up with a low-wage, low-productivity, tax haven?

Accepting the role of employees' engagement in enhancing productivity must involve recognition of the role of trade unions, in the whole process. Barth, Bryson, and Dale-Olsen (2017) looking at the economy of Norway concluded that increasing union density led to improved firm-level productivity and added: our results "imply that an increase in the firm mean of union density of around 1 percentage point raises firm productivity by 1.7–1.8%" (p. 25). More interestingly, a consultation document published by the UK's former Department of Trade and Industry states " there is also evidence that unionised workplace have better training policies and union learning representatives have successfully introduced many thousands of employees to training which has enhanced their productivity" (DTI, 2007, p. 22). The annual productivity gain is estimated between £476 million and £1133 million a year, but adds in the footnote "Annex B also estimates a more general gain of £3.4–10.2 billion from increased productivity"; and reacting to such an impressive productivity gain of more than £10 billion, the report comments "this is a speculative calculation, but its magnitude implies that the benefit is potentially very great" (ibid., p. 22).

Failing to recognize a collective voice and responding positively and effectively to reverse the de-coupling of real wages and productivity growth could only increase economic and political discontent in the years to come. If this link is not re-established, any attempt to enhance employees' engagement to improve productivity would fail as they have little motivation to engage. Government must re-consider the role of trade unions and a serious reassessment of policies relating to labour market institutions in the past four decades should be undertaken. To ensure the success of this new model, trade unions should also change and shift to a more productive economic role. They should enlarge their facilities for training and retraining to speed up the process of reskilling the workforce in the light of changing technologies. It is important to stress that the training and retraining programmes by the trade unions should focus on how to improve low take up of digital technologies by the UK firms to improve the demand for skills too. In order to achieve this aim, it should also pay attention on how to reduce the adoption barriers. The consequence of doing nothing will be devastating on equality, employees' well-being and most probably on tax revenue for the state too (McCombie & Spreafico, 2015; Taylor & Omer, 2018). In the UK, as we move further towards a service-based economy, we face a vital choice. Would there be a focus on raising employees' engagement and skill level to have a highly productive, high wages and prosperous service-based economy?

To achieve this, investment in intangible assets, and more specifically, on training and employee engagement should be encouraged. Investment in UK R&D in 2015 was just 1.7% of GDP and that is too low, given the task faced in this country. It is less than the average in the Euro Area, and slightly more than half of what the US invests on R&D (Tomorrow's Company, 2018, p. 10). As a matter of urgency, investment in R&D should increase. In a service-based economy, human capital plays a bigger role in achieving higher productivity, and to unlock this potential, employee's training and up-skilling and engagement is the key, for which, greater investment is needed. Tax incentives should be used to encourage firms to increase investment in lifelong learning for their employees enabling them to up-skill and re-skill across their working life. The government, in turn, should take measures to improve basic skills, and enhance the availability of technical education as about half of young people in the UK do not go to the universities.

To tackle secular stagnation, a number of measures were used, that is, cutting interest rate to a very low level, and via the medium of quantitative easing, trying to increase the provision of credit. Neither of these policies was successful. Part of the reason may be, on the one hand, the public were told that there was no more money to finance public services and investment. At the same time, the Bank of England created substantial amount of new money through quantitative easing which was injected directly into financial markets—£375 billion for the period between 2008 and 2014 (Bunn, Pugh, & Yeats, 2018, p. 2). Overlooking the main issues, weak aggregate demand, and weak investment, flooding financial markets with more money than they were willing to invest has hugely inflated the value of finance-related assets. This policy did not address the main problems, but added to the growing divide which was already plaguing the economy. Bunn et al. (2018, p. 25), who studied the distributional impact of QE between 2008 and 2014, pointed out "The 10% of least wealthy households are only estimated to have seen a marginal increase in their measured real wealth of around £3000 between 2006–08 and 2012–14, compared to £350,000 for the wealthiest 10%".

More than ten years passed since the GFC, the UK economy is not out of its predicament and the outcome is a fragile economy sustaining its less-than-historical rate of growth by increasing debt and a stock market financial bubble. It is true that in the long run, we will all be dead, but it looks obvious that focusing to meet short-term outcomes will lead to a decline in long-term investment. There is no doubt that attention to short-term aims is needed for the firm to remain competitive, but ignoring or paying lip services to long-term objectives harms the value creating capacity of the firm, and at the end of the day, the shareholders. Looking at the UK, investment in fixed assets (gross) has fallen from 19% of GDP in the early 1990s to a low of 14% in 2016 and, while it has subsequently recovered to 17% " it is still lower than thirty years ago" (Tomorrow's Company, 2018. p. 11). For the good of the economy in general, public policy should try to reverse this declining trend.

It goes without saying that practical details of how this policy could or should change goes beyond the scope of this contribution.

While reforming labour market institutions would contribute to higher productivity, these reforms would not solve this problem fully. There are still two other essential issues to be addressed.

There is no doubt that dualism in productivity distribution is a contributing factor to the growth of inequality (Andrews et al., 2016; OECD, 2017). At the same time, this growing divide perpetuates and intensifies inequality further as it also means that less people can afford education and training to improve their skill level, and thereby, end up in a trap of low-productivity, low-paid jobs. Haldane (2017, p. 16) suggested that had the Bank of England not drastically reduced the interest rate, it would have increased productivity by 1–2% by causing 10% of firms to go bust, at a cost of 1.5 million jobs. This may be true, but we have argued in this contribution that there are better ways to promote productivity, that is, promoting investment. Highly productive economy has a better potential of protecting jobs instead of destroying them.

In Europe, in 2014, total investment was about 15% below 2007 figure and in certain member states; the decline has been even more dramatic (European Investment Bank, 2015, p. 1). In the US, net fixed capital formation, which stood at 12% of GDP in 1950, declined to 4% of GDP in 2014 (McKinsey Global Institute, 2016, p. 2). These are significant falls with serious implications for the rest of the economy. Weak investment dampens aggregate demand in the short run but more importantly hallows out productive capacity in the long run. This would take us to the final section of our policy recommendations, that is, re-assessing the role of the state. The conventional view on the role of the state in modern capitalism is primarily concerned with dealing with market failures. In this section, we only focus on the assertion that markets could not produce full employment. The possibility of underemployment equilibria meant that at such level where demand and supply aggregate would be equal; there is no automatic internal mechanism to move the economy towards full employment. Consequently, the state should intervene by managing aggregate demand to push the economy towards full-employment equilibrium. We would argue that given the complexity of challenges that we face, a new approach is needed.

Setting aside issues relating to the environment, for the past few years, we had historically low and exclusive growth, manifested in rising inequality in most industrialized societies. Across the board, compared with the historical trends, average productivity is low and its growth, essential for our long-term prosperity, slowed down. Increasing inequality and a growing divide manifests itself into aggravated social tensions—for example, France, Chile and Lebanon (Brand, 2019; Ruiz Caro, 2020; Salti, 2019). There may have been some positive movements in wages (The Guardian, 13 August 2019), but for years, real wages remained stagnant and declining in many cases. De-coupling of real wages and productivity was almost complete and even in the superstar firms, real earnings do not rise in line with productivity growth (Qureshi, 2017).

We argue that over and above the state intervention to correct market failure in its traditional sense, the quality of state intervention must change because the challenges that society faces are far deeper and a lot more complex than ever. What is needed now is a proper innovation-led growth, which is both inclusive, to tackle the growing inequality, and sustainable, to reduce the cost of ecological crisis. As to what this new direction should look like, consider Keynes's (1926) view that "the most important Agenda for the state relate not to those activities which private individuals are already fulfilling, but to those functions which fall outside the sphere of the individual, to those decisions which are made by no one if the state does not make them" (p. 11). More interestingly, Keynes (op. cit.) states openly and clearly "the important thing for government is not to do things which individuals are doing already, and to do them a little better or a little worse, but to do those things which at present are not done at all" (p. 11).

We would argue that the investment in productive sector of our economy comes very close to what Keynes so clearly depicted nearly 100 years ago. We suggest setting up a publicly owned investment bank with a clearly defined mission of financing productive investment at a level conducive of promoting the overall growth rate (Macfarlane, 2018; Mazzucato & Macfarlane, 2018; Mazzucato & Penna, 2015). The economic justification for this rests on two further propositions.

First, markets are inherently unstable and second, we share Keynes's (1936) view that when the economy is in a recession, markets tend to remain "in a chronic condition of sub-normal activity for a considerable period without any marked tendency, either towards recovery or toward complete collapse" (p. 157). To put it differently, inaction would make secular stagnation a normal state, a point not missed by Keynes when he talks about "an intermediate situation is neither desperate nor satisfactory is our normal lot" (ibid., p. 157).

It is our contention that more than a decade since the GFC is long enough for the magical intervention of the 'invisible hands' to put things right, and hence, something drastic to break the current vicious circle is essential if we are ever to get out of this scramble. In this context, we argue that the state should focus on new direction and creation of new industries informed by epoch making progress in new technologies. In the process, the purpose should be creating good quality employment, that is, high productivity, and coupled with it high real pay, which would take care of inadequate aggregate demand. Higher demand, financed by higher real earnings linked with higher productivity, would also reinvigorate our financial systems towards more stability as it would reduce the need for Ponzi loans, that is, loans to finance consumption that had been on the rise in the recent past.

In this contribution, we would also argue that correcting market failures continue to be an important part of public policy making under modern capitalism. We contemplate that the state could and should do more to shape the market as well. If this function were performed well, the outcome would ease correcting market failures too by reducing the number of cases where market fails.

It is essential that appropriate measures are taken to ensure that the financial system operates in the service of sustainable, stable and equitable economic development. A system that fails to finance long-term investment cannot and will not be sustainable. This is, in fact, a precondition for functional efficiency of the financial system and this is different from the mainstream notion of efficiency. Details could be country specific but it is feasible to use lending targets and tax credits to influence lending towards certain social and economic goals. We could also move towards setting up specialized lending institutions to tackle gender gap, minority's inadequate access to credits, small and medium businesses, and last but not least, promotion of diffusion of new technologies. These may be very ambitious goals, but on the one hand the overall crisis that we face is very serious; and more importantly, our potential capabilities to tackle all these issues are more than sufficient. What is lacking is a political collective will upon taking up the task. Furthermore, it is important to understand that a depressed state of productivity growth and growing inequality are not un-related problems. Inequality has a negative impact on economic growth by causing a lack of investment in human capital among low-income families. Added to inadequate investment in physical capital, insufficient accumulation of human capital would depress productivity further, thus perpetuating and potentially intensifying the problem. For the recovery to be sustained, reducing inequality should be a top priority. To that end, it should be comprehended that low growth of productivity in some sectors and companies—laggard and zombie firms—is a contributing factor to this growing inequality. This growing divide also means that less people can afford training and up-skilling, which in turn leads to skill mismatch. It is common sense that with technological changes, these programmes should be more widely available to reduce the costs of dislocation in the labour market. We would argue that our current situation, if left to its own internal mechanisms, would lead to a gradual but serious decline in living standards. Such economic policies are particularly relevant for a Post Neo-Liberal World.

6 Concluding Remarks

From the discussion offered in this chapter, five general conclusions could be drawn. First, the proposed conflict between jobs and productivity is indeed an after-effect of de-coupling of productivity growth and real earnings. Cost savings from productivity improvement should be put back to work elsewhere in the economy, partially in the form of higher wages and also, in the form of lower prices, leaving households and businesses with more money to spend. Strong demand would ensure that sector employment expands at the same time that productivity was growing (Berg & Ostry, 2011; Bell, 2019; McKinsey Global Institute, 2011; Cingano, 2014).

Second, the slowdown in productivity growth and the rise in inequality are interconnected. Third, unless there is effective intervention in the economy to change and transform underlying processes, various components of this flawed economic model reproduce and reinforce one another. Forth, given the common causes of productivity growth slowdown and growing inequality, efforts to boost productivity and enhance equity would be positively interconnected. Fifth, in view of the complexity of the situation, the role of the state in the economy should be re-defined because as Qureshi and Dervis (2019) pointed out "the era of smart machines will demand smarter policies" (p. 4).

References

ACAS. (2015). *The Productivity Challenge and What the Next Government Should Do About It*. Available at: https://archive.acas.org.uk/media/4228/The-productivity-challenge%2D%2D-and-what-the-next-government-should-do-about-it-Ian-Brinkley/pdf/Acas-Employment-Relations-Comment-Ian-Brinkley-February-2015.pdf

Acharya, V. V. Eisert, T., Eufinger, C., & Hirsch, C. (2019). *Whatever It Takes: The Real Effects of Unconventional Monetary Policy*. Available at: http://pages.stern.nyu.edu/~sternfin/vacharya/public_html/pdfs/Acharya%20et%20al%20Whatever%20it%20takes.pdf

Albrizio, S., Conesa, M., Dlugosch, D., & Timiliotis, C. (2019). *Unconventional Monetary Policy and Productivity: Evidence on the Risk-Seeking Channel from US Corporate Bond Markets*. Available at: https://www.oecd-ilibrary.org/docserver/06d2cce0-en.pdf?expires=1583248529&id=id&accname=guest&checksum=375E7081C4C530EEC15E1AA65E2DC482

Alexander, L., & Eberly, J. (2016). *Investment Hallowing Out*. Available at: https://www.imf.org/external/np/res/seminars/2016/arc/pdf/Alexander_Eberly_Session2.pdf

Andrews, D., Criscuolo, C., & Gal, P. N. (2016). *The Best versus the Rest: The Global Productivity Slowdown, Divergence Across Firms and the Role of Public Policy*. Available at: https://www.oecd-ilibrary.org/docserver/63629cc9-en.pdf?expires=1583248674&id=id&accname=guest&checksum=8746469DEFBC513E587B6FD06C0C2988

Askenazy, P., & Erhel, C. (2015). *The French Productivity Puzzle* (IZA Discussion Papers, No. 9188). Bonn, Germany: Institute for the Study of Labor (IZA).

Autor, D., Dorn, D., Katz, L. F., Patterson, C., & Van Reenen, J. (2017). Concentration on the Fall of the Labour Share. *American Economic Review: Papers and Proceedings, 107*(5), 180–185.

Bahar, D., & Foda, K. (2019). *The Technology-Productivity Paradox: Why Had Productivity Growth Slowed?* Available at: https://www.brookings.edu/wp-content/uploads/2019/05/productive_equity_190522.pdf

Baily, M. N., & Montalbano, N. (2016). *Why Is US Productivity Growth So Slow? Possible Explanations and Policy Responses.* Available at: https://www.brookings.edu/wp-content/uploads/2016/09/wp22_baily-montalbano_final4.pdf

Banerjee, R., Kearns, J., & Lombardi, M. (2015). *(Why) Is Investment Weak?.* Available at: https://www.bis.org/publ/qtrpdf/r_qt1503g.pdf.

Barclays. (2019). *Increased Corporate Concentration and the Influence of Market Power.* Available at: https://www.investmentbank.barclays.com/content/dam/barclaysmicrosites/ibpublic/documents/our-insights/MarketPower/Barclays-ImpactSeries5-MarketPower_final_2.4MB.pdf

Barkai, S. (2016). *Declining Labour and Capital Share.* Stigler Centre for the Study of the Economy and the State (New Working Paper Series, No. 2). Chicago: University of Chicago.

Barnett, A., Batten, S., Chiu, A., Franklin, J., & Sebastia-Barriel, M. (2014). The UK Productivity Puzzle. *Bank of England, Quarterly Bulletin, Q2,* 118.

Barnett, A., Chiu, A., Franklin, J., & Sebastia-Barriel, M. (2014). *The Productivity Puzzle A Firm Level Investigation into Employment Behaviour and Resource Allocation Over the Crisis.* Available at: https://www.bankofengland.co.uk/-/media/boe/files/working-paper/2014/the-productivity-puzzle-a-firm-level-investigation-into employment.pdf?la=en&hash=E880774027E6284FE498964717690E8611D08925

Barth, E., Bryson, A., & Dale-Olsen, H. (2017). *Union Density, Productivity and Wages* (Discussion Paper No. 481). Available at: https://www.niesr.ac.uk/sites/default/files/publications/DP481.pdf

Bell, J., & Dervis, K. (2019). *The Dynamics of Productive Equity.* Available at: https://www.brookings.edu/wp-content/uploads/2019/05/productive_equity_190522.pdf

Bell, T., & Tomlinson, D. (2018). *Is Everybody Concentrating?* Available at: https://www.resolutionfoundation.org/app/uploads/2018/07/Is-everybody-concentrating_Recent-trends-in-product-and-labour-market-concentration-in-the-UK-2.pdf

Berg, A. G. (2013). *Equality and Efficiency: Is There a Trade-Off Between the Two?* Available at: http://regardssurlaterre.com/en/equality-and-efficiency-there-trade-between-two

Berg, A. G, & Ostry, J. D (2011). *Inequality and Unsustainable Growth: Two Sides of the Same Coin.* Available at: https://www.imf.org/external/pubs/ft/sdn/2011/sdn1108.pdf

Bivens, J., & Blair, H. (2017). *Competitive Destruction, Cutting Corporate Tax Rates Will Not Create Jobs or Boost Incomes for the Vast Majority of American Families.* Available at: https://www.epi.org/files/pdf/114189.pdf

Bivens, J., &, Mishel, L. (2015). *Understanding the Historic Divergence Between Productivity and a Typical Worker's Pay: Why It Matters and Why It's Real.* Available at: https://www.epi.org/files/2015/understanding-productivity-pay-divergence-final.pdf

Blonigen, B. A., & Pierce, J. R (2016). *Evidence for the Effects of Mergers on Market Power and Efficiency.* Available at: https://www.federalreserve.gov/econresdata/feds/2016/files/2016082pap.pdf

Blundell, R., Crawford, C., & Jin, W. (2013). *What Can Wages and Employment Tell Us About the UK's Productivity Puzzle?* (IFS Working Paper, W13/11).

Brand, M. (2019). *The Yellow Vests, the Crisis of the Welfare State and Socialism.* Available at: https://www.counterpunch.org/2019/01/25/the-yellow-vests-the-crisis-of-the-welfare-state-and-socialism/

Bunn, P., Pugh, A., & Yeats, C. (2018). *The Distributional Impact of Monetary Policy Easing in the UK Between 2008 and 2014.* Available at: https://www.bankofengland.co.uk/-/media/boe/files/working-paper/2018/the-distributional-impact-of-monetary-policy-easing-in-the-uk-between-2008-and-2014.pdf

Bussiere, M., Ferrara, L., & Miloxvich, J. (2015). *Explaining the Recent Slump in Investment: The Role of Expected Demand and Uncertainty.* Available at: https://www.semanticscholar.org/paper/Explaining-the-Recent-Slump-in-Investment%3A-the-Role-Bussi%C3%A8re-Ferrara/1880e091fb9a256e3bf74d7972739f3a13da2ce8

Calligaris, S., Del Gatto, M., Hassan, F., Ottaviano, G. I. P., & Schivardi, F. (2015). *Italy's Productivity Conundrum.* Available at: http://www.lse.ac.uk/business-and-consultancy/consulting/assets/documents/italys-productivity-conundrum-a-study-on-resource-misallocation-in-italy.pdf

Centre for Cities. (2018). *The Wrong Tail, Why Britain's Long Tail Is Not the Cause of Its Productivity Problems.* Available at: https://www.centreforcities.org/reader/wrong-tail-britains-long-tail-not-cause-productivity-problems/

Cingano, F. (2014). *Trends in Income Inequality and its Impact on Economic Growth* (OECD Social, Employment and Migration Working Papers, No. 163). OECD Publishing. https://doi.org/10.1787/5jxrjncwxv6j-en

Corfe, S., & Gicheva, N. (2017). *Concentration Not Competition: The State of UK Consumer Markets*. Available at: http://www.smf.co.uk/wp-content/uploads/2017/10/Concentration-not-competition.pdf

Coulter, S. (2016). *The UK Labour Market and the 'Great Recession'*. Available at: http://eprints.lse.ac.uk/65615/1/Coulter_The%20UK%20labour%20market%20and%20the%20great%20recession.pdf

DeLoecker J., Eechhout, J., & Unger, G. (2019). *The Rise of Market Power and the Macroeconomic Implications*. Available at: http://www.janeeckhout.com/wp-content/uploads/RMP.pdf

Disney, R., Jin, W., & Miller, H. (2013). *The Productivity Puzzle*. Available at: https://www.ifs.org.uk/docs/34598THZZ12.pdf

Dolphin, T., & Hatfield, I. (2015). *The Missing Pieces, Solving Britain's Productivity Puzzle*. Available at: https://www.ippr.org/files/publications/pdf/missing-pieces-britains-productivity-puzzle_Aug2015.pdf.

Dottling, R., Gutierrez, G., & Philippon, T. (2017). *Is There an Investment Gap in Advanced Economies? If So, Why?* Available at: https://www.ecb.europa.eu/pub/conferences/shared/pdf/20170626_ecb_forum/T_Philippon_Is_there_an_investment_gap_in_advanced_economies_If_so_why_with_R_Dottling_and_G_Gutierrez.pdf

DTI. (2007). *Consultation Document: Workplace Representatives: A Review of Their Facilities and Facility Time*. Available at: https://webarchive.nationalarchives.gov.uk/+/http:/www.berr.gov.uk/files/file36336.pdf

Ellis, M. (2016). *Britain Loses 385,500 Manufacturing Jobs Since 2008....* Available at: http://www.mirror.co.uk/news/uk-news/britain-loses-385500-manufacturing-jobs-8127448

Elstner, S., Feld, L. P., & Schmidt, C. M. (2018). *The German Productivity Paradox- Facts and Explanations*. Available at: https://www.cesifo.org/DocDL/cesifo1_wp7231.pdf

European Investment Bank. (2015). *Why Does the EU Need an Investment Plan?* Available at: https://ec.europa.eu/commission/sites/beta-political/files/factsheet1-why_en.pdf

Foda, K. (2019). *The Evolution of Growth, Productivity and Income Inequality*. Available at: https://www.brookings.edu/wp-content/uploads/2019/05/productive_equity_190522.pdf

Furman, J., & Orszag, P. (2018). *Slower Productivity and Higher Inequality: Are They Related*. Available at: https://pdfs.semanticscholar.org/5856/72d3d75103c60ab929f39275 95c084b93e08.pdf?_ga=2.104053952.1173740182.1581887677-747560336.1558616796
Gieve, J. (2006). *The Puzzle of UK Investment*. Available at: https://www.bankofengland.co.uk/-/media/boe/files/speech/2006/the-puzzle-of-uk-business-investment
Goldin, I., Koutroumpis, P., Lafond, F., Rochowicz, N., & Winkler, J. (2019). *The Productivity Paradox: Reconciling Rapid Technological Change and Stagnating Productivity*. Available at: https://www.oxfordmartin.ox.ac.uk/downloads/reports/Productivity_Paradox.pdf
Gordon, C. (2017). *Growing Apart, A Political History of American Inequality*. Available at: http://scalar.usc.edu/works/growing-apart-a-political-history-of-american-inequality/index
Gouveia, A. F., & Osterhold, C. (2018). *Are Zombie Firms Curbing the Growth of Viable Firms?*. Available at: https://www.bportugal.pt/sites/default/files/anexos/cep_6_2_en.pdf
Gregg, P., Machin, S., & Fernandez-Salgado, M. (2014). *The Squeeze on Real Wages- and What It Might Take to End It*. Available at: http://personal.lse.ac.uk/machin/pdf/gmf-s%20february%202014.pdf
Gutierrez, G., & Philippon, T. (2017). *Declining Competition and Investment in the US*. Available at: https://www8.gsb.columbia.edu/faculty-research/sites/faculty-research/files/finance/Macro%20Lunch/IK_Comp_v1.pdf
Haldane, A. G. (2017). *Productivity Puzzle*. Available at: https://www.bankofengland.co.uk/-/media/boe/files/speech/2017/productivity-puzzles.pdf?la=en&hash=708C7CFD5E8417000655BA4AA0E0E873D98A18DE
Haldane, A. G (2018). *The UK's Productivity Problem: Hub No Spokes*. Available at: https://www.bankofengland.co.uk/-/media/boe/files/speech/2018/the-uks-productivity-problem-hub-no-spokes-speech-by-andy-haldane.pdf
HM Government. (2017). *Industrial Strategy: Building a Britain Fit for the Future*. Available at: https://assets.publishing.service.gov.uk/government/uploads/system/uploads/attachment_data/file/664563/industrial-strategy-white-paper-web-ready-version.pdf
IMF. (2015). *World Economic Outlook: Uneven Growth- Short and Long Term Factors*. Available at: https://www.imf.org/en/Publications/WEO/Issues/2016/12/31/World-Economic-Outlook-April-2015-Uneven-Growth-42382

Institute of Directors. (2018). *Lifting the Long Tail.* Available at: https://www.iod.com/Portals/0/PDFs/Campaigns%20and%20Reports/Economy/Lifting-the-long-tail.pdf?ver=2018-10-11-124501-460

Jones, C., & Philippon, T. (2016). *The Secular Stagnation of Investment?* Available at: http://pages.stern.nyu.edu/~tphilipp/papers/Q_ZLB.pdf

Jones, C. I. (2017, June). *The Productivity Growth Slowdown in Advanced Economies.* Available at: https://web.stanford.edu/~chadj/JonesSintra2017.pdf

Keynes, J. G. (1936). *The General Theory of Employment, Interest, and Money.* Available at: http://cas2.umkc.edu/economics/people/facultypages/kregel/courses/econ645/winter2011/generaltheory.pdf

Keynes, J. M. (1926). *The End of Laisses Faire.* Available at: http://www.stephen-hicks.org/wp-content/uploads/2015/03/Keynes-J-The-End-of-Laissez-Faire.pdf

Kose, M. A., Ohnsorge, F., Ye, L. S., & Islamaj, E. (2017). *Weakness in Investment Growth: Causes, Implications and Policy Response*s. Available at: https://cama.crawford.anu.edu.au/sites/default/files/publication/cama_crawford_anu_edu_au/2017-03/19_2017_kose_ohnsorge_ye_islamaj_0.pdf

KPMG. (2019). *Zombies in Our Midst.* Available at: https://assets.kpmg/content/dam/kpmg/uk/pdf/2019/05/zombie-in-our-midst.pdf

Lazonick, W. (2014). *Profits Without Prosperity: How Stock Buybacks Manipulate the Market, and Leave Most Americans Worse Off.* Available at: https://www.ineteconomics.org/uploads/papers/LAZONICK_William_Profits-without-Prosperity-20140406.pdf

Lazonick, W. (2016). *The Value-Extracting CEO: How Executive Stock-Based Pay Undermines Investment in Productive Capabilities.* Available at: https://www.ineteconomics.org/uploads/papers/WP_54-Lazonick-Value-Extracting-CEO-2016.pdf

Lazonick, W., Tulum, O., Hopkins, M., Sakine, M. E., & Jacobson, K. (2019). *Financialization of the US Pharmaceutical Industry* (Working Paper). Institute for New Economic Thinking.

Levy, F., & Temin, P. (2007). *Inequality and Institution in 20th Century America* (MITIPC-07-002). Available at: https://ipc.mit.edu/sites/default/files/documents/07-002.pdf.

Macfarlane, L. (2018). *The UK Needs a State Investment Bank to Support Its Industrial Strategy.* Available at: https://medium.com/iipp-blog/why-the-uk-needs-a-state-investment-bank-to-support-its-industrial-strategy-6fe2d61d756e

Maito, E. E. (2014). *The Historical Transience of Capital: The Downward Trend in the Rate of Profit Since XIX Century*. Available at: https://mpra.ub.uni-muenchen.de/55894/

Marin, D. (2017). *Inclusive Globalization in a Digital Age: Analysis*. Available at: https://www.g20-insights.org/wp-content/uploads/2017/04/Marin_INCLUSIVE-GLOBALIZATION-IN-A-DIGITAL-AGE.pdf

Martin, B., & Rowthorn, R. (2012). *Is the British Economy Supply Constrained II? A Renewed Critique of Productivity Pessimism*. Available at: https://pdfs.semanticscholar.org/64c4/264ecaec6182d72d18283b92c4e6426477b4.pdf

Mazzucato, M. (2018). *The Value of Everything: Making and Taking in the Global Economy*. London: Penguin Random House.

Mazzucato, M., & Macfarlane, L. (2018). *State Investment Banks and Patient Finance: An International Perspective*. Available at: https://www.ucl.ac.uk/bartlett/public-purpose/sites/public-purpose/files/iipp_wp_2018-01.pdf

Mazzucato, M., & Penna, C. C. R. (2015). *The Rise of Mission-Oriented State Investment Banks: The Cases of Germany's KFW and Brazil's BNDES*. Available at: http://www.isigrowth.eu/wp-content/uploads/2015/11/working_paper_2015_1.pdf

McCombie, J. S. L., & Spreafico, M. R. M. (2015). *Income Inequality and Growth: Problem with the Orthodox Approach*. Available at: https://www.landecon.cam.ac.uk/research/real-estate-and-urban-analysis/centres/ccepp/copy_of_ccepp-publications/copy_of_IncomeInequalityandGrowthPaperWP0115.pdf

McGowan, M. A., Andrews, D., & Millot, V. (2017). *The Walking Dead? Zombie Firms and Productivity Performance in OECD Countries*. Available at: http://www.oecd.org/economy/growth/The-Walking-Dead-Zombie-Firms-and-Productivity-Performance-in-OECD-Countries.pdf

McKinsey Global Institute. (2011). *Why US Productivity Can Grow Without Killing Jobs*. Available at: https://www.mckinsey.com/~/media/McKinsey/Featured%20Insights/Employment%20and%20Growth/Why%20US%20productivity%20can%20grow%20without%20killing%20jobs/Why%20US%20productivity%20can%20grow%20without%20killing%20jobs.ashx

McKinsey Global Institute. (2016). *Secular Stagnation and Low Investment: Breaking the Vicious Cycle*. Available at: https://www.mckinsey.com/~/media/McKinsey/Featured%20Insights/Europe/Secular%20stagnation%20and%20low%20investment%20Breaking%20the%20vicious%20cycle/Secular-stagnation-and-low-investment-Breaking-the-vicious-cycle-Working-paper.ashx

McKinsey Global Institute. (2017). *The Productivity Puzzle: A Closer Look at the United State*. Available at: https://www.mckinsey.com/~/media/mckinsey/featured%20insights/employment%20and%20growth/new%20insights%20into%20the%20slowdown%20in%20us%20productivity%20growth/mgi-the-productivity-puzzle-discussion-paper.ashx

Mitchell, S. (2016). *Monopoly Power and the Decline of Small Business*. Available at: https://ilsr.org/wp-content/uploads/downloads/2016/08/MonopolyPower-SmallBusiness.pdf

OECD. (2017). *The Great Divergence(s)*. Available at: https://www.oecd-ilibrary.org/docserver/953f3853-en.pdf?expires=1581891025&id=id&accname=guest&checksum=E5AADC1EF94434728D27FEB3309413EE

Okun, A. (1975). *Equality and Efficiency: The Big Trade off*. Washington, DC: Brookings.

Oulton, N. (2018). *The UK Productivity Puzzle: Does Arthur Lewis Hold the Key?* Centre for Macroeconomics, LSE. Available at: https://scholar.harvard.edu/files/jorgenson/files/pl05b_oulton.pdf

Pessoa, J. P., & Van Reenen, J. (2013). *Wage Growth and Productivity Growth: The Myth and Reality of Decoupling*. Available at: http://cep.lse.ac.uk/pubs/download/cp401.pdf

Qureshi, Z. (2017). *The Age of Perplexity: Rethinking the World we Knew. Advanced Tech, But Growth Slow and Unequal: Paradoxes and Policies*. Bilbao/Madrid, Spain: BBVA, OpenMind, Penguin Random House Grupo Editorial.

Qureshi, Z., & Dervis, K. (2019). *Overview: Booming Technology, Slowing Productivity and Rising Inequality*. Available at: https://www.brookings.edu/wp-content/uploads/2019/05/productive_equity_190522.pdf

Ramsden, D. (2018). *The UK's Productivity Growth Challenge*. Available at: https://www.bankofengland.co.uk/-/media/boe/files/speech/2018/the-uks-productivity-growth-challenge

Roberts, M. (2016). *The Long Depression: How It Happened, Why It Happened, and What Happens Next?* Chicago: Haymarket Books.

Roberts, M. (2019). *Productivity, Investment and Profitability*. Available at: https://thenextrecession.wordpress.com/2019/05/11/productivity-investment-and-profitability/

Roland, I. (2018). *Unlocking SME Productivity, Review of Recent Evidence and Implications for the UK's Industrial Strategy*. Available at: http://cep.lse.ac.uk/pubs/download/is05.pdf

Ruiz Caro, A. (2020). *The Dramatic Fall of Chile as Latin America's Neoliberal Role Model*. Available at: https://www.counterpunch.org/2020/02/05/the-dramatic-fall-of-chile-as-latin-americas-neoliberal-role-model/

Sablik, T., & Trachter, N. (2019). *Are Markets Becoming Less Competitive?*. Available at: https://www.richmondfed.org/-/media/richmondfedorg/publications/research/economic_brief/2019/pdf/eb_19-06.pdf

Salti, N. (2019). *No Country for Poor Man: How Lebanon's Debt Has Exacerbated Inequality*. Available at: https://carnegieendowment.org/files/8-8-19_Salti_Inequality.pd

Schneider, P. (2018). *Decomposing Differences in Productivity Distribution*. Available at: https://www.bankofengland.co.uk/-/media/boe/files/working-paper/2018/decomposing-differences-in-productivity-distributions.pdf?la=en&hash=3875660487AD8ADF2D1A98553169940541 16CF65

Schwellnus, C., Kappeler, A., & Pionnier, P. (2017). *Decoupling of Wages from Productivity: Macro-Level Facts* (OECD Economics Department Working Papers, No. 1373). Available at: https://doi.org/10.1787/d4764493-en.

Sisson, K. (2014). *The UK Productivity Puzzle- Is Employment Relations the Missing Piece?* Available at: https://archive.acas.org.uk/media/4129/The-UK-Productivity-Puzzle%2D%2D-is-employment-relations-the-missing-piece/pdf/The-UK-Productivity-Puzzle-is-employment-relations-the-missing-piece.pdf

Sumner, J., & Blond, P. (2018). *A New Bargain: People, Productivity and Prosperity*. Available at: https://www.respublica.org.uk/wp-content/uploads/2018/03/A_New_bargain-ResPublica-Report.pdf

Szczepanski, M. (2018). *The Productivity Riddle: Supporting Long-Term Economic Growth in the EU*. Available at: https://www.europarl.europa.eu/RegData/etudes/BRIE/2018/630319/EPRS_BRI(2018)630319_EN.pdf

Taylor, L., & Omer, O. (2018). *Race to the Bottom: Low Productivity, Market Power, and Lagging Wages*. Available at: https://www.ineteconomics.org/uploads/papers/Lance-Taylor-Race-to-Bottom.pdf

Tenreyro, S. (2018). *The Fall in Productivity Growth: Causes and Implications*. Available at: https://www.bankofengland.co.uk/-/media/boe/files/speech/2018/the-fall-in-productivity-growth-causes-and-implications

The IPPR. (2017). *Why the Adult Skills System Is Failing to Build an Economy that Works for Everyone*. Available at: https://www.ippr.org/files/publications/pdf/skills-2030_Feb2017.pdf

The IPPR. (2018). *Prosperity and Justice, A Plan for the New Economy*. Available at: https://www.ippr.org/files/2018-10/cej-final-summary.pdf

Tily, G. (2017). *Productivity: The Long Global View*. Available at: https://touchstoneblog.org.uk/2017/05/productivity-the-long-global-view/

Tomorrow's Company. (2018). *A Question of Investment, Have We Stopped Taking the Plunge?* Available at https://www.tomorrowscompany.com/wp-content/uploads/2018/11/Investment-Report_.pdf

Tracey, B. (2019). *The Real Effects of Zombie Lending in Europe*. Available at: https://www.bankofengland.co.uk/-/media/boe/files/working-paper/2019/the-real-effects-of-zombie-lending-in-europe.pdf?la=en&hash=CCA9E1918D63205AA778C90D08681E8E44D57574

TUC. (2015). *Productivity: No Puzzle About It*. Available at: https://www.tuc.org.uk/sites/default/files/productivitypuzzle.pdf

TUC. (2017). *The Gig Is Up*. Available at: https://www.tuc.org.uk/research-analysis/reports/gig

Uguccioni, J., Sharpe, A., & Murray, A. (2016). *Labour Productivity and the Distribution of Real Earnings in Canada, 1976–2014*. Available at: http://www.csls.ca/reports/csls2016-15.pdf

UNCTAD. (2018). *World Investment Report*. Available at: https://unctad.org/en/PublicationsLibrary/wir2018_en.pdf

Yang, A. (2018). *The War on Normal People: The Truth About America's Disappearing Jobs and Why Universal Basic Income in Our Future*. New York: Hachette books.

5

Environmental Policies to Save the Planet

Richard Lewney

1 Introduction

Neoliberal economics has generally opposed or rolled back policy measures designed to protect the environment. In June 2017, President Trump[1] announced the decision for the United States to withdraw from the Paris Agreement, and in November 2019, Secretary of State confirmed that the United States had initiated the process of withdrawal (to be completed a year later). Burke, Hagen, Höhne, Nascimento, and Bals (2019) ranked the United States as bottom of its Climate Change Performance Index league table of 61 countries on a variety of indicators,

[1] It is debatable whether President Trump and politicians with similar convictions can be classified as 'neoliberal' given their predilection for protectionism in trade policy. But they do share and draw support from the neoliberal suspicion of strong government intervention when it comes to environmental policy.

R. Lewney (✉)
Cambridge Econometrics and Cambridge Trust for New Thinking in Economics, Cambridge, UK
e-mail: rl@camecon.com

P. Arestis, M. Sawyer (eds.), *Economic Policies for a Post-Neoliberal World*, International Papers in Political Economy, https://doi.org/10.1007/978-3-030-56735-4_5

including a 20% weighting for policy. Australia remains a signatory to the Paris Agreement, but ranked 56 out of 61 in Burke et al. (op. cit.); in November 2019, the Swedish central bank announced[2] that it had divested from bonds issued by the states of Queensland and Western Australia, also the Canadian province of Alberta, because of sustainability concerns. Brazil's President Bolsonaro threatened withdrawal from the Paris Agreement when running for office in 2018, but has so far decided not to carry out the threat. However, he has been openly critical of Greta Thunberg and vowed to reduce tribal rights to land and allow commercial exploitation of protected reservations.[3]

Neoliberal economics typically draws on neoclassical economics for intellectual support, although the two are far from coterminous. Neoclassical economics does not necessarily prescribe neoliberal policies, but its benchmark of perfectly competitive markets is consistent with neoliberal ideals. Neoclassical economics recognises environmental degradation as a classic example of an externality and frames its response in terms of correcting that market failure, but the limitations of its marginal cost-benefit approach have been exposed in the climate change debate. This chapter explores the role that the key insights of post-Keynesian and Schumpeterian economics (such as path dependence, radical uncertainty, the presence of heterogeneous actors, the role of money and finance, and the representation of endogenous technical change) are playing in forming an analysis of environmental policy that is better adapted to the challenge of tackling global warming.[4]

The chapter initially presents an introduction to environmental pressures, concluding that, among the various threats, climate change poses the biggest challenge. The relationship between neoliberal politics and mainstream (neoclassical) economics is then discussed and the response of the latter to the climate change challenge is critically reviewed. A subsequent section discusses possible technological pathways to reach

[2] Available at: https://www.riksbank.se/en-gb/press-and-published/speeches-and-presentations/2019/floden-riksbank-selling-bonds-for-climate-reasons/

[3] Available at: https://uk.reuters.com/article/uk-climate-change-greta-bolsonaro/brazils-bolsonaro-calls-activist-thunberg-a-brat-idUKKBN1YE27U

[4] See Pollitt (2019) for a modeller's perspective on the opportunity for post-Keynesian analysis to meet the needs of policymakers seeking to confront the climate crisis.

net-zero greenhouse gas (GHG) emissions by 2050. The next section discusses key obstacles to be overcome and policies to address those. The final section summarises and concludes.

2 Economic Development and Environmental Degradation

2.1 The Concept of Natural Capital

The concept of *natural capital* provides a framework within which to understand how environmental degradation affects *human* well-being.[5] The UK Department for Environment, Food, and Rural Affairs (2018) draws on the Natural Capital Committee (2013) to provide a succinct definition of natural capital as

> the elements of nature that directly and indirectly produce value or benefits to people (now or in the future), including ecosystems, species, freshwater, land, minerals, the air and oceans, as well as natural processes and functions. (Department for Environment, Food and Rural Affairs, 2018, p. 6)

Natural capital is therefore understood as one of four types of capital that provide services to individuals and society, the other three being:

- manufactured or produced capital (e.g. buildings, roads or machinery),
- human capital (e.g. knowledge and skills) and
- social capital (e.g. trust, behavioural norms and institutions).[6]

Natural capital provides *ecosystem services*, categorised in the European Environment Agency's Common International Classification of Ecosystem Services[7] into three broad sections. Table 5.1, taken from

[5] The concept of natural capital embodies an anthropocentric approach to the question of why we should take care of the environment. See Williams (1995) for a discussion of this ethical stance.

[6] Natural Capital Committee (2013, p. 10).

[7] Haines-Young and Potschin (2018).

Table 5.1 Sources of economic value from ecosystem services

Category	Example	Source of economic value	Direct implication of depletion/ degradation
Provisioning	Crops and livestock Fisheries Water supply Timber	Inputs to production/ direct consumption	Lower/costlier production
Regulation and maintenance	Air quality regulation Flood regulation Global climate regulation	Maintenance/ protection of human and physical assets	Impaired productive capacity Costs of defence/ repair Costs of alternatives
Cultural	Recreation	Intrinsic (amenity) value	Lost welfare/ well-being Costs of maintenance/ repair

Source: White et al. (2017)

White et al. (2017), shows the three sections and gives key examples of particular services that support human well-being, including economic activity. It also indicates the direct economic implications that might be expected to arise from the loss of each type of ecosystem service, as a result of environmental degradation.

To give some idea of the scale of ecosystem services (Costanza et al., 2014), and as IPCC (2019, chapter 1) reports,

> [t]he annual value of the world's total terrestrial ecosystem services has been estimated [in 2011] to be … approximately equivalent to the annual global Gross Domestic Product. (p. 81)

The stresses placed by human activity upon natural capital, and hence upon the ecosystem services it provides, come about through unsustainable use of resources (overfishing, overuse of ground and surface water resources, repurposing of natural habitats, forestland and flood plains for agricultural use or building, etc.), and through the unsustainable use of environmental sinks (disposal of waste pollutants at a higher rate than the capacity of the environment to process, absorb and render harmless the pollutants).

2.2 The Key Threats to Ecosystem Services

The latest in the European Environment Agency's (2019, p. 35 and following) five-yearly assessments of the state of the environment and prospective changes makes the following key points:

- Population and economic activity have put huge pressure on our planet's life support systems, reflected in climate change, loss of biodiversity and changes in the chemical composition of atmosphere, oceans and soil.
- More species are now facing the threat of extinction than at any time in human history.
- The period since the 1950s has seen an unprecedented acceleration in global temperature change due to anthropogenic greenhouse gas emissions, the result in turn of fossil fuel combustion, agricultural practices and deforestation.
- The plans submitted by countries under the Paris Agreement are consistent with an increase in global temperatures of about 3 °C compared with pre-industrial levels by 2100.
- There is great uncertainty over what change in temperature would trigger tipping points leading to self-reinforcing feedback loops, but some estimates are in the range of 2–3 °C.
- Europe's consumption of goods and services depends on the extraction of resources outside of the continent and so Europe is responsible for environmental impacts felt in other parts of the world.

Thus, while some improvements to environmental quality have been made in some countries, because of more stringent environmental standards (e.g. reduction in certain local air pollutants in cities in the West), the threats associated particularly with declining biodiversity and global warming are very high.

2.3 The Response of Neoliberal Economics

The 'neoliberal' label is used in a variety of ways. Here we adopt the definition offered by Castree (2010) for 'neoliberalism as policy discourse' and summarise it as the following agenda for government (Castree, 2010, p. 10):

- privatisation, including the assignment of clear, legally enforceable private property rights to environmental assets;
- marketisation: introducing market exchange, for that might not previously have been subject to a market logic;
- state roll-back or deregulation, including the contracting-out of delivery of some state services;
- market-friendly reregulation and tax policies;
- use of market proxies in the residual (non-privatised) state sector;
- strong encouragement of 'flanking mechanisms' in civil society to provide social support mechanisms that the state no longer provides; and
- creation of 'free', 'self-sufficient', and self-governing individuals and communities with a strong ethic of individual responsibility.

In principle, this agenda does not preclude the adoption of policies intended to meet ambitious targets to prevent and reverse environmental degradation, but it does circumscribe tightly the permissible policy tools used to pursue those targets (limited essentially to market-based instruments). However, there are two reasons why, in practice, neoliberal economics ends up with at best a very limited policy intervention for environmental goals.

Firstly, its philosophical standpoint gives primacy to the individual as the arbiter of value. If someone chooses to drive a diesel car in the city even in the face of a substantial hike in the tax on fuel designed to reflect the environmental externality, that shows that the cost (in terms of lost welfare) of a policy that leads or forces them to switch to a zero-emissions vehicle is very high. It makes no difference if the saving in their total cost of driving over time, suitably discounted, is greater than the additional purchase cost of the vehicle: the fact that they could have realised that saving but choose not to do so is proof that they prefer not to make the change. If they persist in driving the diesel car when the fuel price has been raised to reflect the cost that their behaviour imposes as an externality on others, that is a more desirable outcome than one in which policy leads or forces them to curb their emissions (say, by regulating the maximum emissions permissible from cars). The consequence is that, in a cost-benefit calculation, a high value is placed on *behavioural inertia*, interpreting it as a freely made, informed choice. If, in contrast, the behaviour has a more complex explanation that does not allow such a straightforward interpretation of welfare to be made, the neoliberal approach to welfare has an inherent bias towards the status quo rather than action to improve the environment. In addition, if a completely different ethical yardstick is adopted, the choice to pay a fine and continue to pollute may not be regarded as socially acceptable.

Secondly, it places a very high priority on individual freedom as against state action that limits such freedom, even if the action itself uses a market-based instrument rather than, say, regulation as the tool. Raising the price of carbon constrains the freedom of individuals to drive internal combustion engine cars, to travel by aeroplane and to turn up the heat instead of insulating their home. Raising the price of goods whose production is intensive in methane emissions constrains the freedom to eat beef and consume milk. The scale of state intervention required to implement widespread greenhouse gas taxes goes well beyond the minimalist state envisaged in neoliberal political philosophy. For the neoliberal, the individual freedom that has to be sacrificed is so precious that there is almost no prospective benefit that could make it a price worth paying.

In trying to reconcile an unwillingness to countenance the loss of that freedom with the prospect of an existential threat to human life, one solution is to deny the validity of the climate science. Hornsey, Harris, Bain, and Fielding (2016) undertake a meta-analysis of earlier studies testing for an association between individuals' characteristics and acceptance of or scepticism about climate change. and conclude:

> [T]he data suggest that 'evidence' around climate change is searched, remembered, and assimilated in a way that dovetails with people's own political loyalties and their worldviews. For some, this may lead to a disre-

gard for (or misunderstanding of) the scientific consensus around climate change. (Reported in 'Implications' of Hornsey et al., 2016)

2.4 The Response of Mainstream Economics

The best-known economist working on climate change economics from the mainstream neoclassical tradition is William Nordhaus, who shared the 2018 Sveriges Riksbank Prize in Economic Sciences in Memory of Alfred Nobel.

Nordhaus developed the influential DICE (Dynamic Integrated model of Climate and the Economy) integrated assessment model (IAM),[8] which combines an economic growth model with a calculation of emissions of carbon dioxide (CO_2) (which respond to a carbon price and the cost of abatement technology) and a reduced-form model of the consequent global warming and damages suffered. Society has a choice whether or not to abate emissions in any given time period, trading off the cost of doing so with the discounted cost of damages from global warming in the future. The model can determine the 'optimal' (within its own terms) rate of trade-off and hence the time profile for the carbon price required to prompt the necessary expenditure on abatement in each period.

DICE has a single-good neoclassical economic growth function, with population-driven assumptions for labour-supply growth and an assumption for total factor-productivity growth. Gross investment (and hence changes in the capital stock once depreciation is deducted) is determined by saving, where the saving rate is optimised over time (reflecting a choice made by consumers between consuming today or investing to consume more tomorrow). Hence, output is either consumed (providing utility now) or invested (to provide utility tomorrow). Assumptions are included for the time profile of carbon emissions produced per unit of GDP, and then an endogenous abatement factor is applied to determine the emissions that go into the atmosphere. The abatement factor is determined by a decision whether to pay a carbon price or invest in a zero-emissions 'backstop' technology which has an assumed (initially high but declining

[8] The first version of DICE was published in Nordhaus (1992). The current version of DICE is documented in Nordhaus (2018a).

over time) cost per tonne of CO_2 abated. Assumptions for land-use CO_2 emissions are added to give total emissions. A set of geophysical equations link emissions to temperature change. Finally, a damage function, with a quadratic form to represent a non-linear impact of temperature on damages, determines the reduction in GDP associated with global warming.

Critics of DICE, from the environmental side, regard its conclusions for mitigation action as insufficiently radical. Nordhaus (2018a, Table 4, p. 353) reports a 'no-policy' projection of a 4.1 °C temperature increase above pre-industrial levels by 2100 under 'best-guess' parameters, which is within the 3.7 °C–4.8 °C range for median estimates of temperature increase reported in the IPCC's (2014, p. 20) 5th Assessment Report. But the 'optimal' scenario in Nordhaus' (2018a) work has only modest mitigation measures producing a temperature increase of 3.5 °C, much higher than the Paris Agreement's objectives (well below 2 °C and towards 1.5 °C). In his own qualitative conclusions, Nordhaus (op. cit.) regards the implications of his work as supporting a call for coordinated global mitigation action in the form of a global carbon price, not a justification for inaction. However, he positions his analysis between the relatively weak action taken by governments so far and excessively ambitious (i.e. too much cost in the near future for too little gain in the long term) objectives such as those recommended by Stern (2007).[9]

Why might the conclusions from DICE understate the urgency for substantial mitigation action and the speed with which it should be carried out? The answers relate to: (i) the choice of discount rate used to weight losses of future consumption (due to damages) against losses of present consumption (due to mitigation); (ii) the estimates of the relationship between the scale of greenhouse gas emissions and damages; (iii) estimates of the cost of abatement/mitigation; and (iv) the treatment of uncertainty in the cost-benefit calculation.

[9] See also Nordhaus (2007, pp. 26–27) and Nordhaus (2018a, Table 2, p. 349).

2.5 The Choice of the Discount Rate

When Stern (2007) was published, an element that proved controversial was its choice of a lower discount rate than was used conventionally by economists. Since a lower discount rate gives more weight to the well-being of future generations compared to the present, it results in policy prescriptions with a greater emphasis on mitigation action.

Nordhaus (2007) argues for the 'descriptive'[10] approach in the choice of interest rate, which is to use the estimated real market rate of return on capital. The justification is that this approach captures the way people today behave when comparing the weight given to consumption now compared with consumption in the future. In contrast, 'normative' approaches like that of the Stern Review take an ethical stance that, according to descriptivists, governments impose on society's choices vis-à-vis future generations. The suspicion of government typical of neoliberal economics can be clearly seen in Nordhaus' (2007) characterisation:

> The *Review* takes the lofty vantage point of the world social planner, perhaps stoking the dying embers of the British Empire, in determining the way the world should combat the dangers of global warming. The world, according to Government House utilitarianism,[11] should use the combination of time discounting and consumption elasticity that the *Review's* authors find persuasive from their ethical vantage point. (pp. 148–149)

The Stern Review is therefore characterised not as a contribution to debate in a democratic society, but as the imposition of the views of an imperial elite.

Apparently reluctant to rest his argument about the appropriate choice of discount rate on political philosophy, Nordhaus (2007) does not proceed to the logical next step of making the argument that governments should respect the preferences revealed by the individuals who make up society collectively to value present consumption substantially more than future consumption. Rather, he seeks to distinguish his approach as one

---

[10] Following the terminology of Arrow et al. (1996).

[11] A term coined by Sen and Williams (1982).

of empirical realism in contrast to moralising that is irrelevant to the way the world actually works, hence the term 'descriptive'. Nevertheless, there is no escaping the need for additional justification for moving from 'is' to 'ought'. If DICE is intended as a model of how people actually behave, the 'optimal' path that it derives must be interpreted not as 'desirable' but merely as capturing the choice that actors would *actually* make to adjust consumption over time. Together with the associated social cost of carbon, this can only become a policy recommendation if we accept that the discount rate implied by the observed rate of return on capital is an *acceptable* rate by which society should trade off the consumption of future generations against consumption now.

Consider a mitigation opportunity that involves a consumption sacrifice of €1bn today to prevent damages worth €100m per year in perpetuity. The descriptivist's logic is that if the rate of return for that opportunity is less than the market rate, future generations will be worse off if society invests in the mitigation opportunity than in the alternative opportunity available on the market. Hence, the market rate becomes the benchmark by which any investment, including mitigation, should be judged. Society, the argument goes, should undertake mitigation up to the point where the rate of return falls below the market rate and then stop. On this argument, the discount rate applied to mitigation is not to determine the trade-off between consumption today and consumption tomorrow: that trade-off has already been decided by choice of how much to save. Rather, the discount rate is used to allocate scarce investment resources between mitigation and other kinds of investment. Future generations are going to receive income from the saving (=investment) undertaken by today's generation: it is just a question of whether they receive it in the form of reduced damages or higher GDP (arising from the alternative, non-mitigation investment).

However, can the market rate of return on capital be interpreted as representing society's preferences about the value of consumption today versus the consumption of future generations? As far as individuals are concerned, the long tradition in the literature on myopia in economic behaviour[12] casts doubt on whether the observed tendency to choose earlier over later rewards should be interpreted as a pure time preference (i.e. that individuals actually care less about tomorrow's consumption than today's). Gabaix and Laibson (2017) develop a model in which *imperfect information* leads a 'perfectly patient' (i.e. with zero pure time preference) Bayesian decision-maker to act as if they have time preferences, and that agents who are better informed in various ways exhibit less 'as if' discounting.

When behaviour is aggregated, there is clearly a problem with regard to who is represented in the financial market transactions that determine the market rate. For the generation alive today, wealth is very highly concentrated both within and across countries, and so the observed choices made in financial markets are not representative of the general population. Even if they were, future generations are not represented at all. The calculation based on the rate of return in capital markets of any trade-off between consumption today and consumption tomorrow is, at best, lifetime consumption smoothing for relatively wealthy individuals who are not infinitely lived (but may, if they are wealthy enough, make some allowance to provide an inheritance for children and grandchildren).

Thirdly, if we abandon the notion that the rate of return in capital markets is the price that clears the market for saving (sacrificed consumption) and investment in favour of one in which the supply of investible funds depends upon the creation of money by private banking institutions, the observed rate of return can no longer be interpreted as a measure of society's willingness to trade off consumption today against consumption tomorrow. Rather, it is a measure of the extent to which expected returns exceed banks' cost of capital, in which the rate of interest that has to be paid to depositors (the price that could influence consumption/saving decisions) plays only a small part.

The choice by neoclassical economists of the market rate of return as the discount rate to use in assessment of environmental policy, therefore, builds in a bias towards today's consumption versus tomorrow's, and

[12] See, for example, Kahneman and Lovallo (1993), Larson, List, and Metcalfe (2016), and Thaler, Tversky, Kahneman, and Schwartz (1997).

against mitigation action, consistent with the limited 'optimal' scenario recommended by Nordhaus (2007).

2.6 The Damages That Will Arise from GHG Emissions

Even if a zero pure time preference rate is accepted, the discount rate used in cost-benefit analysis (CBA) also incorporates[13] a factor that captures diminishing marginal returns to additional consumption, or, equivalent in the mathematics but more relevant for environmental policy, the idea that an additional unit of consumption is worth more to the poor than to the rich (and that social welfare is treated as an aggregation of individuals' utility). If economic growth permits per capita consumption to be higher in the future than today, and if mitigation action imposes costs on today's generation (see below on each of these assumptions), the impact of the policy is to transfer consumption from this generation (including the population of poor countries) to its richer descendants. Unabated carbon emissions may increase the number of very hot days in what are currently temperate climates, but (so the argument goes) those who suffer the consequences will be better able to afford air conditioning than their parents and grandparents were able to afford abatement measures.

An external critique of that argument is that it accepts the premise built into IAMs like DICE that we value climate damages on the same scale as consumption so that they can be traded off against each other, rather than treating them as incommensurable.[14] An alternative approach, and the one effectively adopted by the governments that have committed to the most ambitious targets for climate change mitigation, is to set an objective for the time profile of net emissions and to rank alternative pathways to achieve that objective according to the each pathway's economic and social impacts.

---

[13] In the formula developed by Ramsey (1928).

[14] One way of extending CBA under these circumstances is to use multi-criteria decision analysis, an approach now included in the UK government's economist's toolkit. Available at: https://www.gov.uk/government/publications/green-book-supplementary-guidance-multi-criteria-decision-analysis

Within its own terms, the argument assumes that mitigation undertaken in the present period imposes a cost on consumers in the present period. Even if mitigation comes at a cost (see discussion below), the measures could, of course, be funded by borrowing so that the cost is spread at least partly over future generations. An obvious example is the cost of investment in a power generation plant based on renewable sources, for which future electricity consumers will pay the debt servicing costs in their electricity bills over the life of the plant. IAMs like DICE do not represent the role of finance in spreading repayments explicitly; if saving determines investment in the present period, then there is no need to take account of borrowing: those who are funding the loans must cut their consumption to effectively support the consumption of those for whom the cost burden is deferred.

The argument also depends on the assumption of continued growth in per capita consumption under business-as-usual (so that future generations are richer) and on the scale of damages that mitigation would avoid. The DICE quadratic damage function is quadratic in temperature increase, meaning that there is a non-linear (accelerating) impact on GDP as temperature rises. However, the scale of impact is relatively modest: 2.1% of global income at a 3 °C warming, and 8.5% of income at a 6 °C warming (Nordhaus, 2017).

Strikingly, even analysis that yields a damage function with similar modest impacts at a national level can comprise much larger impacts at the regional or local level. Hsiang et al. (2017) report a negative correlation between county-level damage impacts and per capita incomes, with damages in 2100 in the range 2%–20% of county income for what are currently the poorest third of counties under business-as-usual emissions.

Weitzman (2009) notes that any extrapolation to high-temperature outcomes of a damage function that fits low-temperature conditions, including the quadratic form assumed in DICE and other IAMs, is highly uncertain:

> High-temperature damages extrapolated from a low-temperature damages function are remarkably sensitive to assumed functional forms and parameter combinations because almost anything can be made to fit the low temperature damages assumed by the modeler. Most IAM damages func-

> tions reduce welfare-equivalent consumption by a quadratic-polynomial multiplier equivalent to $1/[1 + \gamma(\Delta T)^2]$, with γ calibrated to some postulated loss for $\Delta T \approx 2^\circ C - 3^\circ C$. There was never any more compelling rationale for this particular loss function than the comfort that economists feel from having worked with it before. (p. 16)

Burke, Hsiang, and Miguel (2015) use the World Bank country-level panel data for 166 countries over 1960–2010 and find that

> the slope of the damage function is large even for slight warming, generating expected costs of climate change 2.5–100 times larger than prior estimates for 2°C warming, and at least 2.5 times larger for higher temperatures. (p. 239)

Burke et al. (2019) follow this up with a panel data study of 11,000 districts across 37 countries, arguing that a more granular geographical approach allows for more precise estimates than using country averages (in which within-country variations are lost). The implications for the relationship between GDP and temperature change are similar to those in the earlier relevant study.

Burke et al. (2015) note that the estimates are conservative in the sense that these kinds of damage function equations, estimated over historical data (as is the case also for the IAMs), yield estimates that

> are based only on temperature effects (or effects for which historical temperature has been a proxy), and so do not include other potential sources of economic loss associated with climate change, such as tropical cyclones or sea-level rise. (p. 239)

Keen (2019) argues that the exclusion of these kinds of system effects is the critical weakness in the Nordhaus approach. Even wide variations in temperature across places during a period in which global temperatures are less than 1 °C higher than pre-industrial levels do not provide a representative evidence base for the kind of damages that could occur when global temperatures are, say, 4 °C higher than pre-industrial levels: the geophysical consequences are different when there is so much more energy stored up in the system. However, Nordhaus (2007) recognises that the form of the damage function used in DICE (and other IAMs) does not include sharp thresholds or tipping points, and justifies this on the basis of a reference to a literature survey which Keen (2019) identifies as Lenton et al. (2008). Keen (2019) cites text from Lenton et al. (2008) to show that the reference actually warns *against* smooth projections of climate change and explores various potential tipping points. Keen (2019) concludes:

> So the very reference that Nordhaus uses to justify **not** having a tipping point in his Damage Function establishes that *his Damage Function should have a tipping point.* (Emphasis in the original)

Nordhaus (2007) himself acknowledges that the optimal policy conclusions from DICE would change radically if damage impacts were higher/non-linear for temperature increases above 2 °C, although he does not regard current damages studies as supporting either of these (IRENA, 2019). Dietz and Stern (2015) provide a demonstration that, indeed, the implied optimal policy recommendation from DICE is for much stronger action if DICE is amended to include a stronger non-linear response of GDP to warming, a mechanism for endogenous technical change/growth and an explicit treatment of uncertainty over climate sensitivity to emissions.

2.7 The Costs of Abatement/Mitigation

Reflecting the underlying assumptions of neoclassical economics, DICE assumes that mitigation must be costly: if a choice were available that could provide the same of higher level of welfare at a lower cost, agents would already have chosen it. The question then arises as to how to interpret the existence of 'no regrets' opportunities, the classical example of which is roof insulation, which typically has a very short payback period for owner-occupiers. Conventionally, the failure of some consumers to undertake such opportunities is interpreted as showing that the welfare loss associated with the inconvenience outweighs the value of the cost savings available or that the consumer's rate of time preference is very high (so that future energy bill savings count for little). Hence, *by assumption*, mitigation measures must be welfare-reducing (before taking account of the environmental benefits of reduced emissions).

Inertia in take-up of mitigation options combines with endogeneity in technological change to produce pathways for mitigation in which costs are strongly path-dependent. The outstanding example in renewable energy is the dramatic fall in the costs of solar photovoltaic technology (PV) over the last two decades, as a direct result of greater sales. The idea that solar PV would already be competitive with fossil fuel generation in many situations (IRENA, 2019) would have seemed ridiculously optimistic even a decade ago.

However, even relying on conventional IAMs, IPCC (2014, p. 24) reported mitigation costs that are small in the context of expectations of long-term income and consumption growth (a median estimate of 4.8% of 'business-as-usual' (BAU) consumption in 2100).

2.8 The Treatment of Uncertainty

Nordhaus (2007) places considerable emphasis on uncertainty in his analysis, but not the consequences of uncertainty for the behaviour of agents in the economy and society. Rather, his treatment of uncertainty relates to *parameter uncertainty*, and he examines the consequences for the key outputs of his model (such as the social cost of carbon) of different draws from probability distributions assumed for parameter estimates. As far as it goes, this is clearly a commendable approach, acknowledging the uncertainty that the modeller faces in trying to predict the future. However, if the modeller faces uncertainty about the future, so do the agents whose behaviour the modeller is seeking to capture, and so it is inconsistent not to incorporate that uncertainty into the representation of behaviour and the interpretation of elasticities.

Weitzman (2007) shows how the motivation for mitigation is affected by a recognition that the scale of impact of future warming is uncertain:

> The basic issue here is that spending money to slow global warming should perhaps not be conceptualized primarily as being about consumption smoothing as much as being about how much insurance to buy to offset the small chance of a ruinous catastrophe that is difficult to compensate by ordinary savings. (p. 703)

Daniel et al. (2019) pursue this idea, drawing on the financial economics literature for decision-making under risk and uncertainty. In contrast to the implications of DICE, their analysis suggests a profile for the carbon price that begins high and then is likely to decline over time as the insurance value of mitigation falls (we know, increasingly over time, the extent and impact of global warming) and technological change makes emissions cuts cheaper.

Nevertheless, uncertainty in the behaviour of economic agents extends much further, into decisions to take up and to commit finance to new (and therefore unfamiliar) technology. If there is an uncertainty penalty for new, clean technologies, we can no longer interpret low responses to carbon price signals as indicating the preferences of fully informed, rational individuals. In other words, what looks like a high mitigation cost in a world of perfect information (agents will not act unless the price signal is very high) becomes a case of herding behaviour (agents will not act until they see other agents doing so).

2.9 Is Raising the Carbon Price an Adequate Policy Response?

The policy recommendation of the neoclassical tradition emphasises 'correcting' prices as the way to address externalities such as carbon emissions. Nordhaus (2007) argues strongly for action to raise the carbon price, concluding:

> To a first approximation, raising the price of carbon is a necessary and sufficient step for tackling global warming. The rest is largely fluff. (p. 28)

Nordhaus is urging policymakers to grasp the painful nettle of raising the price of carbon rather than produce call-for-action soundbites that fail to include this essential step for fear of political unpopularity. Similarly Weitzman (2007), applauding the Stern Review's unequivocal call for a higher carbon price, argues:

> [S]teady pressure from the predictable presence of a high carbon price reflecting social costs (whether imposed directly through taxes or indirectly via tradable permits) would do more to unleash the decentralized power of capitalistic American inventive genius on the problem of researching, developing, and finally investing in economically efficient carbon-avoiding alternative technologies than all of the piecemeal command-and-control standards and patchwork subsidies making the rounds in Washington these days. (p. 723)

So, raising the carbon price is indeed a necessary step for tackling global warming, but it is far from sufficient, for reasons that neoclassical analysis typically ignores.[15] Reliance on this single policy assumes that agents are certain that the policy will be maintained, and even strengthened as necessary, in the future, so that they will be willing to commit to investment in long-lived assets. Imperfect information, uncertainty and institutional obstacles (where privately rented tenure is important, separating the dwelling owner from the household that would benefit from an investment in energy efficiency) act to make households less responsive to energy price signals, making a much higher carbon price necessary to squeeze out consumption. But the distributional impact of a very high carbon price will be severe, with a substantial increase in energy poverty, unless action is also taken to ensure a large improvement in the thermal efficiency of the homes that poor households inhabit. Some of the key green technological advances such as the dramatic cost reduction in solar PV, improvements in the energy efficiency of cars and the development of battery electric vehicles (BEVs) have come about not because of a commitment to a high carbon price but through a mixture of initial R&D support, regulation and a growing general shift in the public policy stance. To insist on reliance on the carbon price instrument alone is to misunderstand key features of the world we actually live in.

[15] See Grubb et al. (2014, Section 8.8, pp. 302–305) for a fuller discussion.

3 What Would Getting to Net-Zero Greenhouse Gas Emissions by 2050 Look Like?

3.1 Possible Futures

A number of different pathways to achieve net-zero greenhouse gas (GHG) emissions by 2050 can be envisaged, depending on the rate of change in candidate, and sometimes competing, clean technologies, and on the extent of changes that might occur in personal and social behaviour. The scale of the challenge also depends on what is assumed for economic and demographic growth over the period, since that increases the scale of pressure on energy and other resources that needs to be curbed.

The EU's long-term climate strategy (European Commission (2018)) presented five different scenarios for the EU that would achieve an 80% reduction in net GHG emissions by 2050 (hence falling short of net zero). All five scenarios involve almost complete decarbonisation of electricity generation, on the assumption that there is not sufficient progress in bringing down the cost and improving the efficacy of carbon capture and storage (CCS) technology for this to be applied to fossil fuel power generation on a large scale. Renewable technologies expand their share of generation dramatically and nuclear continues to play a role. However, the scenarios differ in the way that final energy demand is met. One scenario focuses on electrification of most energy applications, for example, with heat pumps and electric vehicles. Another focuses on the production of 'green' (by electrolysis) or 'blue' (by steam reforming of natural gas coupled with CCS) hydrogen by electrolysis and its use as a feedstock in industry, in space heating and in hydrogen fuel-cell vehicles. A third assumes that synthetic hydrocarbons in the form of both liquid fuels and methane are produced using electricity and CO_2 (sourced from biomass or direct air capture), and then used in the same way that their fossil fuel-derived counterparts are today. A fourth scenario assumes deep energy efficiency improvements across all sectors, including deep renovation of buildings and modal shift in transport towards more sustainable modes.

The fifth focuses on the contribution that circular economy measures could make via increased resource efficiency and recycling.

In order to make the further cuts in emissions required to go from an 80% reduction by 2050 to net zero, two further scenarios are produced. In one, a technology-driven solution is followed, with the most cost-efficient options from the first four scenarios combined with 'bio-energy with carbon capture and storage' (BECCS) plants to remove carbon from the atmosphere. In the other, the emphasis is on lifestyle changes, extending the circular economy measures to include changes in diet and transport choices, while natural carbon sinks are also enhanced.

In analysis carried out for the European Climate Foundation's Net Zero 2050 series, Cambridge Econometrics and Element Energy (2019) also developed a number of alternative pathways for the EU with the same distinction scenarios with high electrification of final demand and those with more of a role for hydrogen. The study emphasised the impact that demand-side choices have on the costs of the energy system, particularly a system dominated by renewable energy in electricity generation. Power generation is then subject to intermittency and seasonal variations in supply and lacks the flexibility to meet demand peaks provided currently by fossil fuel-based dispatchable capacity. The use of smart technology to smooth electricity demand peaks reduces the need for extra generation capacity to ensure adequate supply, particularly in countries with a cold winter that face a large power deficit on a cold evening. Battery storage, including vehicle-to-grid technology, can be used to achieve short-term load shifting. Investment in energy-efficient buildings both reduces peak demand and reduces the capacity required of heat pumps to achieve the required ambient temperature. The study also considered the need for seasonal storage of energy, to make use of surplus renewables capacity to produce hydrogen in summer and use it in power generation or direct final demand applications in winter.

On present assumptions, both the European Commission (2018) and Cambridge Econometrics and Element Energy (2019) find that scenarios with substantial behaviour change including deep energy efficiency, dietary changes and enhanced circular economy measures permit a lower-cost energy system than do scenarios that put most of the weight on technological solutions. The question, therefore, is the extent to which we are willing to adopt the behaviour changes or, instead, to pay higher energy costs.

In its global analysis, IEA (2019) has a Sustainable Development Scenario which achieves net zero by 2070 rather than 2050 with similar features to those already discussed for the EU. Electricity generation is largely decarbonised, but there is some CCS with fossil fuel plants in a few countries. Energy efficiency measures keep the scale of final energy use broadly stable despite economic and population growth. There is substantial electrification of final demand, substitution of hydrogen for methane and some CCS to capture industrial emissions. To go further, to stabilise the global temperature increase at 1.5 °C (50% chance), either a scaling-up of negative emissions solutions or shutting-down/retrofitting with CCS of existing fossil fuel power plants would be required.

IPCC (2018) reviews a range of model-based scenarios that keep temperature increase to 1.5 °C. It notes that scenarios that include a temporary overshoot in emissions (to permit a slower and, perhaps, less costly transition) rely on the future deployment of carbon dioxide removal (CDR) technologies, typically either BECCS or afforestation, to make up for the overshoot, and the availability of such technologies is far from certain. In summarising the findings of its review, IPCC (2018) notes the need for action in both energy and non-energy sources of emissions of all the greenhouse gases:

> Limiting warming to 1.5°C implies reaching net zero CO2 emissions globally around 2050 and concurrent deep reductions in emissions of non-CO2 forcers, particularly methane (high confidence). Such mitigation pathways are characterized by energy-demand reductions, decarbonization of electricity and other fuels, electrification of energy end use, deep reductions in agricultural emissions, and some form of CDR with carbon storage on land or sequestration in geological reservoirs. Low energy demand and low demand for land- and GHG-intensive consumption goods facilitate limiting warming to as close as possible to 1.5°C. (p. 95)

4 Obstacles and Policies

4.1 The Macroeconomic Impact

One of the key political obstacles to the transition to net zero is the fear that it entails a significant economic cost, experienced in constrained choices, higher prices, lower returns on investment, lower incomes and fewer jobs. The capacity of governments to protect or compensate losers would be reduced if the transition entailed a macroeconomic cost: it is harder to redistribute pieces of the pie if the overall pie is smaller.

Paroussos, Fragkiadakis, and Fragkos (2019) provide a review of recent studies that use integrated assessment models (IAMs) to assess the macroeconomic impacts of the transition. They categorise the studies into two broad groups according to the modelling methodology adopted:

> The first group includes IAMs that assume optimising behaviour agents that operate in a closed resource system (where capital and labour resources are sscarce (Type I–IAMs) … The second group includes IAMs that consider an open resource system with no capacity constraints (Type II–IAMs). (Section 1)

And their review finds:

> For green growth to take place, it requires that GHG emission reduction takes place at such rate that allows clean energy technologies to become market competitive, while at the same time sufficient financial resources at a low cost exist. The studies that find negative impacts from reducing GHG emissions attribute this either to the factor that clean energy technologies do not achieve price parity with fossil-fuel technologies or because there is no sufficient financing available that eventually puts a stress in the capital markets and reduces financing for alternate investment projects. (Section 2)

Hence, the answer to the question whether the transition would have a positive or negative impact on indicators of national economic performance such as GDP, or consumer spending, depends critically on what is assumed about the way that the economy works. Suppose that agents make choices that maximise their intertemporal welfare, and that their collective behaviour has no impact on the rate of technological advance in clean technologies. In that case, action by government to price the externality of GHG emissions into product prices or to regulate to prevent certain choices being made must result in a sub-optimal outcome (i.e. with lower welfare before the benefits of curbing emissions are counted in). And if investment is determined by an interest rate that equilibrates the supply of and demand for saving, then an alternative future with much higher investment in decarbonisation technologies must drive up the interest rate and crowd out consumption or other kinds of (and more productive) investment.

In the European Commission (EC)'s Long-Term Strategy, the estimates of impact on the level of EU GDP in 2050 in decarbonisation scenarios that meet 2 °C and 1.5 °C targets by that date range from −1.3% to +2.2% (European Commission, 2018, Table 12, p. 219). The small negative impacts are found using GEM-E3,[16] a hybrid global Computable General Equilibrium (CGE) macro-sectoral model, while the small positive impacts are found using E3ME,[17] a macroeconometric macro-sectoral model in the post-Keynesian tradition.

In its discussion of alternative pathways to achieving 1.5 °C target, IPCC (2018) does not present macro GDP impacts. Instead, it highlights qualitatively the potential synergies and trade-offs between the whole set of UN Sustainable Development Goals (SDGs),[18] an approach that has the clear merit of highlighting fundamental objectives (e.g. eliminating poverty, promoting decent work and living standards) rather than the means to an end represented by the GDP measure. It also forces attention on the extent to which raising GDP is likely to achieve those fundamental objectives, taking account of distributional considerations and impacts on the full range of ecosystem services. Of course, the impacts on SDGs depend critically on how mitigation is achieved. IPCC (2018) expresses the view that the synergies between action to curb

[16] Available at: www.e3mlab.eu/e3mlab/index.php?option=com_content&view=category&id=36%3Agem-e3&Itemid=71&layout=default&lang=en

[17] Available at: www.e3me.com

[18] Available at: https://sustainabledevelopment.un.org/?menu=1300

warming and the promotion of many of the SDGs outweigh the trade-offs (IPCC, 2018, p. 20), in part no doubt because global warming damages are estimated to fall more heavily on poor countries/communities.[19]

4.2 Winners and Losers and Higher Costs for Those Unable to Mitigate the Impact of Carbon Taxes

Unsurprisingly, there is general agreement that the transition involves substantial restructuring of economies. In the absence of economically viable technological solutions that capture, use and store carbon at the time of fossil fuel combustion or which extract and store carbon dioxide from the atmosphere, the economic activities that depend on the extraction, processing and distribution of fossil fuels must be phased out. Similarly, there are very significant challenges for energy-intensive industries that currently depend heavily on fossil fuels and for industries that emit carbon dioxide or other GHGs in process emissions: they must find alternative energy sources and ways to capture process emissions or we must reduce our use of their products. At the same time, the economic activities that depend on the development and production of the green technologies and products needed to take the place of GHG-intensive activities would flourish.

Even models in the neoclassical tradition that find a negative impact of the transition on GDP can report net positive employment impacts[20] because their production functions include a substitution of labour (as well as capital) for energy, while models that find a positive impact on GDP also find a positive net impact on jobs. European Commission (2018, p. 226) reports net positive impacts on jobs for the EU from both GEM-E3 and E3ME. Models such as these that distinguish sectoral detail also capture the feature that output and job losses are mostly in sectors with low labour intensity (fossil fuel extraction, oil refining), while some of the sectors that gain have higher labour intensity,

[19] See the discussion of Hsiang et al. (2017) above in this chapter.

[20] Unless they assume full employment in the 'business as usual' scenario against which the transition scenario is compared.

particularly refurbishment to make buildings more energy efficient. However, there are counter-examples. The shift from internal combustion engine to battery electric vehicles (BEVs) involves a shift in the location of value added in the supply chain from engine to capital-intensive battery manufacture; BEV engines last longer and need less maintenance, and refuelling does not require petrol stations and fuel delivery. ILO (2018) provides global estimates that in a 2 °C scenario there would be an additional 24 million jobs in the sectors that benefit from the transition against some 6 million lost in fossil fuel extraction processing and power generation.

The transition would therefore create both losers and winners. The restructuring impact is made more severe by the fact that the activities that would be phased out tend to be geographically concentrated (regionally and internationally) either as a consequence of geology or because they are subject to economies of scale and so tend to have large plants that are major local employers.

The European Commission's Long-Term Strategy notes that there are three NUTS 2 (i.e. level 2 of the Nomenclature of Territorial Units for Statistics) regions in the EU in which the extraction of fossil fuels and the associated support activities account for more than 1% of the region's total employment. The area around Aberdeen in Scotland is particularly vulnerable, with over 11% of jobs directly related to the oil and gas industry. Silesia in Poland and SudVest Oltenia in Romania have a dependence on coal and lignite production, accounting for 5% and nearly 2% of each region's jobs respectively (and, obviously, larger shares in the particular communities where the mines are located). While fossil fuel sectors face job losses, energy-intensive industries, such as metals and chemicals, and motor vehicle manufacturers will need to transform their processes and products. The Strategy reports that there are 24 NUTS 2 regions in which these sectors account for more than 1% of employment, and the higher shares are in less prosperous Member States. In Strední Cechy in the Czech Republic, Közép-Dunántúl in Hungary and Vest in Romania, these industries account for about 10% of each region's jobs (European Commission, 2018, p. 232). The prospect of these kinds of job losses can be expected to lead to a strong political reaction in favour of political parties opposed to green policies: the success of the Alternative für

Deutschland party in state elections in eastern Germany has been attributed in part to reaction to the closure of coalmines.[21]

What these findings highlight is the critical need for policies to support reskilling of workers so that they can adapt to the change in the jobs market and to support the development of alternative employment in the localities whose economies are specialised in the vulnerable sectors.

Cedefop (2019) reported a review of policies to support green skills and employment in six EU countries. It found that all the countries covered had some sort of sector-based skills anticipation mechanisms, within which the particular needs associated with the transition could be included. Similarly, programmes for skills development for the unemployed or those in work existed, but most did not have a specific focus on green skills (Cedefop, op. cit., p. 14).[22] It remains to be seen whether, without that focus, these mechanisms would identify skill mismatches that arise during the transition quickly enough and steer funding into the training programmes that can meet those needs.

Examples of local communities whose social and economic life has been torn apart by the closure of a major industrial employer are not hard to find, with legacy effects that span more than one generation. Beatty, Fothergill, and Gore (2019) describe the continuing evidence of deprivation in the former coal fields of Great Britain, encompassing a population of 5.7 million (9% of the UK total), where major job losses in coal mining mostly occurred more than 30 years ago. There remains a large jobs deficit, with just 55 employee jobs per 100 residents of working age (the national average is 73) and low wage rates for those in work.

The biggest policy shift intended to anticipate job losses due to the transition came in August 2019 when the German federal government announced a €40bn plan to support coal mining regions over the coming two decades during which coal-fired power generation is due to be phased out. Elements of the plan include improved broadband access and transport infrastructure and locating research institutes and federal authorities

[21] Available at: www.bbc.co.uk/news/world-europe-49544781

[22] Exceptions to this general rule were reported for the French public employment service and charitable/not-for-profit organisations, for example, in the United Kingdom.

in the areas losing jobs.[23] In January 2020 the European Commission launched its Just Transition Mechanism designed to mobilise at least €100b over the period 2021–27 to be targeted at the most affected regions, including €30–50bn of grants to support reskilling of workers, promotion of new employment opportunities and energy efficiency investments.[24]

The question is whether governments have the will and capacity to bring about the transformation of opportunities in these regions. The Long-Term Strategy (European Commission, 2018, p. 235) notes that there are other prospective long-term trends, unrelated to climate change mitigation, that present significant labour market challenges. Illustrating this, Lewney, Alexandri, and Storrie (2019) undertake scenarios using the E3ME macro-sectoral global model to assess the potential impact of a radical acceleration in job automation and find much larger potential job shifts and losses than in climate transition scenarios. Job losses in industries vulnerable to the transition will likely be happening at the same time as widespread labour market restructuring, the social implications of which could prove to be a major challenge, perhaps *the* major challenge, to sustained political commitment to decarbonisation.

The restructuring will also require households and individuals to change the way that they use energy. There are technological solutions that would involve less behavioural change, namely to produce synthetic versions of refined oil and methane in a way that is carbon neutral (extracting the carbon from the atmosphere), but these currently look to be very expensive. The lower-cost alternatives involve a combination of heavy investment in buildings to improve their thermal efficiency and a switch to greater use of electricity or hydrogen in transport and heat applications. In some cases technological advances are likely to reduce the cost of the zero-carbon alternative to the point where it is competitive with fossil fuels so that users will be no worse-off as a result of the transition. However, this will be true only if energy users are in a position to make the change. Policy would have to ensure that the price of fossil fuel

[23] 'Germany to spend up to $44 billion to cushion coal exit', as reported in: apnews.com/f3e79e70c2e547428db34a9f1b073f42

[24] Available at: https://ec.europa.eu/commission/presscorner/detail/en/ip_20_17

energy products rises; anyone who continues to rely on those products for transport and heating and who cannot make their home more energy efficient would face higher energy bills. This threatens to penalise those in privately rented accommodation and those who cannot afford to pay (or arrange to borrow to finance) the higher upfront investment cost for zero-carbon heating and transport solutions even if the saving in running costs would ultimately pay back that investment. The *gilets jaunes* movement in France remains a powerful reminder of what can happen when a government seeks to raise the price of fossil fuels.

To tackle the threat of increased fuel poverty as energy prices rise, very substantial investment in housing is needed to raise the standard of thermal efficiency of homes (to reduce the need for both heating and cooling). This is clearly a case where market signals are not strong enough to promote change. In England, for example, less than 2% of homes are in one of the top two energy efficiency rating bands and the owner-occupied or privately rented homes tend to be in the lower bands (Ministry of Housing, Communities,, & Local Government, 2019). More worryingly, only 1% of new homes in 2018 were built to the highest Energy Performance Certificate rating (Band A), in part because policies to support low-carbon measures had been weakened (Committee on Climate Change, 2019, p. 11). The UK Committee on Climate Change (CCC) has recommended that retrofitting energy efficiency measures in existing homes be undertaken as a national infrastructure priority with substantial public funding. It has also called for new homes to be required to meet ultra-high efficiency standards and that, from 2025 at the latest, no new homes should be connected to the gas grid. Local authorities (the planning authorities charged with ensuring compliance with regulations) need to be adequately resourced to act vigorously to promote energy efficiency.

4.3 The Take-Up and Cost of Clean Technologies

The pace of decarbonisation clearly depends on the speed of take-up of clean technologies.

Take-up is complicated by the fact that many of the key physical assets have a long life: motor vehicles can remain in the stock for ten years or more, while the useful life of power generation plant, industrial plant and buildings is measured in decades. Decisions made now can lock us into carbon-intensive technologies just when the pace of decarbonisation needs to be stepped up. Shearer, Yu, and Nace (2019) report that while the rest of the world outside of China collectively reduced its coal-fired power generation capacity over January 2018–June 2019, this reduction is more than offset by the scale of new build in China:

> China's recent growth is due to a brief but massive spree of project permitting that occurred from September 2014 to March 2016, a period when the central government delegated permitting to provincial authorities who had strong incentives to approve and build coal plants to hit province-level economic targets … Today, 147.7 GW of coal plants are either under active construction or under suspension and likely to be revived – an amount nearly equal to the existing coal power capacity of the European Union (150 GW). (Shearer et al., op. cit., p. 3)

Shearer et al. (2019, p. 13) estimate China will only be able to achieve Paris-compatible reductions in CO_2 emissions from power generation if its coal-fired plant is retired after operating for just half of the normal lifetime. Similar issues arise for other fossil fuel assets. Mercure et al. (2018) estimate that the adoption of Paris-compliant policies worldwide could result in a discounted global wealth loss of $1–4 tn. The greater the scale of such prospective losses, the greater is the incentive for those whose wealth is at risk to commit resources to persuade governments to delay action.

The path dependence implied by technological lock-in is strengthened by the endogenous nature of technological change and the role played by radical uncertainty in decisions to invest in innovation and to adopt new technologies.

Heuberger, Rubin, Staffell, Shah, and Dowell (2017) provide a short discussion of the tradition of technology cost reduction and the cost learning curves that are included in empirical models in which technology costs are endogenised. They note a range of technology cost-reduction drivers, including: market push (competition driving investment in R&D), demand pull (the stimulus to technological development given by a step increase in demand, for example, through government R&D policy or subsidy) and process advancement (e.g. through the exploitation of economies of scale). All can support the general principle of a virtuous circle in which increased deployment and production of a technology stimulate further cost reductions and hence greater deployment and so on. The relationship between deployment and cost reductions may be non-linear and typically varies with the maturity of the technology. The case of photovoltaic modules has been extensively studied. Kavlaka, McNerneya, and Trancikab (2018) note a variety of factors that drove the 97% reduction in module costs over 1980–2012, with government-funded and private R&D the most important driver, while economies of scale became increasingly important after 2001.

Drawing on Grubb et al. (2014), Mercure et al. (2016) review the barriers at various stages in the development of a new technology following a Schumpeterian approach. They note that the costs of investment in the innovation stage are often considerably greater than in the basic research stage and so uncertainty over prospective returns is a key obstacle. They cite the analysis of the innovation chain for power generation technologies of Murphy and Edwards (2003), who identify a 'technology valley of death' for technologies that receive early-stage public finance but fail to attract subsequent private finance for the commercialisation stage.

Mercure et al. (2016) also review barriers to take-up of new technologies: the diffusion stage. Here, again, uncertainty is key, in that take-up is low and slow even when technologies are cost-effective ('no regrets' opportunities). A critical factor informing potential policies on how to accelerate take-up is recognition of the importance of heterogeneity among potential users of a technology. The standard S-curve of market penetration over time, in which adoption rates are initially slow, then accelerate sharply, then level off again, is understood to reflect the different attitudes to risk of different market segments ('innovators', 'early adopters', 'early majority', 'late majority' and 'laggards').

The lessons for policy from this application of innovation and diffusion theory to the case of power generation and energy using technologies are therefore as follows. The risk of lock-in is high because the technology assets have a long life. The players in the industry sector are typically large because of the economies of scale that are present in fossil fuel extraction and processing, power generation and energy-intensive manufacturing. Once technology lock-in occurs, these players have a very strong incentive to lobby governments to delay decarbonisation policy action and even to fund 'spoiler' research to make the scientific consensus on climate change appear to be less coherent. Hence, the technology lock-in leads to political lock-in: the time is never right for strong action. Because of the dependence of future technology cost reductions on the scale of investment and deployment, there is a potential virtuous circle to be triggered once deployment passes a certain threshold. However, firms and households are wary of adopting new technology until market penetration reaches a level that gives confidence, even it appears cost-effective. Similarly, financial investors require a higher risk premium for 'unproven' technologies (those with a lower market share).

All of this points to the need for decisive early policy action to head off lock-in, promote take-up of new clean technologies past the early adopter stage and trigger the virtuous circle of greater deployment, innovation and cost reductions. Once the barriers to a new technology have been overcome, government support can be redirected to less mature technologies. A policy approach that is limited to incorporating the climate warming externality in the price of fossil fuels would prove inadequate because it is not adapted to the dynamics of economics and technological innovation. While commitment to raise the cost of fossil fuels through a carbon tax is important to ensure that price and cost incentives are aligned with the decarbonisation goal, those incentives would fall short in a world in which people operate with bounded rationality in a context of radical uncertainty.

4.4 The Mobilisation of Finance

Most of the changes required to decarbonise the energy system involve the substitution of capital equipment for the burning of fossil fuels. In power generation, renewable energy sources such as solar photovoltaic panels and wind turbines have a high capital cost and low running cost (including a zero cost for the energy captured from the sun and wind). The same is true in road transport, where zero-carbon vehicles (battery electric or fuel cell vehicles) have a higher purchase cost but lower running costs, and for heat pumps in buildings. Heavy investment will be needed in energy efficiency, particularly to renovate existing buildings. Furthermore, the energy system will require substantial investment in electricity transmission and distribution networks to meet the much higher demand and investment in smart technology and in short-term and seasonal storage solutions to balance demand with renewable supply.

Some of this investment will take the place of what would be needed in a fossil fuel future. However, because the net-zero technologies are more capital intensive, the overall scale of investment in the energy system would be higher, especially in the period up to 2050 when the entire new system needs to be put in place. Estimates of what that level of investment would be vary quite widely, depending on the pathway by which emissions reductions are achieved. For example, 'reduce' measures (changes in consumer lifestyles and energy efficiency investments) permit lower investment requirements than 'pure technology' solutions.

For a 1.5 °C pathway, IPCC (2018) draws on existing studies to present an average estimate that annual global investment in the energy system amounting to \$2.4tn (at 2010 prices) would be needed between 2016 and 2035, equivalent to 2.5% of world GDP. This is a gross figure, meaning that the energy system would in any case require substantial investment in a 'current policies' baseline case (about 1.8% of global GDP) (IPCC, op. cit., p. 373), but the additional investment is still substantial. The figure is for the energy system (supply-side and demand-side) only. IPCC (2018) cites analysis by OECD (2017) suggesting that when investment in transport and in other infrastructures is included, the gross figure could be nearly three times the figure for the energy system alone. However, because cars have a shorter asset life than energy system equipment, much of that investment could take the form of substitution of the purchase of zero-carbon instead of fossil fuel vehicles and so the additional cost, relative to a fossil fuel future, would be much lower.

IEA (2019) presents an estimate of global annual investment needed in the energy system under its Sustainable Development Scenario, which achieves net-zero carbon emissions by 2070, consistent with limiting global warming to 1.65 °C (50% chance)–1.8 °C (66% chance). Over 2019–40, average annual investment of $3.2tn (at 2018 prices) is needed, including some $0.75tn in energy efficiency (IEA, op. cit., Table 7, p. 50).

Broadly, comparable figures to those of IPCC (2018) are estimated for the EU. In the analysis carried out for the EU's long-term climate strategy, European Commission (2018) presented an estimate for the EU that suggested averaged annual investment in the energy system of €550bn (2013 prices) would be needed in the period 2031–50 for a 1.5 °C, equivalent to 2.8% of GDP. This compares with investment amounting to 1.9% of GDP in a baseline that already includes some decarbonisation actions.[25] When transport investment is included, the annual investment figure rises to €1.4tn (2013 prices), some 20% higher than in a 'current policies' baseline (European Commission, 2018, pp. 201–202). EU Technical Expert Group on Sustainable Finance (2019, Table 17, p. 95) presents an analysis of the difference between estimated annual investment required under a business-as-usual scenario and various scenarios of greater ambition prepared for the EC.[26] By far the largest increase over business-as-usual, both in absolute and in percentage terms, is reported for buildings; 95% of that increase is expected to be funded by loans.

What are the economic implications of a finance requirement on this scale? In a traditional neoclassical model, investment must be 'financed' by saving in the same period, where 'saving' here is the national accounts concept: disposable income less final consumption. The rate of interest is determined as the price of saving that equilibrates demand (for investment) and supply. There is no role for banks (except, conceivably, as an intermediary between savers and investors, in the same way that a market stallholder acts as an intermediary between farmers and households).

Paroussos et al. (2019) cite the comment by Flaherty, Gevorkyan, Radpour, and Semmler (2017) that,

[25] The Long-Term Strategy baseline is a 'current policies' scenario, sufficient to achieve a cut in EU CO2 emissions by 65% compared with the 1990 level, rather than the reductions of between 80% and 100% in net emissions required to meet the Paris Agreement's objectives (well below 2 °C and towards 1.5 °C).

[26] The business-as-usual scenario is the Commission's REF2016 projection for energy use, and the scenarios with greater ambition are the various EUCO scenarios.

> [i]n most current models, the burden of enacting mitigation and adaptation policies falls on current generations. (p. 468)

which motivates a theoretical model designed to show that intertemporal borrowing through a vehicle such as green bonds would result in a Pareto improvement for both current and future generations.

In effect Flaherty et al. (2017) provide the motivation for modelling to represent a role for banking to allow agents in the present period to borrow on the expectation of repayment out of future income. Paroussos et al. (2019, Section 6) report the application of a hybrid applied CGE model that implements the possibility of intertemporal borrowing. That model allows three alternative macroeconomic closures for the treatment of the money supply: (1) money supplied by agents within the same period, (2) money supplied by agents across periods (implying a bank that creates money at the time of borrowing and then destroys it as the loan is repaid) and (3) 'unlimited money supply at exogenously defined interest rates' (in which all investments that are viable at the exogenous interest rate are funded). The latter two modifications, therefore, relax the constraint that would otherwise require that additional investment for decarbonisation must crowd out other investment or consumption in the current period.

A post-Keynesian approach to finance rejects entirely the notion that bank lending is constrained by the decisions of savers to supply deposits, which is why models like E3ME do not impose a trade-off between consumption and investment. For an individual bank, the deposit it creates for the borrower would, when the borrower spends the proceeds, become deposits held throughout the banking system, and so the bank needs to raise finance to replace its lost deposits on its balance sheet. However, for the banking system as a whole, the deposits that banks create at the time of initiation of loans collectively match the value of the new loans on their balance sheets.

Rather than channel saving to investors, banks bear liquidity and credit risk: they convert the risk attitudes of those from whom they raise finance (depositors, bondholders, shareholders) into terms that match the risk profile of those to whom they lend. For example, a bank chooses to offer loan finance to a customer to build a wind farm. The loan has a long term and there is some credit risk (moderated by the presence of equity investors in the same project). The deposit created by the bank is drawn on by the project developer to pay contractors, who in turn pay workers, who deposit the proceeds in (for simplicity[27]) the same bank. The workers are holding their additional wealth in the form of a demand bank deposit, highly liquid and very low credit risk (and very low or zero interest payable). The loan has created the deposit needed to finance the bank's loan asset. The bank bears some liquidity risk (because it has lent long-term but raised short-term finance) and also bears a particular form of credit risk (through exposure to the wind farm operation), neither of which is borne by households (except indirectly).

The critical issue is, therefore, not the availability of current saving to 'finance' current investment but rather, on the one hand, the willingness/capacity of financial institutions, and especially banks, to bear risk and, on the other, the risk profile of probable returns to investment.

The lessons for policy from this understanding of the role of finance is therefore to focus on: (i) derisking investments for which uncertainty is the key obstacle, notably policy risk, R&D risk and various aspects of technology risk; and (ii) improving the information flow to financial investors seeking to align their portfolio to a net-zero emissions objective.

Policy risk reflects uncertainty over the commitment of governments to decarbonisation. The United Kingdom has taken a strong lead in this respect and the Climate Change Act 2008 established a legal framework that probably sustained the policy commitment at times during the last decade when short-term priorities were focused elsewhere. Similarly, the EU's commitment to successively more ambitious decarbonisation targets provided important leadership in the 2015 Paris Agreement negotiations. Policy also has a key role in promoting the development of supporting infrastructure where it is needed to promote take-up (e.g. of BEVs).

---

[27] In practice, as already noted, an individual bank will not receive back all the deposits it creates from any loan it makes. However, collectively, the banking system holds the deposits that match all the new loans. If agents decide to repay loans rather than hold deposits, the deposits are destroyed and the banking system's loan assets fall by a matching amount. In an open economy; a country undertaking additional investment may see a deterioration in its balance-of-payments current account. To that extent, the initial deposits created by the loan come under the ownership of foreign banks who create matching foreign-currency deposits for the foreign residents who supplied the imported investment goods.

A whole-innovation chain approach to technology policy is needed. This includes R&D support for new technologies that are far from the market and which will be essential for long-term mitigation, recognising that some technologies will fail along the way. Nevertheless, the approach also includes incentives for early take-up of new technologies in the early phase of diffusion so that investors gain familiarity and confidence and risk perceptions are reduced.

There are signs that policy action is already shifting the market. Growing confidence in the prospect of sustained policies to promote the transition was reflected in Mark Carney's, 2015 speech (Carney, 2015) to Lloyd's of London when he was the then Governor of the Bank of England. This represented a turning point for the commitment of regulators towards the integration of climate-related risks into their financial stability monitoring and micro-supervision, a programme taken forward by the grouping of central banks and regulatory authorities, the Network for Greening the Financial System.[28]

With regard to improving information for financial investors, the European Commission has taken the lead in establishing a taxonomy[29] that is intended to ensure that investment products labelled as 'sustainable' genuinely contribute to achieving a climate-neutral economy. Outside of public authorities, the Task Force on Climate-related Financial Disclosures[30] has developed recommendations for voluntary climate-related financial risk disclosures for use by companies in providing information to the financial community, covering physical, liability and transition risks. In his annual letter to CEOs in January 2020, BlackRock's CEO Larry Fink wrote:

> Climate change is almost invariably the top issue that clients around the world raise with BlackRock. From Europe to Australia, South America to China, Florida to Oregon, investors are asking how they should modify their portfolios... And because capital markets pull future risk forward, we

[28] Available at: https://www.ngfs.net

[29] Available at: https://ec.europa.eu/commission/presscorner/detail/en/IP_19_3034

[30] Available at: https://www.fsb-tcfd.org

will see changes in capital allocation more quickly than we see changes to the climate itself. In the near future – and sooner than most anticipate – there will be a significant reallocation of capital.[31]

4.5 A Green New Deal

Many of the features of policy argued for here have been included in the various versions of Green New Deal proposals that have been advanced since the phrase was coined as a response to the 2007–08 financial crisis. All have had the goals of promoting the decarbonisation transition, achieving a just transition and creating high-quality jobs. In the United States, the Green New Deal resolution, proposed to Congress in February 2019[32] by Senator Edward Markey and Representative Alexandria Ocasio-Cortez, called for a ten-year mobilisation plan covering a wide range of environmental, economic and social projects. Senate Republicans blocked it in March 2019. In the United Kingdom, Green New Deal proposals were incorporated in the Labour Party's November 2019 election manifesto,[33] including a specific commitment to bring almost all of the United Kingdom's 27 million homes up to the highest energy efficiency standards and eliminate energy poverty. Labour lost the election, but campaigners such as the New Economics Foundation continue to promote it.[34]

A version that is going ahead is the European Green Deal[35] launched in January 2020, incorporating the European Green Deal Investment Plan, the Just Transition Mechanism and proposals for a carbon border tax to limit carbon leakage. This represents a significant policy development, but the European Commission has limited funds and powers to bring about many of the Plan's goals and much will depend on the enthusiasm with which Member States take it up and supplement it.

[31] Available at: https://www.blackrock.com/hk/en/larry-fink-ceo-letter

[32] Available at: https://www.congress.gov/bill/116th-congress/house-resolution/109/text

[33] Available at: https://labour.org.uk/manifesto/a-green-industrial-revolution/

[34] Available at: https://neweconomics.org/campaigns/green-new-deal

[35] Available at: https://ec.europa.eu/info/sites/info/files/european-green-deal-communication_en.pdf

4.6 Making Space for Conservative Environmentalism?

At the same time as pressure from the Left has mounted for a Green New Deal in the United States, the Climate Leadership Council (2017) launched a 'conservative case' for an escalating carbon 'dividend' (i.e. a tax in all but name) levied on fossil fuels to be recycled in equal shares to individuals, accompanied by a 'border carbon adjustment' import tariff. The plan has garnered significant support from former senior Republican politicians, business leaders and mainstream economists. Its proposals formed the Energy Innovation and Carbon Dividend Act of 2019 introduced into Congress as a bipartisan initiative by Representative Ted Deutch, a Florida Democrat, in January 2019. The prospects for the bill improved in early 2020 when Jamie Dimon, CEO of JP Morgan, embraced the initiative, now supported by Goldman Sachs, MetLife and ten energy companies, including BP.[36] The focus on carbon pricing alone makes the initiative more palatable to small-government conservatives, while the border carbon adjustment can appeal to the populist trade agenda ('We will call it a Trump tariff if this helps'.[37]). It remains to be seen whether Republican politicians and voters will coalesce behind the plan and whether it will be implemented at a level of tax that makes a real difference, given the prospective impact on gasoline prices and the fossil fuel energy industry.

5 Summary and Conclusions

The response of mainstream economics to the climate crisis has been weak, reflecting key inadequacies in its understanding of human behaviour, the consequences of imperfect information and radical uncertainty, the nature of finance and the contribution policy can make to reduce risk perceptions and the critical importance of just transition considerations in determining the social acceptability and hence longevity of

[36] Reported in Tett (2020).

[37] Tett (2020).

commitment to decarbonisation targets. Mainstream economics focuses on the carbon price as a sufficient policy instrument and this is misleading and uninformative to policymakers.

Mainstream economics assumes that the impact of environmental degradation can be measured in terms of lost human consumption and compensated for by higher economic growth. It treats the rate of return in capital markets as the measure of societal preferences with regard to consumption now or in the future, when most of the human population now and in the future play little or no part in the functioning of capital markets. It is far too sanguine about the scale of potential damages from global warming and is willing to stake the planet's future on the assumption that tipping point thresholds will not be crossed. In this it makes the dangerous mistake of treating large uncertainty (we do not know how close we are to the tipping points) as 'no evidence'. It assumes that mitigation opportunities necessarily represent a more costly path. It places a high value on inertia, interpreting it as the preference of an informed individual who takes account not only of their own welfare but that of future generations, instead of the heuristic response of an imperfectly informed individual faced with an uncertain future.

A serious response to the climate crisis necessarily involves substantial policy action, which, in turn, would accelerate the shift in financial markets that is already happening. It requires a focus on derisking key investment decisions. It requires a major commitment to mitigate policy impacts on energy poverty and to provide alternative, decent work opportunities for those dependent on fossil fuel-related jobs, or else social divisions will ultimately undermine political commitment. The challenge we all face is whether our political and economic system can find the way.

References

Arrow, K. J., Cline, W., Maler, K. G., Munasinghe, M., Squitieri, R., & Stiglitz, J. (1996). Intertemporal Equity, Discounting and Economic Efficiency. In J. Bruce, H. Lee, & E. Haites (Eds.), *Climate Change 1995: Economic and Social Dimensions of Climate Change* (pp. 125–144). Cambridge, UK: Cambridge University Press.

Beatty, C., Fothergill, S., & Gore, T. (2019). *The State of the Coalfields 2019*. Coalfields Regeneration Trust. https://www4.shu.ac.uk/research/cresr/sites/shu.ac.uk/files/state-of-the-coalfields-2019.pdf

Burke, J., Hagen, U., Höhne, N., Nascimento, L., & Bals, C. (2019). *Climate Change Performance Index Results 2020*. Bonn, Germany: Germanwatch, NewClimate Institute and Climate Action Network.

Burke, M., Hsiang, S. M., & Miguel, E. (2015). Global Non-linear Effect of Temperature on Economic Production. *Nature, 527*, 235–239.

Cambridge Econometrics and Element Energy. (2019). *Towards Fossil-Free Energy in 2050*. Brussels: European Climate Foundation. https://european-climate.org/wp-content/uploads/2019/03/Towards-Fossil-Free-Energy-in-2050.pdf

Carney, M. (2015). *Breaking the Tragedy of the Horizon – Climate Change and Financial Stability*. Speech Given to Lloyd's of London. London: Bank of England. https://www.bankofengland.co.uk/-/media/boe/files/speech/2015/breaking-the-tragedy-of-the-horizon-climate-change-and-financial-stability.pdf?la=en&hash=7C67E785651862457D99511147C7424FF5EA0C1A,29.9

Castree, N. (2010). Neoliberalism and the Biophysical Environment: A Synthesis and Evaluation of the Research. *Environment and Society: Advances in Research, 1*, 5–45.

Cedefop. (2019). *Skills for Green Jobs 2018 Update European Synthesis Report* (Cedefop Reference Series; No 109). Luxembourg: Cedefop. https://www.cedefop.europa.eu/files/3078_en.pdf

Committee on Climate Change. (2019). *UK Housing: Fit for the Future?* London: Committee on Climate Change. https://www.theccc.org.uk/wp-content/uploads/2019/02/UK-housing-Fit-for-the-future-CCC-2019.pdf

Costanza, R., Groot, R., Sutton, P., Van der Ploeg, S., Anderson, S., Kubiszewski, I., et al. (2014). Changes in the Global Value of Ecosystem Services. *Global Environmental Change, 26*, 152–158.

Daniel, K.D., Littermanc, R.B., & Wagnerd, G. (2019). Declining CO2 price paths. Proceedings of the National Academy of Sciences October 15, 2019 116 (42) 20886-20891; https://doi.org/10.1073/pnas.1817444116

Department for Environment, Food & Rural Affairs. (2018). *A Green Future: Our 25 Year Plan to Improve the Environment, Annex I Supplementary Evidence Report*. H M Government. https://assets.publishing.service.gov.uk/government/uploads/system/uploads/attachment_data/file/673492/25-year-environment-plan-annex.1.pdf

Dietz, S., & Stern, N. (2015). Endogenous Growth, Convexity of Damages. *Economic Journal, 125*, 574–620.
EU Technical Expert Group on Sustainable Finance. (2019). *Taxonomy Technical Report*. Brussels: European Commission. https://ec.europa.eu/info/sites/info/files/business_economy_euro/banking_and_finance/documents/190618-sustainable-finance-teg-report-taxonomy_en.pdf
European Commission. (2018). *In-Depth Analysis in Support of the Commission Communication COM(2018) 773 ('The Long-Term Strategy')*. Brussels: European Commission. Available at https://ec.europa.eu/clima/sites/clima/files/docs/pages/com_2018_733_analysis_in_support_en_0.pdf
European Environment Agency. (2019). *The European Environment – State and Outlook 2020*. Brussels, Belgium: European Environment Agency. https://www.eea.europa.eu/publications/soer-2020
Flaherty, M., Gevorkyan, A., Radpour, S., & Semmler, W. (2017). Financing Climate Policies Through Climate Bonds – A Three Stage Model and Empirics. *Research in International Business and Finance, 42*(December), 468–479. https://doi.org/10.1016/j.ribaf.2016.06.001.
Gabaix, X., & Laibson, D. (2017). *Myopia and Discounting* (NBER Working Paper No. 23254). https://www.nber.org/papers/w23254
Grubb, M., Hourcade, J-C. & Neuhoff, K.(2014). Planetary Economics: energy, climate change and the three domains of sustainable development. Routledge.
Haines-Young, R., & Potschin, M. B. (2018). *Common International Classification of Ecosystem Services (CICES) V5.1 and Guidance on the Application of the Revised Structure*. Nottingham, UK: Fabis Consulting Ltd. Available at www.cices.eu
Heuberger, C. F., Rubin, E. S., Staffell, I., Shah, N., & Dowell, N. M. (2017). Power Capacity Expansion Planning Considering Endogenous Technology Cost Learning. *Applied Energy, 204*, 831–845. https://doi.org/10.1016/j.apenergy.2017.07.075.
Hornsey, M. J., Harris, E. A., Bain, P. J., & Fielding, K. S. (2016). Meta-Analyses of the Determinants and Outcomes of Belief in Climate Change. *Nature Climate Change, 6*, 622–626.
Hsiang, S., Kopp, R., Jina, A., Rising, J., Delgado, M., Mohan, S., et al. (2017). Estimating Economic Damage from Climate Change in the United States. *Science, 356*, 1362–1369.
IEA. (2019). *World Energy Outlook*. Paris: International Energy Agency.
ILO. (2018). *Greening with Jobs: World Employment Social Outlook 2018*. ILO. https://www.ilo.org/weso-greening/documents/WESO_Greening_EN_web2.pdf

IPCC. (2013). *Climate Change 2013: The Physical Science Basis: Contribution of Working Group I to the Fifth Assessment Report of the Intergovernmental Panel on Climate Change*. Cambridge, UK: Cambridge University Press.

IPCC. (2014). *AR5 Synthesis Report: Climate Change 2014*. IPCC. https://www.ipcc.ch/site/assets/uploads/2018/02/SYR_AR5_FINAL_full.pdf

IPCC. (2018). *Global Warming of 1.5°C. an IPCC Special Report on the Impacts of Global Warming of 1.5°C above Pre-Industrial Levels and Related Global Greenhouse Gas Emission Pathways, in the Context of Strengthening the Global Response to the Threat of Climate Change*. Intergovernmental Panel on Climate Change.

IPCC. (2019). *Climate Change and Land*. IPCC. https://www.ipcc.ch/srccl/

IRENA. (2019). *Renewable Power Generation Costs in 2018*. IRENA. https://www.irena.org/-/media/Files/IRENA/Agency/Publication/2019/May/IRENA_Renewable-Power-Generations-Costs-in-2018.pdf

Kahneman, D., & Lovallo, D. (1993). Timid Choices and Bold Forecasts: A Cognitive Perspective on Risk Taking. *Management Science, 39*, 17–31.

Kavlaka, G., McNerneya, J., & Trancikab, J. E. (2018). Evaluating the Causes of Cost Reduction in Photovoltaic Modules. *Energy Policy, 123*, 700–710. https://doi.org/10.1016/j.enpol.2018.08.015.

Keen, S. (2019). *Playing DICE with Life on Earth: Nordhaus's Damage Function*. https://www.patreon.com/posts/26781733

Larson, F., List, J. A., & Metcalfe, R. D. (2016). *Can Myopic Loss Aversion Explain the Equity Premium Puzzle? Evidence from a Natural Field Experiment with Professional Traders* (NBER Working Paper No. 22605). https://www.nber.org/papers/w22605

Lenton, T. M., Held, H., Kriegler, E., Hall, J. W., Lucht, W., Rahmstorf, S., & Schellnhuber, H. J. (2008). *Tipping Elements in the Earth's Climate System*. https://www.pnas.org/content/105/6/1786. Accessed 14 Jan 2020.

Lewney, R., Alexandri, E., & Storrie, D. (2019). *Technology Scenario: Employment Implications of Radical Automation*. Eurofound. https://www.eurofound.europa.eu/sites/default/files/ef_publication/field_ef_document/fomeef18009en.pdf

Mercure, J.-F., Knobloch, F., Pollitt, H., Lewney, R., Rademakers, K., Eichler, L., van der Laan, J., & Paroussos, L. (2016). *Policy-Induced Energy Technological Innovation and Finance for Low-Carbon Economic Growth*. Research Prepared for Study on the Macroeconomics of Energy and Climate Policies. European Commission. https://ec.europa.eu/energy/sites/ener/files/documents/ENER%20Macro-Energy_Innovation_D2%20Final%20%28Ares%20registered%29.pdf

Mercure, J.-F., Pollitt, H., Viñuales, J. E., Edwards, N. R., Holden, P. B., Chewpreecha, U., et al. (2018). Macroeconomic Impact of Stranded Fossil Fuel Assets. *Nature Climate Change*, 588–593. https://doi.org/10.1038/s41558-018-0182-1.

Ministry of Housing, Communities & Local Government. (2019). *English Housing Survey, Headline Report, 2017–18*. Ministry of Housing, Communities & Local Government. https://assets.publishing.service.gov.uk/government/uploads/system/uploads/attachment_data/file/834603/2017-18_EHS_Headline_Report.pdf

Murphy, L. M., & Edwards, P. L. (2003). *Bridging the Valley of Death: Transitioning from Public to Private Sector Financing*. Golden, CO: National Renewable Energy Laboratory.

Natural Capital Committee. (2013). *The State of Natural Capital: Towards a Framework for Measurement and Valuation*. https://www.gov.uk/government/publications/natural-capital-committees-first-state-of-natural-capital-report; https://assets.publishing.service.gov.uk/government/uploads/system/uploads/attachment_data/file/516707/ncc-state-natural-capital-first-report.pdf

Nordhaus, W. D. (1992). An Optimal Transition Path for Controlling Greenhouse Gases. *Science, 258*, 1315–1319.

Nordhaus, W. D. (2007). *The Challenge of Global Warming: Economic Models and Environmental Policy*. http://www.econ.yale.edu/~nordhaus/homepage/OldWebFiles/DICEGAMS/dice_mss_072407_all.pdf

Nordhaus, W. D. (2017). *Revisiting the Social Cost of Carbon*. https://www.pnas.org/content/114/7/1518. Accessed 14 Jan 2020.

Nordhaus, W. D. (2018a). Projections and Uncertainties about Climate Change in an Era of Minimal Climate Policies. *American Economic Journal: Economic Policy, 10*, 333–360.

OECD. (2017). *Investing in Climate, Investing in Growth*. Paris: Organisation for Economic Co-operation and Development Publishing. https://doi.org/10.1787/9789264273528-1-en

Paroussos, L., Fragkiadakis, K., & Fragkos, P. (2019). Macro-Economic Analysis of Green Growth Policies: The Role of Finance and Technical Progress in Italian Green Growth. *Climatic Change*. https://doi.org/10.1007/s10584-019-02543-1.

Pollitt, H. (2019, May). *The Contribution of Post-Keynesian Economics to Climate Policy and Meeting Global Decarbonisation Targets*. Paper Presented to the 29th Annual Workshop of the Post-Keynesian Economics Society, University of London. http://www.perc.org.uk/project_posts/29th-pkes-annual-workshop-29th-may/

Ramsey, F. P. (1928). A Mathematical Theory of Savings. *Economic Journal, 38*, 543–559.

Sen, A., & Williams, B. (1982). *Utilitarianism and Beyond*. New York: Cambridge University Press.

Shearer, C., Yu, A., & Nace, T. (2019). *Out of Step – China Is Driving the Continued Growth of the Global Coal Fleet*. Global Energy Monitor. https://endcoal.org/wp-content/uploads/2019/11/Out-of-Step-English-final.pdf

Stern, N. (2007). *The Economics of Climate Change: The Stern Review*. Cambridge, UK: Cambridge University Press.

Tett, G. (2020) Wall Street is trying to catch up on climate change, Financial Times, 14 February 2020.

Thaler, R. H., Tversky, A., Kahneman, D., & Schwartz, A. (1997). The Effect of Myopia and Loss Aversion on Risk Taking: An Experimental Test. *Quarterly Journal of Economics, 112*, 647–661.

Weitzman, M. L. (2007). A Review of the Stern Review on the Economics of Climate Change. *Journal of Economic Literature, 45*, 703–724.

Weitzman, M. L. (2009). On Modeling and Interpreting the Economics of Catastrophic Climate Change. *Review of Economics and Statistics, 91*, 1–19.

White, C., Thoung, C. Rowcroft, P., Heaver, M., Lewney, R., & Smith, S. (2017). *Developing and Piloting a UK Natural Capital Stress Test*. Prepared by AECOM and Cambridge Econometrics, WWF-UK. https://www.wwf.org.uk/sites/default/files/2017-09/Developing%20%26%20Piloting%20a%20Natural%20Capital%20Stress%20Test_AECOM-WWF%20Sept2017.pdf

Williams, B. (1995). Must a Concern for the Environment Be Centred on Human Beings? In B. Williams (Ed.), *Making Sense of Humanity and Other Philosophical Papers 1982–93* (pp. 233–240). Cambridge, UK: Cambridge University Press.

6

Public Ownership in the Pursuit of Economic Democracy in a Post-Neoliberal Order

Andrew Cumbers and Helen Traill

1 Introduction

As we enter the third decade of the twenty-first century, the neoliberal order that has dominated global political economy since 1980 is increasingly being called into question (Bell & Christoph, 2019; Jacques, 2016). Overlapping and unresolved social, ecological and political crises problematise the dominant economic model of free markets and private property that has hitherto been the unquestioned governance superstructure for national and global elites. This was evident at the time of the global financial crisis but is especially the case, as we return to later in the chapter, in the failing efforts to tackle the climate emergency. It has also been

This chapter has benefited from funding under the European Union's Horizon 2020 programme, specifically the project 'MPOWER: Municipal Action, Public Engagement and Routes Towards Energy Transition'.

A. Cumbers (✉) • H. Traill
Adam Smith Business School, University of Glasgow, Glasgow, UK
e-mail: Andrew.Cumbers@glasgow.ac.uk; Helen.Traill@glasgow.ac.uk

P. Arestis, M. Sawyer (eds.), *Economic Policies for a Post-Neoliberal World*, International Papers in Political Economy, https://doi.org/10.1007/978-3-030-56735-4_6

sadly true of the slow responses by some governments to get to grips with the coronavirus pandemic. Cultural mindsets that have been forged through a period of deregulation, viewing human behaviour through the lens of individual rationality, and with a stubborn adherence to a business as usual approach and liberalised market solutions, have at times got in the way of collective responses, serious strategic planning and effective regulations and social institutions (see, e.g. Lent, 2020).

Nowhere are the flaws in market-driven forms of economic and social provision more evident than in neoliberal's flagship policy of privatisation. Its manifest failings to deliver affordable, reliable or sustainable public provision, particularly in vital services such as water, energy and transport, provide the litmus test of the contradictions of marketised and private forms of capital (Cumbers, 2012, chapter 2). Not only has private capital proved ineffective in providing the promised investments, modernisation and know-how promised in the 1980s and 1990s by Thatcherite dogma or Washington Consensus rhetoric, but overwhelmingly privatisation's mechanisms and modes of delivery have proved ineffectual in delivering effective governance and management, requiring constant change to counteract its contradictions. Its only achievement, when taken as a whole, seems to have been to greatly accelerate inherent capitalistic tendencies towards short termism and financialisation (Lapavitsas, 2013).

As privatisation fails, the presence of the state is gradually expanding, as both a social actor and increasingly critical institution, to processes of economic development. While the state—despite the early euphoria of market enthusiasts in the 1990s that it was withering away under globalisation—remained a key institution and arena for the playing out of political and social relations, from the 1980s onwards it was increasingly taken over by private and corporate interests at the expense of labour and the broader public. These interests were thus able to significantly re-write the rules of the global economy around free trade, financial deregulation and the protection of private property on behalf of vested interests (to use Veblen's, 1919, terms).[1] However, as the contradictions and serious flaws

[1] Writing over a hundred years ago, Veblen's term vested interests as those within a society who have "a legitimate right to get something for nothing" (1919, p. 169) seems prescient to our times. The vested interest is a way of seeing a ruling class as a combination of wealth holders who benefit from intangible assets without involving productive work. A range of contemporary commentators has

of these neoliberal rules have been exposed, the relations between state, society and economy are now being restructured and re-organised. On one level, this means a greater role for state actors and institutions in processes of economic development, signified by the growing role of state enterprises and corporate vehicles—such as sovereign wealth funds—but also in the increased levels of state investment driving infrastructural change and renewal. More worrying is the retreat from international and global rules and agreements, and the growth of far right nationalism and populism through which the state is increasingly being used to attack minority rights and pluralism on behalf of ethno-nationalist projects of "imagined community" (Anderson, 1983), and to the exclusion and demonisation of the Other.

The return of public ownership is one of the crucial elements of the quantitative and qualitative resurgence of the state in economic development. At a national level, this was most evident during the 2007–9 financial crisis when large swathes of the banking sector were brought back into public ownership around the world, as well as in the nationalisation of some key sectors and enterprises to keep them afloat (Cumbers, 2012). In the UK, there have also been 'temporary' nationalisations in the failing private rail industry plus the more permanent nationalisation of the track and infrastructure after the disastrous collapse of the whole network in 2002. However, there has also been a less widely acknowledged global trend for municipal authorities to take formerly privatised assets back into public ownership, at the local level, which has gathered pace since 2000 (Kishimoto & Petitjean, 2017).

In this chapter, we explore what the return of public ownership means for broader processes of economic governance. How does the trend sit with continuing stubborn adherence by political and economic elites (at national and supranational levels such as the EU and International Monetary Fund (IMF) to ideologies and policies of marketisation and privatisation? Moreover, what is the potential to create forms of public

---

of course made similar arguments about twenty-first-century capitalism (e.g. Hudson, 2012; Piketty, 2014). Effectively 'free income', and crucially, applies more broadly than Marx's category of a Bourgeois class to corporations benefiting from monopoly positions, landowners able to appropriate rent, or clergy or nobility who have a recognised 'customary' social claim to wealth and privilege.

ownership that are democratic and accountable that can be linked to advancing the common good over private vested interests? How might a renewed agenda around democratic public ownership assist in tackling key public policy questions, notably in dealing with the climate emergency? The chapter does not presume to offer definitive answers to these questions but rather seeks to contribute to the debate through a critical assessment of the possibilities inherent in the revival of public ownership. Nevertheless, it also assesses the continued barriers and constraints from oppositional power blocs (at national and international levels) wedded to a decaying neoliberal regime. Its arguments are developed through an ongoing engagement with examples from the energy sector, which, given its strategic role at the heart of the mainstream economy and the sphere of social reproduction, is seen as vital to the construction of progressive alternatives.

The rest of the chapter is divided into six parts. In the next section, we outline the increasingly evident contradictions and failings of privatisation and the way state intervention is returning in the economy. The subsequent section explores the return of public ownership particularly at the local level with the global remunicipalisation wave. We then explore the limits to a renewed municipalism through the lens of EU energy transition, focusing on its continued adherence to market-based rhetorics and policies and the subsequent constraints on local action. An alternative approach, centred upon Denmark's successful wind-power-based renewables transition, is used to highlight the merits of a non-market-based model of decentralised public and cooperative ownership. The penultimate section of the chapter engages with a number of other actually existing examples of public ownership and the Labour Party's recent proposals for the energy sector to set out some broader principles and values for twenty-first-century public ownership geared to the common good and tackling social and ecological injustices. The chapter then concludes with a summary of the basic themes and a call for greater recognition of the necessity of 'imperfect' solutions (whether planned or market-based) to resource allocation and the importance of democracy and deliberation in economic decision-making.

2 Privatisation's Contradictions, Failings and Mutations

Privatisation emerged as one of the key elements of the increasingly hegemonic neoliberal global policy tool kit in the 1980s, although beginning earlier with Chilean dictator's shock therapy privatisations after the military coup against Salvador Allende's democratically elected government in 1973. Under successive Conservative Governments, although it is worth recording that the Labour Government also sold shares in BP in the late 1970s,[2] the UK became the subsequent pioneer of privatisation. Accounting for 40% of the total privatisation of public assets across the OECD between 1980 and 1996 (HM Treasury, 2002) reduced the share of state-owned enterprises from 10% of GDP in 1980 to less than 1% by the late 1990s (Megginson & Netter, 2001). Although privatisation peaked in the mid-1990s, succeeding UK governments, both of the centre left under Labour administrations and recently under the Conservatives, have continued to be ideologically committed to privatisation and opposed to public ownership. While, as we detail below, the Labour Party has now endorsed public ownership, the Conservative Government remains ideologically opposed to it, although, as noted, it has been forced into emergency nationalisations within the rail sector.[3]

One of Thatcher's original stated intentions with privatisation was to create a shareholding democracy. This quickly fizzled out and, over the longer term, individual shareholding as a proportion of total shares has declined markedly, as can be gauged from the trends in the London stock market (Fig. 6.1). Privatisation has actually been associated with increased foreign ownership of the UK economy, having perverse effects in a growing presence of foreign state ownership in recent years, as we detail further below with regard to the energy sector.

---

[2] The 1970–74 Conservative Heath Government made some relatively minor privatisations of pubs in the city of Carlisle and the travel operator Thomas Cook (personal communication with Malcolm Sawyer).

[3] The government quietly carried out an effective renationalisation of the passenger rail network in March 2020 as a response to the coronavirus pandemic (Gill, 2020).

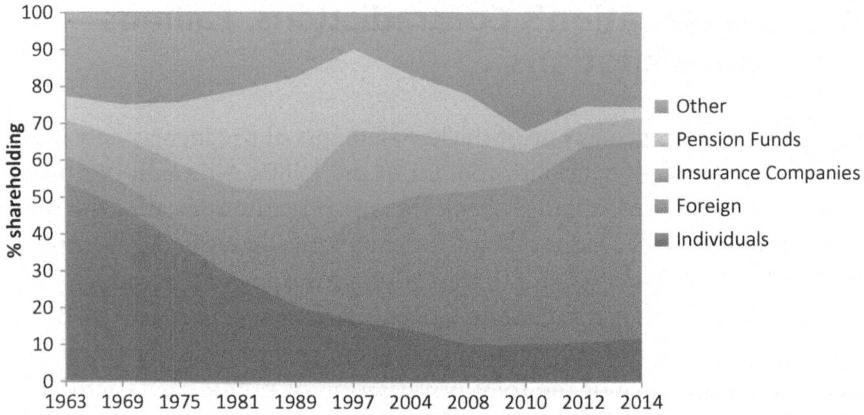

Fig. 6.1 Ownership of share capital in UK's quoted companies 1963–2014. (Derived from Office for National Statistics, Ownership of UK quoted shares: https://www.ons.gov.uk)

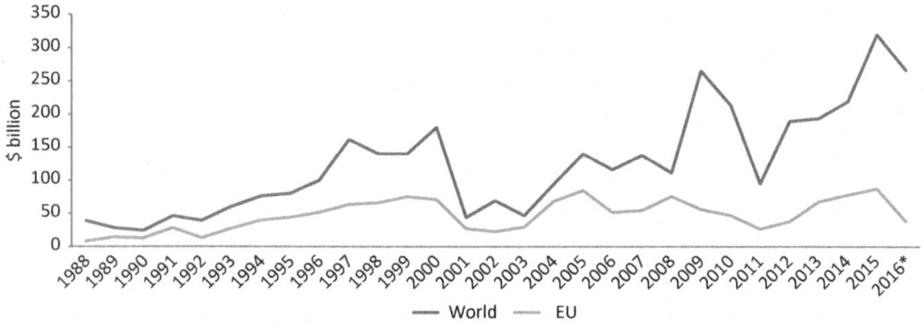

Fig. 6.2 Privatisation proceeds ($ billion). (Data derived from Privatisation Barometer: www.privatizationbarometer.net)

As is now well known, privatisation was rolled out across all continents in the 1990s and into the 2000s, becoming part of increasingly dogmatic neoliberal policy agenda; linked to shrinking state intervention in the economy and an economic governance mantra of reducing budget deficits (Fig. 6.2). Privatisation was part of the marketisation and deregulation agenda foisted upon cash-strapped governments in the global south in return for World Bank and IMF loans, with particularly disastrous effects and subsequent pushback and political mobilisation against it in Latin America. A particularly salutary tale comes from Ecuador where, in return for IMF funds in the 1990s, the country was obliged to accept 167 loan conditions that included axing 26,000 jobs in the public sector. Moreover, a halving of the wages of the remainder, an 80% increase in the price of cooking gas and the privatisation of its water system (Palast, 2000). In Africa, Tanzania was forced to introduce charges for hospital visits (at a time when 8% of the population has AIDS) and school fees, leading to a drop in enrolment from 80% to 66% (Palast, 2000). The privatisation of the capital Dar Es Salaam's water system in 2003 was reversed only two years later after a disastrous experience with the private consortium (Pigeon, 2012). In the post-communist countries, one mainstream economist (Goldman, 2003) referred to the imposition of shock market therapy and privatisation on the former Soviet Union and Eastern Europe as "piratization". The transfer of public assets to a small private elite, fostering growing inequalities, has resulted in an increasing scepticism about the liberal democratic model and contributed to the growth of autocratic states and right wing populism.

Countries that choose to depart from such policies risk either having investment cut by the IMF or World Bank or "disciplining" by now heavily integrated global financial markets.[4] In passing, it is worth noting that countries that have been able to pursue more developmentalist, "statist" planned approaches, notably China in the recent past, have seen the most dramatic steps forward in economic development over the period of neoliberalism (Arrighi, 2007).

For much of the 1990s and early 2000s, European countries also enthusiastically adopted privatisation (see Fig. 6.2), as much a centre left as a centre right project, as part of the EU's Single Market agenda to marketise and deregulate utility sectors. Despite increased evidence of poor performance and failure to deliver promised modernisations, it was also revived as a policy in the 2010s as part of the rolling out of austerity packages in the wake of the Eurozone crisis (Blyth, 2013), mimicking the policy prescriptions dished out to countries of the global south in the 1990s. Governments in Greece, Italy, Spain, Portugal and Ireland in particular were mandated privatisations alongside socially harmful cuts to government expenditure, public sector jobs and wages in return for

---

[4] See Fine and Saad-Filho (2014) for a useful recent summary and discussion.

financial assistance from the European Central Bank (ECB), IMF and European Commission.

While there is now very well documented evidence of the failings of privatisation (e.g. Bowman et al., 2013; Hall, Thomas, & Corral, 2009; Lobina & Hall, 2007) the UK provides the exemplar par excellence. Nowhere has this been more evident than in the disastrous break-up of the nationally integrated rail sector, where the virtual collapse of the privatised network in 2001 led to the renationalisation of the network operator Railtrack, and the regular take-back of passenger operator franchises, the most recent being Northern Rail in 2019. Bowman et al.'s (2013) forensic analysis of the effects of rail privatisation come to the scathing conclusion that "Rail privatisation created a situation whereby risk and investment averse private companies positioned themselves as value extractors, thanks to high public subsidies" (Bowman et al., op. cit., p. 14). While public subsidy has increased rather than contracted following privatisation, investment has slumped dramatically. To provide one example, investment in rolling stock in the five years prior to rail privatisation was over 60% higher than in the five-year period to 2012 (Bowman et al., 2013, p. 43). Despite such evidence, neoliberalism and privatisation dogma still reign supreme in the European Commission, where under the Commission's Fourth Rail Package, countries are forced to open up their networks to competition and the private sector by 2023.

Some of the greatest failings of privatisation are evident in the energy sector where key public policy goals are supposedly about delivering cheap and affordable energy to consumers, providing security of supply, and shifting away from carbon fuels towards renewable energy as part of tackling global warming. However, under the privatised regime that currently exists, the UK is monumentally failing on all three counts. Taking the affordability issue first, studies over a number of years have consistently concluded that electricity prices are between 10% and 20% higher than they would have been without privatisation (Hall et al., 2009). The distributional effects of privatisation have been particularly unequal. By the late 1990s it was already evident that the main impact of energy privatisation was one of "considerable redistribution between different groups" (Waddams Price & Hancock, 1998, p. 68); permitting corporate strategies of "monopoly exploitation" (ibid., p. 68) rather than the promised effects of lowering prices to all consumers. Privatisation permitted companies to develop differential pricing, moving away from an average-cost basis, which had allowed the cross-subsidisation of lower income groups under public ownership, to one that favoured higher income consumers by giving price reductions based on quantity used. One authoritative study found that poorer customers who use pre-payment metres can pay up to 40% higher in some parts of the UK, compared to those on direct debit (Thomas, 2008). One important effect in the gas and electricity sectors is that prices can rise during periods of peak demand, during wintertime, precisely when the poorest and most vulnerable groups need heating supplies the most. Furthermore, the UK has some of the worst statistics in Europe for fuel poverty. Particularly shocking are the number of pensioners that die from extreme cold every winter with rates for the UK as a whole double that of Finland, with its much colder winter climate, and far higher also than countries with similarly severe winter weather such as Sweden and Germany (Cumbers, Danson, Whittam, Morgan, & Callaghan, 2013).

Taken overall, the UK's energy privatisation stimulated the profit motive and short-term rent seeking at the expense of the most vulnerable groups, while also encouraging greater energy use rather than tackling stated climate change goals of reducing energy use and developing efficiencies. It has also had the effect of failing to deliver on the most basic of energy policy goals: "keeping the lights on", with massive implications for the UK's strategic energy requirements (e.g. Bradshaw, 2012). Under privatisation, and up until the establishment of the Renewables Obligation, which gave renewable power generators a financial subsidy, large established power utilities had little incentive to switch from conventional sources of power. Because they could make vast profits from the status quo, whereas they would have had to make massive investments to put in place the infrastructure necessary for renewables, the UK was for a long period Europe's renewable energy laggard.

Rectifying this situation, while continuing with the perverse logic of privatisation and flawed rhetoric of the 'energy market', has meant that given the lack of local capacity, skills and knowledge, the UK is increasingly dependent on massive government subsidy of foreign and largely state-owned enterprises. This is to deliver on its energy policy commitments, whether this is in securing energy supply or meeting its climate change obligations to decarbonise.[5]

Perhaps the best example of this is the decision to commit to a new generation of nuclear power plants (as part of the decarbonisation strategy) despite the exorbitant costs, social and environmental risks. The new Hinckley Point C power station, commissioned in 2016 at an estimated £18 billion (NAO, 2017), which when completed will deliver 7% of the UK's electricity by the mid-2020s, will be operated by a consortium of French company Électricité de France (EDF), which is 83.6% owned by the French state (https://www.edf.fr/en/the-edf-group/dedicated-sections/investors-shareholders/the-edf-share/capital-structure) and the fully state-owned, China General Nuclear Power Group (CGN). Although the construction of the power station is supposed to be financed by private partners, the guaranteed price for the subsequent production of electricity was agreed in 2013 at £97.50/MWh. This has been described as "ridiculous" by one energy sector commentator,[6] particularly when compared to the recent equivalent price guarantee to a new offshore wind farm on Dogger Bank in the North Sea of £39.65/MWh. In a somewhat damning indictment of the scheme, the National Audit Office in its report concluded:

> the [Business and Industry] Department's deal for HPC has locked consumers into a risky and expensive project with uncertain strategic and economic benefits. While committing the developer to bearing the construction risks means taxpayers and consumers are protected from costs overrunning, consumers could end up paying more for HPC's electricity than if the government had shared these risks. Past experience shows that ultimately these risks could shift back to taxpayers or consumers. (NAO, 2017, p. 12)

---

[5] The UK has a statutory duty (set up by the Labour Government in 2008) to reduce its carbon dioxide emissions to 80% of 1990 levels by 2050.

[6] "There are two areas today's results highlight, however, chiefly how ridiculous Hinkley Point C's £97.50/MWh agreement looks in comparison. EDF is not due to energise that plant until 2025, a year after swathes of Dogger Bank come onstream, and that energy is going to cost consumers more than twice that" (Liam Stoker, editor in chief, https://www.current-news.co.uk/news/offshore-wind-smashes-price-records-in-third-cfd-auction-round)

A similar experience prevails in the growth of the offshore wind sector, where it has been estimated that almost £28 billion will be invested by 2021 (Labour Energy Forum, 2017). Although there have been some important achievements in recent years—with offshore wind increasingly from virtually zero to a predicted 10% of electricity generation by 2020—the massive up-front costs of capital investment have deterred smaller private and community groups and necessitated considerable government subsidies for larger, and predominantly foreign, enterprises.

Of the 38 projects commissioned and operational in 2018 (Crown Estate, 2018), 13 were awarded either singly or as the major operator to the Danish energy corporation, Ørsted. In terms of the latter, 50% owned by the Danish government, five to Vattenfall (100% Swedish state owned), three to Equinor (Norwegian majority state-owned enterprise formerly known as Statoil) and two to EDF. Significantly, local and national state-owned organisations also own significant stakes in multi-consortia initiatives such as the London Array (which is led by German multinational E.ON with Ørsted and the Abu Dhabi state-owned enterprise, Masdar). Ørsted also have 50% ownership of the Hornsea 1 offshore wind farm, which will be the largest in the world when it comes onstream in mid-2020.

Three critical points arise from the analysis above in terms of broader issues of economic ownership and control. The first is that under privatised regimes, there is a direct conflict between the profit-making concerns of business and important public policy goals, with the latter coming a distant second if markets and private entities are left largely to their own devices. In private hands, decision-making and investment will deliver for short-term shareholder value more often than not at the expense of workers, customers or user groups. The increasing presence of hedge funds, private equity firms and other forms of financialised institutions in privatised sectors seems to be a logical outcome of market-centred designs in this sense.

The second is that, to square this circle, governments have to provide massive and perverse subsidies and incentives to encourage private investment, particularly where long-term investment in infrastructure is required. These usually end up being more costly than funding and operating services in-house as the UK's experience with the disastrous Private

Finance Initiative has shown.[7] A third point that we can make here is that far from the decentralised, competitive markets of crude neoliberal ideology, the levels of finance and risk needed for the largest infrastructure projects make it impossible for new and innovative firms and solutions to compete in energy markets. Thus, many smaller firms and community enterprises struggle to both compete with larger established entrants, lacking the capacity and size to develop a sustainable presence. In this respect, one key flaw of marketised and privatised sectors, observed over time, is the tendency towards oligopoly. Even where publicly owned or community-owned firms are set up to 'compete', such as in the electricity supply sector, they struggle against larger vested incumbent interests (as we illustrate further below), particularly in period when costs rise and revenues are squeezed.

3 The Return of the State, Public Ownership and the Remunicipalisation Wave

Both the nuclear example and the offshore wind sector offer an interesting snapshot of the broader trend for some kind of state capital to underpin privatised sectors in what are faux market contexts. This is also evident in a wider sense with the return of the state through different institutional forms. Notably, sovereign wealth funds (particularly as a means for oil-rich states to channel revenues into longer term investment vehicles), but also the increased operation overseas of state-owned corporations, operating little differently to privately owned transnational corporations. With the growing attempts by states to develop greater regulation and tax powers at the national scale (King, 2017), even the *Financial Times* has acknowledged the return of the state as being one of the key features of

[7] A House of Commons Treasury Committee report found that private finance has always been more expensive than direct government borrowing to fund infrastructure projects but following the 2007–9 financial crisis, the borrowing costs were double than that of the public sector (HOC Treasury Committee, 2012). See, also the work of Parker (2012), who calculates that the 860 PFI projects that have been constructed in the UK since 1991 have resulted in £239 billion of liabilities for future generations of taxpayers.

twenty-first-century capitalism (ibid. See also see Dolfsma & Grosman, 2019). This is most significant in the emergence of state capitalism in China. It is also evident through the widespread emergency nationalisations of the financial crisis, and furthermore in the shift back to state ownership in some of the heavily privatised former eastern European economies such as Poland and Hungary (Kozarzewski, Bałtowski, & Mickiewicz, 2022).

Whether this represents a decisive shift away from a neoliberal regime of economic governance is a little too early to tell. Neoliberalism in its original forms needs to be seen as an elite political project to wrestle back control of the economy from labour and state management towards private and corporate interests (Harvey, 2005). The more perceptive observers have identified an ongoing, mutating and stumbling process of neoliberalisation (Brenner, Peck, & Theodore, 2010), where it is always having to wrestle with its own economic and social contradictions (e.g. Hall, 2017) and subsequently prone to crisis tendencies (Peck & Theodore, 2019). In particular, the ongoing negative consequences of market-based dogmatism have to be continually addressed and resolved, usually through new forms of state regulation and action. In practice, this leads to variegated forms of neoliberalism (Brenner et al., 2010), taking different forms, whilst interacting with other political and economic cultures and social relations, and as such, different variants of capitalism across space and time.

Some have pointed towards a shift from a more progressive neoliberalism under centrist Third Way politics in the late 1990s and early 2000s to a more authoritarian form associated with austerity policies, regressive state incursions on liberty and human rights and increasingly nationalist and xenophobic tendencies in the 2010s (Bruff, 2014, 2019; Peck & Theodore, 2019). Returning to the core themes of the chapter—privatisation and public ownership—there is little doubt that, even as elite opinion makers continue to encourage privatisation and marketised models of governance, public ownership is making a stubborn return, particularly at the local level, as the failings of privatisation for public service delivery and critical policy goals mount.

Although official bodies like the IMF, World Bank and the OECD prefer for their own reasons to ignore the trend, recent research by the

Amsterdam-Based Transnational Institute (TNI) has identified a remarkable and largely 'under the radar' process of de-privatisation taking place around the world in the past two decades. As a phenomenon, it is notably a sub-national process, taking place at the local and regional scales and referred to as "remunicipalisation" (Kishimoto, Steinfort, & Petitjean, 2020). TNI recorded 1408 cases either of privatised assets being taken back into public ownership (924 cases) or instances of new public enterprises being established (484) cases. De-privatisation is evident in over 2400 cities and across 58 countries on all continents. Alongside remunicipalisation, there have also been instances of renationalisation at the national scale (in 23 countries), notably in the energy sector across Latin America; but also in other sectors as diverse as transport, telecoms and postal services (Kishimoto & Petitjean, 2017).

Latin America was the epicentre of a de-privatisation wave in the early 2000s, with a growing revolt against negative consequences of failed water privatisations. Bolivia witnessed several "water wars", with grassroots social mobilisations in La Paz and Cochabamba forcing governments to cancel private contracts and set up new public enterprises. These were one element of a broader challenge to foreign capital and in particular US and European multinational incursion across the continent in the 1990s, with a pushback against broken promises to invest and modernise water and waste infrastructure running alongside massive hikes in prices (Lobina & Hall, 2007). Remunicipalisations also occurred in Argentina, Colombia, Brazil and Venezuela with Uruguay seeing the full renationalisation of its water services (Lobina & Hall, 2013).

Remunicipalisations in the water sector, sparked by similar poor experiences of private contractors, have become a more pronounced global phenomenon, catalogued by the excellent work of TNI, the Public Services International Research Unit (operating out of the University of Greenwich) and the Municipal Services Project, led by David McDonald of Queens University, Canada (https://www.municipalservicesproject.org/). From 2 cases identified in 2000, the number increased dramatically to 235 by 2015 (Kishimoto, Lobina, & Petitjean, 2015). The diversity of cities and towns turning their back on privatisation has been remarkable; from Houston and Atlanta in the US to Paris and Berlin, to Odessa, Dar Es Salaam, Johannesburg and Samarkand (Kishimoto et al.,

2015; Lobina & Hall, 2013). France has the greatest number of remunicipalisations in water (and sanitation services with 106 case recorded by 2019 (Kishimoto et al., 2020), although it is thought that the real number may be double this figure (Petitjean, 2017). In addition, there is a major trend in the sector in the United States with 61 cases identified (Kishimoto & Petitjean, 2017).

Alongside water, energy has been the sector with the greatest number of remunicipalisations globally, with 374 cases documented by TNI in its second study in 2019 (Kishimoto et al., 2020). Germany has been at the forefront of this trend where, as part of the country's Energiwende (the political and social pressure to tackle climate change), many towns, cities and in some cases sub-national regions bring formerly privatised energy utilities back into public hands (see also Cumbers & Becker, 2018). As with France, Germany's privatisation problems were as much a centre left "third way" phenomenon as a right-wing project, as a multi-scalar neoliberal governance discourse (Cumbers, 2012). It took hold: reflecting the growing sway of the EU Single Market project and market liberalisation pressures (which have been, in practice, more about opening the public sector up to private sector incursion and capital accumulation processes than competition). Germany like elsewhere also experienced the shift towards a national policy discourse of private sector innovation and management allied to greater fiscal austerity and subsequent pressures on cash-strapped towns and cities to generate revenues (Cumbers & Becker, 2018; Streeck, 2014).

However, neoliberal policy hegemony never really took hold in the way that it had in the UK, so that privatisation was more constrained, occurring through the franchising out of local services (still under local state control in a more decentralised and federated polity) rather than full sectoral sell-offs. Because constitutionally, basic services are supposed to be a municipal obligation in the German context, the private sector could in effect only be partners of local authorities. As privatisation's failings mounted across the country's energy sector, and it became clear that private energy utilities (with the sector dominated by the big four of Vattenfall, E.ON, RWE and EnBW) continued to invest in fossil fuels while being too slow to invest in renewable energy, municipalities began to take assets and services back into public ownership—either as franchises expired, or in some case through grassroots mobilisations and campaigns to take over concessions (Cumbers & Becker, 2018).

While remunicipalisation is an important straw in the wind of a shift in economic governance away from marketised and private solutions, without a broader transformation in policy thinking and discourses at national and international scales away from neoliberal dogma and hegemony, critical issues such as achieving social and ecological justice are likely to be stymied. To illustrate this further, the next section considers some of the constraints and problems facing European municipalities, which are attempting to pursue public solutions to facilitate the energy transition.

4 Two Cheers for Europe's Municipal Energy Transition[8]

As this brief overview shows, thus far it has been local actors prosecuting the new trend towards public ownership, seeking to gain more ownership and control over local vital assets for key public policy purposes. What is clear, however, is that there is a sense of dislocation between increased collective action and public ownership at the local level and a continuing business as usual approach at national and international policy scales.

Although the remunicipalisation trend has been considerable in the European energy sector, it is important to recognise its limitations either for tackling climate change or for stimulating a broader alignment towards public ownership and non-marketised solutions at higher scales. The TNI report recorded 352 energy remunicipalisations across the continent with the lion's share being in Germany (with 305 cases) for the reasons noted above. There have been some celebrated municipal success stories here both in large cities such as Hamburg and smaller rural towns where new municipal enterprises and also a flourishing local energy cooperative movement have flourished in recent years, a trend common in other countries such as Belgium and Denmark (discussed further below).

[8] This section draws upon ongoing research from EU Horizon 2020 project MPOWER: Municipal Action, Public Engagement and Routes towards Energy Transition.

The Hamburg case is illustrative both for demonstrating the potential for local public ownership in a decentralised state context with strong federated regions, but also for its limits as a model than can be replicable elsewhere in more centralised polities. Hamburg became an iconic remunicipalisation case when a local grassroots citizens' movement successfully mobilised against the main establishment parties and trade unions to win a referendum to take back public control and ownership of the city's energy grid from privatised operator Vattenfall in 2013 (see Becker, Moss, & Naumann, 2017). This came on the back of an earlier decision in 2009 by the Greens (in coalition at the time with the Christian Democrats) to set up a new public electricity utility, Hamburg Energie, with the vision to eventually create a full integrated local public energy and heating company.

Because the Social Democrats, as the largest party in the ruling coalition (with the Greens), were tasked with implementing the remunicipalisation, despite having opposed it, further proposals to bring the district heating grid into public ownership to provide the potential for a fully integrated energy transition strategy were initially blocked. However, the departure in 2018 of the more conservative Social Democrat Mayor of Hamburg, Olaf Scholz, to become federal government finance minister led to a regime change resulting in district heating remunicipalisation. This has given the city the potential to embark upon a highly ambitious 'game changer' strategy of converting 400,000 of the city's homes away from coal and gas fired heating toward renewables and CHP (interview with former Green Member of Parliament, February 2020). This will have a massive impact on the city's CO_2 emissions if successful. Hamburg has been in a position to do this because of the city's political capacity, as a city region with devolved powers over energy and significant legislative power, its ability as one of the wealthiest cities in Europe to borrow at cheap rates on the private markets to fund the remunicipalisation policies and its broader green investments. Its political agency as a fully fledged Bundesland within the German system has even allowed it to amend federal laws on district heating to support its plans (ibid.).

Like other German municipalities, Hamburg can also borrow at very low interest rates from the German state development bank, the KfW (see below). Across the country, this has meant that even relatively small towns and rural districts can finance energy transition and efficiency initiatives beyond the reach of larger cities elsewhere.

More broadly, it is significant that in a recent survey of municipalities and energy transition experiences across Europe, out of 96 cities and towns for the MPOWER project, the top 10 ranked cities were all from northern and western Europe. Some of the strongest performing towns and cities are not surprisingly from Nordic countries where municipal energy is both devolved to the local level (see below) and usually remaining in public hands, allowing innovative initiatives in terms of both energy transition and democratisation. One far from unusual example is the Danish town of Frederikshavn, which is well advanced in a transition to renewable energy with a plan to be 100% renewable by 2030. An important element of its capacity and success is its considerable local public ownership and control of the local energy system, including municipal electricity companies that operate as public-consumer cooperatives, typical of many Danish cities. This allows Frederikshavn to plan their energy transition in an integrated, holistic fashion.

Frederikshavn has also developed some innovative democracy and citizen participation projects. By law, Danish municipal organisations, already require employee- and citizen-elected representatives (with four-year cycles) on their boards. Nevertheless, the municipality has gone beyond these stipulations to institute two new schemes aimed at greater citizen engagement. 'My Energy City' is an initiative to bring citizens together across the local authority territory to consider their own role in sustainable development; also, what barriers exist to maximising this role. A second project, described as a 'youth climate concept' brings schoolchildren and teenagers together to discuss sustainability and practical problem-solving and the discussions are then integrated into local school policies and calendars.

The picture is less rosy in other parts of Europe. Spain has seen a number of new public energy companies, established in cities such as Barcelona and Cadiz, but the lack of a supportive national policy framework. The previous right-wing government introduced what became known as the 'Sunshine Tax', under pressure from the large power utilities who were concerned at the growing competition from smaller scale solar power producers, which has thus far stymied attempts to develop renewable energies. In the UK, there has been a recent trend for cities to establish their own electricity supply companies. However, the inability to develop fully integrated companies (with grid and distribution capabilities) within a highly competitive privatised landscape, and lack of local control over a heavily concentrated and centralised private energy system, has meant that they have struggled to establish a foothold against the established private utility companies. Two of the most prominent public companies, Bristol Energy and Nottingham based Robin Hood Energy, have posted heavy losses in the last financial year following rising prices on wholesale markets which, without their own energy generating capacities, they have little control over. Another non-profit energy company, 'Our Power', owned by a coalition of Scottish social housing associations, went bust for similar reasons in January 2019.

With a continental energy landscape reflecting broader processes of spatially uneven development, municipalities in central and eastern Europe are often more disadvantaged, with a lack of effective national energy transition policy making them dependent on funding and support from EU initiatives and their corresponding terms of reference. Ljubljana, which received the accolade of European Green Capital in 2016, has, in the absence of available funding from its own national government, had a measure of success in drawing upon funding from the European Investment Bank's ELENA (European Local Energy Assistance) scheme (interviews with local municipal officials, March 2020). This has been used in three phases to refit municipally owned buildings to improve energy efficiency. The agreement with the EIB required the use of third-party private companies (Energy Savings Companies, or ESCOs) in order to access the project development funds that were crucial for the pursuit of their energy goals. This created a steep learning curve for the municipality, who had never utilised such a funding model, and introduced the mirage of competitivity within the process, when there are only two ESCOs in all of Slovenia capable of carrying out the work (interviews with local municipal energy actors, March 2020). This is in keeping with the kinds of neoliberal disciplinary policies applied to peripheral EU countries since the Eurozone crisis. It also reflects Slovenia's adherence to being a "good student" in integrating into a European neoliberal status quo, though it is undermined by the sham of competitivity de facto created by the ESCO stipulation. Activists in Ljubljana critique this focus on energy efficiency and the running of the municipality as a business, which focuses public officials' attention on publicity projects at the expense of considerations of democratic representation or more crucial maintenance and infrastructure investment (interviews, March 2020).

Another relatively successful Eastern European case is the Bulgarian city of Dobrich, which, in the absence of national government funding or support, has developed partnerships across Europe to forge networks for support and dissemination of advice and to access sources of funding in order to pursue energy efficiency transitions. Again, its focus has largely been on energy efficiency, perhaps in reflection of the EU's notion of energy efficiency as the 'first fuel', though it is also notable that there is again no national financing mechanism for renewables investment. Instead, Dobrich has worked with a range of EU funding streams to develop municipal capacity, a sustainable energy action plan (SEAP) and to train municipal staff in Green Public Procurement. What these networks and actions cannot often provide, beyond a pilot stage, is concrete investment, which instead has to come from private sources, for example again through ESCOs for energy efficiency retrofits and in financing the development of a 60,000 panel PV power station—the largest in the region—which was funded by a private energy company. Despite this welcome investment, Dobrich is likely to miss its renewable energy targets, sitting at only 25% of the expected 32% renewables in its final energy consumption.

Both Dobrich and Ljubljana demonstrate a broader point: namely, what funding is available shapes the possible landscape of transition. Despite political will in both contexts at a local level, a need for project development support, greater municipal capacity and funding limits the possibilities of municipal actions for sustainability. In contrast with the Danish example above, where the protection and prioritisation of democratic and citizen-led schemes was made possible by political will and economic policy, both Dobrich and Ljubljana are pushed towards marketised, private sector solutions. Despite, in Ljubljana's case owning a large Public Holdings company, including an energy branch, which with the right funding could be transitioned from its current emphasis on coal to something far greener.

Lurking behind this uneven landscape of municipal capacities and agency is the EU's evolving energy policy, which in its most recent outing is purportedly geared towards decarbonisation and delivering "clean energy for all citizens" (European Directive, 2019). However, it is instead a classic example of the application of flawed market logics to critical public policy issues, notably the "trilemma" of energy security, delivering affordable energy, and transitioning to renewables.[9] The original 1990s Single Market vision of creating one unified internal European energy market to enhance competition and market dynamics was rooted in mainstream neoclassical and public choice theory, with a discourse steeped in actions and policy responses, "determined through calculations and evaluations in quantitative language of efficiency" (Hatzisavvidou, 2020, pp. 106–107) divorced from social and political contexts. Set against this however, national governments have retained the right under different EU provisions and the principle of subsidiarity to retain control over 'services of general economic interest' with residual powers to decide how these are financed and organised.

Because national governments have retained considerable powers in the energy sector, although with varied capacities as the Ljubljana and Dobrich examples demonstrate, much of the EU discourse and attention has been driven towards eliminating barriers to a single unified market, which are seen as stifling efficiency and competitiveness. At the same time, there has been a growing (though rarely explicit) recognition that privatised energy market logics have tended to strengthen larger established players and particular dominant utilities, which span different national markets. Until very recently, these actors have been wedded more to centralised established fossil fuel technologies—rather than facilitating a transition to renewable energy—and have used their considerable political leverage to stifle more radical transition strategies at the national level.

[9] The failure of the European Union's market-driven approach to energy transition is most evident in the widely critiqued and derided ETS (Emissions Trading System). A disastrous attempt to add a cost for CO2 into the market price, adroitly summarised by one set of experienced policy commentators as "a failed system where emission costs neither reflect environmental costs nor provides any incentive for carbon-neutral electricity production" (Hvelplund, Østergaard, & Meyer, 2017).

EU energy policy has evolved along diverse and at times slightly contradictory lines to address this situation. Until relatively recently much of its funding was going towards projects that connected up infrastructure across borders to address energy security issues although still framed within a discourse of strengthening single market competition. For example, funding has been available as part of the Connecting Europe Facility (CEF) promotion of 'Projects of Common Interest', but only for 'impacting the market' through grants for electricity and gas pipelines such as the Southern Gas Corridor. It has received a €173 m CEF grant, or integrating the Iberian peninsula grids, which gained €588 m from the fund. Often this funding has been put to good use, such as enabling investments for carbon capture and storage facilities and smart grids, but the overriding focus has been on an integrated market and boosting competition as the solution especially to potential issues of supply.

Alongside this has been a somewhat belated recognition in the 2010s of the importance of action at local and city level to tackle climate change, allied to the need to engage citizens. This has resulted in increased rhetoric—though significantly no real binding legislation—around the importance of Local Energy Communities and municipal action. Pressure has come from other parts of the European Commission, notably those directorates concerned with territorial cohesion and regional policy. In addition, and from less prosperous parts of the EU, especially Eastern Europe, to create both a level playing field throughout the EU for a just energy transition as well as for specific measures to support municipal action in the establishment of local renewable initiatives. In a recent communique, the Romanian rapporteur for the European Committee of the Regions evoked this spirit:

> We believe that the future of energy production is the hands of citizens. We need to make sure that local energy communities can fully contribute to the decentralisation and democratisation of energy systems and foster sustainable economic and social development locally. Local production, distribution and consumption of energy are key to fighting energy poverty. (ECR, 2018)

The communiqué went on, however, to note the lack of support for local action, the continuing blockages at national level and the difficulties of competing against larger established private and corporate sector interests—all issues that resonate with ongoing themes here.

Revealing too in this context has been the shift in the EU's own position from an active support for local action in its espousal of 'Local Energy Communities', and non-profit-based initiatives, in its initial Winter Package proposals in 2017 to a much vaguer notion of Citizen Energy Communities in its eventual legislation. This is evident in the following two citations from the relevant texts:

> local energy community' means: an association, a cooperative, a partnership, a non-profit organisation or other legal entity which is effectively controlled by local shareholders or members, generally value rather than profit-driven, involved in distributed generation and in performing activities of a distribution system operator, supplier or aggregator at local level, including across borders. (European Commission, 2017, Article 2, p. 52)

> citizen energy community' means a legal entity that [...] is based on voluntary and open participation and is effectively controlled by members or shareholders that are natural persons, local authorities, including municipalities, or small enterprises; [...] has for its primary purpose to provide environmental, economic or social community benefits to its members or shareholders or to the local areas where it operates rather than to generate financial profits. (European Directive, 2019, L158/140)

While the concept of a Citizen Energy Community does provide some important impetus to community and local authority initiatives, and arguably might facilitate broader collective actions (such as non-localised cooperative formation), it is striking that the legislation also permits SMEs and possibilities for profit generation, although not as the primary focus. What is also striking is the couching of increased support for citizen and community initiatives as part of improving market functioning by facilitating consumer-centric initiative seen in individualised terms redolent of mainstream economic rationalities: "Community energy offers an inclusive option for all consumers to have a direct stake in producing, consuming or sharing energy. [...] Community energy also enables certain groups of household customers to participate in the electricity markets, who otherwise might not have been able to do so" (EU Directive, 2019, L158/130).

In essence, the EU's approach expresses an underlying tension between stimulating local action and citizen engagement and higher level political drivers to reinforce market-oriented and competitiveness agendas. What is also striking in these policy documents is the failure to acknowledge the shift back towards public ownership at the municipal level or its potential in delivering on stated ambitions to restructure and decentralise the energy system to encourage renewables or enhance public participation and engagement in tackling climate change (see Energy Cities, 2017).

5 Decentralised Public Ownership Beyond the Market

As we have written about elsewhere in greater depth, a good example of a decentralised non-market-based approach to public ownership, which has had some measure of success in achieving a transition away from fossil fuels to renewable energy, is Denmark's remarkable development of its wind power sector (Cumbers, 2012, chapter 9, 2018). Since 1980, the country has transitioned from being almost totally reliant upon imported oil for its energy needs, to a situation where renewable energy accounts for 34% of final energy consumption and 64% of total electricity consumption.[10] Alongside this, the country's wind turbine manufacturers created a new industrial sector comprising 20,000 jobs and 50% of world market share by 2000—a remarkable feat for a country of 5 million.

A lot of international attention on the Danish success story has focused upon the achievements of the small-scale private sector turbine manufacturers, who through collaborative action and decentralised forms of organisation successfully competed against larger and more capital-intensive state-backed US producers to develop their global leading position. Because it does not fit with the heroic David versus Goliath narrative

[10] 2017 figures available at: https://ens.dk/en/our-services/statistics-data-key-figures-and-energy-maps/key-figures

of neoliberal global competitive advantage, rather less is made of the crucial role played by decentralised forms of cooperative and public ownership, allied to non-market state-driven institutional supports. What is particularly interesting here is the way a variegated but heavily democratic collectively owned energy system emerged that was neither a centrally planned hierarchical state model of ownership, nor a privatised system driven by (faux) market rationalities.

Particularly important to the establishment of renewables were three forms of state interventionism: an infant industry strategy whereby the government provided 30% funding for all new wind turbines; protecting the domestic sector from a wildly fluctuating world market in the 1980s, and compelling local publicly owned electricity suppliers to accept a certain quota of renewable energy culminating in the establishment of Feed-In-Tariffs (FITs) with guaranteed prices in the 1990s; and, a set of residency and consumption criteria established to facilitate small-scale local ownership, rather than allowing wealthy individuals or corporations to absorb the benefits (Cumbers, 2018). The main effect of the latter was to encourage a cooperative renewables sector to develop alongside the existing decentralised and publicly owned energy system. The incentive for families and individuals to combine to build wind turbines was strong leading to a situation where, by the mid-1990s, it was estimated that cooperatives and individual family holdings accounted for 80% of wind turbine ownership (Cumbers, 2012). A more recent figure has suggested that cooperative ownership still represents around 15% of the sector, despite the shift to larger offshore wind projects. Alongside this, and in common with Germany, Denmark's electricity supply and distribution system has historically been split between rural cooperatives and municipal enterprises (Hadjilambrinos, 2000) with regional transmission networks. Although there has been some amalgamation and mergers across the sector over time to afford economies of scale, this publicly owned system remains largely intact. The renewables revolution has effectively been highly adaptive in adding a local cooperative and small privately owned wind dimension into the mix.

Although these laws and initiatives have been relaxed over time—allowing greater amalgamation and growth of corporate interests—they were critical in setting in train a publicly owned and controlled system that involved a multi-scalar governance approach integrating national, regional and local state planning and institutions; yet one which enables local collective action and initiative. Since the late 1990s neoliberal imperatives from the European Union and accommodationist politics from both centre left and centre right parties have eroded the collectively owned system, enabling greater incursion by corporate and financial interests.

Two trends are symptomatic of broader themes identified in this chapter. The first was the ditching of the FIT by the Social Democrat led coalition in 1999 in favour of the more market-oriented tradeable green certificate (TGC), effectively replacing a guaranteed price for renewable producers with a quota system whereby electricity companies source a certain proportion of energy but where prices can fluctuate in an unregulated fashion. Like many 'open and free market solutions', TGCs have ended up benefitting larger producers and well-established incumbents who can weather price fluctuations and work against smaller and newer enterprises (such as community enterprises or cooperatives) and more innovative technologies. The integration of the Danish electricity system into the Nordpool spot market—a common Nordic energy market—has further eroded government ability to provide stability for renewables, especially older wind turbine producers (see Hvelplund et al., 2017, for a more updated assessment).

Second, the growing acceptance of private and corporate capital by the political class in the sector has led to a shift towards commercial and financial imperatives. A pivotal moment was the 20% sale of state energy company DONG to private investors, including Goldman Sachs in 2013 (Lockwood, 2015). Like most established energy utilities, DONG faced the problem of disinvesting from its carbon sources of energy and shifting towards renewables. The decision by the Social Democrats to use private equity capital rather than state financing to invest in its offshore wind strategy drew much opprobrium at the time—which only grew after a subsequent stock market listing of the company, which delivered an estimated £16 billion return for Goldman (Milne, 2016), and led to the split of the governing coalition.

Following the return of the left to government in 2019, it was notable that the sale of DONG's (now renamed Orsted with government maintaining a 50.1% stake) distribution and retail business was to the largest Danish energy cooperative SEAS-NVE. Significantly, its sale to foreign interests had been blocked in parliament with opposition leader (and subsequently Prime Minister) Mette Frederiksen quoted as saying: "It's not a question about whether it should be sold or not. It is a question about who it should be sold to .... It's important that we keep critical infrastructure including the power network in hands where we keep democratic control" (Jacobsen, 2019).

Despite such rhetoric there are clear tensions remaining in Denmark—as with elsewhere—between a more progressive agenda of developing community and public ownership of key resources against creating avenues for financial encroachment and capital accumulation. In the context of continuing austerity and restrictions on public financing at national and European levels, financialising assets can leverage the kind of large-scale capital investment required for post-carbon transition, but having the level of guarantees for private investors means that the public purse is usually short-changed in the long term, either through state subsidy or higher prices for consumers. Like the UK, its offshore and large-scale onshore wind sectors, despite the presence of Orsted as a "national champion", are increasingly dominated by corporate and foreign interests, including pension funds, which has sparked considerable resistance in a country with a tradition of local collective ownership (Hvelplund et al., 2017). Although existing regulations force companies to give a 20% shareholding in new ventures—except those over 16 km from the coast—to local residents, there are pressures to create expanded and more robust 'common good' shareholdings. Because Danish municipalities still retain considerable planning powers and governance responsibilities, local citizen groups and campaigners, not because of resistance to wind farms per se but because of an absence of local ownership and control, often block large private developments.

6 Envisaging Democratic Public Ownership

As the limits to EU energy policy and the more recent adaptation dilemmas of Denmark's energy transition demonstrate, progressive national and local actors can only do so much in coming to terms with the broader limitations and contradictions of existing political economy. Innovations in local public and collective ownership will fail to effectively tackle climate change or deliver more socially just and sustainable solutions without a broader critique and overhaul of economic institutions.

In the context of this chapter, this implies challenging marketised and privatised solutions that still attempt to preserve the hegemony of neoliberal thinking and mainstream economic narratives. While the complex global economy of the twenty-first century requires a mixed economy of both markets and planning, neoliberalisation has extended market mechanisms and values into essential public services and utilities such as energy and water where they should have no place in a civilised society. Even from a narrower economic perspective of productivity and cost effectiveness, sectors with natural monopolies are better suited to planning and forms of public ownership, a point reinforced by the neoliberal experience of privatisation in sectors as diverse as rail, energy and water.[11]

However, in advocating public ownership, it is important to avoid the mistakes of past forms of state ownership, whether under post-1945 capitalist nationalisation projects or those of state socialism. In the UK as elsewhere, older models of state ownership tended to be heavily top-down, prone to capture by elite corporate or technocratic interests. One lesson from the past is the importance of opening up public ownership to diverse and competing interest groups, to full public participation and deliberative processes as a means of securing broader social values beyond commercial norms. This is especially important in a world of growing inequalities and ecological crisis.

These issues were taken up in the UK Labour Party's recent policy review of public ownership, of which one of the authors of this chapter was a participant. Although its decisive defeat at the 2019 General

[11] A case in point is the water sector where in the UK a positive comparison can be made between the financial stability of Scottish Water and its debt-laden private counterparts (Hall, 2018).

Election make it unlikely that these proposals will be enacted any time soon, there has nevertheless been some important new thinking in terms of how public ownership might be more democratic, accountable and shaped by non-marketised values (e.g. Cumbers & Hanna, 2019; Labour Party, 2017). There is an important emerging consensus in particular on the need for fuller economic democracy in public ownership that includes user groups as well as workers including engagement with a diverse range of democratic collective ownership and alternative experiences such as the Mondragon cooperative or the public-employee hybrid, Banco Popular, in Costa Rica (Marois, 2017).

There has also been a welcome debate in the UK in particular about the failings of older forms of state ownership and the need for more diverse and decentralised forms of public ownership—where economic effectiveness and technical feasibility make this possible (e.g. Cumbers, 2012). In particular, there is a need to go beyond older monolithic, bureaucratic and top-down forms of nationalisation to a broader spectrum of citizen engaged and participatory public enterprises (Cumbers & Hanna, 2019). Two important points need to be made up-front. First, that there is no 'one-size-fits-all' solution. Moreover, the forms that democratic public ownership would take would differ according to the diverse technical requirements and social needs of particular sectors and places. Second, that there is an inevitable trade-off—sometimes a tension—between higher level co-ordination and the devolution of power to the local level to enable greater public and community participation. Overall, what this discussion suggests is that we might envisage very different forms of public and collective ownership depending on the policy objectives in question (see relevant table in Cumbers & Hanna, 2019, p. 3).

Not only should public ownership be sensitive to spatial and sectoral diversity but it should also be adaptive, and also able to change over time as the relations between economy, society and environment change. One of the relevant Hayekian criticisms made of older forms of centralised state ownership was that they were unresponsive to changes on the ground and the dynamics processes of economic development. Nevertheless, whereas Hayek saw the solution in terms of the tacit forms of knowledge in decentralised market systems, privatisation experiences remind us of similar flaws in the scientific rationality of mainstream economics and the misapplication of universalising market logics to diverse and evolutionary social and economic practices (see O'Neill, 2003).

The energy sector example is apposite here. Transitioning to a post-carbon economy means a shift away from the centralised grids and massive power stations of the fossil fuel era towards diverse and decentralised forms of energy. This will require the refashioning of energy grids to smarter and more adaptive networked systems, which are capable of harnessing multiple different forms and sources of power. Complex and flexible governance arrangements are needed that go beyond both traditional forms of state-driven central planning and the flawed regulation of the electricity markets of the European Union.

However, more positively, it offers the opportunity to provide more local autonomy and decision-making power to towns, cities and rural communities to develop their own integrated renewable energy systems. Such a transformation will only be possible with higher level co-ordination at regional, national and international scales; in other words, strategic planning of grids, infrastructure and networks, by the relevant public and state authorities. This is also true for transport, water and health care sectors.

In its paper on energy sector renationalisation (Labour Party, 2019), the Labour Party recently set out the kind of multi-scalar structure of public ownership that might be envisaged here, with four key levels of democratic public ownership replacing the current privatised system. A National Energy Agency tasked with strategic co-ordination including managing the national grid, setting decarbonisation targets, regulating the energy system, and co-ordination of skills and workforce planning; Regional Energy Agencies responsible for electricity and gas distribution, decarbonising heat and energy, and having an industrial policy role; Municipal Energy Agencies (MEAs) and Local Energy Communities (LECs) (Fig. 6.3).

While the national and regional agencies are tasked with basic infrastructure provision, regulating and distribution functions, the model envisages scope for the lower level agencies to take on more responsibility and develop more locally integrated system where required. Therefore, for example, the MEAs could realise a full democratic municipalism by having key powers at the regional level over the supply and distribution

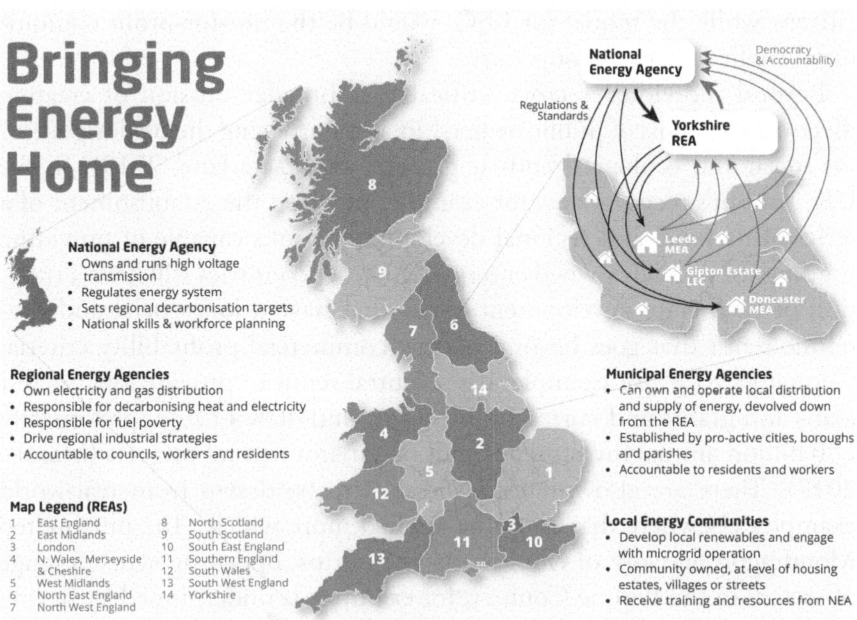

Fig. 6.3 Labour's plan for a publicly owned energy network. (Source: Labour Party 2019, pp. 8–9: Bringing Energy Home)

of energy devolved, while LECs could be the scale at which rural communities or urban neighbourhoods develop even more radical energy solutions, which empower communities by developing their own renewables and even creating micro-grids.

All forms of public enterprise would have democratic participation and accountability written into their constitutional structure but in varying forms consonant with the scale of activity but all with the requirement to have 50% women on boards. The NEA would have a board with national government appointees, members from Regional Energy Agencies (REAs), elected members from the LEC sector, worker representatives and civil society members. REAs would have similar set-up but with local government and devolved regional members (as opposed to national government appointees). MEAs would be under local municipal government control but with democratic fora to represent workers and citizens while the model for LECs would be the not-for-profit community benefit society or cooperative.

Beyond individual sectors, critical to a broader mission of creating diverse ecosystems of public ownership, is repurposing the banking sector for social and ecological ends (e.g. Berry & Macfarlane, 2019). In the UK, Labour's recent plans, for example, involved the establishment of a series of national and regional development banks capable of providing funding for publicly owned enterprises. Other countries still have a tradition of such state development banks that have a long social and economic remit that goes beyond narrow commercial profitability criteria. Germany's KfW, for example, has a central remit to provide low interest loans and grants and currently invests around 40% of its approximately €80 billion annual investment funds on environmental projects (Marois, 2017). There are also interesting lessons to be drawn from real-world examples elsewhere that could be applied more widely. The much-cited Mondragon network of employee-owned firms, operating across a range of sectors in the Basque Country, for example, is underpinned by having its own bank to provide its autonomous financial support in line with its values of democratic governance and "labour sovereignty" (Heales, Hodgson, & Rich, 2017).

One inspirational model is Costa Rica's Banco Popular y de Desarrollo Comunal (broadly translated as the Popular Bank for Community Development) (Marois, 2017). It is an interesting democratic hybrid as a public bank but legally controlled by the country's workers and citizens and governed by an elected assembly of 290 representatives from across different sectors of economy and society. Since its establishment in 1969, it has been committed to investing 25% of its revenues in social projects and more recently has seen impressive, and progressive, towards environmental objectives, including a partnership with rural energy cooperative, enabling it to become the first Latin American energy utility to achieve carbon neutrality (Marois, 2017).

Also critical to a new generation of democratic public enterprise is the development and pursuit of alternative ecological and social values that challenge mainstream economic growth and profit-seeking agendas. While local public entities need to have autonomy and genuine control in their operations and decision-making, they should be, at the same time, beholden to a broader set of commonly accepted values and norms. Although the principle of 'subsidiarity', devolved decision-making closer to communities and citizens, should be to the fore in a new generation of public enterprise, public enterprises should have a broader remit (without being overly prescriptive) to social and ecologically sustainable values, whatever the conflicts and difficulties of applying this in practice, to a philosophy of the common good. There is still a strong tradition, for example, in Nordic countries to use natural resources for the "whole of society" (see Cumbers, 2012, chapter 8). This has been an important cornerstone of Norwegian energy policy since the country's discovery of North Sea oil—and was critical to setting up the state oil company (Statoil) and subsequently the investment fund—so that its oil wealth is broadly distributed rather than captured by vested interests.

This approach is embedded in a much longer standing tradition common across the Nordic countries (and is apparent in the Danish renewables case) that economic rents from natural resources should be the "common property of the people" (Ryggvik, 2010) rather than open to capture and appropriation by private interests. A second feature of this 'Nordic approach' is that social need and a longer-term development perspective should dictate the use of revenues from natural resources. This principle was behind the formation of the two financial instruments in the Norwegian case to separate out operational oil activities from Statoil from the distribution of revenues, the state's direct financial interest (SDFI) in 1985 and the Norwegian Government Pension which has become the world's biggest sovereign wealth fund valued at around $1 trillion. Although Norway has been accused of 'double standards' by its critics, for continuing to profit and invest in oil activities while pursuing projecting a green image in many of its activities overseas, an active civil society and strong democratic governance institutions are important bulwarks in holding its commercial interests to account.

In this sense, an important third element of the Nordic model that can be applied to public ownership is the importance of collective decision-making and a tradition of strong public deliberation (see Cumbers, 2012, chapters 8/9 for greater elaboration of the Norwegian and Danish cases). While there would always be disagreements and conflicts between competing groups, it is important to develop appropriate institutions and associations between state, the private sector and civil society that allow legitimate differences to be debated and negotiated in the formulation of policy.

Out of the collectivist approach also comes a tradition of collective learning and knowledge construction where technology and innovation are shared across communities rather than being privately appropriated. A remarkable feature in the growth of the Danish wind turbine industry was the absence of patenting of prototypes; indeed, no patents were developed in the industry until the mid-1990s, which in part was due to an 1885 law that banned rural technology patents. This meant that in the early years of the industry, the technology was commonly available to local producers and experiences were shared.

An important argument for public ownership over private, therefore, is to secure the common good against vested interests. But committing public enterprises to a vision of the common good raises a host of philosophical questions stretching back to the earliest civilisations about how and by whom this 'common good' is constituted. Who gets to decide what is the common good? In addition, will democratic solutions necessarily lead to progressive outcomes that protect the common good rather than lead some times to authoritarian outcomes or the rule by an expert or technocratic elite on behalf of the rest of us? There are no easy answers to these questions and no perfect constitutional or institutional mechanisms—as the failings of both market and planned utopias demonstrate (Hodgson, 1999)—that can deliver absolutist solutions.

To some extent common good values are always going to be socially constructed and contingent therefore on time and place. Slavery and many other forms of gender, racialised and social exploitation are considered morally unacceptable and legislated for (although sadly still part of economic practice) in most advanced societies in a way that was not the case in the recent past. One way out of this conundrum is to recognise the importance of local commitment to a set of broader global responsibilities to promote democratic and sustainable societies. It is useful to understand our 'common' shared interests in this respect as being about the sustainable use of resources and assets to lead decent and flourishing lives but set against the environmentalist principles to safeguard the planet for future generations. A set of values that compel present decision-makers to respect the needs and rights of future generations on a planet of finite resources would seem apposite here.

An obvious starting point in this regard is the 17 sustainable development goals agreed by the 193 countries of the United Nations. These goals commit all signatories to tackling climate change, poverty and inequality, providing sustainable production and consumption, promoting peace and justice, and promoting gender equality. Crucially, whatever their weaknesses and the lack of progress in the breach, for our purposes here they have been agreed deliberatively through a process that has established a global consensus. Adhering to these principles, and being held to account through democratic mechanisms and regular reporting, could be a way for public enterprises to exercise the common good, however imperfect this process may be in practice. The effectiveness of public ownership could then be 'measured' according to how well (or poorly) it performs with respect to these goals, rather than more orthodox financial goals and performance targets.

7 Summary and Conclusions

As privatisation continues to fail and the broader problems and contradictions of neoliberal economic governance multiply amidst increasing social, economic and ecological crises, forms of state regulation and public ownership are likely to return to the policy agenda in the 2020s. The growing presence of financialised forms of capital in privatised sectors, often aided and abetted by state action, as in the Danish case of Ørsted and Goldman Sachs, suggests, however, that public assets and services, because of their very inelastic demand properties as sectors that deliver for the basic needs of social reproduction, will continue to be attractive avenues for rent seeking opportunities by private capital. This may well intensify in the next decade given the limited returns likely from a low-growth environment in the rest of the economy.

At present, as the muddled approach by the European Union and indeed the vast majority of national governments across the continent (and for that matter globally) to tackling climate change attests, market-based solutions and neoliberal referents around creating active consumers, private property rights and profit-centred solutions continue to hold sway. This means that there is a sense of dislocation between the upsurge in municipal action and renewed agenda for public ownership locally reported here and the 'business as usual' mantra of national and international political elites. This can frustrate local actions towards addressing the challenges of mitigation and adapting to the climate crisis; though as demonstrated in some northern European contexts an alignment between municipal ownership, local will and national-level political and financial support can lead to innovative and democratic action for transition.

The problems evident in energy illuminate a broader issue in much current public policy thinking in tackling the 'wicked problems' that human society faces. From Hayek onwards, and especially through the work of the Public Choice economists (e.g. Buchanan et al., 1978), the neoliberal attack on the state and public ownership has deliberately obfuscated the boundaries between the different but related issues regarding planning and markets, public and private, the individual and the collective. Growing state intervention in the economy in the 1970s in many western economies—with the handy Bogey Man of the Soviet Union's "actually existing socialism" (Hodgson, 1999)—was successfully portrayed as an existential threat to markets and individual liberties on Hayek's "road to serfdom".

It is difficult to exaggerate the impact of these ideas on today's society where marketised values, founded upon individual rationality and the primacy of consumer choice, have percolated into so many areas of public life, from education to health care and even to the deregulated utility sectors. Public policy thus becomes reduced to providing market metrics and indicators from which idealised consumers are expected to be able to make informed choices, irrespective of diverse and unequal social contexts. As Brown (2016, p. 3) puts it: "While neoliberalism overtly aims to emancipate the individual from webs of state regulation and intervention, it enfolds and binds that same being into every neoliberalised sphere and institution with which they engage. As it specifies entrepreneurial conduct everywhere, it constrains the subject to act in a capital-enhancing fashion everywhere".

Hence, while flawed initiatives such as privatisation continue to fail, the political project to remake society beyond the formal economy (especially through the state and households) in the image of markets continues apace (Bruff, 2019). Hayek's valid critique of state planning and centralised ownership structures is that those at the centre of large hierarchical organisations are often too distant from the actual conditions on the ground. For him, the decentralised anarchy of the market—its spontaneous order—was the best solution to the problems of uncertainty, economic dynamism and evolution, bringing together consumers and producers "on the ground" in an idealised market place.[12] This is the use of the market as a knowledge discovery process—an effective means of tacit learning—rather the neoclassical sense of a mechanism returning to market equilibrium under conditions of perfect competition and information. Nevertheless, markets even as devices for knowledge discovery also have their limits, as various critics have pointed out (see, e.g. O'Neill, 1998, 2007). The 40-year neoliberal experiment suggests that deregulated market forces do not lead to some decentralised utopia but to a concentration of ownership, private elite appropriation of wealth and resources, growing inequalities and myriad deepening social, political and ecological crises.

Privatisation's failings should alert us to the importance of developing an ongoing and open debate about the limits to both markets and planning in economic governance. As the more critical and thoughtful heterodox traditions in economics (e.g. Burczak, 2006; Hodgson, 1999; Nell, 2015) remind us, there is no perfect solution to resource allocation, whether done through the price mechanism or a more directive form of planned economy. The energy examples here show the limitations of attempts at establishing 'market pricing' and incentive structures—premised on neoclassical economics flawed application of rather simplistic market and competition-based assumptions—to a natural monopoly sector. If the stated public policy ambition is to shift from a centralised carbon-based energy system around coal, oil and gas (Mitchell, 2009) to a post-carbon networked structure of diverse and decentralised renewable production, the privatised and marketised approach of the status quo has

[12] These arguments are dealt with in greater length than is possible here in Cumbers (2015).

been found wanting. At the same time, reducing economic decision-making to commercial and profit imperatives across all sectors—as the neoliberal project attempts to do—is clearly flawed both in terms of efficiency but also on moral grounds.

Ultimately, all economic governance institutions and mechanisms, whether these are market or non-market forms are 'imperfect' and work best through an adaptive process of regulation, knowledge exchange and collective learning in response to the realities of the uncertainty and dynamic evolution that characterise the workings of actually existing economic systems. The Danish FIT system of allocated shares for renewable energy, accompanied by non-market-based state institutions, worked well in the 1980s and 1990s but would need adjustment to the very different conditions pertaining today. What it does illustrate well is the possibility of constructing diverse, and more democratic forms of collective ownership, which are not market-based or privatised.

Recent evidence suggests that there is a broad public appetite for public ownership and a different way of doing political economy. In the UK, where Margaret Thatcher's privatisation experiment set down its deepest roots, and despite a generally hostile media environment for public ownership, a remarkable opinion poll undertaken by the right wing Legatum Institute immediately after the 2017 General Election found high levels of support for renationalising water (83%), gas and electricity (77%) and train services (76%) (Elliott & Kanagasooriam, 2017). The danger, in our current situation, is that if the left and broader progressive forces do not come up with their own alternatives to the "failing forward" project of neoliberalism (Peck & Theodore, 2019) and its flawed utopian markets discourse, an authoritarian right will steal some of the left's clothes. There are already signs of this happening with some authoritarians fusing a nationalistic politics with elements of the left agenda around public ownership and services. It is notable in this respect that Hungary, under Orban, has been the leading European country in renationalising formerly privatised activities over the past decade (see Kishimoto & Petitjean, 2017). While a central component of Marine Le Pen's platform in France has been renationalising the banking sector, defending public services, farmers and workers' rights against "wild and anarchic globalisation" (Chassany & Khalaf, 2015).

Hopefully, as we have already shown through the examples in this chapter, there are alternative pathways towards more democratic and inclusive forms of public ownership. In the UK, and despite its resounding defeat at the 2019 General Election, the Labour Party—through a series of policies and papers—has initiated an important debate about the potential of new and democratic forms of public ownership. These are critical to tackling key social and environmental injustices. Through the lens of the energy sector, this chapter has demonstrated the potential of non-market-based public solutions and exposed the hollow promises of markets and privatisation to address climate change and other critical policy arenas. Ultimately, the resurrection of public ownership can also evoke different values and more democratic alternatives to both privatisation and conventional forms of top-down state ownership.

References

Anderson, B. (1983). *Imagined Communities*. London: Verso.

Arrighi, G. (2007). *Adam Smith in Beijing: Lineages of the Twenty-First Century*. London: Verso.

Becker, S., Moss, T., & Naumann, M. (2017). Between Coproduction and Commons: Understanding Initiatives to Reclaim Urban Energy Provision in Hamburg and Berlin. *Urban Research and Practice, 10*, 63–85.

Bell, E., & Christoph, G. (2019). The Slow Retreat of Neoliberalism in Contemporary Britain. In S. Dawes & M. Lenormand (Eds.), *Neoliberalism in Context: Governance, Subjectivity and Knowledge* (pp. 19–38). Cham, Switzerland: Springer Nature.

Berry, C., & Macfarlane, L. (2019). *A New Public Banking Ecosystem; a Report to the Labour Party Commissioned by the Communication Workers Union and the Democracy Collaborative*. London: Labour Party.

Blyth, M. (2013). *Austerity: The History of a Dangerous Idea*. New York: Routledge.

Bowman, A., Folkman, P., Froud, J., Johal, S., Law, J., Leaver, A., et al. (2013). *The Great Train Robbery: Rail Privatisation and After*. Manchester, UK: Centre for Research on Socio-Cultural Change (CRESC).

Bradshaw, M. (2012). *Time to Take Our Foot Off the Gas*. London: Report for Friends of the Earth.

Brenner, N., Peck, J., & Theodore, N. (2010). Variegated Neoliberalization: Geographies, Modalities, Pathways. *Global Networks, 10*, 182–222.

Brown, W. (2016). Sacrificial Citizenship: Neoliberalism, Human Capital, and Austerity Politics. *Constellations: An International Journal of Critical and Democratic Theory, 23*, 3–14.

Bruff, I. (2014). The Rise of Authoritarian Neoliberalism. *Rethinking Marxism, 26*, 113–129.

Bruff, I. (2019). Overcoming the Allure of Neoliberalism's Market Myth. *South Atlantic Quarterly, 118*, 363–379.

Buchanan, J., Rowley, C. K., Breton, A., Wiseman, J., Frey, B., Peacock, A. T., Grimond, J., Niskanen, W. A., & Ricketts, M. (1978). *The Economics of Politics*. London: Institute of Economic Affairs.

Burczak, T. (2006). *Socialism After Hayek*. Ann Arbor: University of Michigan Press.

Chassany, A.-S., & Khalaf, R. (2015, March 5). Marine Le Pen Lays Out Radical Vision to Govern France. *Financial Times*.

Crown Estate. (2018, January–December). *Offshore Wind: Operational Report*. London: Crown Estate.

Cumbers, A. (2012). *Reclaiming Public Ownership: Making Space for Economic Democracy*. London: Zed.

Cumbers, A. (2015). Responding to Hayek from the Left: Beyond Market Socialism on the Path to a Radical Economic Democracy. In G. Nell (Ed.), *Austrian Theory and Economic Organization: Reaching Beyond Free Market Boundaries* (pp. 177–196). New York: Palgrave Macmillan.

Cumbers, A. (2018). The Danish Low Carbon Transition and the Prospects for the Democratic Economy. In P. North & M. Scott Cato (Eds.), *Towards Just and Sustainable Economies: The Social and Solidarity Economy North and South* (pp. 179–194). Bristol, UK: Polity.

Cumbers, A., & Becker, S. (2018). Making Sense of Remunicipalisation: Theoretical Reflections on and Political Possibilities from Germany's Rekommumalisierung Process. *Cambridge Journal of Regions Economy and Society, 11*, 503–517.

Cumbers, A., Danson, M., Whittam, G., Morgan, G., & Callaghan, G. (2013). *Repossessing the Future: A Common Weal Strategy for Community and Democratic Ownership of Scotland's Energy Resources*. Biggar, UK: Jimmy Reid Foundation.

Cumbers, A., & Hanna, T. (2019). *Constructing the Democratic Public Enterprise. Next System Project*. Washington, DC: Democracy Collaborative.

Dolfsma, W., & Grosman, A. (2019). State Capitalism Revisited: A Review of Emergent Forms and Developments. *Journal of Economic Issues, 53*, 579–586.

ECR. (2018). *Press Release: "Unlocking the Potential of Local Energy Communities. European Committee of the Regions"*. Available at: https://cor.europa.eu/en/news/Pages/unlocking-the-potential-of-local-energy-communities-.aspx. Last Accessed 14 Apr 2020.

Elliott, M., & Kanagasooriam, J. (2017). *Public Opinion in the Post-Brexit Era*. London: Legatum Institute.

Energy Cities. (2017). *Local Energy Ownership in Europe: An Exploratory Study of Local Public Initiatives in France, Germany and the United Kingdom*. Energy Cities. Available at: https://energy-cities.eu/wp-content/uploads/2019/01/local_energy ownership_study-energycities-en.pdf. Last Accessed 14 Apr 2020.

European Commission. (2017). *Proposal for a Directive of the European Parliament and of the Council on Common Rules for the Internal Market in Electricity*. Brussels, Germany: European Commission.

European Directive. (2019). *Directive (EU) 2019/944 of the European Parliament and of the Council of 5 June 2019 on Common Rules for the Internal Market for Electricity and Amending Directive 2012/27/EU* (Recast). Published in Official Journal of the European Union: L158/125-199.

Gill, O. (2020, March 23). The Railways Have Been Nationalised – And There's No Turning Back. *Daily Telegraph*.

Goldman, M. I. (2003). *The Piratization of Russia: Russian Reform Goes Awry*. New York/London: Routledge.

Hadjilambrinos, C. (2000). Understanding Technology Choice in Electricity Industries: A Comparative Study of France and Denmark. *Energy Policy, 28*, 1111–1126.

Hall, D. (2018). *Privatised Water: A System in Need of Repair*. Greenwich, UK: Public Services International Research Unit.

Hall, D., Thomas, S., & Corral, V. (2009). *Global Experience with Electricity Privatisation*. Greenwich, UK: Public Services International Research Unit.

Hall, S. (2017). *Selected Political Writings: The Great Moving Right Show*. London: Lawrence and Wishart.

Harvey, D. (2005). *A Brief History of Neoliberalism*. Oxford, UK: Oxford University Press.

Hatzisavvidou, S. (2020). Inventing the Environmental State: Neoliberal Common Sense and the Limits to Transformation. *Environmental Politics, 29*, 96–114.

Heales, C., Hodgson, M., & Rich, H. (2017). *Humanity at Work: Mondragon. Social Innovation Ecosystem Case Study*. London: The Young Foundation.

HM Treasury. (2002). *Implementing Privatisation: The UK Experience*. London: HM Treasury.

HOC Treasury Committee. (2012). *Private Finance Initiative: Seventeenth Report of Session 2010–12*. London: House of Commons.

Hodgson, G. (1999). *Economics and Utopia: Why the Learning Economy Is Not the End of History*. London: Routledge.

Hudson, M. (2012). *The Bubble and Beyond: Fictitious Capital, Debt Deflation and Global Crisis*. Dresden, Germany: Islet.

Hvelplund, F., Østergaard, P. A., & Meyer, N. I. (2017). Incentives and Barriers for Wind Power Expansion and System Integration in Denmark. *Energy Policy, 107*, 573–584.

Jacobsen, S. (2019, September 18). Orsted to Sell Its Danish Power Businesses for $3.2 Billion. *Reuters*. Available at: https://www.reuters.com/article/us-orsted-m-a-seasnve/orsted-to-sell-its-danish-power-businesses-for-3-2-billion-idUSKBN1W31AW. Last Accessed 14 Apr 2020.

Jacques, M. (2016, August 21). The Death of Neoliberalism and the Crisis in Western Politics. *The Observer*.

King, S. (2017, April 20). The Pendulum Swings Between Globalisation and Nation State. *Financial Times*.

Kishimoto, S., Lobina, E., & Petitjean, O. (Eds.), (2015). *Our Public Water Future: The Global Experience with Remunicipalisation*. Amsterdam: Transnational Institute in Collaboration with Multinational Observatory, Public Services International Research Unit, European Federation of Public Services Unions and Municipal Services Project.

Kishimoto, S., & Petitjean, O. (2017). *Reclaiming Public Services: How Cities and Citizens Are Turning Back Privatisation*. Paris/Amsterdam: Transnational Institute.

Kishimoto, S., Steinfort, L., & Petitjean, O. (2020). *The Future Is Public: Towards Democratic Ownership of Public Services*. Amsterdam: Transnational Institute.

Kozarzewski, P., Bałtowski, M., & Mickiewicz, T. (2022). State Capitalism in Poland and Hungary. In M. Wright, G. Wood, A. Cuervo-Cazurra, P. Sun, I. Okhmatovskiy, & A. Grosman (Eds.), *Oxford Handbook on State Capitalism and the Firm*. Oxford, UK: Oxford University Press, forthcoming.

Labour Energy Forum. (2017). *Who Owns the Wind Owns the Future*. London: Labour Energy Forum.

Labour Party. (2017). *Alternative Models of Ownership. Report to the Shadow Chancellor and the Shadow Secretary of State for Business, Energy and Industrial Strategy*. London: Labour Party.

Labour Party. (2019). *Bringing Energy Home: Labour's Proposal for Publicly Owned Energy Networks*. London: Labour Party.

Lapavitsas, C. (2013). *Profiting Without Producing: How Finance Exploits us All*. London: Verso.

Lent, J. (2020, April 12). Coronavirus Spells the End of the Neoliberal Era. What's Next? *Open Democracy*. Available at: https://www.opendemocracy.net/en/transformation/coronavirus-spells-the-end-of-the-neoliberal-era-whats-next/. Last Accessed 14 Apr 2020.

Lobina, E., & Hall, D. (2007). *Water Privatisation and Restructuring in Latin America: A Briefing*. Greenwich, UK: Public Services International Research Unit.

Lobina, E., & Hall, D. (2013). *List of Water Remunicipalisations Worldwide – As of November 2013*. Greenwich, UK: Public Services International Research Unit.

Lockwood, M. (2015). *The Danish System of Electricity Policy-Making and Regulation*. (EPG Working Paper 1504). Exeter, UK: Exeter University.

Marois, T. (2017). *How Public Banks Can Help Finance a Green and Just Energy Transformation*. Amsterdam: Transnational Institute.

Megginson, W. L., & Netter, J. M. (2001). From State to Market: A Survey of Empirical Studies of Privatization. *Journal of Economic Literature, 31*, 321–389.

Milne, R. (2016, June 8). Dong Energy's Debut Sparks Outrage in Denmark Over Goldman Windfall. *Financial Times*.

Mitchell, T. (2009). Carbon democracy. *Economy and Society, 38*, 399–432.

NAO. (2017). *Hinckley Point C*. London: National Audit Office.

Nell, G. (Ed.). (2015). *Austrian Theory and Economic Organization: Reaching Beyond Free Market Boundaries*. New York: Palgrave Macmillan.

O'Neill, J. (1998). *The Market: Ethics, Knowledge and Politics*. London: Routledge.

O'Neill, J. (2003). Neurath, Associationalism and Markets. *Economy and Society, 32*, 184–206.

O'Neill, J. (2007). *Markets, Deliberation and Environment*. London: Routledge.

Palast, G. (2000, October 8). Inside Corporate America: An Internal Study Reveals the Price "Rescued" Nations Pay: Dearer Essentials, Worse Poverty and Shorter Lives. *The Observer*.

Parker, D. (2012). *The Private Finance Initiative and Intergenerational Equity.* London: Intergenerational Foundation.

Peck, J., & Theodore, N. (2019). Still Neoliberalism? *South Atlantic Quarterly, 118*, 245–265.

Petitjean, O. (2017). Remunicipalisation in France: From Addressing Corporate Abuse to Reinventing Democratic, Sustainable Local Public Services. In S. Kishimoto & O. Petitjean (Eds.), *Reclaiming Public Services: How Cities and Citizens Are Turning Back Privatisation* (pp. 24–33). Paris/Amsterdam: Transnational Institute.

Pigeon, M. (2012). From Fiasco to DAWASCO: Remunicipalising Water Systems in Dar Es Salaam, Tanzania. In M. Pigeon, D. A. McDonald, O. Hoedeman, & S. Kishimoto (Eds.), *Putting Water Back into Public Hands.* Amsterdam: Transnational Institute.

Piketty, T. (2014). *Capital in the Twenty-First Century.* Cambridge, MA: Harvard University Press.

Ryggvik, H. (2010). *The Norwegian Oil Experience: A Toolbox for Managing Resources?* Oslo, Europe: Centre for Technology, Innovation and Culture.

Streeck, W. (2014). The Politics of Public Debt: Neoliberalism, Capitalist Development, and Restructuring of the State. *German Economic Review, 15*, 143–165.

Thomas, S. (2008). *Poor Choices: The Limits of Competitive Markets in the Provision of Essential Services to Low-Income Consumers.* London: Energy Watch.

Veblen, T. (1919 [2005]). *The Vested Interests and the Common Man.* New York: Cosimo.

Waddams Price, C., & Hancock, R. (1998). Distributional Effects of Liberalising UK Residential Utility Markets. *Fiscal Studies, 19*, 295–319.

7

Welfare as Freedom, the Human Economy, and Varieties of Capitalist State

Louise Haagh

1 Introduction

Welfare studies have been enriched in recent decades by critical normative perspectives that argue for a freedom-focussed design of welfare institutions. A key objective of the Welfare-as-Freedom (WAF) literature has been to forefront personal choice within economic and social organisation. Whilst agreeing with this objective, I argue that a too singular perspective on individual governance can set the reality of institutional constraints on personal control too much aside. Whilst the WAF literature has tended to focus on reshaping post-war welfare institutions towards a more simple pre-distributive form, I use freedom-orientation as an opportunity to re-assess the foundations and functioning of welfare systems from a multi-level institutional and well-being perspective. I argue that a focus on lifestyle choice gives an unrealistic representation of the scope for personal control, and overdraws the connection between

L. Haagh (✉)
Department of Politics, University of York, York, UK
e-mail: louise.haagh@york.ac.uk

P. Arestis, M. Sawyer (eds.), *Economic Policies for a Post-Neoliberal World*, International Papers in Political Economy, https://doi.org/10.1007/978-3-030-56735-4_7

choice and well-being. Instead, acknowledging the reality of institutions leads to a focus on their design from the perspective of impacts on states of well-being, which filter the real extent and quality of choices people enjoy.

Focussing on the framing of everyday activities and social relations redraws both the characterisation of and explanation for key differences between familiar welfare state varieties and helps to clear up prevailing misconceptions about them. Along with much standard economic analysis, WAF scholars tend to assume more encompassing welfare states exert more direct control over persons because social organisation is formalised, whereas greater personal and political freedoms require more simple forms of social protection and less regulation. Taking a different direction, I argue that examining developmental dimensions of freedom that can be linked with states of well-being is the basis for a more broadly informative characterisation of welfare state evolution and function. Building on insights from the human development approach (HDA), institutionalist political economy, and the systems varieties literature (SVL), I develop a systems approach to well-being and identify ways the form of public sector development is a factor in both system function (coherence) and social foundations for well-being (transcendence). More particularly, I deepen the focus of these literatures with reference to constraints which, in giving rise to key cooperative problems in social life, human economy (HE) exerts within systems of governance.

I argue key forms of control of time and within social relations are mutually affective, so that the more or less egalitarian and developmental bases on which social relations are formalised shapes institutions' function. We have reason to assume that in societies in which formal cooperation around core human activities is more developed at the level of systems, the form of institutions is more likely to involve an orientation to promote developmental forms of control (HE responsiveness). In turn, important historical factors in HE responsiveness include the level of social equality underpinning modern state formation, combined with the degree of embedding of social cooperation in public sector development.

On this basis, this contribution proceeds as follows. I first discuss how my approach challenges freedom-focussed inquiry at a methodological level. Responding, next, I consider how taking the nature of the human economy as reference aids understanding of developmental aspects of freedom and of the role of embedding of cooperation in institutional development. Third, I discuss in more detail how systemic support of human development and related freedoms can be examined in terms of public sector development and systems of public finance in advanced capitalist states, focussing especially on the cooperative structure of public finance, developmental policies, and systems of education, care, and the incorporation of women. Fourth, I compare capitalist states within the Organisation of Economic Cooperation and Development (OECD) along these lines, honing in on the UK and Denmark. Fifth, I set this discussion in relation to specific aspects of HE responsiveness and control of time. Sixth, I discuss implications for contextual and polemical features of the case for a permanent, unconditional, individual, and regularly paid, citizen's subsistence grant, or universal basic income (UBI, or simply 'basic income') as a response to rising insecurity and support of personal control under globalisation. Last, I summarise and conclude.

2 Comparative Capitalism and Human Development

2.1 Welfare as Freedom and Liberal Neutrality

An emerging WAF literature, deriving from Liberal Egalitarian Thought (LET) and the Human Development Literature (HDL), challenges the study of welfare states. This literature draws attention to everyday forms of control of our lives—for example, of activities like leisure, work and care (Goodin, 2001; Haagh, 2007; Goodin et al., 2008; Standing, 2002; van Parijs, 1995), and human reasons for acting, being and doing (Alkire, 2002; Nussbaum, 2006; Sen, 1998). Whilst this promises to provide a constructive input into policy debate by revealing the value of individuals' real or active ends ('real' freedom, van Parijs—henceforth VP, 1995), the WAF has tended to overlook the extent to which opportunity for valuable *developmental* forms of freedom is socially patterned.

First, my account challenges libertarian-inspired approaches in LET (LALET) that prioritise transactional aspects of control of lifestyle and predistributive justice on assuming that regulatory approaches to social and institutional development devalue freedom. Prioritising the frame around production has been Anglo-liberal practice. Beveridge (1942, p. 121), architect of the British welfare state, aimed welfare at supporting the poor. Even whilst Rawls' later (1971, p. 376, pp. 409–417) influential work stressed the role of fellowship—engaging Nozick's (1974, pp. 183–97) critique of society, approaches in LALET have tended to tie persons' control of the structure of their lives to their direct control of resources (Dworkin, 1981; van Parijs, 1995; discussed in Williams, 2008, pp. 499–500). Informed by a shared ideal of neutrality concerning institutions' form, differences have centred on the principle that should regulate the distributive frame. In Rawls (1971, pp. 65–72), this entailed favouring the least well-off; in Dworkin (1981, pp. 304–5), promotion of equal resources or preference-led insurance (Dworkin, 2000, pp. 70–71, pp. 331–40), and in VP (1995, p. 245, n. 18, following Meade, 1964, p. 1989), emphasis on lifetime basic security, as distinct from (eschewing) more complex social organisation and common services. In these ways, LALET has been given to underestimate the collective nature of economic development to make the case for individual property or 'predistribution' (PD), a position often supported by the idea (in Meade, 1964, pp. 25–6; and recently, The Economist, 2014, November) that automation spells an end to the social nature of production. I argue this underestimation in LALET of the collective character of social life points to the salience of feminist critiques of how distributive approaches (empirically) ignore the reality of social relations (Anderson, 1999, pp. 297–300, p. 311; Young, 1990, pp. 29–33, pp. 120–1) and the gender bias of neo-classical economics (Elson, 2014, p. 191; Pearson, 2014) in favour of a focus on personal control and choice. However, further to this, I explore how examining the relation between institutions and personal control entails placing feminists' insights within a broader idea of how human economy constraints shape common institutions and informs cooperative interests that humans in general have.

Dworkin's (2000, pp. 258–260) reasoning concerning ways true freedom (ethical integrity) relies on a person herself defining what constitutes her life's limits or challenges illustrates the problem at hand. Generic HE features, for example, our orientation to learn, life-cycle biology, and dependence on social ties, do not appear in this account. Rather, HE attributes (talent, physical powers, friendships and associations Dworkin, op. cit., p. 260) are listed on a par with specific social arrangements (wealth, technology, culture, being American, pp. 260–1). The way, then, Dworkin (2000) thereby fails to distinguish integrity (lifestyle) challenges that are linked with deeper developmental constraints, reveals how prioritising social neutrality narrows our conception of the problem of freedom and just institutions to how to adjust for particular innate handicaps and talents (see, also, Dworkin, 1981; VP, pp. 68–70, p. 241, n. 49). In turn, this obscures how opportunity for autonomy in the generic form of developing mental powers ('choosing for one's own reasons', Dworkin, 1988, pp. 13–18, n. 19–20) is a basis for discovering and developing talents in everyone. The structure of this opportunity not only—I argue—is informed by how wider cooperative practices impact individual opportunity within specific groups. In addition, the level of cooperative practice in society as a whole shapes the opportunity structure for all—including for the worse and better off. For example, in education systems, separating or not children by means or ability affects other levels of funding (e.g. of diverse occupational choices; Sect. 4), and the scope for allocation of talent predominating over de-selection of ability in the way economic life is structured.

In another example, we can imagine a woman accepting the job market is too much of a challenge, thus making instead her home (and her limits) a positive factor in her life. However, this only illustrates again how the existence of a human economy (e.g. parenting representing the regularity of care) positions individuals in an unregulated competition economy between two logics—of care or occupation—and thus as not free (in this case) to make choices unless more HE features are systemically recognised. In short, a paradoxical aspect of the focus on lifestyle is how features of the human economy that create dependence on others, directly and remotely, entail that HE choices are more socially constrained *for the same reason* as they are of the highest integrity value. Therefore, embedding cooperation in more complex forms of shared security matters for freedom because transforming social relations away from patterns of domination or isolation towards mutual regard is at the root of expanding core forms of personal control.

In this context, the key problem is then how *informational* limits about the stuff of human development imposed by the post-libertarian project produce oversimplified welfare proposals on account, in part, of how said project ends up misinforming analysis of welfare states.[1] To exemplify, VP (1995) pits his proposal for a universal 'basic income' (UBI or BI) for life—aimed to secure choice of alternative lifestyles, against "welfarist or outcome-oriented" (n. 30, p. 248) projects. Specifically, he links the egalitarian-seeking aim of social democracy with "the freedom to consume" (VP, op. cit., p. 33). This indicates VP does not recognise human development as a motive rooted in Nordic states' public institutions, and as a source of the kind of post-materialist values linked with voluntary activity and leisure (evidenced as strong in Nordic states in Inglehart et al., 2001, p. 7, pp. 15–17) that his analysis prioritises. Instead, VP (1995, p. 242) appeals to the liberal egalitarian tradition of development neutralism and concern (in the lineage of and as expressed in Rawls', 1988, pp. 252–3; 1993, p. 13; 2001, p. 52, p. 60) that public policy should remain silent on matters of the good life (anti-perfectionism, p. 28, p. 255). Albeit tentatively recognising a need for some shared services (but not in principle—VP 1995, p. 231), the commitment to anti-perfectionism becomes in turn a reason to associate post-materialist values with individualised resources distribution in the economy (VP 1995, p. 242). In a recent restatement of this position, Vanderborght and van Parijs (2017, p. 99) justify basic income as a scheme of distributive as distinct from cooperative justice (ibid., p. 103). Moreover, a basic income entails "not to equalise outcomes or achievements … rather … to make less unequal and distribute more fairly, real freedom, possibilities and opportunities" (ibid., p. 107).

I argue that discounting developmental freedoms in this way involves a methodological mistake given how both van Parijs (1995) and Rawls

[1] Concern in LALET to restrict intervention to the distributive frame, overshadowed concern with inequality (Williams, 2008, p. 504).

(2001) recognise developmental interests humans have. So, Rawls (1971, p. 274) aims to protect *against* the transactional outcomes of human frailty (differences of talent and energy), and recognises human rationality as developmental (the Aristotelian principle, pp. 372–376). However, with reference to the immoral nature of markets (p. 274), and stressing monetary incentives to train and work, he abandons this developmental account in his analysis of economic relations. Similarly, *social protection* is VP's (1995, p. 46) rationale for wanting the basic income grant to be paid in a regular form (as distinct from as a one-off grant). However, in depicting Labour Markets (LMs) as transactions of inherent talent (VP, op. cit., 121), he sets aside how talent is developed in education and jobs. In linking our scope to be crazy (leisure) to our opportunity to leave jobs—VP (1995) makes leisure a wholesale lifestyle choice. In distinction from this, I argue the patterned reality of the human economy makes the realisation and wider freedom effects of PD policies highly dependent on the pattern of cooperation in general. On that basis, tendencies in WAF to see the informal as a source of control (e.g. of care and work in Standing, 2002, pp. 269–272); to dichotomise the formal-informal (being work-crazy or leisure-lazy, VP, 1995, pp. 89–96, p. 122); to link control with unstructured time (Goodin, 2001; Goodin et al., 2008); or, to view protection outside the mainframe of production as a source of protection for women (VP, 2001, pp. 19–20; Allstott, 2001, p. 77)—as distinct from emphasising institutional sources of equal standing *of* women; all risk recreating the explanatory problems of Dworkin's (1981) account.

Another way to proceed—and bring the concern in WAF with control of human activities to bear on welfare analysis—is to think that control of time and activities matters not on grounds of being unaffected by institutions, but in reference to developmental features of being human. In this case, unstructured and structured forms of time matter for reasons such as that (Sect. 2.2) they enable human well-being and operating. For example, at stake is the more creative thinking arising from knowledge of (secure, regular) access to contemplative thought (slow thinking, Kahneman, 2011, p. 36), patterned learning arising from repetition and structure (Sennett, 2008, pp. 19–39), and (developmental) autonomy that stability of resources and time supports (Haagh, 2011b). Regularity of both structured and unstructured forms of time enables conciliation of control of everyday and long-term activities and relations (Haagh, 2007), aiding self-development (intrinsic motivation) and mutual regard (Sennett, 2003, pp. 54–56, p. 63) and cooperation (Hood, 2014, pp. 203–4, pp. 267–8) in social relations. Micro-studies have found intrinsic forms of motivation that can be linked with well-being are favoured in conditions in which individuals enjoy combined security (in external income security, more stable employment, shorter unemployment), with these effects being stronger for women and reinforced by but not dependent on higher levels of schooling (Haagh, 2011b). In this way, discovering wider reasons for choosing certain institutions and their combination also offers a different account of individual policies, as I exemplify by how on this basis a different—developmental—defence of basic income can be made as part of a reformist agenda with broader aims and supports.

In the same light, some forms of critique of basic income can be judged as too hasty. For example, conceiving lifestyle choice in terms of leisure is not flawed mainly as this promotes selfishness (Anderson, 1999, p. 299), but because of how it entails an overly simple conception of institutions, for example that ignores key features and linked problems of human functioning. Mutual effect between institutions that support forms of autonomy and of cooperation is a reason why the PD *approach* as set up in LET creates explanatory problems.[2] Adopting instead a broader systemic focus on control of time and activities makes it possible to construct answers to the sort of question that Goodin et al. (2008, p. 14, p. 54) left open in their examination of unstructured time as to why its *extent* is higher in high-tax democracies. I argue it is due to the developed formal features of cooperation—including gender equality—that an inclusive and diversified structure of tax indicates and supports, that a high level of tax in GDP is a conduit for promoting developmental policies at the level of systems.

[2] Meade (1964, pp. 35–8) saw different policies as at the root of different *systems* (e.g. progressive taxation, solidaristic unionism, minimum wages, universal unconditional allowances, respectively), and rejected all but the last as out of date.

2.2 The Human Economy, Institutions, and Freedom

The HDL provides forms of the kind of independent elaboration of human freedoms (Nussbaum, 2006), reasons for acting (Alkire, 2002) and social opportunity (Sen, 1998), that I argue is called for. At the same time, the HDL has been characterised by an intention to leave open the field of individual and social choice (Sen, 1992, pp. 46–48, p. 53, p. 72; Arneson, 2013, pp. 11–12; Anderson, 1999, pp. 331–7). This has meant focus on agency aspects of democracy, including women's agency and organisations (Nussbaum, 2000, pp. 270–290, in discussion of the state), and on basic entitlements (public health, initial schooling; Sen, 1998, pp. 40–46), has prevailed over concern with social regulation. To also support an institutional analysis of human development, reference to the broad idea of a human economy can be made against systematic evidence of human functioning in general, such as already indicated. For example, in line with the above discussion of control of time and relations, core human economy constraints can be identified as conditions relating to developmental cognitive patterns, the biological life cycle (daily, long-term and reproductive conditions) and social dependence (the need of care, fellowship, learning; Haagh, 2007, 2019e). Without aiming to give an exhaustive account, identification of core HE traits is useful for understanding cooperative dynamics and governance effectiveness in systems; for instance, by clarifying how different inequalities are created and matter. This includes how relational and resource inequalities within education, gender equality in care and occupations, or access to basic security, are linked and underpin welfare legitimacy, as well as affect policy effectiveness and wider inequalities of income and in social relations (Sects. 4 and 5).[3]

On this account, developmental features of human *cognition* explain how human rationality and behaviour are generally patterned (North, 2005; Rawls, 1971—his Aristotelian principle of human motivation). The same features help explain how long-term health is responsive to the creation of sustained patterns in individuals' lives (as documented in

[3] Piketty (2014, p. 265) links growing earnings inequality in Anglo-Saxon countries to rules which permit 'super-managers' to set their own wage.

Fredrickson et al., 2013). Social surveys (Haagh, 2011b; Parker and Skoufias 2001), and behavioural (Kahneman, 2011) and neuro-science experiments (Callard & Margulies, 2014; Smallwood, 2013), indicate that where the form of (formal and informal) institutions enable stability as a basis for structured learning, more intrinsic forms of motivation result (Haagh, 2011b). Psychologists have identified innate needs for a time structure that fits (regularity and reproductive) constraints of the human life cycle (Cantor & Sanderson, 2003), whereas a range of studies now exist to document how cooperation is a human desire that—when enabled in a stable form—is linked with mental and physical health (Hood, 2014, pp. 134–5, p. 193). Conversely, uncontrollable events in everyday life—including in structures affecting others—have been found to cause feelings of helplessness (Peterson, 2003, pp. 291–292). In turn, when unstable economies make uncontrollable events recurrent, this generates self-fulfilling behaviours, as both society and individuals adapt and learn to be helpless (ibid., p. 293).

The key point here is how reference to developmental aspects of human function suggests generic (cooperative) interests that humans have in institutions that enable personal control in relation to both the structure of human life itself and its social relations, as vulnerability is a central feature of both. Evidence that women plan fertility in relation to their labour market positions (Haagh, 2011b) and that men gradually take on childcare duties (Nordenmark, 2015, pp. 172–3) and care leave (Bloksgaard, 2015, pp. 148–52) when general institutions permit it (Gornick, 2015, pp. 375–376), indicates both men and women seek to attain a balance in their lives between core human activities and social relations, and respond to institutions accordingly.

To better illustrate how different forms of control of the human economy are linked, I distinguish core forms of HE-relevant aspects of control of time, activities and social relations, as follows. I hypothesise that *dynamic* control of the human learning process and relations is linked with developmentally structured education and working life; *static* control is tied to opportunity for regular time for the core activities of occupation, leisure and care (Haagh, 2007), whereas *reproductive control* emerges from arrangements that make combinations of these processes possible (e.g. parental leave and the occupation-competitive structure).

In turn, interests in underlying senses of personal security (*constant control*) express a higher-order interest in enjoying a permanent foundation of personal economic stability that is not dependent on any one relation as a basis for sustaining and exercising innate capacities for independent reason, establishing thus a wider foundation for enjoying developmental forms of motivation and choice acts to prevent direct domination and protect persons' integrity in the Dworkinian sense. Finally, on this basis, *direct political or cooperative control* describes opportunity for social relations based on mutual recognition (contra domination) to include then the nature of the patterning of informal activities and relations in core settings (work, the family, vis-à-vis the state).

Unlike previous studies, I suggest the areas concerned are mutually affective in institutional reality because they have roots in human economy. Put in another way, the above-listed forms of control are important in their own right (they require separate forms of support). However, in practice, (i) their exercise depends on the existence of the others; and (ii) partly for this reason, we can expect that institutions that support control develop in complex affective patterns. Explanatory advantages include to avoid that caution as expressed in the HDL to remain neutral (as explained in Alkire, 2002, p. 194) entails linking human development directly with individual choices of functionings whatever they are (also a fallacy of Dworkin's account). For example, identifying HE features creates a way to analytically and empirically separate human propensities, well-being states, and common and specific forms that institutions take, all three of which feature without differentiation in HD depiction or lists (Alkire, 2002; Anderson, 1999, pp. 331–7; Nussbaum, 2006, pp. 76–79). So, capabilities such as, in Nussbaum (2006, pp. 76–77), practical reason, (biological) life, and (social) affiliation are in my account generic traits of the human condition and deeper causes of patterns in social relations. Material security, political rights, social bases of self-respect (Nussbaum, op. cit., pp. 77–78), and specific forms these take (equal rights to seek employment, in work having relations of mutual recognition, p. 78), are general and more specific corollaries. Notably, in Sen (1998, pp. 37–38), the two categories would be, respectively, general and specific forms of instrumental freedoms, as distinct from capabilities and functionings that have intrinsic value.

In addition, HE reference also supports an account of system functioning and outcomes, as focus on embedded as well as process aspects of cooperation can reveal how these are linked. For example, further to the constitutive role of women's agency (Sen, 1998, pp. 189–203), we can explore how institutions sustain it and gender *relations* count. For example, embedding of cooperation in everyday life and institutional development (the design of public finance and developmental policies) may at once raise the level and differentiate the form of shared security, as well as enable both direct agency and other (more internalised) forms of personal control (as perceptible in Nordic states, Sects. 4 and 5).

In short, taking HE responsiveness in the institutional form cooperation takes as an interceding variable in accounting for freedom impacts, offers a way to bridge the comparative institutions (including feminist) and HDL literatures. Problems of how states treat citizens, how persons can control social relations, and can have access to time, can be understood as related and shaped by the system of institutions as a whole. The reality of HE can help explain how gender equality is central to system coherence.

3 Public Sector Development and Systems of Cooperation in Nordic and Anglo-Saxon States

As in the case of WAF, comparative institutional literatures which claim or aim for value neutrality also end up being locked into a too linear analysis, which involves assuming institutions are a direct product of actors' choices. Focus on human economy as a governing constraint transcends a neutrality/normativity divide within institutional studies by revealing underlying determinants of the functioning of institutions for particular ends.

To illustrate, questions of value are central in distinguishing post-neoclassical and heterodox economics analyses of institutions, in terms of the way institutions are conceptualised as arising and having effect. The two traditions share certain traits, including to recognise (i) the importance of security in individual motivation (North, 2005, pp. 13–15) and (ii) the pivotal role of institutions in transforming uncertainty into calculated risk (Eggertson, 1990, pp. 26–27; North, 2005) and forging underlying forms of coincidence of interest (political security; Bates, 2006, p. 709; Steinmo, 2018).

North's (2005) tradition is post-neo-classical in that it lays emphasis on the state's role in relation to the maintenance of stable institutions in support of market-transacting economies, which are themselves seen as rational (Williamson, 1985, pp. 68–75). In contrast, heterodox approaches such as institutionalist political economy tend to at least implicitly privilege understanding of the role of regulation in generating more egalitarian development outcomes, for example, actively regulating the labour market is both inescapable (You & Chang, 1993) and part of 'civilisation'—as in the case of regulating child labour (Chang, 2003, pp. 542–543; Solow, 1990). Further to this, however, I want to highlight how political choices are constrained by deeper forces. Specifically, we can expect that—irrespective of the motivations at stake—the effect on systems' function of choices about institutions' design depends on the level of HE responsiveness.

The SVL has identified factors that distinguish systems, respectively being 'de-commodification' (protection from marketised relations) in the Welfare State Varieties (WSV) school—led by Esping-Andersen (1990), and the organisation of skills in the Varieties of Capitalism (VoC) approach. I argue, however, that identifying de-commodification and skills organisation gets us only halfway to recognising the human economy as a deeper constraint behind human systems.

Esping-Andersen (1990, p. 37) classified welfare systems by use of a freedom measure, de-commodification. On the other hand, relating his definition to a feature of institutions, for example protection from wage-related employment, like WAF, Esping-Andersen (op. cit.) did not offer a separate definition of freedom itself, which would explain how and why commodification is a problem. This raises the question whether Esping-Andersen's (1990) critique of commodification takes issue with employment per se, or with just a certain form of employment. Since

Esping-Andersen (op. cit.) does explicitly link good and bad work with different welfare systems (pp. 203–17), this suggests the problem at hand—including for him—is *not* the social organisation of work through contract (employment) and commodification in this sense (resourcing productive activity and in some accountable way rewarding individuals for their effort or time). Rather, of concern is the form social work takes and the extent it is backed up by employment-independent security systems. More clearly problematising the (contractual, accountable, stable a.o.) form that employment takes against external criteria is compatible with the human economics approach laid out here, in the terms of which employment systems—linking the form of employment and systems that support it—can be viewed as representing modes of formally recognising and investing in lines of at the same time human and economic activity. The environmental reality of human economy explains why developmental policies and forms of governance and long-term planning are more effective, if not necessarily prevalent. Specifically, the degree of HE sensitivity of employment would depend on the societal-level development of employment-internal and employment-external economic security systems. For example, employment structures can be viewed as HE sensitive in the degree they enable stability of expectations around combinations of forms of control in and outside occupational life in ways which would not be feasible through self-organisation (Sect. 4). Notably, even when neither the WSV or VoC explicitly account for the regulative role of human economy, focussing instead on more incidental factors in systems' evolution, the historical accounts these approaches provide are revealing of human economy constraints acting in shaping how systems work.

Where the WSV starts with state-led social protection in comparing system types, the VoC literature begins with the business-led organisation of skills. In the latter case, giving evidence of how the structuring of a core human capacity and activity—learning—shapes alternative systems, the VoC challenged the central role that conventional economics (and political philosophies resting on it, Sect. 2) gave to transactional freedom. Hall and Soskice (2001, p. 17), Thelen (2004), and Maurice, Sellier, and Silvestre (1986), set out how Germany's 'coordinated' market economy promoted industrial skills systemically. Pagano (1999) showed how more developed property-rights systems have adopted skills development along with social protection as universal goals. In contrast, Schneider (2013) and Haagh (1999, 2002) have documented how weak representation and hierarchy in production systems in Latin America created inequality and weak investment in skills.

On the other hand, to avoid the charge of being normative, the mainstay of VoC became wedded to neutralism (Haagh, 2019b). This involves a claim that all systems are equally 'good', which then prevents more affirmative analyses of institutional designs in relation to explicit criteria (such as skills organisation and implications for well-being). The VoC can be characterised as politically determinist in the sense that political origins and choices are the normative standard. So, the USA form of capitalism—even though it generates a much lower level of skills—is not necessarily worse or better—merely different (Steinmo, 2010, p. 20; Thelen, 2014, p. 3). When Thelen (2014) notes, referring to the USA and Germany, that the VoC in comparing the two has examined "different ways to organise capitalism [in which] *each type operates on a wholly different logic* and *each does different things well*", she is not only explicating the commitment to neutralism (requiring VoC to acknowledge *each does different things well) (p. 3; italics and brackets added).* In addition, it is claimed that the *'logic'* driving each system is '*wholly different*'. This said, the VoC has identified business organisation as a key (common) distinguishing factor in skills organisation (Hall & Soskice, 2001; and Thelen, 2014, p. 39, for the USA). I argue, if further to this we were to say that there are similar constraints and problems acting on all systems, and differences in skills organisation represent *varied responses*, then the scope for a more informed multi-level analysis of and *explanation for* systems' performance would be brought into view.

Business sector organisation would be only one factor in emergence of different systems (Steinmo, 2010), whilst the coordinating role of the state could be recognised as more important in shaping systemic patterns, such as HE responsiveness. In particular, the role of state-led education systems in shaping economic and social organisation would play a bigger role in the explanation. Accordingly, where Steinmo (2010, p. 16) points to dynamic change as driven by how institutions' functions combine, I argue mutual effects between institutions can also be understood more affirmatively in terms of transcendence. This refers to dynamic incentives that a wider embedding of cooperative interests in everyday more equal social relations creates in evolving more HE-referent and system-coherent solutions to problems. In addition, a higher level of skills organisation then becomes a very important intermediary factor in explaining state capacity to evolve and sustain systems of well-being. Besides the underlying constraints presented by human economy, modern societies share the reality of states as the dominant legal frame. On this basis, making sense of how in these ways overall cooperative patterns in public sector development shapes systems, entails paying attention to the level of *resource coordination* and the *formality of incorporation*, respectively. This requires briefly examining the historical importance of two key factors, being, respectively, social equality in the period prior to and during modern state formation, and the extent the rise of industrial capitalism broke the established pattern.

3.1 Actual Equality, State Formation, and Freedom

An important sub-variety within historical institutionalism seeks to understand how social conditions behind state formation shape the character of modern political economies. This literature comprises rich analysis of the role of 'inclusive' reforms and state initiatives in development modernity. Examples include the role of war and taxation in generating more tax-effective states (Bates, 2006; Tilly, 1985), and the role of early land reform and inherited property-rights systems in more inclusive market economies and viable democracies (Acemoglu, Johnson, & Robinson, 2002; Boix, 2003). An interesting aspect of this literature turns on the question, what comes first—conditions of equality, or equalising reforms and institutions? Sokoloff and Engerman (2000) argue that conditions of inequality or equality resulting from the form of new world exploration—for example Spanish and Portuguese colonial settlement in the early modern period—produced lasting differential effects, which attained dynamic features. Once economic elites in Latin America were in a position to control policy and the state, they were able to lock in their power, resulting in omissions or actions in public policy, which restricted competitive entry of other groups, notably natives and slaves. By contrast, comparably greater equality in North America, in particular within the North of the modern USA, generated more transparent political and more inclusive market institutions.

If, however, we add to this comparative exercise the case of Nordic states, we discover an additional key factor in filtering and abating the effect of conditions of relatively greater market-based equality. This factor is the extent of state-initiated property-rights redistribution before the rise of capitalism. In Nordic states, the spread and level of literacy and public organisation of elementary education in the 1700s have been argued to be rivalled only by North America at the time (Sandberg, 1979). At the same time, state-led reforms in Nordic states also entailed a more egalitarian distribution of land and small-scale owner farming (Chang, 2009; Kananen, 2014). On this account, Sokoloff and Engerman (2000) arguably overestimate the extent of social equality in North America (given the contrast with Latin America where inequality was extreme). Specifically, in the USA, contestation of slavery by the Republican North was framed in defence of an alternative freedom of labour in the market space, which in turn suited industrial elites (Foner, 1995). Unlike both North America and Nordic states, the land enclosures in Britain further concentrated land ownership (Fairlie, 2009) and—as in America in the case of ex-slaves and white poor farm labourers—turned a new rural underclass into an impoverished industrial proletariat. In the USA, the consequence was a radical yet disempowered union movement (Archer, 2010), and in both the USA and Britain a persistent legacy of low-skill labour (Finegold & Soskice, 1988).

By contrast, in Nordic states, a tradition of peasant appeal to public authorities to exert justice and regulation of work in the countryside before and during the period of state formation (Haagh, 2019b; Jensen, 1936), embedded the role of the state and public policy in society. Effective and rights-based centralisation of power in individual kingdoms gave the state authority to regulate economic affairs, and override claims of the nobility (Haagh, 2019b; Kananen, 2014). In the nineteenth century, cooperative farmers' movements in Nordic states received public subsidies and moulded into a rural middle-class, which formed alliances with a gradually emerging urban organised working class (Chang, 2009).

On this basis, it can be claimed that Nordic states, whilst market societies, were not exactly a different variety of capitalism as much as they were and have remained *less capitalist.* The rights-basis of Nordic states prevented the arising of an underbelly of informal economy and extensive proletarianisation and precarisation of labour.

In turn, a pattern of simultaneous central resource coordination and formal incorporation of citizens, through multi-pronged forms of social service expansion and legal changes, took place. This may be exemplified as much in state-backed developmental subsidy of land reform (Kananen, 2014, p. 38, pp. 47–9) as in the legal equality of women in education and family law, and educational expansion (Soysal & Strang, 1989).[4]

By contrast, weaker embedding of cooperative capabilities and HE sensitivity characterised the pattern of Anglo-liberal transitions to modern statehood (in the USA symbolised by the North South-divide, Boix, 2003, pp. 118–23). In movements to extend the franchise, women's and tenants' rights were relegated by split working class and left groupings ultimately manipulated by competing factions of capital for larger political ends (Collier, 1999, pp. 62–7). Capital accepted political democratisation only on the basis of special exit (Boix, 2003, p. 228) or rent (e.g. from public debt, Piketty, 2014, pp. 130–133, p. 142) options, which in turn curtailed efforts at redistribution and public investment (Piketty, ibid., pp. 133–136).

In Sweden, the 'Rehn-Meidner' labour-capital accord of the 1950s to support high productivity growth by suppressing low wages was actively supported by fiscal (developmental) policy (Steinmo, 2010, p. 51, p. 54, pp. 57–58), to use tax to favour productive investment over speculation, and encourage women's sustainable inclusion in occupational life through child-care and family subsidies. Counterfactually, a structurally weak business community (in the USA, see Thelen, 2014, p. 39), and a fractured industrial relations in the UK (Crouch, 1994, pp. 13–16; 1977), created fault-lines that after the 1970s crisis made deep deregulatory politics attractive.

[4] Overtaken only by Switzerland and France in Europe, education coverage was uniformly high in Nordic countries by 1870 (at 58, 71 and 61% in Denmark, Sweden and Norway), compared with 49% in the UK and the highest in Southern Europe, at 29% in Italy (Soysal & Strang, 1989).

A key point here is how the two trajectories reviewed respond to vulnerability differently. In the first case, an abstract moral (external) concern gave rise to group-focussed—but ultimately residual—schemes, such as in Skocpol's (1992, pp. 532–535) analysis framed early American welfare. Meanwhile, a gradual flattening of provision (Clasen, 2001; Hay & Farrall, 2014) has shaped the UK welfare state. By contrast, the second—Nordic—trajectory entailed a form of progressive and cumulative systemic recognition of more human needs over time.

Notably, Korpi and Palme (1998) referred to how Nordic states lowered old-age poverty as a 'paradox', as public schemes (also) involved subsidising (higher) earners' savings. Accordingly, Korpi and Palme (op. cit., p. 670) excluded Denmark from the 'encompassing' group because of its simple pension model. However, relatively rights-based income assistance combined with subsidy of generous second-tier unemployment insurance, and of housing stability, care, and all levels of education, training and early retirement (Graphs 7.3 and 7.5), mean Denmark easily (if not better) fits Korpi and Palme's (1998) general model of complex incorporation through publicly supported services. Like other Nordic states, Denmark also combined pre – and re-distribution.

Transcendence is also revealed in the general integration of more (educational, care) services from the 1950s on, and over time their progressive coverage of men (see below), and—more recently—legal changes that promote the care status of fathers after divorce (Friðriksdóttir, 2015, pp. 64–8) and choice in publicly supported care (see Sect. 5). In the UK, policies to support single mothers to become economically active did not take off till the 2000s, and again was a largely reactive development, on the back of a long period of falling benefit levels (Atkinson, 2015, p. 66, p. 226), and in the form of threats of benefit or housing withdrawal (Sect. 4). In comparison, in Nordic states, promotion of a *developmental-allocative* model in education and occupational and family life (see below) aligns *distributions* of resources (e.g. income) and opportunities more effectively than hierarchical-selective competitive systems can achieve. The upshot of a developmental-allocative model is to embed more equal social relations in different ways, for example insofar as individuals do not have to participate directly (though they can; Pettersson, 2007, p. 177; e.g in school boards, labour unions) to be part of (*incorporated* in) systems.

4 Public Finance, Systems of Institutions, and Developmental Coherence in Capitalist States

The point here is not to establish single causes of developmental coherence, since developmental coherence can be attained through different routes and ascertained in different ways. Rather, I want to explore, however established, developmental coherence as well as incoherence function dynamically. This includes investigating how in the contemporary (post-1980s) period, in Anglo-liberal states, greater propensity to pursue reform through the market has entailed fragmentary processes that proceed relatively rapidly. Comparably, institutional resilience and its supports in Nordic states are revealed in ways responses to restructuring have taken a more cooperative form. To exemplify, below I discuss how evidence points to ways public sector development is informed by its progressiveness as defined—in systemic terms—by a dynamic relation between the (i) democratic structure—and related overall level—of tax and (ii) developmental orientation of regulation and spending. Importantly, my understanding of progressiveness here refers to overall system features (cooperative structure of tax, regulation and spend), which contrasts with the OECD's (2008e, pp. 104–105) strict or narrow definition of progressiveness, as the relative share of tax paid by the highest earners. I argue this latter model forms part of a renewed political tendency to suppress the level and scope of common finance, through targeting services in the form of compensatory protection, along with promotion of adversarial and punitive governing as distinct from the promotion of mutual regard in social relations.

To illustrate, in the USA, the high share of the rich's tax contribution stems from the high earnings threshold at which higher tax rates (notably lower however than the Nordic rate) set in (at 9.6 times the average wage in 2009, up from 8.9 in 2000, the highest in the OECD, Table A.1). The way thus the better off appear to pay a lot only as others pay so little—against a background of high inequality (in part a function of the wide span of earnings)[5]—means that there is neither the fiscal means, nor the political climate, to smooth out education and employment inequalities, and thus enable a more even contributions base (for tax). In sum, the low-tax and low-regulation economy legitimises unequal entitlements by diminishing the reality of shared production. A heavily class-redistributive tax structure is thus a source of a low-tax equilibrium. In contrast, the greater formality of sharing under a progressive public finance model—as I define progressiveness—renders the reality of the inter-dependent nature of the modern economy (e.g. to include the human economy) visible. Britain is an interesting hybrid moving in a fragmentary direction by a different route, for example as more inclusive public services (health), better social protection (income, housing), and higher (intermediate) levels of public finance in GDP, are more entrenched (compared with the USA), yet public regulation and services have been over time further withdrawn from production. Median earners pay a higher relative share of tax (than in the USA), but lower marginal rates, combined with declining real wages (and low-income tax receipts), have reinforced deep cuts to universal (and middle-class inclusive) services over time. In turn, this has contributed to bolster the strong hierarchical structure and exclusive nature of private provision (e.g. in schooling), and eventually changed the state (Sect. 5).[6]

Whilst the rise of public austerity has been recognized to generally threaten the democratic function of states (Streeck & Schäfer, 2013), and induce forms of breakdown in state functions (Haagh, 2019a, c, e, 2020) that scholars of institutional change (Streeck and Thelen, 2005) refer to as exhaustion and breakdown, this tendency is met with greater resistance in systems in which HE responsiveness is more embedded. As Thelen (2014) discusses, there are significant differences between countries' liberalisation policies, for example, investment in training; differences however, which—in contrast to Thelen (op. cit.)—I argue are only

[5] OECD (2008e, p. 36).

[6] The UK's 2013 marginal rate tax cut was according to accountants KPMG, reported in the Daily Telegraph (3 December 2014), the largest in the world that year.

in the second instance a (recent) response to global competition. As an example, Nordic responses to global competition that involve greater training and social protection (flexicurity; Kongshøj-Madsen, 2003) ought, I argue, to be seen in the first instance as being the outcome of longer-running systemic features of HE responsiveness, to include Nordic states' more deliberate developmental forms of education, occupation, and integration of women. Involved is, as indicated, a developmental orientation (through regulation and spending) in areas of public policy more central to the organising of human activities, to include leave, training, subsidy of employment, and child-care (Table A.1). Thelen's (2014) characterisation may also be argued to overlook negative aspects of neo-liberalisation in Nordic states, such as how the element of labour flexibilisation involved has challenged the developmental model of governance rather than enhanced it (Haagh, 2019a). Cuts in entitlement to unemployment insurance (such as from four to two years in 2010) meant a large share of the labour market—between 2010 and 2014 an estimated 80,000 persons (Kirk, 2015)—fell out of the developmental (UI) system to become instead reliant on means-tested support. On the other hand, a sustained high level of spending on training (Haagh, 2019e) has played a key role in sustaining a developmental model, even as this has been challenged.

Accordingly, my composite indices below of trends in public sector development give data indicating both HE orientation (tax, regulation and spending) and impact greater weight. Use of composite indices to draw out key traits of public finance, and education, and labour market and other institutions, and to characterise patterns of opportunity, and distributive and cooperative outcomes, reflects the institutional form of explanation pursued. Hence, the graphs to follow depict relevant compound features of systems, and do not indicate direct—but rather mediated—lines of causality between individual policies and outcomes. This is as mutual effects between general *opportunity structures* and stratification of *attainments* are argued to shape interactions between incentives, cooperation, policy effectiveness and legitimacy. This mutual effect between opportunity structures and attainments reflects the patterning of HE responsiveness in systems' evolution.

4.1 Progressive Public Finance and Horizontal-Developmental Versus Hierarchical-Competitive Systems

To first depict the democratic-developmental structure of public finance that the above discussion suggests is indicative of systemic differences, Graph 7.1 presents indices of (y axis) the level and egalitarian dimensions of tax and (x axis) developmental public expenditures in GDP. I focus on the immediately preceding 2008-crises period to show how variant patterns were both well-established and deepened during the intermediate (1990s–2000s) period of neo-liberal globalisation, prior to the 2008 crash.[7]

The index of Progressive Public Finance (PPF) in the dimension of tax (Table A.1) includes marginal rates, the level at which they apply, and the total tax level in GDP: Table A.1 and Graph 7.1 indicate an up-scaling effect between the two. Also included are taxes on production and profits, showing these are geared to incentivise (being higher on dividends and marginal income) in Nordic states. The spending index of PPF (Table A.2) contains, in addition to the level of social expenditure, public spending in GDP on education and services to support occupation stability and balanced time (child-care).[8] Graphs 7.1 and 7.2 use comparable (thus more compressed) data for 2000 and 2007, indicating that the Anglo-Saxon countries show the most dramatic change, especially the UK, due to the rapidly rising influence of educational fees and a significant fall in spending on training and job creation (Table A.1). In the USA, where spending commitments are already low, change occurs on the side of taxation, with a significant drop in the top marginal rate (the opposite occurs in Britain). This difference reflects the (as discussed) different form of stratification of cooperative interests. Concentration of tax in the USA on top earners is politically unsustainable, whereas in the UK, where tax is already higher and broader, the top marginal rate—effective

[7] For 2010 trends, see Haagh (2019e).

[8] Public health, as well as long-term care expenditure in GDP, is high in Nordic countries (and in Denmark the highest; OECD, 2011a, pp. 36, 165, 72, 177, 163).

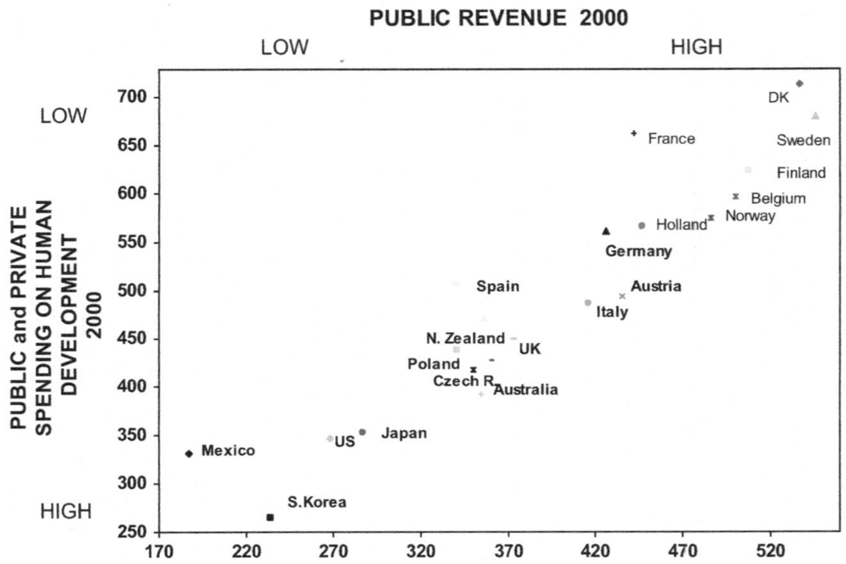

Graph 7.1
PUBLIC REVENUE: Index of 1. Top marginal tax rate and multiple of average wage where set in. 2. Total tax revenue as % of GDP. 3. General Government Revenue in GDP

PUBLIC SPENDING ON HUMAN DEVELOPMENT: Index of 1. Public social expenditure as a percentage of GDP. 2. Training and job creation public expenditure in GDP. 3. Share of public expenditure on tertiary educational institutions. 4. Public/private education spending in GDP. 5. Public spending on family services in GDP (Sources and calculations see Table A.1 in Appendix.)

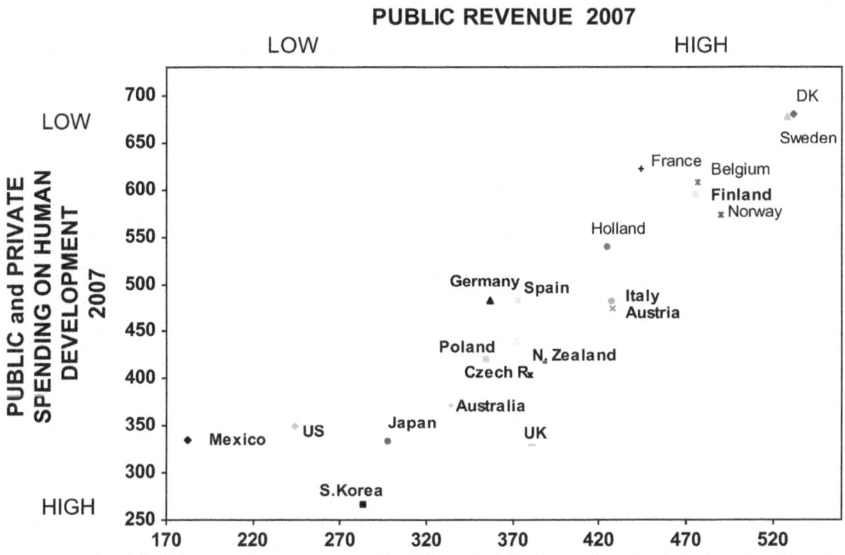

Graph 7.2
PUBLIC REVENUE: Index of 1. Top marginal tax rate and multiple of average wage where set in. 2. Total tax revenue as % of GDP. 3. General Government Revenue in GDP

PUBLIC SPENDING ON HUMAN DEVELOPMENT: Index of 1. Public social expenditure as a percentage of GDP. 2. Training and job creation public expenditure in GDP. 3. Share of public expenditure on tertiary educational institutions. 4. Public/private education spending in GDP. 5. Public spending on family services in GDP (Sources and calculations see Table A.1 in Appendix)

at a lower threshold—is temporarily increased in response to the (2007 onwards) crisis.

A depiction of impact on distributional outcomes is shown in Graph 7.3, illustrating how countries with more features of PPE, combining tax and spend in one index (from Table A.1), also tend to have more diversified structures of shared security and more effective targeted policies (column 2.b, Table A.2), lower inequality (columns 1, 3, 4) and more universal coverage of services (column 6).

Ways in turn in which cooperative features of public finance support developmental-allocative institutions, mutual regard, and everyday forms of control in this context, include as redistributive properties of PPF, and incorporating initiatives in public policy, reinforce each other.[9] In the case of education, broad-based tax raises available resources and the legitimacy of promoting universal (e.g. equal quality) schooling. Meanwhile, high average but also progressive tax reinforce this effect by keeping income inequalities that give rise to elite education at bay. Unusually high public spending on education in GDP (Table A.1, column 4) is evidence of this dynamic. In Nordic states, either or both a direct cap on fees (ban in Sweden, Steinmo, 2010, p. 73), or/and a policy to reduce incentives for schools to charge fees (by public subsidy), as well as strong common curricula requirements and elimination of grading (ibid., p. 71), also promote *general opportunity* (e.g. to discover different talents through delayed examinations). These measures are a source of more widely dispersing occupational *attainments,* as this structure generates support for high spending on different opportunities (university and vocational); with apprenticeships covering up to 40% of school leavers in Denmark, and 21% of private firms participating, in the late 1990s (Anker, 1998).[10] Mixed-ability teaching within and across classes and schools embeds forms of mutual regard in the relation of peers through the educational process—and extension into occupational life of public policies embeds support across generations. Flexicurity corroded this system to some extent, with a fall in youth participation in manual occupational training systems to around 20% by the late 2010s (Tesfaye, 2013). A government long-term target of upping participation to 30% (Jyllandsposten, 2020), however, suggests continued efforts to evolve and maintain the developmental systems of occupational inclusion in the face of strain.

By counterfactual reference, a long-standing practice in the UK education system leaves the fee-paying sector outside the purview of public subsidy (except indirectly through the claiming of non-tax charitable status) in exchange for a framework of self-regulation. This exemplifies the emphasis on the distributive frame in Anglo-liberal public policy (and analysis, as above) and systemic impacts it has, for example, as weak

[9] Sweden's support for paying higher taxes—and trust in other citizens' honesty—grew dramatically in the 2000s during a period of cutbacks and recession (Svallfors, 2011, pp. 811–812).

[10] This compares with only 64 companies overall in Britain, reportedly taking apprentices at the height of pro-apprenticeship policy in 2007 under Labour's flagship Job-Centre Plus network (Financial Times, 10 September 2007).

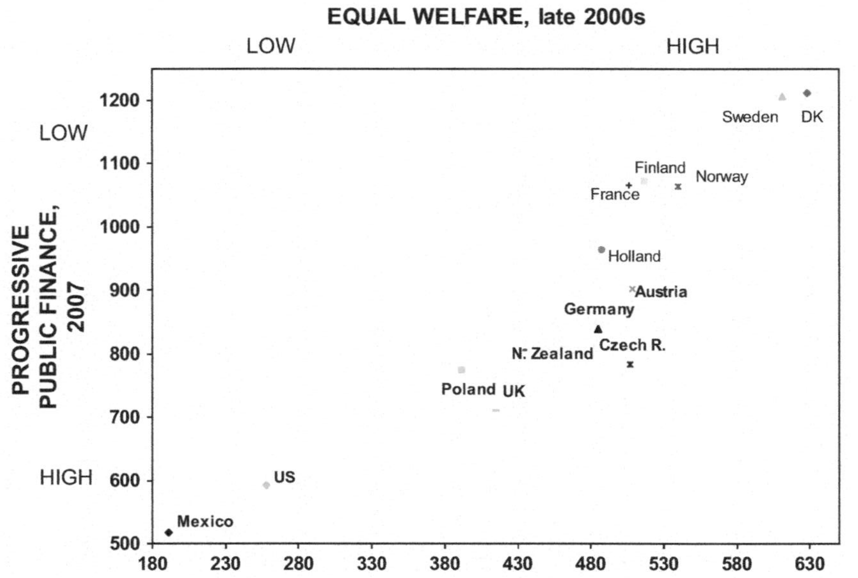

Graph 7.3
PROGRESSIVE PUBLIC FINANCE: Index of X and Y axes, Graph. 7.3
PUBLIC REVENUE: Index of 1. Top marginal tax rate and multiple of average wage where set in, 2007. 2. Total tax revenue as % of GDP, 2007. 3. General Government Revenue in GDP, 1007, and

PUBLIC SPENDING ON HUMAN DEVELOPMENT: Index of 1. Public social expenditure as a percentage of GDP. 2. Training and job creation public expenditure in GDP. 3. Share of public expenditure on tertiary educational institutions. 4. Public/ private education spending in GDP. 5. Public spending on family services in GDP. EQUAL WELFARE: 1. Disposable income poverty rate, late 2000s, and trend. 2. Difference in inequality before and after taxes and transfers, mid 2000s. 3. Redistribution of cash transfers to lowest quintile, mid-2000s 4. Ratio of rich to poor. Mid-2000s, and trend. 5. Gini, late 2000s and trend. 6. Higher scores for lower private social expenditure, 2007, and trend. 7. The level and relative evenness of the value of public services at top and bottom of income quintiles (Sources and calculations see Table A.2 in Appendix) regulatory capacity has undermined effectiveness of individual policies and lowered incentives for common finance of higher education and training.[11] To illustrate, rapidly rising fees to independent schools meant growth of private finance in the UK between the mid-1990s and 2005 (at 174%) discounted effects of public investment in the same period (at 146%, OECD, 2008a), as the opportunity structure grew more vertical.[12] In 2006, Britain had one of the most unequal distributions of class sizes between the public and fee-paying sector in the OECD (a ratio of 18.6 to 7.2 between state and fee-paying schools).[13] Private pupils' chances of entering elite universities (Oxbridge) (as compared with other pupils) were estimated at about 55–1 in the late 2000s (Sutton Trust, 2014b, p. 7). Reinforcing the effect of this inequality at the base was a more radical shift in higher education funding, where the share of public spending dropped radically, from 80% to 36%, transforming the UK from a continental European to a US model in the space of 12 years (1995–2007). Inequalities of access to top professions in Britain, already high, rose as well (Sutton Trust, 2007, p. 7). These trends are captured and compared with other OECD countries in an index of education inequality, covering 22 OECD countries, in order to give an overview of inequality structure and direction of change. Notably, a fragmentary trait of the HC trajectory is how at the same time it permits new (e.g. schooling, income) inequalities to rise that less developmentally focussed public policies are in turn less able to contain. Furthermore, in the UK, as employment policy spending was dramatically cut (from 0.37 to 0.05% in GDP in the 2000s), real costs of private care grew (along with

[11] There are more students in independently (parent-) governed schools in Nordic states (13% in Denmark—39% in the capital Copenhagen—against 7% in the UK). Many charge a small fee though—as noted earlier—the level and effect are contained through public policy. For the same type of school—Steiner, the fees are about 5.6 times higher in the UK (Kr. 15,500 or about £1737 per year in Århus in Denmark in 2013, and £9800 in Hounslow, UK). Available at: http://www.steinerskolen-aarhus.dk/information/skolepenge/; and also at: http://www.stmichaelsteiner.hounslow.sch.uk/information/finance.html

[12] Thus, in only seven years, between 2000 and 2007, the share of public finance for elementary education in Britain fell from 88.7% to 78.1% (the lowest level in the OECD) whilst the share of pupils attending state schools remained constant.

[13] Private educational fees rose by 83% in real terms between 1992 and 2010, almost three times the rise in average incomes (Daily Telegraph, 18 June 2010). Half of this rise occurred since 2005 (Daily Telegraph, 15 January 2010).

Switzerland and Ireland), seeing the highest net costs to parents within the sample (Table A.6).[14]

As developmental policies are not extended into occupational life, in turn female equal standing in education is hard to sustain, as care—and so employment—become less affordable at lower levels of education and income. To accordingly reflect the difference life-cycle policies, in particular, make for women's positions, an index of occupational inclusion (Table A.4) compares female return rates in addition to the level and stratification of employment security in the form of data on unemployment and earnings, showing the Nordic states are distinctive—and the UK's position is extreme (Graph 7.4). The upshot is to evidence how a more effective developmental-allocative institutional structure—reflecting HE responsiveness—appears to contribute elements of a systemic explanation for more equal occupational inclusion in Nordic (HD) states.

Assessing underlying factors is also revealing (Table A.3, column 4). For example, the UK's low position in 2007 is shaped by structurally deeper shifts in core background distributions, like schooling.[15] In Nordic countries, what above I called dynamic control—for example of occupational life, is noticeably higher, with several different dimensions of dynamic control—tied to equality in education and occupational life—contributing to this (Table A.3), as I now further examine.

5 Public Sector Incorporation and Control of Time, Activities, and Social Relations

System varieties are—as indicated—shaped by—among other factors—the composite form of their responsiveness to the human economy and, in turn, this shapes the incidence of more opportunities for control. In the case of education in Britain, growing competition with the fee-paying

[14] Between 2009 and 2014 child-care costs in Britain rose by 27%, whilst real wages remained stagnant (The Family and Childcare Trust, 2014).

[15] Zero-hour contracts, permitting employer discretion in work-hours are especially prevalent in Britain (EOWL, 2010) and in services for vulnerable groups (adult domiciliary care, Pyper & McGuinness, 2013, p. 5)—typically carried out by women—at 61% of such jobs against 3–4% of all jobs in England.

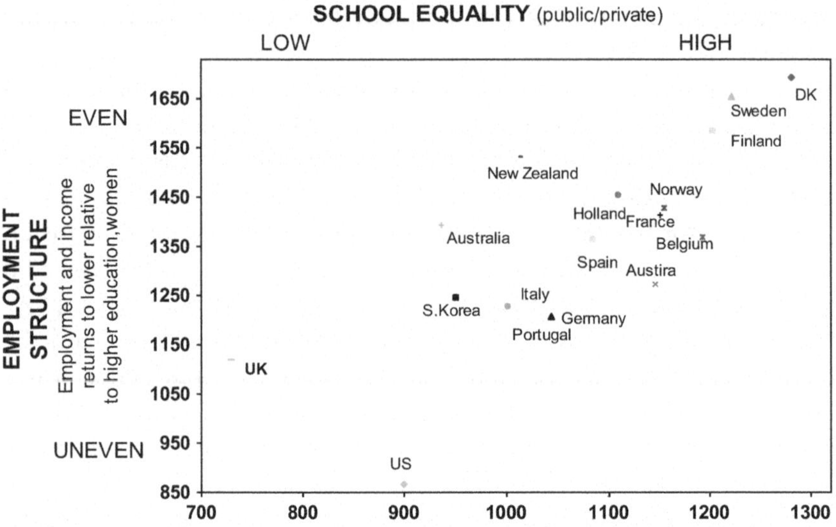

Graph 7.4
X: SCHOOL EQUALITY Index of: 1. Public expenditure on education in GDP 2007, and trend. 2. Public expenditure on education in public expenditure, 2007, and trend. 3. Population that has attained upper secondary, 25–34 age cohort, 2007, and trend. 4. Public/private education spending in GDP, 2007, and rate of change. 5. Public/private ratio of students to teaching staff. 6. Lower scores for level of private household expenditure on education, 2007. 7. Students in publicly funded schools, 2007 and trend. 8. Unit of funding attained by public/private school students, 2007, and trend

Y: EMPLOYMENT STRUCTURE: Index of: 1. Education-employment return rate, females (lower secondary, and lower secondary to tertiary), 2008, and trend. 2. Education unemployment return rate, females, (lower secondary, and lower secondary to tertiary), 2008, and trend. 3. Relative education income return rates (lower secondary as % of tertiary), 2007, and trend. 4. Higher scores for low earnings dispersion. 5. Incidence of long-term unemployment in total unemployment, females. 2009, and trend. 6. National unemployment rate, 2009, and trend. 7. Employment security index, ILO 2004)

(Sources and calculations see Tables A.3 and A.4 in Appendix)

sector in the 1990s, meant state-led practices of early de-selection of weaker students intensified with more segregated ability-teaching. A scheme of school competition for pupils and funding through league tables had schools working to statistical projections of children's grades from entry to exit, where then students' initial performance levels set (and delimited) their personal targets and peer groups (Sutton Trust, 2014a).

Counterfactually, developmental emphasis at the level of systems can be shown, in Nordic states, to have been a source of integrating the function, quality, and effectiveness of services, and of increasing cooperative control, through embedded voice opportunities (e.g. in services like schools, Pettersson, 2007, pp. 155–164; OECD, 2007e, p. 147; Piketty, 2014, p. 486). Integration is exemplified in how the high spending on family services and child-care already observed (Table A.1, c 8.b) has been driven by the educational content of care (OECD, 2007e, p. 138, pp. 144–146). A qualifications-driven approach is cited as reason the quality of care for under 3s is highest in Denmark, followed by Sweden (European Commission, 2013, p. 7; Mahon, 2010) and (gradually) men are drawn to the profession (ibid., p. 15) as well.[16] A more prevalent use of school buildings for afterschool care (OECD, 2007e, p. 146) shows concern to prioritise and align children's and parents' needs. Class stratification of formal child-care is highest in the UK and Italy, high in mid-European countries, and almost negligible in Denmark, and low in other Nordic states (European Commission, 2013, p. 7). Time spent in care activity is more equal between men and women in Nordic states. Greater public support for life-work balance combined with greater gender equality and senses of control and well-being in work generate combined more overall control of time in Nordic states (Table A.6, col. 7).

What results in the form of a broad scaffolding of embedding of cooperative interests has implications for the overall level and structure of control of core activities, forms of time, and social relations. As noted earlier, much of the literature on control of time in the WAF has focussed on leisure defined as non-work time. Including this measure, my index also covers the gender structure of (part-time) work, sources of reproductive control (parental leave access and cost of child-care), and data presented earlier of stability in occupational life (dynamic control).

[16] In 10 out of a total of 32 countries in the report, the figure for children in informal care was over 40%, at 42% in the UK, and 54% in Holland. (European Commission, 2013, p. 33), compared with under 5% in Nordic states.

Graphs 7.5 and 7.6 show how countries are positioned on this composite index (x-axis) as set against an index (y-axis) of the public finance nexus as it extends property rights in stability through the school system and public support for occupation, employment transitions and families (combining the indices of Tables A.1, A.3 and A.5).

These graphs indicate a tendency for more forms of (static, dynamic and reproductive) control—being embedded forms of empowerment—to be higher in countries where property rights in stability are stronger. The more equal sharing of housework in Nordic states shows the direct impact on female empowerment—for example, in informal settings—of institutions' design.

Relatedly, the way overall developmental coherence shapes the developmental nature of institutions can also be depicted as a likely factor behind (relatively) less punitive employment systems of Nordic states. In Holland, a target-based contracted out model of job placement is reported to generate more intense control over persons (compared with Denmark and Sweden, OECD, 2007a, p. 215), though less than in the UK (OECD, op. cit., p. 223). Finally, in the Nordic states, dynamic responsiveness to new HE-referent needs and choices is indicated in early expansion of lifestyle options through Home Childcare Allowance (HCAs) systems, alongside subsidised (and so less class-differentiated, Meagher & Szebehely, 2009, p. 102) high-quality formal care (ibid., pp. 90–97). Notably, male take-up is greater in longer standing and more fully funded care-leave schemes (Leira, 2006; Duvander & Johansson, 2015, p. 361)—and more so when embedded in legally enshrined occupational norms (in Sweden; Duvander & Johansson, 2015, pp. 352–353). The way women's equal standing in occupational life positively affects fathers' view of care and housework (Nordenmark, 2015, p. 181) indicates how in general men's choice to suppress time for care has a strong institutional basis.

The British case illustrates counterfactually how prioritising the distributive frame is a precarious and incoherent redistributive strategy. For example, deregulation begun in the 1980s, over time saw the rapid expansion of use of ('zero-hour') contracts that do not guarantee regular work or pay, led by sectors (care services) in which both (primarily female and many foreign) workers and users are vulnerable.[17] On the other hand, as

[17] By July 2013, 1 in 5 firms used the contracts (Guardian Friday, 16 August 2013), up from 4% in 2004 (Pyper & McGuinness, 2013, p. 4).

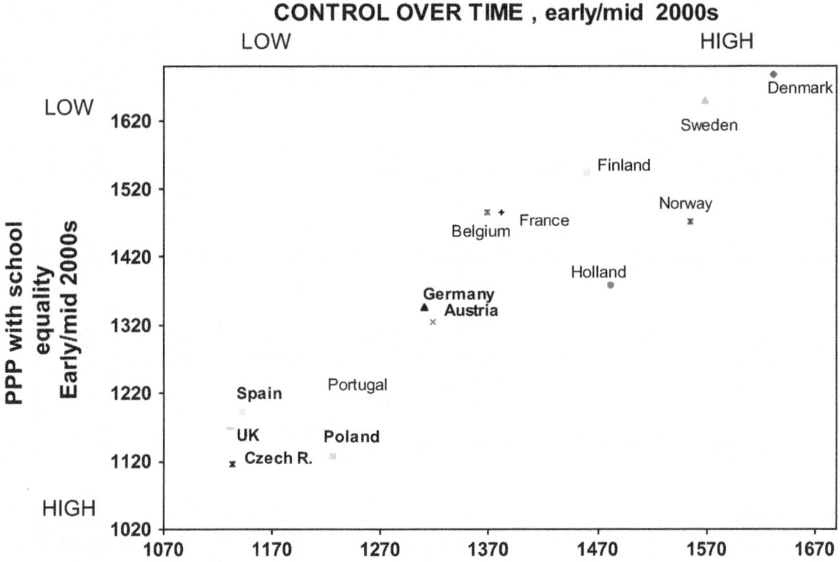

Graph 7.5

Y axis: *WELFARE STATE INSTITUTIONS*: Index combining SCHOOL EQUALITY, composed of 1. Public expenditure on education in GDP 2000; 2. Public expenditure on education in public expenditure, 2000; 3. Population that has attained upper secondary, 25–34 age cohort, 2000; 3. Share of public expenditure on tertiary educational institutions, 2000; 4. Public/private education spending in GDP, 2000 Table A.5, columns 1–4—for 2000); and PUBLIC REVENUE, composed of 1. Top marginal tax rate and multiple of average wage where set in; 2. Total tax revenue as % of GDP; and 3. General Government Revenue in GDP; and PUBLIC SPENDING ON HUMAN DEVELOPMENT, composed of 1. Public social expenditure as a percentage of GDP; 2. Training and job creation public expenditure in GDP; 3. Share of public expenditure on tertiary educational institutions; 4. Public/private education spending in GDP; and 5. Public spending on family services in GDP, all 2000 (Table A.1, column 9 (1 & 2—for 2000) Combined, as given in Table A.6, column 7,e).

X Axis: *CONTROL OF TIME*: Index composed of 1. Average annual leisure hours 2. Males' share of part-time jobs in total male employment as a share of females' share of part-time jobs in female total employment; 3. Paid paternity, maternity and parental leave, months; 4. Task and time control and well-being at work (able to choose order of tasks, able to set work time, work gives feeling of work well done); 5. Employment security (share of job tenure over 10 years, lower scores for share of long-term unemployment in total) 55–59 age cohort with more than 5 years job tenure; and 6. Net cost of child-care fees, and EMPLOYMENT STRUCTURE (pattern of employment returns to education), composed of: 1. Education-employment return rate, females (lower secondary, and lower secondary to tertiary), 2002; 2. Education unemployment return rate, females, (lower secondary, and lower secondary to tertiary), 2002; 3. Relative education income return rates (lower secondary as % of tertiary), 2000; 4. Higher scores for low earnings dispersion; and 5. Training and job-creation public spending in GDP 2000 (Combined, as given in Table A.6, column 7,c)

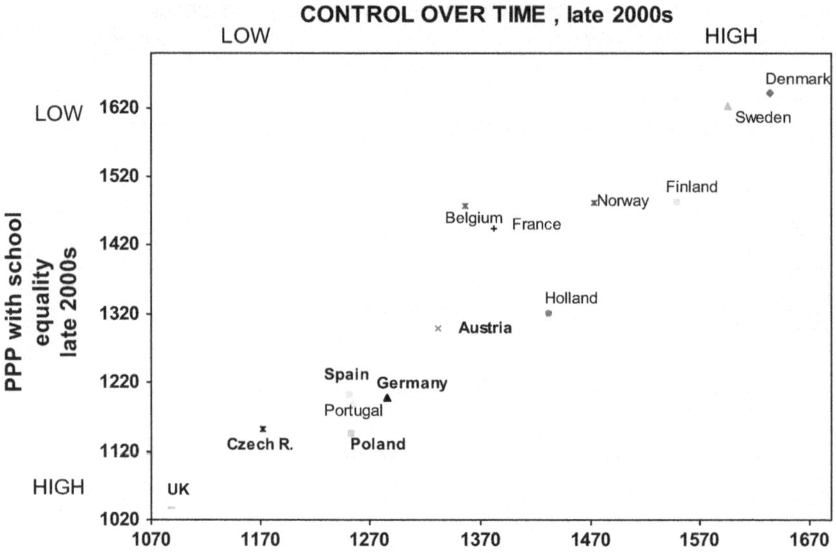

Graph 7.6

Y axis: *WELFARE STATE INSTITUTIONS*: Index combining SCHOOL EQUALITY, composed of 1. Public expenditure on education in GDP 2007; 2. Public expenditure on education in public expenditure, 2007; 3. Population that has attained upper secondary, 25–34 age cohort. 2007; 3. Share of public expenditure on tertiary educational institutions, 2007; and, 4. Public/private education spending in GDP, 2007, and PUBLIC REVENUE: composed of 1. Top marginal tax rate and multiple of average wage where set in; 2. Total tax revenue as % of GDP; 3. General Government Revenue in GDP; and PUBLIC SPENDING ON HUMAN DEVELOPMENT composed of 1. Public social expenditure as a percentage of GDP; 2. Training and job creation public expenditure in GDP; 3. Share of public expenditure on tertiary educational institutions; 4. Public/private education spending in GDP; and, 5. Public spending on family services in GDP, all 2007 (Table A.1, column 9 (1 & 2—for 2007). Combined as given in Table A.6, column 7,f).

X Axis: *CONTROL OF TIME*: Index composed of 1. Average annual leisure hours; 2. Males' share of part-time jobs in total male employment as a share of females' share of part-time jobs in female total employment; 3. Paid paternity, maternity and parental leave, months; 4. Task and time control and well-being at work (able to choose order of tasks, able to set work time, work gives feeling of work well done; 5. Employment security (share of job tenure over 10 years, lower scores for share of long-term unemployment in total) 55–59 age cohort with more than 5 years job tenure, and, 6. Net cost of child-care fees; and EMPLOYMENT STRUCTURE (pattern of employment returns to education), composed of 1. Education-employment return rate, females (lower secondary, and lower secondary to tertiary), 2002; 2. Education unemployment return rate, females, (lower secondary, and lower secondary to tertiary), 2002; 3. Relative education income return rates (lower secondary as % of tertiary), 2000; 4. Higher scores for low earnings dispersion; and, 5. Training and job-creation public spending in GDP, 2000. (Combined, as given in Table A.6, column 7,d) real wages have fallen, the value of income assistance in Britain over time came to exceed that of low-paid employment—the only OECD country in which this was the case, and not because the value of income assistance was high (Atkinson, 2015, pp. 226–9; Haagh, 2019b). More so than in other countries, educational stratifications determine labour market outcomes, as already shown, reproducing stratifications including among women, and increasingly youth.[18] In this context, Britain's unusual systemic stratification of work time—whereby high-income groups overwork and low-income groups under-work, in international comparison, is worthy of note.[19] This indicates how choices and options to parent are structured by occupational class, and so care has become informalised and stratified at the same time as formal work has grown more precarious.

The period after the economic crisis saw state policies to condition benefits on return to work for single parents (the vast majority women) increase, without, however, the accompanying role of occupational policies of Nordic states. Though the UK spent one-sixth on passive (income) support as compared with Denmark (in 2010, at 0.3% and 1.78% of GDP; OECD, 2013), and twenty times less on training (in 2007); the UK spent five times more than Denmark on the administration of benefits and recipients' behaviour (at 0.21% of GDP against 0.04% in Denmark). In the same year as a unification of benefits proceeded, in 2013, previously universal (child) benefits became subject to heavier means-tests (introduced for the first time in 2009). Access to income assistance became detached from housing stability (the so-called bedroom tax), and punitive conditions on benefits were strengthened.[20] Unification of schemes (Universal Credit) was combined with an intention to align benefits with flexible work (raising the frequency of reporting of earnings—the 'real-time information system'). New measures were introduced to remove benefits where claimants refuse to take work on zero-hour contracts, which were considered a form of 'enabling'

[18] Britain in 2013 had an average level—but by education the most divided share—of youth (15-to-29-year-olds) not in education or employment in the OECD: 24 per cent with low schooling were inactive as compared with 8 per cent with high education. In Denmark, Sweden and Norway, the figures are (10.3, 8.2; 8.1, 4.9; 9.8, 6.6). (OECD 2014, 103).

[19] According to Burtless et al. (2010), in the UK top earners work 3 times as many hours as the lowest earners, as compared with 1.6 in the US and 1.5 in Austria.

[20] Introduced in April 2013, the 'under-occupancy tax' is intended to entice residents with an extra room to move or take a tenant.

work by the then-Employment Minister, Ms. McVey (Guardian, 8 May 2014). Impacts of benefit unification reforms (Universal Credit) combined with more intensive policies of sanction have been found to have had significant adverse mental health impacts in Britain (Wickham et al., 2020), whereas in Denmark legal provisions to protect have played a role in comparably countering such effects in implementing sanctions (Haagh, 2019b).

Again, it is relevant to compare this pattern of change with Denmark where, despite a radical cut, in 2010, to coverage of earnings-related benefits (from four to two years), the level and length of protection, along with investment in re-education and child-care (OECD, 2014, p. 115), remained the most generous (bar for Luxembourg, for the level of Unemployment Insurance—UI) in the OECD. This contrasts with the way collapse, in the 1980s, of wage-related coverage in Britain was followed by the state imposing what amounted to a flat-rate system (Clasen, 2001). These policy initiatives induced policy incoherence and were at the same time counterintuitive given the stress in the dominant discourse on work incentives. They involved ending the added risk pooling and structured incentives that can be linked with contribution-based top-up of basic entitlements (e.g. as Atkinson, 2015, pp. 229–230, stresses; Haagh, 2013, 2019b). Notably, in Nordic states, the crisis also entailed introduction of new means-tests, including in Denmark child benefit (for the first time, in 2014). But whilst, in Britain, the benefit falls away altogether with higher earnings, in Denmark, it was cut by 2% of high earnings (e.g. about the equivalent cut-off point of Dkr. 712,000), indicating continuation of a universalist structure.[21] Danish neo-liberalisation has thus been notable but systematically less penetrative compared with the UK's.

6 Universal Basic Income and Systems of Well-Being

Alternative arguments for basic income as a response to contemporary changes in capitalism illustrate the importance of placing freedom-oriented analysis within a well-being systems perspective. A Universal

[21] Børnepenge – børne og ungeydelserne, Babyxplore.dk, 3. December 2014.

Basic Income is an institutional reform, which would entail guaranteeing a small regular income to all individuals in a territory (Standing, 2017) and for life (Haagh, 2019e). The proposal for UBI has been central to debates in WAF in ways which involve a critical view of the role of the state and a redistributive focus (Sect. 1). Alternatively, I argue it is plausible to consider the relevance of UBI historically and today as contributing to consolidate systems of well-being, by enabling the political security *of* well-being. As already discussed, institutional literatures conceive of political security historically in terms of the establishment of effective insurance of social risk by the state (Bates, 2006). In this context, recognising the constraint of human economy on human function and social cooperation can be argued to entail by extension that state insurance of developmental security should be recognised as a central component of political security in terms of relatedly effective governance and states of well-being. Viewed from this angle, insuring individuals' subsistence is arguably a long-overdue development. Its importance can be demonstrated by failings in the systems we have that are based in policing access to income security through means-tests and behaviour controls that inevitably leave gaps, the more so as the labour market has become more complex (Haagh, 2019e; Sect. 5 above).

Seeing basic income as contributing to political security of well-being is basis for critique of a neutralist defence of basic income discussed in Sect. 1. As far as both orthodox economics and post-libertarian egalitarianisms tie freedom to personal choice, they conceal how translating choice into well-being is parasitic on developmental measures and institutions, which both approaches deny or take for granted and which are eroding today, as demonstrated above. On this basis, we can argue that outcomes of Anglo-liberal globalisation have revealed weaknesses at the same time in the neutralist defence of UBI, which has been influential in freedom-oriented conceptions of welfare, and in the orthodox development economics, which forms a background for the neutralist case. The preceding sections have shown how policies and institutions that support outcomes linked with control of time, and valued in new freedom-oriented welfare approaches, are more developed in horizontal capitalist states. The upshot is to call post-libertarian forms of defence of basic income, which frame the case *at the same time* on development neutralist grounds, and as a defence of control of time, into question.

Neutralist normativity ('non-perfectionism', Birnbaum, 2012, pp. 9–10) can be considered heavily prescriptive in terms of advocating a market-neutralist normativity today, even whilst adapting this defence to include more explicit recognition (Birnbaum, 2012; Vanderborght & van Parijs, 2017, op.cit) of the need for universal services. A risk inherent in a neutralist defence of basic income is to exaggerate a basic income's viability and impact within the system of institutions. Whilst there is a strong moral case for basic income in more insecure and unequal societies, the very grounds for inequality, for example as represented in weak public finance systems, compromise the likelihood and freedom-enhancing effect of a prospective basic income reform. This generates in turn what I have referred to as equality and crises paradoxes in basic income narrative, characterised by a tendency to overdraw a basic income's effects precisely where such effects are least likely (Haagh, 2019d).

As occupation-based education, stable employment, and state support for secure relocation and education, are weaker and corroding at a more rapid rate in Anglo-liberal states, a moral case for basic income—tied to alleviating poverty—may not translate into an effective one—linked with securing control of time. To the extent the latter is true, this undermines the case for basic income as a feasible mechanism of 'exit' (Haagh, 2007, 2011a, b), which involves an underlying premise that implies freedom lies squarely in movement, which thereby enables control (Taylor, 2017). The effectiveness of this argument relies (unrealistically) on individuals being able to directly control their surrounding environment, or—alternatively—that conditions both *in* jobs and *in* informal activities are universally good. This in turn depends on a strategically incorporating form of public sector development, which then weakens the neutralist defence of basic income reform. Even if one can easily accept Taylor's (2017) case that exit options are necessary for and part of freedom, they *can* be wholly ineffective, and are insufficient.

A predominant neutralist-universalist perspective has contributed to shape subsequent and contemporary polemics, including the idea that a case for basic income specifically raises concerns about reciprocity (White, 2003; Atkinson, 2015, p. 121), community (Anderson, 1999), equity (Sen, 2002) or a more expanded view of basic public services (Universal Basic Service, or UBS, Portes et al., 2017, p. 6, p. 13). An outcome of the polemical character of basic income debates has been to leave out of view the broader importance of basic income as both (i) a missing piece in the post-war more developmental universal welfare state (Haagh, 2011a, 2017), and (ii) as an important but not omnipotent response to the consolidation of a more illiberal state in the wake of post-crisis global public austerity.

Framed as an addendum to the post-war rights project, a basic income could help resolve contradictions in it (Haagh, 2017). These arise from the way post-war state policies sought to promote stability in human development, by limiting market corrosion of rights in housing, employment, and welfare, but failed to do so with regard to the right to subsistence. Once labour protections began to fall away after the 1980s, and access to housing and income support became more restricted, the way modern systems reinforce direct market-dependence was laid bare. Consider that individuals in contemporary economies have in some ways less security than serfs in feudal systems, who—albeit in expectation of labour contributions and no property of their own—enjoyed some expectation of stable subsistence and place—through access to dwellings and land use and thus livelihoods. In today's economy, individuals who enjoy a high wage and a notional independence in asset ownership may have very little real autonomy, if untied to a local community, or if in losing jobs or becoming ill, they face losing housing and everything they own.

There is no inherent reason why the value or form of basic income should be defended in anti-perfectionist terms. Basic income can be defended pragmatically as a contribution to the development and political security of well-being systems, without it being necessary to argue a basic income is sufficient for control. An institutional, developmental defence of basic income is consistent with actual institutional dynamics—for example, developmental policies tend to enable universalist policies (Haagh, 2011a, 2019e). The alleged trade-offs between basic income and social democracy are objectively false, even if stacking up the case this way has become a self-fulfilling prophecy, generating opposition to basic income among social democrats (Haagh, 2019d). We have evidence (Sects. 4 and 5) that multiple sources of more independent economic security support intrinsic motivation. In addition, basic income can bolster the stability of other institutions and policies—including health policies—by embedding a stable layer of financial security within the economy (Haagh, 2013; Haagh, 2019e; Haagh & Rohregger, 2019), providing the basic income is not financed through more ad hoc mechanisms, but given a stable and legal funding frame. Having such a system in place would also contribute to generate more resilient responses to crises such as presented by the 2008 crash and Coronavirus, where we have seen countries with more plan-rational economies and established social funds and systems—such as East Asian and Nordic states, respectively, have been better placed. For example, in response to Coronavirus, in Denmark, all behaviour conditionalities on claimants were lifted in early March to synchronise with social distancing measures, and anyone losing their employment would get access fairly quickly to income support via electronic systems up and running already (DR, 2020).[22] Nordic states benefit from electronic citizens' registers, whereas financial information about citizens in Britain is weak and patchy, on some estimates covering between half to three-quarters of the population—and there is not a single integrated system. Consequently, it would be more costly and very difficult for Britain to enact an equivalent effective response to guarantee individuals' financial security, and sustain it. If income security systems have been weakened in Denmark by sanctions, a fairly robust structure remains in place, including through the unemployment insurance system, which complements public income assistance and enjoys public subsidy to enable wide inclusion. Whilst rates have fallen after separation from union affiliation, and under other influences, the majority of the work-force are still paying in to this voluntary system. During the first lock down in Spring 2020, there was a very significant rise in re-affiliations to unemployment insurance, a form of return to safer structures, which would not have been possible without such institutional options being in place.

The potential contribution of basic income to support the political security of well-being is thus counterfactually demonstrated in the recent transformation of especially Anglo-liberal states towards a more illiberal

[22] In Britain, the initial financial response to Coronavirus comprised cash for businesses, though mainly in the form of loans (BBC, 2020, March 17). A scheme to support 80% of individuals' wages, an equivalent package for the self-employed, and upping the level of Universal Credit payments (albeit by much less) for those depending on assistance, followed (Financial Times, 2020). The UK in this sense in effect mimicked—albeit only temporarily—the two-tier more comprehensive economic security system of Nordic and East Asian states, comprising of both wage-linked and basic security systems.

form. The fact that income security as a right was never guaranteed on the same basis as education or health made legal encroachment on the security of the poor and vulnerable groups a hallmark of every economic downturn. The intensification under austerity in the period after the financial crisis of 2008 of sanctions policies—which entail using state policies to compel individuals' labour market participation on the pain of subsistence—marks the emergence of a new illiberal state as a form of adaptation to financial globalisation (Haagh, 2019e). At the height of sanctions policies during the 2010s, one-quarter of benefit claimants in both the UK and Denmark received at least one sanction—one episode of reduction in income assistance payments or of curtailment of entitlement for a time period—every year. Sanctioning involves a flaw rate of 40% or more in appealed case, and has been found to be overly reliant on agent discretion in all states practising such policies (Adler, 2016; Haagh, 2019b). The impact of austerity on this illiberal form in the UK is evidenced through a documented lack of research into the effects of sanctions-based income assistance reforms (NAO, 2016) as compared with other countries (Haagh, 2019a, b). Guaranteeing a share of income as a right is in this context a way of remedying design flaws in the emergence of modern income assistance schemes as reactive structures in the course of the nineteenth and twentieth centuries, flaws the significance of which re-appear during crises.

At the same time, the case for basic income needs to be carefully interpreted in the context of the alternative paths of hierarchical and horizontal capitalist development discussed in this chapter. A relevant difference between the British and Nordic states is that the latter are not just—as Britain has been recently depicted (Sloman, 2019)—'transfer states'—dominated by a monetary redistributive perspective. This chapter has argued that the UK's 'transfer state' status is a feature of the hierarchical capitalist trajectory. If a transfer state is insufficient, it is not on account of using transfers (Denmark spends more money on transfers in GDP) but because of what it is *not*; for example, transfers are not accompanied by wider efforts to stabilise conditions for control of skills, time, social relations and cooperation in society.

A compensatory logic, when embedded in welfare state evolution, affects the treatment the poor receive. Recent studies confirm the connection between punitive welfare designs and ill mental health in Britain (Wickham et al., 2020), and elsewhere (Haagh & Rohregger, 2019). Comparison of sanctions policies in the UK and Denmark has shown that their form and effect are systemically highly variant between the two cases (Haagh, 2019b, 2019e). This reinforces the need to recognise a basic income's importance contextually. Recent debates about UBI in Britain are evidence of the danger that UBI becomes a part and indeed the source of a new diminished welfare reform debate centred on *basic universalism*. Although Universal Basic Services (UBS) has been pitted against UBI (Portes et al., 2017), both proposals can be situated as a familiar conflict within a very British anti-poverty paradigm. A concern is that a basic income, which supports a welfare state construct aiming primarily at securing against absolute poverty, might not in fact eradicate coercive forms of economic organisation, in the labour market or even the state. Whilst a basic income would in principle get rid of punitive sanctions and behaviour-testing policies on *basic* support, it may do nothing to alleviate punishing competition systems, which crush well-being in work (Sect. 5), and drive down tax (Sect. 4). On this basis, a basic income cannot be itself a solution to contemporary crises. If rising insecurity is caused by the pursuit of orthodoxy and neutralism in economic governance, a basic income cannot be a response to the failure of that orthodoxy. Whilst the case for basic income is to end assistentialism and enable individual independence, in a context of Anglo-liberal globalisation a singular case for basic income may in fact be a case for assistentalism—and thus orthodoxy—in a new form. To illustrate, the present-day polemic surrounding the alleged conflict between UBI and UBS (Portes et al., 2017) arguably represents an extension of the austerity paradigm by seemingly endorsing the view that the public ought to choose between services or cash under conditions of rationing of public expenditure. Global pressure to induce countries into low-tax equilibria through low-tax competition is made to appear as a natural and moral constraint under the paradigm that states' adaptation to global constraints is a social utilitarian feature of competitiveness, which demands public restraint.

In all, the ways in which changes in the welfare state have generated a new basis for a defence of universal basic income, yet this defence is also potentially treacherous, reveals the importance of seeing a basic income's contribution to political security from a well-being systems perspective.

On the one hand, it is possible to make the case for basic income as a form of political security in terms of the importance of stabilising institutional foundations for individual inclusion in society. Crises and pandemics—including the recent Coronavirus—which in Britain immediately generated a debate about entitlement to sick-pay—because the poor in society could not afford to self-isolate—to help contain the virus (Daily Mirror, 2020), show how fragile societies are in which income and economic security are wholly tied to the labour market, and effective, common universal security structures, or citizens registers, are non-existent. Weak incorporation of society, involving the social security of the persons in it, has been at stake in both the rise of economic precarity, and how this has affected the state.

On the other hand, contemporary downward pressure on public finance and rising precarity are not good conditions for basic income in terms of its sustainability or effects (Columbino, 2009; Haagh, 2015, 2019c), which rely on also promoting other developmental policies and collective savings systems. Hence, the need to support people financially during crises, such as including under the Corona lockdown, should not lead UBI advocates to make a case for UBI *contra* other measures to stabilise employment and services in this or other crisis scenarios. The biggest long-term risk from Coronavirus may be the disappearance on a mass scale of cooperative structures of production in favour of deregulated work and a flat assistance structure. The implication is that a robust case for basic income reform will continue to depend on the success of wider efforts with respect to bolstering public ownership and democratisation of inclusion structures and of sustainably raising the level of public finance in GDP.

7 Summary and Conclusions

In summary, this contribution has compared cases of mature capitalist democracies in terms of their systemic promotion of well-being, arguing that reference to constraints exerted by human economy aids our understanding of systems' character, evolution, and function. Reference to regulatory features of human economy adds new dimensions to the contributions of the SVL and WAF, and derives a new institutional field of study of human development, by clarifying how the pattern of human economy generates general cooperative interests yet varied political responses. Where these general interests have greater representation in common institutions and mechanisms of shared security, transcendental effects in terms of the systemic promotion of developmental policies are more likely. Conversely, where political systems promote more market-compensating institutions, the outcome is a tendency towards fragmentation of cooperative interests and to reinforce sources of incoherence in governance.

System incoherence can be shown to affect the effectiveness of individual policies. In Britain, effects of growing public education spending were undermined by hierarchy. In the employment system, spending less (on training and production strategies) undermined the effectiveness of (relatively high) spending on administration to allocate persons to jobs.

Using the same approach, I set the proposal for universal basic income in a wider political and institutional context, focussed on the systemic development of control of time as a multi-level cooperative problem. Seeing UBI as an institution with the potential to contribute an elementary form of stability in response to complex developmental and cooperative interests arising from human economy directs attention from too sufficient distributive arguments in the modern welfare debate, whilst also highlighting a UBI's prerequisites. The proposal for a UBI significantly brings the topic of universal and stabilising inclusion structures back into the centre of public discussion at a time of corrosion of public capacity and crisis. And yet, there is a risk that UBI may be interpreted as a stand-alone distributive scheme given the conditions behind modern crises in state governance, illustrating thereby the problems discussed in this paper in terms of the developmental determinants of governance efficacy for human well-being and senses of settlement. As we have learnt from history, conditions of developmental equality in society shape the form and impact of individual policies. In this context, a basic income's contribution to freedom is—as in the case of other welfare institutions—mediated by the level of political development, defined in terms of the formation of shared risk structures in response to fundamental cooperative problems in human society.

Appendix

Table A.1 The welfare state, revenue and spending on human development: 2000, 2007

	Column 1. a. Top marginal tax rate, b. multiple of average wage where rate sets in (2000, 2007)				Column 2. Total tax revenue as a per-cent-age of GDP		Column 3. General government revenue in GDP		Column 4. Public social expenditure as a % of GDP 2000 2007 (*Public expenditure on education in GDP % 2007, ** 2000 as 100)			
	2000		2007		2000	2007	2000	2007	2000	2007	*	**
	a	b	a	b								
Denmark	63.3	1.0	63.0	1.0	49.4	48.7	55.5	55.1	25.8	26.1	7.8	107
Finland	59.8	2.1	56.1	1.9	47.2	43.0	55.2	52.6	24.3	24.9	5.9	87
Sweden	55.4	1.5	56.5	1.5	51.8	48.3	60.7	55.1	28.5	27.3	6.7	94
Norway	55.3	2.6	47.8	1.5	42.6	43.6	57.7	58.7	21.3	20.8	6.7	85
Germany	53.8	1.7	47.5	5.9	37.2	36.2	46.4	43.8	26.2	25.2	4.5	98
Holland	60.0	1.6	52.0	1.2	39.7	37.5	46.1	45.7	19.8	20.1	5.3	104
Belgium	68.0	1.2	59.4	1.0	44.9	43.9	49.1	48.2	25.3	26.1	5.9	–
Switz.	49.5	4.0	47.9	3.4	30.0	28.9	35.2	33.9	17.9	18.5	5.2	91
Austria	42.4	2.3	42.7	1.9	43.2	42.3	50.3	48.2	26.4	26.4	5.4	89
France	46.5	2.9	49.8	2.8	44.4	43.5	50.1	49.6	27.9	28.4	5.6	89
France	48.0	4.4	43.0	2.6	34.2	37.2	38.1	41.1	20.3	21.6	4.3	93
Portugal	46.6	3.4	48.8	4.3	34.1	36.4	40.2	43.2	19.6	22.5	5.3	104
Italy	51.9	3.9	50.7	3.3	42.3	43.5	45.3	46.4	23.3	24.9	4.3	91
Hungary	77.7	0.9	71.0	0.8	38.0	39.5	43.9	44.8	20.0	23.1	5.2	100
Czech R.	40.5	2.4	40.5	1.5	35.3	37.4	37.9	41.1	19.8	18.8	4.2	88
Poland	45.1	3.3	42.7	3.1	32.8	34.9	38.1	40.3	20.5	20.0	4.9	94
Slovak R.	35.0	3.2	17.5	0.4	34.1	29.4	39.9	32.5	17.9	15.7	3.6	78
Ireland	50.5	1.0	47.0	1.0	31.3	30.8	36.1	36.5	13.6	16.3	4.9	98
UK	40.0	1.4	41.0	1.2	36.4	36.1	40.3	41.4	19.2	20.5	5.4	108
US	48.0	8.9	42.7	9.1	29.9	28.3	35.4	34.0	14.5	16.2	5.3	113
Australia	48.5	1.2	46.5	2.6	31.1	30.8	36.1	36.0	17.8	16.0	4.3	88
N. Zeal.	39.0	1.7	39.0	1.3	33.6	35.7	41.1	45.2	19.4	18.4	5.8	104
Japan	49.5	4.5	47.8	4.5	27.0	28.3	31.4	33.5	16.5	18.6*	3.4	94
S. Korea	43.4	5.5	38.3	3.2	22.6	26.5	27.9	33.3	5.0	7.5	4.2	–
Mexico	42.9	49.3	22.5	1.4	16.9	18.0	20.5	19.6+	5.8	7.2	4.8	114

(*continued*)

Table A.1 (continued)

	Column 5. Training and job creation public spending in GDP		Column 6. Share of public expenditure on tertiary educational institutions		Column 7. Public/private education spending in GDP Primary, secondary and post-secondary non-tertiary				Column 8. Public spending on a. family services in GDP		
					A.	B.	i.	ii.			
	2000	2007	2000	2007	Public	Private	2000	2007	a		b
					A. i	ii	B. i	ii	00	07*	05
Denmark	1.58	1.02	97.6	96.5	97.8	98.1	2.2	1.9	1.6	1.8	0.8
Finland	1.00	0.71	97.2	95.7	99.3	99.0	0.7	1.0	1.3	1.3	0.7
Sweden	1.37	0.89	91.3	89.3	99.0	100	0.1	0.0	1.4	1.9	0.6
Norway	0.74	0.45	96.3	97.0	99.0	–	1.0	–	1.2	1.5	0.5
Germany	1.23	0.45	88.2	84.7	87.3	86.3	13.7	12.7	0.7	0.8	0.1
Holland	1.68	0.72	76.5	72.4	85.6	86.7	14.3	13.3	0.7	1.4	0.1
Belgium	1.34	1.22	91.5	90.3	94.7	95.2	5.3	4.8	0.8	1.0	0.2
Switz.	0.49	0.47	–	–	89.2	86.1	10.8	13.9	0.3	0.3	0.1
Austria	0.50	0.51	96.3	85.4	95.8	96.0	4.2	4.0	0.5	0.4	0.3
France	1.31	0.68	84.4	84.5	92.6	92.7	7.4	7.3	1.5	1.7	0.4
France	0.94	0.60	74.4	79.0	93.0	92.9	7.0	7.1	0.7	0.7	0.4
Portugal	0.61	0.39	92.5	70.0	99.9	99.9	0.1	0.1	0.4	0.4	0.0
Italy	0.60	0.37	77.5	69.9	97.8	96.8	2.2	2.3	0.6	0.8	0.2
Hungary	0.39	0.23	80.3–	77.9+	–	–	–	–	1.1	1.1	0.1
Czech R.	0.22	0.12	85.4	83.8	90.7	91.7	8.3	9.3	0.5	0.5	0.1
Poland	0.79	0.40	66.6	71.5	95.4	98.6	4.6	1.4	0.2	0.3	–
Slovak R.	0.32	0.12	91.2	76.2	97.6	89.3	2.4	10.7	0.4	0.4	0.1
Ireland	1.14	0.52	79.2	85.4	–	–	–	–	0.2	0.3	0.3
UK	0.37	0.05	67.7	35.8	88.7	78.1	11.3	21.9	0.9	1.1	0.4
US	0.15	0.10	31.1	31.6	91.6	91.4	8.4	8.6	0.6	0.6	0.1
Australia	0.46	0.30	49.6	44.3	82.9	81.1	18.9	17.1	0.6	0.7	0.2
N. Zeal.	0.56	0.25	62.5*	65.7	–	85.6	–	14.4	0.6	0.8	0.1
Japan	0.29	0.05	38.5	32.5	89.9	89.9	10.2	10.1	0.4	0.4	0.2
S. Korea	0.49	0.10	23.3	20.7	80.8	77.8	19.2	22.2	0.1	0.5	0.1
Mexico	0.06	0.01	79.4	71.4	86.1	82.1	13.9	17.9	0.5	0.7	0.0

(*continued*)

Table A.1 (continued)

	Column 9. Progressive Public Finance Scores: 1. Revenue: ((1a*2) – (1b*10)) + (2*4) + 3*4. 2. Spending: (4*4) + (5*100) + 6 + (7A*2) + (8a*100)			
	1. 00	07	2. 00	07
Denmark	537	532	714	680
Finland	508	476	623	594
Sweden	546	528	680	678
Norway	486	490	574	573
Germany	426	357	561	483
Holland	447	425	565	538
Belgium	500	477	596	607
Switz.	319	313		–
Austria	435	428	494	474
France	442	444	662	622
France	341	373	506	482
Portugal	356	372	472	439
Italy	416	428	486	480
Hungary	518	472	–	–
Czech R.	350	380	418	404
Poland	341	355	438	419
Slovak R.	334	279	430	370
Ireland	270	354	–	–
UK	373	381	449	328
US	268	244	347	349
Australia	354	334	393	371
N. Zeal.	360	388	427	416
Japan	287	298	353	332
S. Korea	234	284	264	266
Mexico	187	182	331	335

Source: Columns 1 and 2: OECD Tax database, Stat.extract. Column 3: OECD Factbook 2010. Figures for Mexico are from 1995 and 2006 (from OECD Government at a Glance). Column 4: OECD Social Expenditure database. * is for 2005 where the 2007 data is not available. Column 5: Includes training, employment incentives, supported employment, employment rehabilitation, direct job-creation and start-up incentives. OECD Employment Outlook. C olumns 6 and 7: Education at a Glance 2011.– Figure is for 1995. + Figure is for 2006. * is for 2002. Column 8: OECD Family database. Family services include, direct financing and subsidising of providers of childcare and early education facilities, public spending on assistance for young people and residential facilities, public spending on family services, including centre-based facilities and home help services for families in need

Table A.2 Direct and indirect sources of equal welfare, OECD

	1. a Disposable income poverty rate, i. 1985 ii. 2005, iii. Late 2000s b. point reduction in rate from market income by taxes and transfers, i. 1985 ii. 2005. Score (S): ((20-a. iii)*10) + (ai – aiii) + (bii) + (bii-bi)						2. a. Inequality before & after taxes & transfers mid 2000s b. redistribution of cash transfers to lowest quintile, mid-2000s c. child poverty rates after taxes & transfers 2000			3. Ratio of rich to poor, a. mid 1990s, b. mid-2000s		4. A Gini. a. mid-80s, b. mid 2000s, c. late 2000s. B 80/20 quintile ratio. a. mid-2000s. b. % point change from mid-1980s. Score (S): (100-(Ac*100)*3) + (10-Ac-Aa)) (100-(Ba*10)*3) + (30-(Bb*10))					
															B		
	a. i	ii	iii	b. i	ii	S	a.	b.	c	a.	b.	A a.	b.	c.	a.	b.	S
Denmark	14.1	5.3	6.1	6.0	18.3	178	0.41	9.2	2.4	3.2	4.6	0.221	0.232	0.248	3.3	0.1	553
Finland	10.0	7.3	7.9	5.1	10.3	139	0.28	4.7	2.8	2.7	5.7	0.207	0.269	0.263	3.9	0.9	520
Sweden	23.2	5.3	8.4	5.8	21.4	168	0.40	8.5	4.2	2.6	4.7	0.198	0.234	0.259	3.3	0.6	541
Norway	12.3	6.8	7.8	6.4	17.2	155	0.31	6.0	3.4	–	6.6	0.234	0.276	0.250	4.0	0.6	527
Germany	19.2	11.0	8.9	7.2	22.5	159	0.31	4.9	10.2	–	7.7	0.257	0.298	0.295	4.8	1.1	483
Holland	19.2	7.7	7.2	3.1	17.0	171	0.31	5.4	9.8	–	6.3	0.259	0.271	0.294	4.0	0.5	513
Belgium	10.8	8.8	9.1	25.9*	23.9	133	0.37	7.3	7.7	3.3	5.8	0.274	0.271	0.269	4.0	0.4	526
Switzl.	7.5	8.8	8.7	12.0**	9.4	119	0.14	4.7	6.8	–	6.9	0.279+	0.276	0.276	4.3	+	519
Austria	–	6.6	7.2	–	16.4	155+	0.23	5.1	10.2	3.7	6.0	0.236	0.265	0.265	4.0	0.5	523
France	–	7.1	7.2	–	23.6	162+	0.22	5.3	7.5	3.5	6.2	0.300	0.270	0.293	4.1	–0.6	526
Spain	–	–	13.7	–	–	–	–	–	–	4.0	9.1	0.371	0.319	0.309	5.5	–1.3	492
Portugal	14.6	12.9	13.6	11.6*	16.2	86	–	–	15.6	–	12.4	0.329	0.385	0.361	7.1	0.6	430

Italy	9.8	11.4	11.4	10.3	22.4	119	0.26	3.7	–	4.8	10.7	0.309	0.352	0.337	6.0	1.1	435
Hungary	–	–	6.4	–	–	–	–	–	8.8	–	6.6	0.273	0.291	0.272	4.3	0.3	517
Czech R.	4.3	5.8	5.4	20.8*	22.4	171	0.14	5.6	6.8	3.0	5.8	0.232	0.268	0.255	3.8	0.5	532
Poland	–	14.6	10.1	–	22.9	136+	0.17	3.2	12.5	4.1	13.5	0.316+	0.372	0.314	7.2	+	420
Slovak R.	–	–	6.7	–	–	–	–	4.9	–	6.1	–	–	0.268	0.246	4.0	+	543
Ireland	15.4	14.8	9.8	10.3**	16.1	131	0.31	5.4	15.7	–	8.4	0.331	0.328	0.299	5.4	–0.3	478
UK	19.3	8.3	11.3	6.9	18.0	124	0.27	4.6	15.4	–	8.6	0.325	0.335	0.341	5.4	0.4	460
US	7.7	17.1	17.3	17.9	9.2	18	0.18	2.3	29.9	5.6	16.0	0.338	0.381	0.378	7.9	1.4	363
Australia	11.4	12.4	14.6	17.0*	16.3	69	0.33	5.9	–	–	7.2	0.309*	0.301	0.336	4.8	–0.2	485
N. Zeal.	14.0	10.8	11.0	6.2	15.8	118	0.26	4.4	16.3	–	9.1	0.271	0.335	0.330	5.6	1.5	443
Japan	0.6	14.9	15.7	11.9	11.9	40	0.13	3.1	–	4.2	10.1	0.304	0.321	0.329	5.8	0.9	443
S. Korea	–	14.6	15.0	–	2.9	55	0.05	0.9	–	–	10.1	0.312	0.315	–	5.7	+	464

(continued)

Table A.2 (continued)

	5. Private social expend. a. 1990 b. 2007 Score (S): ((15-b)*10) + ((10–(b-a))			6. The value of public services [in household income?] a-e: 1st – 5th quintile Score (S): ((a+e)*100) + ((a/b)*2)2a*20						(GS)*: (1/2) + (2a *200) + (2b*10) + (50-2c) + (1003b*10) + (4/4) + (5/2) + (6/2)
	a	b	S	a	b	c	d	e	Score	
Denmark	2.1	2.6	134	0.89	0.55	0.38	0.28	0.17	116	628
Finland	1.1	1.1	149	0.68	0.42	0.30	0.23	0.12	89	517
Sweden	1.2	2.9	129	0.98	0.63	0.44	0.31	0.18	127	611
Norway	1.9	2.0	140	0.89	0.54	0.37	0.27	0.14	116	540
Germany	3.1	2.9	131	0.73	0.43	0.32	0.23	0.14	92	485
Holland	6.1	6.9	98	0.49	0.32	0.22	0.16	0.10	64	488
Belgium	1.6	4.7	110	–	–	–	–	–	–	–
Switzl.	5.3	8.3	74	0.55	0.30	0.23	0.17	0.10	70	410
Austria	2.2	1.8	142	0.65	0.39	0.28	0.21	0.13	83	508
France	1.9	2.9	130	0.80	0.51	0.38	0.27	0.16	101	506
Spain	0.2	0.5	155	0.72	0.39	0.27	0.19	0.10	89	–
Portugal	0.9	1.9	140	0.86	0.47	0.32	0.23	0.11	105	–
Italy	4.0	2.1	141	0.83	0.45	0.31	0.21	0.11	102	–
Hungary	0.0+	0.2	158	0.69	0.44	0.33	0.23	0.13	89	–
Czech R.	0.0	0.4	156	0.69	0.43	0.31	0.23	0.13	87	507
Poland	0.0	0.0	160	0.61	0.35	0.26	0.19	0.09	77	392

Slovak R.	0.0	1.0	149	–	–	–	–	–	–	–
Ireland	1.4	1.5	145	0.73	0.37	0.26	0.18	0.11	91	469
UK	5.1	5.8	101	0.62	0.36	0.24	0.16	0.08	78	415
US	7.61	0.5	52	0.88	0.40	0.26	0.17	0.09	107	258
Australia	4.5*	3.8	121	0.91	0.51	0.30	0.20	0.11	110	–
N. Zeal.	0.2	0.4	156	0.77	0.49	0.30	0.20	0.10	95	434
Japan	3.7+	–	123	0.73	0.37	0.27	0.19	0.11	91	–
S. Korea	0.4	2.6	132	–	–	–	–	–	–	–

Sources: *Column 1*: Effects of taxes and transfers in reducing poverty among entire population, mid-2000s and changes since mid-1980s. OECD Growing Unequal 2008, a. Per cent difference made in bringing individuals above the 50% of median income poverty line. p. 141. Late 2000s poverty figures are from Society at a Glance 2011. *second set of figures refer to 1995. ** second set of figures refer to 2000. + To calculate this rate there is assumed a 10 point increase in the reduction rate, and where the 1985 figure for poverty is missing the 2005 rate is used—which likely produces a conservative estimate. In the case of Korea and Mexico, the estimates are 2.9 and 6.0. For Mexico figures for mid-1980s and mid-2000s are from OECD (2008), Growing Unequal – Mexico country note. *Column 2*: a. OECD 2008 Growing Unequal? Income Distribution and Poverty in OECD Countries, pp. 108–110 (OECD income distribution questionnaire), Fig. 4.5. Figure refers to the percentage point reduction in the concentration co-efficient achieved by household taxes and public cash transfers, based on people ranked by their household disposable income. b. Same source, p. 166:The ratio refers to (Average ratio cash transfers in household disposable income of population)* (share of public transfers paid to lowest quintile)/100.c. UNICEF Innocent Report Card, Issue no. 6. *Column 3*:.a. Smeeden 2002, p. 40. b. Growing Unequal OECD 2008, p. 36, based on OECD. Income Distribution Questionnaire a.o. *Columns 4*: a. Growing unequal, Gini mid-1980s, p. 25, * figure is for mid-1990s, + figure is for 2000. b. Gini and inter-quintile share ration (S80/S20), mid-2000s, Growing Unequal, p. 52. c. Society at a Glance 2011. + Change in ratio not available. Estimate figure based on the rise in Gini. For Switzerland, Poland and Korea no change is assumed. For Poland a change of 0.5 is assumed. For Poland and Korea the Gini for mid-1980s is not available so mid-2000s is used for trend. *Column 5*: 1990 figure: OECD Factbook 2010. * Figure is for 1995, + figure is for 2000. 2007 figure: OECD Social Expenditure database. For Japan there is no figure for 2007. No change is assumed. *Column 6*: OECD 2008 Growing Unequal? Income Distribution and Poverty in OECD Countries, figures estimated at around 2000. *Column 7*: * In cases where (3b*10) is over 100, the value above 100 is subtracted from the final score

Table A.3 Education equality

	1. A. Public expenditure on education in GDP (a) 1995 (b) 2007 (c) 1995 as 100 B. Public expenditure on education in public spending (a) 1995 (b) 2007 (c) 1995 as 100). Score (S): (Ab*10) + (Ac/20) + (Bb) + (Bc/20)							2. Population w upper secondary education 25–34 year-olds, %, a. 2001, b. 2007. Score: (a+b)/2+ (b-a – max15)			3. Share of public spending on tertiary educational institutions. a. 1995 b. 2000 c. 2007. Trend (T) 95 as 100. Score: Trend+c					4. Public/private education spending in GDP. Primary, secondary and postsecondary non-tertiary, A. Public. i. 2000, ii. 2007 B. 2000=100 (i. public. ii. private). C: Bi/ii * 100 (to maximum of 130). Score: (Aii * 2) + C					
	A a	b	c	B a	b	c	S	a	b	S	a.	b.	c.	T	S	A i	ii	B i	ii	C	S
Denmark	7.3	7.8	107	12.2	15.4	126	105	86	85	85	99	98	97	97	194	97.8	98.1	116	101	115	311
Finland	6.8	5.9	87	11.0	12.5	114	82	87	90	92	98	97	96	98	194	99.3	99.0	126	186	68	266
Sweden	7.1	6.7	94	10.7	12.7	119	90	91	91	91	94	91	89	95	184	99.0	100	128	130+	98	298
Norway	7.9	6.7	85	15.5	16.4	106	93	93	83	78	94	96	97	104	201	99.0	–	114	–	*	298
Germany	4.6	4.5	98	8.5	10.3	121	66	85	85	85	89	88	85	96	181	87.3	86.3	101	93	109	282
Holland	5.1	5.3	104	9.1	11.7	129	76	74	83	88	79	77	72	95	167	85.6	86.7	126	115	110	283
Belgium	–	5.9	–	12.1*	12.4	102	82	75	82	86	–	92	90	99	189	94.7	95.2	114	103	117	302
Switzl.	5.7	5.2	91	13.5	12.2	90	73	92	90	89	–	–	–	–	–	89.2	86.1	106	141	75	247
Austria	6.1	5.4	89	10.8	11.1	103	75	83	87	81	96	96	85	89	174	95.8	96.0	105	100	105	297
France	6.3	5.6	89	11.6	11.5	99	77	78	83	86	85	84	85	100	185	92.6	92.7	103	101	102	287
Spain	4.6	4.3	93	10.3	11.1	108	64	57	65	70	74	74	79	106	185	93.0	92.9	117	119	98	284
Portugal	5.1	5.3	104	11.7	11.6	99	75	32	44	46	97	93	70	72	142	99.9	99.9	97	93	104	304
Italy	4.7	4.3	91	9.0	9.0	100	62	57	68	73	83	76	70	90	160	97.8	96.8	103	154	67	261

Hungary	5.2	5.2	100	12.9	10.4	81	71	81	85	87	80	–	78+	97	175	–	–	–	151	–	–
Czech R.	4.8	4.2	88	8.7	9.9	114	62	92	94	95	72	85	84	98	182	90.7	91.7	133	150	89	272
Poland	5.2	4.9	94	11.9	11.6	97	70	52	92	87	67	67	72	107	179	95.4	98.6	120	35	343	327
Slovak R.	4.6	3.6	78	14.1	10.5	74	54	94	94	94	95	91	76	84	160	97.6	89.3	131	643	20	198
Ireland	5.0	4.9	98	12.2	13.5	111	73	73	83	88	70	79	85	108	193	–	–	176	–	–	–
UK	5.0	5.4	108	11.4	11.7	103	76	68	75	79	80	68	36	45	81	88.7	78.1	120	264	45	201
US	4.7	5.3	113	12.3	14.1	111	78	88	87	87	37	312	32	86	118	91.6	91.4	121	124	98	281
Australia	4.9	4.3	88	13.8	13.7	99	66	71	81	86	65	50	44	89	116	82.9	81.1	121	137	88	250
N. Zeal.	5.6	5.8	104	16.5	18.1	110	87	82	80	79	–	63*	66	105	171	–	85.6	123	126+	98	269
Japan	3.6	3.4	94	9.5	9.4	98	53	94	*	94	35	39	33	84	116	89.9	89.9	102	101	100	280

(continued)

Table A.3 (continued)

	5. Ratio of students to teaching staff, 2006 Schools: i. state ii. private iii. ii % of i			6. A. Private household spending on education 2007 = x (10-x). B. Students in publicly funded schools, primary, secondary. a. 2000. b. 2007 (x). C. unit of funding (share of 100%) attained by privately & publicly funded students+ i. 2000 ii. 2007. Score (S): (Bc.ii – (Bcii-ci)) *2 – (A*3)						7. Score: (1*3) + (2*2) + 4 (5*3) + 6 + 7 + (8*3)
	i.	ii.	iii.	A	Ba	b	Ci	ii	S	
Denmark	11.8	12.6	107	4	100	100	1.00–0.98-98/1.00–0.98-98		184	1281
Finland	9.9	12.5	126	3	100	100	1.00–0.99-99/1.00–0.99-99		189	1204
Sweden	12.1	11.4	94	3	100	100	1.00–0.99-99/0–0-100		193	1222
Norway	–	–	100	–	100	100	1.00–0.99-99/1.00–0.99-99		198	1155
Germany	15.8	13.0	87	15	100	100	1.00–0.87-87/1.00–0.86-86		125	1044
Holland	16.2	16.2	100	7	99	100	1.00–0.86-86/1.00–0.87-87		155	1110
Belgium	9.1	9.7	107	4	100	100	1.00–0.95-95/1.00.0.95–95		178	1193
Switzl.	–	–	–	–	96	96	2.7–0.93-82/3.48–0.90-74		132	–
Austria	10.5	11.8	112	5	100	100	1.00–0.96-96/1.00–0.96-96		177	1146
France	13.9	15.5	111	7	100	100	1.00–0.93-93/1.00–0.93-93		165	1151
Spain	11.2	15.0	134	12	94	97	1.6–0.99-93/0.96–0.96-100		150	1086
Portugal	8.0	8.9	111	7	88	94	1.00/1.00		179	1052
Italy	10.3	7.3	71	7	95	95	1.00/1.00		179	–
Hungary	11.3	11.1	99	–	100	100	1.00/1.00		200	–
Czech R.	10.4	10.3	84	8	100	100	1.00–0.91-91/1.00–0.92-92		158	–
Poland	12.8	9.2	77	9	100	98	1.00–0.95-95/1.00–0.99-99		163	1131
Slovak R.	14.1	13.2	94	8	100	100	1.00–0.98-98/1.00–0.89-89		136	938
Ireland	15.5	16.3	105	–	99	99	–		–	–
UK	18.6	7.2	39	20	95	95	2.26–0.93-87/4.38–0.82-64		22	730
US	15.7	10.7	68	20	95	91	1.68–0.96-93/0.96–1.00–100		126	900

Australia	12.3	11.9	111	23	100	100	1.00–0.83-83/1.00–0.81-81	89	936
N. Zeal.	17.0	15.9	80	19	95	96	2.88–0.90-80/3.60–0.89-73	75	1013
Japan	15.2	13.2	87	22	88	95	0.84–1.02-100/2.02–0.10-81	58	888

Column 1: Education at a Glance 2011. * Figure is for 2000. *Column 2*: a. OECD Education at a Glance 2002. b. OECD Education at a Glance 2009.* The figure for Japan 2007 is not available and assumed the same as 2000. *Column 3*: Education at a Glance 2010. * is for 2002 figures where 2000 not available. + is for 2006 where 2007 not available. *Columns 4 and 7A*: Education at a Glance 2011. + where data more available for all levels of education. For New Zealand, where the private funding figure for 2007 is not available, the 2000 figure is used (for calculation in Column 7). * for column 4, the figures for 2007 are assumed the same in 2007 for Norway where figure not available. *Column 5*: Education at a Glance 2008. *The Danish figure is not disaggregated between lower and upper secondary because this formal division in schools does not exist. For Australia and Ireland only the secondary overall figure was available. In countries where enough independent school students exist for public records to be kept the figure used is the ratio in independent schools (Greece, Ireland, Italy, Japan, Mexico, New Zealand, Poland, Portugal, Spain, Turkey, UK, US, Brazil, Chile). For other countries, the figure for the private sector is for publicly subsidized schools (Australia, Austria, Finland, France, Germany, Hungary, Iceland, Korea, Slovak Rep., Sweden). + For Holland the Ministry of Education publishes one figure for both sectors. Education, Culture Science of the Dutch Education Ministry Key Figures 2003–2007. +++ For Norway and Canada figures are not available but private funding is negligible in primary and lower secondary schools, with less than 3 per cent attending publicly subsidized private schools. Hence an equal ratio is assumed so as to provide a neutral score for the overall indicator of the private–public resource balance (column 7). For Canada, where there is a significant independent sector, it is not possible to provide a realistic proxy. *Column 6*: OECD Education at a Glance (2002) for 2000 figure and (2009) for 2007 figure. The figure in the table is an average of the ratio in primary, lower secondary and upper secondary. For most countries the ratio across the three is very similar. For Portugal, Japan, New Zealand, Mexico and Switzerland there is more private participation in secondary education and the reverse is the case for Italy. + The c. figure is attained by first calculating the ratio of the share of total funds that are available to private (or public) school students to the share of private (or public) school students in all students; then, second, subtracting the public from the private ratio; and, third, multiplying this with 10 and then subtracting from 100. In cases where there is no significant presence of independent private schools, 99% (students in publicly-funded education) is counted as 100. Where nearly all the funding (as in Portugal 99.9%) is public, all students are counted as in publicly funded schools. Where, as in Italy, the ratio of public students is higher than ratio of private finance, the ratio is considered even

Table A.4 Relative employment and income returns to education, females

	1. Education employment return rate, females* a. 2002 b. 2008. i. lower secondary. ii. i as % of tertiary (to max. of 80)+Score (S): (bi*3) + (bii/2) + (bi-ai) + (bii-aii)					2.*Education unemployment return rate Females. a. 2002 b. 2008. i. lower sec. ii. A: ter. as % of lower sec. (to max. of 100) Score: ((20 – bi)* 20) + (bii) + ((500 –(trend a. i to b. i with ai as 100))/10) + ((100(aiibii))/3)					3. Relative education income return rates, females (upper secondary/ postsecondary non tertiary as 100) a. 1999/00. b. 2007 i. lower secondary ii. tertiary				4. 3i as % of 3ii (3a, b) Score (S): (b*2) + (b–a)		
	a.i	ii	b.i	ii	S	a.i	ii	b.i	bii		a i	ii	b i	ii	a	b	S
Denmark	52	62	60	67	227	4.6	100	3.4	65	484	90	123	83	124	73	67	128
Finland	54	64	61	73	236	8.1	38	9.8	38	293	99	145	96	146	68	66	130
Sweden	69	78	65	72	222	3.9	54	6.9	42	366	88	126	84	127	70	66	128
Norway	57	66	60	67	218	2.1	81	4.5	33+	389	83	135	81	134	61	60	119
Germany	45	56	51	63	198	6.4	59	13.5	30	212	72	137	84	159	53	53	106
Holland	50	61	55	64	205	2.2	91	4.0	37	404	72	155	75	159+	46	47	95
Belgium	45	55	47	57	173	6.0	65	11.4	32	264	82	132	81	134+	62	60	118
Switzl.	62	76	62	74	221	2.7	100	8.4	34	312	72	144	76	156	50	49	97
Austria	48	56	50	61	188	2.9	83	6.9	32	305	74	156	73	160+	47	46	91
France	56	70	58	73	216	9.4	5	10.6	42#	269	79	145	82	147	55	56	111
Spain	44	58	52	64	202	10.1	83	15.7	39	178	64	125	70	149	51	47	90

Portugal	77	80	73	80	255	5.0	96	11.0	62	286	63	170	67	173	37	39	80
Italy	39	51	42	56	162	6.1	97	12.7	42	232	84	137	74	143+	61	52	95
Hungary	35	45	35	46	129	3.1	48	15.3	16	133	71	164	71	185	43	38	71
Czech R.	42	53	42	54	154	8.6	19	17.3	9	121	72	170	74	165	42	45	93
Poland	32	39	32	39	116	11.2	54	11.9	29	235	76	148	76	165	51	46	97
Slovak R.	33	36	30	37	106	16.0	19	34.8~	10	62	–	–	–	–	–	–	–
Ireland	47	56	48	58	176	2.5	44	5.3	4	347	65	163	67	178	40	38	74
UK	48	56	43	50	143	6.8	37	8.2	23	349	69	176	70	181	39	39	78
US	49	62	46	58	160	5.5	38	9.7	22	310	62	164	61	167	38	36	70
Australia	51	63	57	72	222	3.4	59	5.2	35	391	89	146	86	146	61	59	116
N. Zeal.	54	68	59	74	227	3.0	80	4.1	56	436	86	126	85	126	68	67	133
Japan	53	78	–	–	–	2.6	100	4.0	80	461	–	–	–	–	–	–	–
S. Korea	60	80	58	80	212	1.0	100	1.6	100	502	69	141	97	167+	49	58	125
Mexico	48	80	49	67	169	0.5	20	2.7	3.9	378	–	–	–	–	–	–	–

(*continued*)

Table A.4 (continued)

	5. Earnings dispersion 9th to 1st earnings deciles Score (s): (5-5ii)*50)		6. Incidence of long-term unemployment. Females % of total i. 1994. ii. 2008 iii. 2009. Score (S): ((60-6iii) *2 + trend from i to iii with i as 100 (200-trend)/2				7. Unemployment rate, i. 2000, ii. 2008, iii. 2009 Score (S): ((20-iii)*2) +(50–(trend to 2009 with 2000 as 100/5))				Employment security index (ILO), 2004	Overall score: Cols. (1*2) + (2/2) + 4 + (5*3) + 6 + 7 + (8*3)
			i	ii	iii	S	i	ii	iii	S		
Denmark	2.73	114	32.4	12.7	9.4	187	4.3	3.3	6.0	52	96	1693
Finland	2.57	122	21.8*	16.2	14.7	158	9.8	6.4	8.2	57	84	1582
Sweden	2.28	137	20.5	11.3	12.4	162	5.6	6.2	8.3	44	95	1654
Norway	2.28	137	29.8	6.0	8.0	191	3.2	2.5	3.1	65	76	1427
Germany	3.32	84	47.2	51.0	47.0	76	7.5	7.3	7.5	55	72	1207
Holland	2.91	105	48.7	32.2	26.1	141	2.8	2.8	3.4	59	77	1453
Belgium	2.33	134	62.6	48.1	45.0	94	6.9	7.0	7.9	51	75	1368
Switzl.	2.69	116	35.4	39.9	33.6	106	2.6	3.5	4.4	47	61	–
Austria	3.32	84	18.5	22.6	21.0	131	3.6	3.8	4.8	54	72	1273
France	2.91	105	39.5	36.5	34.7	107	9.0	7.8	9.5	50	88	1414
Spain	3.28	137	63.0	28.9	34.4	124	11.1	11.3	18.0	22	74	1362
Portugal	4.26	37	44.3	46.6	47.5	72	4.0	7.7	9.6	23	76	1167
Italy	2.69	116	63.3	47.5	46.9	89	10.2	6.7	7.8	55	66	1225
Hungary	4.11	50	37.6	46.3	42.8	77	6.4	7.8	10.0	39	47	–
Czech R.	3.15	143	22.8	50.1	33.4	80	8.7	4.4	6.7	61	53	–
Poland	3.55	123	43.8	30.8	27.3	102	16.1	7.1	8.2	60	–	–
Slovak R.	–	–	43.5	66.4	54.4	38	18.8	9.5	12.0	53	–	–
Ireland	3.79	111	57.4	19.3	21.7	107	4.2	6.3	11.9	23	69	–
UK	3.63	69	33.9	18.1	21.5	145	5.4	5.6	7.6	47	60	1118
US	4.89	6	10.2	10.3	16.1	110	4.0	5.8	9.3	25	56	866

Australia	3.34	83	30.5	14.0	14.4	118	6.3	4.2	5.6	61	70	1393
N. Zeal.	2.92	104	26.4	3.4	6.4	195	6.2	4.2	6.1	58	53	1529
Japan	3.02	99	12.2	23.8	18.8	155	4.7	4.0	5.1	58	–	–
S. Korea	4.78	11	3.2	0.4	0.3	195	4.4	3.2	3.6	66	50	1244
Mexico	–	–	2.3	1.8	2.1	–	2.5	4.0	5.5	–	39	–

Sources: *Column 1*: 2002 Figure Education at a Glance 2004, 2008 Figure, Education at a Glance 2010.+ For the calculation of the score: where a minus is indicated 0 is used. + The Japan figure is for upper secondary. Norway figure is for 2006. From Education at a Glance 2008. *Column 2*: Females, 25–64 age cohort. Education at a Glance OECD 2010.* Where both years (1999/2000) are available 2000 is used. + for Holland 2002 and 2006 figures are used. For Austria 2005 is used in place of 2000. For Belgium 2005 is used for 2007 where figure not available. 2006 is used for Italy instead of 2007. Korea is 1998 for 2000. The Slovak Republic's level of female unemployment is a strong outlier. To prevent adjusting the score to accommodate it, the score for the S.R. assumes a level of 20%, but subtracts the additional 14.8 points from the final score to take account of the high unemployment. # For France, the calculation of the trend in relative unemployment rates by education is set at 0. *Columns 3 and 4*: Education at a Glance 2010. *Columns 5 and 6*: OECD Employment Outlook 2010. Column 6: *1994 figure for Finland not available, 2006 used instead. *Column 7*: OECD Employment Outlook 2010. *Column 8*: The ILO's Employment Security index is composed of 8 indicators, 3 for ratification of conventions, 1 for coverage of collective bargaining, 1 for existence of independent labor tribunals, and the last three are share of waged and public sector employment, and the ratio of female to male employment. ILO (2004) 161–2, 401–2

Table A.5 Equality of education and employment returns, 1998–2002, 2007–8

	1. A. Public spending on edu. in GDP (a) 2000 (b) 2007 B. Public spending on edu. in public spending (a) 2000 (b) 2007				2. Pop. with upper sec. Edu., age 25–34, %		3. Share of public spending on tertiary educational Institutions A 2000 B 2007		4. Public/private education spending in GDP. Primary, secondary and post-secondary non-tertiary, A. Public. B. Private i. 2000, ii. 2007				5. Edu. Empl. return rate +, female* a. 2002 b. 2008. i. Lower sec. ii. i as % of ter. (to max of 80)				6. Education Unemployment return rate females* a. 2002 b. 2008 i. Lower secondary. ii. Tertiary as % of lower secondary (to a max. of 100)			
	Aa	b	Ba	b	00	07	A	B	Ai	ii	Bi	ii	a.i	ii	b.i	ii	a.i	ii	b.i	ii
Denmark	8.3	7.8	15.3	15.4	86	85	99.4	97.6	97.8	98.1	2.2	1.9	52	62	60	67	4.6	100	3.4	65
Finland	6.0	5.9	12.5	12.5	87	90	97.8	97.2	99.3	99.0	0.7	1.0	54	64	61	73	8.1	38	9.8	38
Sweden	7.2	6.7	13.4	12.7	91	91	93.6	91.3	99.0	100.0	0.1	0.0	69	78	65	72	3.9	54	6.9	42
Norway	5.9	6.7	14.5	16.4	93	83	93.7	96.3	99.0	–	1.0	–	57	66	60	67	2.1	81	4.5	33+
Germany	4.4	4.5	9.8	10.3	85	85	89.2	88.2	87.3	86.3	13.7	12.7	45	56	51	63	6.4	59	13.5	30
Holland	5.0	5.3	11.2	11.7	74	83	79.4	76.5	85.6	86.7	14.3	13.3	50	61	55	64	2.2	91	4.0	37
Belgium	5.9	5.9	12.1	12.4	75	82	–	91.5	94.7	95.2	5.3	4.8	45	55	47	57	6.0	65	11.4	32
Switzl.	5.4	5.2	15.6	12.2	92	90	–	–	89.2	86.1	10.8	13.9	62	76	62	74	2.7	100	8.4	34
Austria	5.6	5.4	10.7	11.1	83	87	96.1	96.3	95.8	96.0	4.2	4.0	48	56	50	61	2.9	83	6.9	32
France	6.0	5.6	11.6	11.5	78	83	85.3	84.4	92.6	92.7	7.4	7.3	56	70	58	73	9.4	5	10.6	42#
Spain	4.3	4.3	10.9	11.1	57	65	74.4	74.4	93.0	92.9	7.0	7.1	44	58	52	64	10.1	83	15.7	39
Portugal	5.4	5.3	12.6	11.6	32	44	96.5	92.5	99.9	99.9	0.1	0.1	77	80	73	80	5.0	96	11.0	62
Italy	4.5	4.3	9.8	9.0	57	68	82.9	77.5	97.8	96.8	2.2	2.3	39	51	42	56	6.1	97	12.7	42
Hungary	4.9	5.2	14.1	10.4	81	85	80.3	–	–	–	–	–	35	45	35	46	3.1	48	15.3	16
Czech R.	4.0	4.2	9.5	9.9	92	94	71.5	85.4	90.7	91.7	8.3	9.3	42	53	42	54	8.6	19	17.3	9

Poland	5.0	4.9	12.7	11.6	52	92	66.6	66.6	95.4	98.6	4.6	1.4	32	39	32	39	11.2	54	11.9	29
Slovak R.	3.9	3.6	14.7	10.5	94	94	95.4	91.2	97.6	89.3	2.4	10.7	33	36	30	37	16.0	19	34.8~	10
Ireland	4.3	4.9	13.6	13.5	73	83	69.7	79.2	–	–	–	–	47	56	48	58	2.5	44	5.3	4
UK	4.3	5.4	11.0	11.7	68	75	80.0	67.7	88.7	78.1	11.3	21.9	48	56	43	50	6.8	37	8.2	23
US	4.9	5.3	14.4	14.1	88	87	37.4	31.1	91.6	91.4	8.4	8.6	49	62	46	58	5.5	38	9.7	22
Australia	4.5	4.3	13.8	13.7	71	81	64.6	49.6	82.9	81.1	18.9	17.1	51	63	57	72	3.4	59	5.2	35
N. Zeal.	6.8	5.8	14.5	18.1	82	80	–	62.5*	–	85.6	–	14.4	54	68	59	74	3.0	80	4.1	56
Japan	3.6	3.4	9.5	9.4	94	*	35.1	38.5	89.9	89.9	10.2	10.1	53	78	–	–	2.6	100	4.0	80
S. Korea	3.7	4.2	16.3	14.8	95	97	–	23.3	80.8	77.8	19.2	22.2	60	80	58	80	1.0	100	1.6	100
Mexico	4.4	4.8	23.4	21.7	25	39	77.4	79.4	86.1	82.1	13.9	17.9	48	80	49	67	0.5	20	2.7	4

(continued)

Table A.5 (continued)

	7. Relative edu. Income return rates, females (upper sec/ postsecondary non tertiary as 100) a. 1999/00 b. 2007. i. lower sec. ii. tertiary iii. Lower sec. as a % of tertiary						8. A. Female long-term unemploy. Rate (as % of total) (70 – x). B. unemployment rate both gender Score A + B ((20 – x)*2)					9. Earnings disp.~ 9th–1st deciles (Score: 2 00 – (*10)) i. 98 ii. 08(5×)*100			10. Returns to equal education score:*** i. 98/02 ii. 07/8 Education (E) Returns (R) i ii i ii*		
							00		08	00	08				i	ii	i	ii
							A		B	S	S							
	a i	ii	b i	ii	iii	a b	00		08	00	08							
Denmark	90	123	83	124	73	67	50	57	4.3	3.3	81	90	2.48	2.73	436	430	731	643
Finland	99	145	96	146	68	66	44	54	9.8	6.4	64	82	2.42	2.57	412	412	597	588
Sweden	88	126	84	127	70	66	47	50	5.6	6.2	76	78	2.24	2.28	423	417	696	613
Norway	83	135	81	134	61	60	67	62	3.2	2.5	101	97	1.95	2.28	412	419	660	565
Germany	72	137	84	159	53	53	19	23	7.5	7.3	44	48	3.07	3.32	360	359	543	491
Holland	72	155	75	159+	46	47	30	38	2.8	2.8	64	72	2.88	2.91	349	356	658	524
Belgium	82	132	81	134+	62	60	13	22	6.9	7.0	39	48	2.39	2.33	390	394	597	553
Switzl.	72	144	76	156	50	49	40	30	2.6	3.5	75	63	2.53	2.69	–	–	–	505
Austria	74	156	73	160+	47	46	47	47	3.6	3.8	80	79	–	3.32	396	397	528	474
France	79	145	82	147	55	56	27	33	9.0	7.8	49	57	3.05	2.91	381	379	531	523
Spain	64	125	70	149	51	47	18	41	11.1	11.3	37	58	–	3.28	343	347	508	456
Portugal	63	170	67	173	37	39	30	23	4.0	7.7	62	50	–	4.26	379	379	531	453
Italy	84	137	74	143+	61	52	9	22	10.2	6.7	25	49	–	2.69	362	357	522	444
Hungary	71	164	71	185	43	48	24	24	6.4	7.8	51	48	4.21	4 11	–	–	–	–
Czech R.	72	170	74	165	42	45	20	20	8.7	4.4	43	51	2.90	3.15	348	368	386	355
Poland	76	148	76	165	51	46	29	39	16.1	7.1	37	67	–	3.55	346	370	434	394
Slovak R.	–	–	–	–	–	–	15	4	8.8	9.5	37	25	–	–	–	–	–	–
Ireland	65	163	67	178	40	38	22	51	4.2	6.3	54	78	3.93	3.79	–	–	491	415

UK	69	176	70	181	39	39	51	52	5.4	5.6	80	81	3.47	3.63	345	327	443	381
US	62	164	61	167	38	36	65	60	4.0	5.8	97	88	4.51	4.89	328	297	406	345
Australia	89	146	86	146	61	59	46	56	6.3	4.2	73	88	2.91	3.34	325	309	545	512
N. Zeal.	86	126	85	126	68	67	56	67	6.2	4.2	84	99	2.64	2.92	357	350	609	567
Japan	–	–	–	–	–	–	53	46	4.7	4.0	84	78	2.98	3.02	–	–	–	–
S. Korea	69	141	97	167+	49	58	69	69	4.4	3.2	100	103	3.83	4.78	286	283	515	548
Mexico	–	–	–	–	–	–	68	68	2.5	4.0	103	100	–	–	–	–	–	–

***Final score: Education: (1A*10) +(1B) + (2/2)+3 +(4A*2) Returns: (5i)+(5ii)+((20-6i)*2)+(6ii) +(7i)+ (7iii) + 8 + ((5–9)*100)/3)) +(col. 5 Table A.3*100) @ *Column 1*: OECD Education at a Glance 2010. *Column 2*: Education at a Glance 2010. * is for 2002 figures where 2000 not available. + is for 2006 where 2007 not available. *Columns 3 and 4*: Education at a Glance 2011. + where data more available for all levels of education. *Column 5*: 2002 Figure Education at a Glance 2004, 2008 Figure, Education at a Glance 2010.+ For the calculation of the score: where a minus is indicated 0 is used. + The Japan figure is for upper secondary. Norway figure is for 2006. From Education at a Glance 2008. *Column 6*: Females, 25–64 age cohort. Education at a Glance OECD 2010.* Where both years (1999/2000) are available 2000 is used. + for Holland 2002 and 2006 figures are used. For Austria 2005 is used in place of 2000. For Belgium 2005 is used for 2007 where figures are not available. 2006 for Italy instead of 2007. Korea is 1998 for 2000. The Slovak Republic's level of female unemployment is a strong outlier. To prevent adjusting the score to accommodate it, the score for the S.R. assumes a level of 20 per cent, but subtracts the additional 14.8 points from the final score to take account of the high unemployment. # For France, the calculation of the trend in relative unemployment rates by education is set at 0. *Column 7*: Education at a Glance 2010. *Column 8*: OECD Employment Outlook, various years. For Holland and Ireland 2000 data is not available, so 1999 is used. *Column 9*: ~ For countries where observations for one year is absent, no change between the two periods is assumed for those variables. @ Column 5 in Table A.3 figures public spending on training and job creation in GDP, for which the levels are also assumed to be influenced by the level of initial school equality

Table A.6 Structure of employment and non-employment time, early to mid2000s, late 2000s

	1. Annual leisure hours, (3000 – average annual employment hours)*00, 2010		2. Male part-time share as % of female Share 00 09		3. Paid maternity and parental leave, full-rate equivalent weeks 98–02 2008		4. Task and time controls A 2005, B 2010 i. able to choose/ change order of tasks a. low skilled manual. b total ii. Some control of work-time (working time arrangements not set by employer), iii. Work gives feeling of work well done											
							i				ii				iii			
							Tasks				Time				Well-being			
							A		B		A		B		A		B	
							a	b	a	b	a	b	a	b	a	b	a	b
Denmark	1419	1458	39	55	24.0	32.2	77	85	74	85	43	59	46	59	88	90	88	91
Finland	1249	1303	51	55	12.0	35.7	70	89	84	91	36	55	31	54	61	70	72	74
Sweden	1358	1376	34	51	14.4	37.7	76	85	65	78	42	66	48	62	81	84	78	82
Norway	1545	1586	26	37	42.0	38.8	65	78	57	82	25	47	28	53	89	87	89	87
Germany	1527	1581	14	21	14.0	54.6	33	52	39	57	28	43	34	45	58	78	80	86
Holland	1565	1623	23	28	16.0	21.3	60	79	64	80	50	63	43	65	71	86	84	90
Belgium	1455	1449	21	21*	11.0	14.4	53	73	56	71	22	47	29	45	73	83	83	86
Switzl.	1312	1360	19	20	16.0*	12.8	–	–	–	–	–	–	–	–	–	–	–	–
Austria	1342	1413	11	21	16.0	35.3	43	65	47	69	35	52	30	47	95	76	91	88
France	1409	1449	22	23	18.0	43.8	53	72	49	68	29	46	81	39	83	87	82	84
Spain	1269	1337	16	21	16.0	16.0	50	40	45	63	28	33	20	87	68	73	77	83

Portugal	1235	1286	33	43	6.0	17.0	44	58	55	63	16	25	22	25	81	83	77	85
Italy	1139	1222	24	19	16.0	23.8	39	60	71	69	30	51	33	41	84	87	84	87
Hungary	943	1039	33	46	17.0	76.1	56	63	44	64	21	28	11	28	75	74	67	78
Czech R.	908	1053	30	34	19.0	63.4	42	59	36	55	32	37	30	40	77	75	67	79
Poland	1012	1061	49	38	16.0	39.1	47	63	47	64	29	38	55	22	81	83	77	85
Slovak R.	1156	1214	35	54	15.4	46.1	–	–	–	–	–	–	–	–	–	–	–	–
Ireland	1281	1336	24	29	12.6	6.6	57	71	39	67	32	47	22	38	72	82	72	82
UK	1300	1353	21	28	5.4	12.8	50	66	52	70	34	47	25	42	68	74	59	75
US	1036	–	–	–	–	–	–	–	–	–	–	–	–	–	–	–	–	–

(continued)

Table A.6 (continued)

	5. Employment security i. % of employment 10 years +. ii. 50-% of unemployment 1 year < (if over 50 score of 0) iii. Unemployment iv. population with more than 5 years job tenure, age 55–59, 2009 Score (S): i + ii + (30-iii) + (iv/10) 2000, 2009								
	i	ii	iii	iv	S i	ii	iii	iv	S
Denmark	30.9	26.6	4.8	77.9	91/27.0	40.9	6.0	72	99
Finland	39.7	25.2	8.4	85.7	107/39.6	33.3	8.2	90	104
Sweden	42.2	21.1	7.6	82.9	114/42.2	37.2	8.3	72	108
Norway	35.6	35.5	4.5	83.3	97/34.5	32.3	3.1	68	101
Germany	41.8	0.0	10.6	84.6	80/42.4	4.5	7.5	76	77
Holland	39.8	7.0	5.3	85.0	80/40.7	25.2	3.4	75	100
Belgium	45.9	0.0	8.5	90.2	76/44.5	5.8	7.9	79	80
Switzl.	35.5	10.9	4.2	82.7	109/33.8	19.9	4.4	69	86
Austria	41.2	24.7	5.2	86.6	99/40.8	28.7	4.8	78	103
France	45.6	8.1	9.2	89.0	83/43.2	14.8	9.5	79	86
Spain	35.0	0.5	9.2	82.8	65/36.6	19.8	18.0	72	76*
Portugal	47.0	0.0	7.7	87.6	78/47.0	5.9	9.6	79	81
Italy	45.6	0.4	7.7	87.8	77/46.4	5.6	7.8	80	101
Hungary	35.9	3.9	7.2	82.7	71/35.0	7.4	10.0	73	70
Czech R.	37.6	6.3	7.9	82.4	74/39.9	18.8	6.7	78	90
Poland	43.4	0.0	17.8	84.1	64/40.0	24.5	8.2	75	94
Slovak R.	36.4	26.9	16.3	78.2	85/36.4	0.0	12.0	77	62
Ireland	29.2	18.4	4.4	77.9	81/33.5	21.0	11.9	74	82
UK	30.6	17.7	4.8	71.6	81/30.8	25.5	7.6	68	86
US	–	–	–	–	–	–	–	–	–

Table A.6 (continued)

	6. a. Net costs of child-care 2004/5, 2008, Score (S)* (100-x) (*b. Diff in female/male time for unpaid work, late 2000s (min per day) Score=300-x Source			7. Overall score: a, b 1/50+2*2+3+4ia+4ib+4iia+4iib+4iiia+4iiib+5*2+6a*2 With employment returns (Table A.5): c, d, PPF score Table A.1 and returns to school equality score Table A.5: e, f					
				a	b	c	d	e	f
Denmark	92	89	243	900	991	1631	1634	1687	1642
Finland	91	88	209	865	962	1460	1550	1543	1482
Sweden	92	93	228	872	983	1568	1596	1699	1623
Norway	90	83	227	894	908	1554	1473	1472	1482
Germany	91	86	195	768	795	1311	1286	1347	1199
Holland	86	87	190	824	909	1482	1433	1377	1319
Belgium	95	94	206	772	803	1369	1356	1486	1478
Switzl.	61	22	–	–	–	–	–	–	–
Austria	81	87	166	791	857	1319	1331	1325	1299
France	85	83	178	850	859	1381	1382	1485	1445
Spain	70	92	113	635	796	1143	1252	1190	1202
Portugal	93	92	68	746	802	1277	1255	1207	1190
Italy	–	–	77	–	–	–	–	–	–
Hungary	92	94	159	717	733	–	–	–	–
Czech R.	90	89	–	747	817	1133	1172	1116	1152

(*continued*)

Table A.6 (continued)

	6. a. Net costs of child-care 2004/5, 2008, Score (S)* (100-x) (*b. Diff in female/male time for unpaid work, late 2000s (min per day) Score=300-x Source				7. Overall score: a, b 1/50+2*2+3+4ia+4ib+4iia+4iib+4iiia+4iiib+5*2+6a*2 With employment returns (Table A.5): c, d, PPF score Table A.1 and returns to school equality score Table A.5: e, f				
				a	b	c	d	e	f
Poland	95	93	161	793	860	1227	1254	1125	1144
Slovak R.	89	93	–	–	–	–	–	–	
Ireland	55	55	133	719	685	1210	1100	–	–
UK	57	59	177	688	708	1131	1089	1167	–
US	–	–	196	–	–	–	–	–	–

Column 1: * For Switzerland 2008 is used in place of 2010. *Column 2*: Elaborated from OECD Employment Outlook: The calculation made is based on the share (per cent) of part-time employment in male total employment as a share of the total part-time employment as a share of female employment.: The 2006 figure for Belgium was not available, so no change is assumed. *Column 3*: * Switzerland's figure is 2006 in place of 2008, and France and Slovak Repl. is 2006 in place of 1998/2002. From OECD Family data-base, 2006/7, (Table PF A.1), and 2011. 1998/2002 figure is elaborated from The Clearinghouse on International Developments in Child, Youth and Family Policies at Columbia University. Flat rate leave is not included, only the period covered at 100% of wage. *Column 4*: Fifth European Survey on Working Conditions, 2010. *Column 5*: OECD Stats Extracts. Column 6a: Net childcare costs for a dual earner family with full-time arrangements of 167% of the average wage, after tax deductions, benefits and rebates. *The Spanish figure for 2004/5 is for pre-school care. OECD Family database and Doing Better for Families OECD 2011. *Column 6*: b OECD Society at a Glance 2011

Source for all columns, unless otherwise specified, Employment Outlook 2010, Statistical Annex

References

Acemoglu, D., Johnson, S., & Robinson, J. A. (2002). Reversal of Fortune. *Quarterly Journal of Economics, 117*, 1231–1294.

Adler (2016). A New Leviathan. *Journal of Law and Society, 43*(2), 195–227.

Allstott, A. (2001). Good for Women. In P. van Parijs (Ed.), *What's Wrong with a Free Lunch*. Boston: Beacon Press.

Alkire, S. (2002). Dimensions of Human Development. *World Development, 30*(2), 181–205.

Anderson, E. (1999). What Is the Point of Equality? *Ethics, 109*, 287–337.

Anker, N. (1998). *Eleverne, Virksomhederne og de Nyudlærte*, PhD serie 7.98, *SocialForskningsinstitutet*, Danmark.

Archer, R. (2010). *Why Is There No Labour Party in the United States?* Princeton, NJ: Princeton University Press.

Arneson, R. (2013). From Primary Goods to Capabilities to Well-Being. *Critical Reviews in Social and Political Philosophy*. http://philosophyfaculty.ucsd.edu/faculty/rarneson/my%20papers/Senrev.pdf

Atkinson, A. B. (2015). *Inequality*. Cambridge, MA: Harvard University Press.

Bates, R. (2006). The Role of the State in Development. In *The Oxford Handbook of Political Economy* (pp. 708–721). Oxford, UK: Oxford University Press.

Beveridge, W. (1942). *Social Insurance and Allied Services*. London: HMSO.

Birnbaum, S. (2012). *Basic Income Reconsidered*. Basingstoke, UK: Palgrave.

Bloksgaard, L. (2015). Negotiating Leave in the Workplace. In G. B. Eydal & T. Rostgaard (Eds.), *Fatherhood in the Nordic Welfare States*. Bristol, UK: Policy Press.

Boix, C. (2003). *Democracy and Redistribution*. Cambridge, UK: Cambridge University Press.

British Broadcasting Corporation (BBC). (2020, March 17). *Coronavirus: Chancellor Unveils £350bn Lifeline for Economy*. https://www.bbc.co.uk/news/business-51935467

Burtless, G., et al. (2010). *Income Distribution, Weekly Hours of Work, and Time for Child-Rearing*. (Luxembourg Income Study Working Paper 489).

Callard, F., & Margulies, D. S. (2014). What We Talk About When We Talk About the Default Mode Network. *Frontiers in Human Neuroscience, 8*, 619.

Cantor, N., & Sanderson, C. A. (2003). Life-Task Participation and Well-Being. In D. Kahneman et al. (Eds.), *Well-Being*. New York: The Russell Sage Foundation.

Chang, H.-J. (2003). Breaking the Mould. *Cambridge Journal of Economics, 26*(5), 539–559.

Chang, H.-J. (2009). Under-Explored Treasure Trovers of Development Lessons. In M. Kremer, P. van Lieshoust, & R. Went (Eds.), *Doing Good or Doing Better*. Amsterdam: Amsterdam University Press.

Clasen, J. (2001). Social Insurance and the Contributory Principle. *Social Policy and Administration, 35*(6), 641–657.

Collier, R. (1999). *Paths Toward Democracy*. Cambridge, UK: Cambridge University Press.

Columbino, U. (2009). *Evaluating Alternative Basic Income Mechanisms* (Discussion Paper No. 578). Bergen, NJ: Statistics Norway, Research Department.

Crouch, C. (1994). *Industrial Relations and European State Traditions*. Oxford, UK: Oxford University Press.

Crouch, C. (1977). *Class Conflict and Industrial Relations Crisis*. Heinemann.

Daily Mirror. (2020, March 4). New Coronavirus Sick Pay Law Announced. https://www.mirror.co.uk/news/politics/breaking-new-coronavirus-sick-pay-21629942

Danish Radio (DR). (2020). *Ledige fredes i coronakrise*. https://www.dr.dk/nyheder/penge/ledige-fredes-i-coronakrise-skal-ikke-i-aktivering-faa-understoettelse

Duvander, A.-Z., & Johansson, M. (2015). Parental Leave Use for Different Fathers. In G. B. Eydal & T. Rostgaard (Eds.), *Fatherhood in the Nordic Welfare States*. Bristol, UK: Policy Press.

Dworkin, G. (1988). *The Theory and Practice of Autonomy*. Cambridge, UK: Cambridge University Press.

Dworkin, R. (1981). What Is Equality. *Philosophy and Public Affairs, 10*, 185–246; 283–345.

Dworkin, R. (2000). *Sovereign Virtue*. Cambridge, MA: Harvard University Press.

Eggertsson, T. (1990). *Economic Behaviour and Institutions*. Cambridge: Cambridge University Press.

Elson, D. (2014). Economic Crises from the 1980s to the 2010s. In S. M. Rai & G. Waylen (Eds.), *New Frontiers in Feminist Political Economy*. London: Routledge.

Esping-Andersen, G. (1990). *The Three Worlds of Welfare Capitalism*. Cambridge, UK: Polity Press.

European Commission. (2013). *Barcelona Objectives: The Development of Childcare Facilities for Young Children in Europe*. Brussels, Belgium: European Commission.

European Observatory of Working Life (EOWL). (2010, March). Flexible Forms of Work: 'Very Atypical' Contractual Arrangements.

Fairlie, S. (2009). *A Short History of the Enclosure in Britain* (The Land, No. 7).

Financial Times. (2020, March 27). *Sunak Unveils £3bn-a-Month Rescue Deal for Self-Employed.*

Finegold, D., & Soskice, P. (1988). The Failure of Training in Britain. *Oxford Review of Economic Policy, 4*(3), 21–53. https://doi.org/10.1093/oxrep/4.3.21.

Foner, E. (1995). *Free Soil, Free Labor, Free Men*. New York: Oxford University Press.

Fredrickson, B., et al. (2013). A Functional Genomic Perspective on Human Well-Being. *Proceedings of the National Academy of Sciences of the United States of America, 110*(33), 13684–13689.

Friðriksdóttir, H. (2015). Nordic Family Law. In G. B. Eydal & T. Rostgaard (Eds.), *Fatherhood in the Nordic Welfare States*. Bristol, UK: Policy Press.

Goodin, R., et al. (2008). *Discretionary Time*. Cambridge, UK: Cambridge University Press.

Goodin, R. E. (2001). Work and Welfare. *British Journal of Political Science, 31*, 13–39.

Gornick, J. (2015). Parental Leave and Fathers: Extending and Deepening the Knowledge Base. In G. B. Eydal & T. Rostgaard (Eds.), *Childcare among Fathers' in Fatherhood in the Nordic Welfare States*. Bristol: Policy Press.

Haagh, L. (2007). Developmental Freedom and Social Order. *Journal of Philosophical Economics, 1*(1), 119–160.

Haagh, L. (2011a). Basic Income, Social Democracy and Control Over Time. *Policy and Politics, 39*(1), 41–64.

Haagh, L. (2011b). Working Life, Well-Being and Welfare Reform. *World Development, 39*(3), 450–573.

Haagh, L. (2013). The Basic Income and Different Egalitarian Rights to Security. In *Council of Europe. Trends in Social Cohesion* (p. 25).

Haagh, L. (2017, March). Basic Income Should Be Seen as a Democratic Right. *Royal Society of Arts Journal.* https://medium.com/rsa-journal/basic-income-should-be-seen-as-a-democratic-right-b249ab6078b0

Haagh, L. (2019a, April). The Developmental Social Contract and Basic Income in Denmark. *Social Policy and Society, 18*(2), 301–317.

Haagh, L. (2019b). Public Ownership Within Varieties of Capitalism. *International Journal of Public Policy*: Angela Cummine and Stuart White (Eds.), *15*(1/2), 153–186.

Haagh, L. (2019c). The Political Economy of Governance Capacity and Institutional Change. *Social Policy and Society, 18*(2), 243–263.

Haagh, L. (2019d). The Philosophy and Political Economy of Basic Income Revisited. In M. Torry (Ed.), *International Handbook of Basic Income*. London: Routledge.

Haagh, L. (2019e). *The Case for Universal Basic Income*. Cambridge, UK: Polity.

Haagh, L., & Rohregger, B. (2019). *UBI Policies and Their Potential for Addressing Health Inequities, WHO Policy Paper Series* (Vol. 1). Venice, CA: WHO.

Haagh, L. (2020, Winter). Rethinking Democratic Theories of Justice in the Economy after COVID-19. *Democratic Theory, 7*(2), 110–123.

Hall, P. A., & Soskice, D. (2001). *Varieties of Capitalism*. Oxford, UK: Oxford University Press.

Hay, C., & Farrall, S. (2014). Interrogating and Conceptualizing the Legacy of Thatcherism. In C. Hay & S. Farrall (Eds.), *The Legacy of Thatcherism: Assessing and Exploring Thatcherite Social and Economic Policies*. Oxford: Oxford University Press.

Hood, B. (2014). *The Domesticated Brain*. London: Penguin.

Inglehart, R., Basanez, M., & Moreno, A. (2001). *Human Values and Beliefs*. Ann Arbor: The University of Michigan Press.

Jensen, H. (1936). *Dansk Jordpolitik 1757–1919*. Gyldendanske Boghandel – Nordisk Forlag, København.

Jyllandsposten. (2020, March 26). *Tredje Aar i Traek*. https://www.altinget.dk/artikel/tredje-aar-i-traek-flere-unge-soeger-en-erhvervsuddannelse

Kahneman, D. (2011). Thinking Fast and Slow. *Penguin*, 496.

Kananen, J. (2014). *The Nordic Welfare State in Three Eras*. Surrey, UK: Ashgate.

Kirk, V. S. (2015), 15th October. 'Salami-metoden: Så skæres der igen et par skiver af dagpengesystemet'. Politiken.

Kongshøj-Madsen, P. (2003). Flexicurity through Labour Market Policies and Institutions in Denmark. In P. Auer & S. Cazes (Eds.), *Employment Stability in an Age of Flexibility*. Geneva, GE: International Labour Organisation.

Korpi, W., & Palme, J. (1998). The Paradox of Redistribution and Strategies of Equality. *American Sociological Review, 63*(5), 661–687.

Leira, A. (2006). Parenthood Change and Policy Reform in Scandinavia. In A. L. Ellingsæter & A. Leira (Eds.), *Politicising Parenthood in Scandinavia*. Bristol, UK: The Policy Press.

Mahon, R. (2010). After Neo-Liberalism? *Global Social Policy, 10*(2), 172–192.

Maurice, M., Sellier, F., & Silvestre, J.-J. (1986). *The Social Foundations of Industrial Power*. Cambridge, MA: MIT Press.

Meade, J. (1964). *Efficiency, Equality and the Ownership of Property*. London: Allen and Unwin.

Meagher, G., & Szebehely, M. (2009). Equality in the Social Service State. In J. Kvist et al. (Eds.), *Changing Social Equality*. Chicago: The Policy Press.

National Audit Office. (2016). *Benefit Sanctions*. London: National Audit Office.

Nordenmark, M. (2015). Gender Regime, Attitudes Towards Childcare. In G. B. Eydal & T. Rostgaard (Eds.), *Fatherhood in the Nordic Welfare States*. Bristol, UK: Policy Press.

North, D. C. (2005). *Understanding the Process of Economic Change*. Princeton, NJ: Princeton University Press.

Nozick, R. (1974). *Anarchy, State and Utopia*. London: Blackwell.

Nussbaum, M. (2000). *Women and Human Development*. New York: Cambridge University Press.

Nussbaum, M. (2006). *Frontiers of Justice*. London: The Belknap Press.

OECD Family Database. (2006/7).

OECD. (2007a). Employment Outlook.

OECD. (2007b). OECD Revenue Statistics.

OECD. (2007c). Society at a Glance.

OECD. (2007d). Taxation of Wage Income.

OECD. (2007e). Babies and Boss.

OECD. (2008a). Education at a Glance.

OECD. (2008b). OECD Revenue Statistics.

OECD. (2008c). Employment Outlook.

OECD Family Database. (2008d).

OECD. (2008e, July). Reforming Corporate Income Tax, Policy Brief.

OECD. (2008f). Growing Unequal, Report.

OECD. (2009a). OECD Tax Database.

OECD. (2009b). Society at a Glance.

OECD. (2010a). National Accounts at a Glance.

OECD. (2010b). OECD Tax Database.

OECD. (2010c). OECD Stat. Extracts.

OECD. (2010d [a]). Benefits and Wages.

OECD. (2010e). Employment Outlook.

OECD. (2011a). Health at a Glance.

OECD Family Database. (2011b).

OECD. (2011c). Society at a Glance.

OECD. (2013). Employment Outlook.

OECD. (2014). Society at a Glance.

OECD. (2018). Employment Outlook, Society at a Glance, Family Database.

OECD. (2019). Employment Outlook, Society at a Glance, Family Database.

Pagano, U. (1999). Property Rights, Asset Specificity and the Division of Labour Under Alternative Capitalist Relations. *Cambridge Journal of Economics, 15*(3), 315–342.

Parker, E., & Skoufias, S. W. (2001, Fall). Conditional Cash Transfers and Their Impact on Child Work and Schooling: Evidence from the PROGRESA Program in Mexico. *Economía, 2*(1), 45–96.

Pearson, R. (2014). Gender, Globalisation and the Reproduction of Labour. In S. M. Rai & G. Waylen (Eds.), *New Frontiers in Feminist Political Economy*. London: Routledge.

Peterson, C. (2003). Personal Control and Well-Being. In D. Kahneman et al. (Eds.), *Well-being*. New York: The Russell Sage Foundation.

Pettersson, M. (2007). The Relationship Between Public Service Dissatisfaction and Political Action. In S. Svallfors (Eds.), The Political Sociology of the Welfare State. Stanford, CA: Stanford University Press.

Piketty, T. (2014). *Capital in the Twenty-First Century*. Harvard University Press.

Portes, J., et al. (2017). *Social Prosperity for the Future*. London: Institute for Global Prosperity, University College London.

Pyper, D., & McGuinness, F. (2013, August 5). Zero Hour Contracts. In *House of Commons Library*. Standard Note SN/BT/6553.

Rawls, J. (1971). *A Theory of Justice*. Oxford, UK: Oxford University Press.

Rawls, J. (1988). The Priority of Right and Ideas of the Good. *Philosophy and Public Affairs, 17*, 251–276.

Rawls, J. (1993). *Political Liberalism*. New York: Columbia University Press.

Rawls, J. (2001). *Justice as Fairness*. Cambridge: Harvard University Press.

Sandberg, L. G. (1979). The Case of the Impoverished Sophisticate. *The Journal of Economic History, 39*(1), 225–241.

Schneider, B. R. (2013). *Hierarchical Capitalism in Latin America*. Cambridge, UK: Cambridge University Press.

Sen, A. (1992). *Inequality Re-examined*. Oxford, UK: Clarendon Press.

Sen, A. (1998). *Development as Freedom*. Oxford, UK: Oxford University Press.

Sen, A. (2002). Why Health Equity? *Health Econ., 11*, 659–666.

Sennett, R. (2003). *Respect*. London: Penguin.

Sennett, R. (2008). *The Craftsman*. London/New York: Allen Lane/ Penguin Books.

Skocpol, T. (1992). *Protecting Soldiers and Mothers*. Cambridge, MA: Harvard University Press.

Sloman, P. (2019). *Transfer State*. Oxford, UK: Oxford University Press.

Smallwood, J. (2013). Distinguishing how from Why the Mind Wanders. *Psychological Bulletin, 139*(3), 519–535.

Sokoloff, K. L., & Engerman, S. L. (2000). History Lessons: Institutions, Factor Endowments, and Paths of Development in the New World. *Journal of Economic Perspectives, 14*(4), 217–232.

Solow, R. (1990). *The Labour Market as a Social Institution*. Oxford, UK: Wiley-Blackwell.

Soysal, Y., & Strang, D. (1989). Construction of the First Mass Education Systems in Nineteenth Century Europe. *Sociology of Education, 62*(4), 277–288.

Standing, G. (2017). *Basic Income*. London: Penguin.

Standing, G. (2002). *Beyond the New Paternalism*. London: Verso.

Steinmo, S. H. (2018). *The Leap of Faith*. Oxford, UK: Oxford University Press.

Steinmo, S. (2010). *The Evolution of Modern States*. Cambridge, UK: Cambridge University Press.

Streeck, W., & Schäfer, A. (Eds.). (2013). *Politics in the Age of Austerity*. Cambridge, UK: Polity.

Streeck, W., & Thelen, K. (2005). Introduction. In W. Streeck & K. Thelen (Eds.), *Beyond Continuity*. Oxford, UK: Oxford University Press.

Sutton Trust. (2007). *The Educational Backgrounds of 500 Leading Figures*.

Sutton Trust. (2014a, October). *Ability Groups and Too Much Praise Can Harm Students*.

Sutton Trust. (2014b, June). *Open Access,* by Hubkau, C. Broughton, N., Keohane, N., Ezeyi, O., and Shorthouse, R.

Svallfors, S. (2011). A Bedrock of Support? *Social Policy and Administration, 45*(7), 806–825.

Taylor, R. A. (2017). *Exit Left*. Oxford, UK: Oxford University Press.

Tesfaye, M. (2013). *Kloge Hænder*. Copenhagen, DK: Gyldendal.

The Economist. (2014, October 4–10). *Special Report: The World Economy*.

The Family and Childcare Trust Annual Report. (2014). UK.

Thelen, K. (2004). *How Institutions Evolve*. New York: Cambridge University Press.

Thelen, L. (2014). *Varieties of Liberalization*. Cambridge, UK/New York: Cambridge University press.

Tilly, C. (1985). War Making and State Making as Organized Crime. In P. Evans et al. (Eds.), *Bringing the State Back in*. Cambridge, UK: Cambridge University.

van Parijs, P. (1995). *Real Freedom for all*. Oxford, UK: Clarendon Press.

van Parijs, P. (2001). 'A Basic Income for All' in What's Wrong with a Free Lunch? In Philippe van Parijs (Ed.), Boston: Beacon Press.

Vanderborght, Y., & van Parijs, P. (2017). *Basic Income*. London: Harvard University Press.

White, S. (2003). *The Civic Minimum*. Oxford, UK: Oxford University Press.

Wickham, et al. (2020). Effects on Mental Health of a UK Welfare Reform. *The Lancet Public Health, 5*(5), 157–164.

Williamson, A. O. (1985). *The Economic Institutions of Capitalism*. New York: Free press.

Williams, A. (2008). Liberty, Equality and Property. In J. S. Dryzek et al. (Eds.), *The Oxford Handbook of Political Theory*. Oxford, UK: Oxford University Press.

You, J.-I., & Chang, H.-J. (1993). The Myth of the Free Labour Market in Korea. *Contributions to Political Economy, 12*, 26–49.

Young, I. M. (1990). *Justice and the Politics of Difference*. Princeton, NJ: Princeton University Press.

8

Employment and Wage Policies in a Post-Neoliberal World

Simon Deakin

1 Introduction

It has become urgent to reduce inequality. For nearly five decades, income and wealth disparities were condoned by the social sciences and tolerated or promoted by governments. Precisely when and how the tipping-point was reached may be debated. The global financial crisis of 2008, and the decade of austerity which then ensued in many countries, played a role. The rise of the authoritarian right in Western democracies after 2016, a symptom of austerity, has focused minds. In this fluid environment, research conducted on the fringes of social science disciplines has begun to enter the mainstream, and the previously conventional wisdom is not looking secure. However, it is too soon to speak of any new consensus, either on the origins of inequality or on what can be done to address it. Modes of thought, which are all too clearly past their peak, still have the power, it seems, to sway debates, in particular when they are invoked to

S. Deakin (✉)
CBR, Judge Business School, University of Cambridge, Cambridge, UK
e-mail: s.deakin@cbr.cam.ac.uk; sfd20@hermes.cam.ac.uk

P. Arestis, M. Sawyer (eds.), *Economic Policies for a Post-Neoliberal World*, International Papers in Political Economy, https://doi.org/10.1007/978-3-030-56735-4_8

defend the argument that there is little that can be done by way of purposive action to address collective ills.

For progress to be made on these questions, the marshalling of evidence on the causes of rising inequality, and on its consequences for the social and political fabric, is needed. The evidence is substantial but dispersed across different disciplines and paradigms, and not always straightforward to interpret. To understand the processes at work requires, on the one hand, a close focus on what has been happening within nation states as a consequence of changes in economic policy, public finance, and market regulation. And, on the other, an examination of the ways in which international economic law and transnational governance more generally have been reshaping trade, capital, and labour flows between states.

Progress on these issues also requires some rethinking of the way institutions and institutional change are theorised in the social sciences. Institutions are not ignored in contemporary social and economic theory—far from it—but they tend to be portrayed as self-organising and so beyond the reach of effective political action. Relatedly, instrumental policy change and its implementation through regulation tend to be seen as external interferences in an otherwise self-adjusting economy. It follows that, if not simply ineffective in the face of indifference or resistance by economic actors, regulation can achieve social policy goals such as the reduction of poverty and inequality only through various trade-offs, that is to say, at the expense of development and growth. These theorisations of the role of institutions turn a blind eye to the essential interdependence of state and market in capitalist economies, and so significantly underplay the scope of politics to reform, reshape and, ultimately, transform capitalism.

With this context in mind, the present paper will attempt firstly to restate the case for seeing capitalism as process which is 'instituted' through particular legal and regulatory mechanisms, and to show that these mechanisms are amenable, within certain constraints, to political influence and hence to conscious and deliberate change (Sect. 2). It will then go on to chart what we know about the institutional causes of the rise in inequality, which has occurred worldwide in recent decades, beginning in Anglo-American systems in the 1970s and then becoming a generalised phenomenon. The focus here will be on the ways in which labour, product and capital markets have been both deregulated and *reregulated*, nationally and internationally, in line with a neoliberal policy agenda, which, in broad terms, empowered capital at the expense of labour (Sect. 3). Section 4 will look at some specific aspects of regulatory trends including the use of 'offshore' jurisdictions to avoid fiscal and regulatory compliance. This is a result of changes to the transnational coordination of legal and regulatory systems, which are eroding state capacity and the rule of law.

Section 5 will consider possible responses. It will analyse specific substantive measures, which could be taken to mitigate and reverse the rise in inequality, such as reviving progressivity in taxation, modernising social insurance, and enhancing collective bargaining over wages and conditions. These measures would be consistent with the restoration of a role for demand management in macroeconomic policy, a key dimension of a post-neoliberal economy, which other chapters in this collection are addressing. Measures of this kind, if taken in a concerted way, would do much to reverse the trend of rising income and wealth disparities, while also rebalancing capitalism away from its current extractive and opportunistic phase. The wider issue to consider concerns the institutional means needed to achieve these policy reforms, as they will not be self-enacting. This last point directs attention to the importance of investment in state capacity. Whatever else it may achieve, the COVID-19 crisis, which began in the early months of 2020, has thrown into stark relief the need for both national and global public goods.

2 Capitalism as Instituted Economic Process

A very familiar refrain in any debate about reforming or rebalancing capitalism is that not much can be done by way of conscious policy making to change the way things are, have always been, and will always remain. A pertinent, and prominent, example of this is the World Bank's insistence, in its *Doing Business Report 2008*, that 'laws created to protect workers often hurt them' (World Bank, 2007, p. 19). The logic of this position is that labour laws, which, for example, set minimum wages and maximum working time, regulate termination of employment, and provide for workers' freedom of association, distort the workings of the labour market, artificially raising employers' costs and so reducing labour demand. The result is involuntary unemployment and related effects, which 'hurt' the intended beneficiaries of the laws, namely workers. On closer inspection, it turns out that a view such as this is not based on evidence, since empirical studies are not clear-cut on these issues (see Adams et al., 2019 for a recent review), as much as certain theoretical priors. Above all: the belief that markets are in general self-organising and will arrive at a welfare-maximising equilibrium, as long as supply and demand can operate freely. This belief rests on nothing more or less than a *naturalisation* of the market: the market is a natural order, and regulation an artificial interference with it.

A slightly more nuanced position is that some laws may be needed to facilitate market-based exchange, but only laws of a certain type, namely rules of private law, which protect property rights and enforce contracts freely made. The idea that the specification through law of property rights is sufficient to generate market-based exchange is associated with a particularly influential interpretation of the 'Coase theorem' (Coase, 1960), which, nonetheless, is open to multiple understandings. Coase himself, reflecting on the reception of his work, wrote that 'if self-interest does promote economic welfare, it is because human institutions have been designed to make it so' (Coase, 1988, p. 134), not exactly a naturalistic understanding of law or the market.

The claim that private law enjoys the property of self-organisation in common with the market is associated with F.A. Hayek's concept of 'catallaxy' or 'spontaneous order' (Hayek, 1982). Hayek's (op. cit.) observation that knowledge in society is decentralised, in the sense of being possessed by individual agents, and so unavailable to a centralised legal 'sovereign', was the basis for his objection to legislative action the field of labour law, among others. Coase's (1960) critique of Pigovian welfare economics can be thought of as making a similar point about the difficulties of the sovereign legal agent setting an optimal tax to deal with environmental externalities (Coase, op. cit.). This argument exaggerates the emergent features of the common law, while neglecting the error-correction role played by legislation, particularly in unblocking the evolutionary 'dead ends' to which judge-made law is prone (Roe, 1996).

In the course of the 1990s, there emerged a further, empirically orientated variant on the theme of the common law's inherent efficiency, in the form of 'legal origins theory'. This approach maintained that national legal systems, which can trace their origin to the English common law, in contrast to the French or German civil law, were, for that reason, more likely to generate legal rules, which are efficient in the sense of wealth- and welfare-maximising (La Porta et al., 1996, 2008). Empirical studies dating from the mid-1990s (and financed at the time partly by the World Bank) appeared to show that cross-country differences in the content of company and insolvency laws were correlated with differences in the ownership structure of firms, with stronger shareholder protection favouring more dispersed ownership, and in the availability of external finance for firms, with higher levels of both shareholder and creditor protection reducing the cost of capital (La Porta et al., 1996). Conversely, stronger labour laws were correlated with distortions of the type predicted by Hayek, including higher unemployment and a larger informal economy (Botero et al., 2004). When it was observed that common-law origin systems (those colonised by the British or otherwise drawing on English law antecedents) tended to have a higher level, on average, of shareholder protection, and a lower average level of worker protection, the final link in the chain was made. Legal origin was a deep-rooted, institutional cause of divergences in levels of economic development across countries.

Claims have been made for the direct influence of legal origins theory on 'structural' reforms in 'dozens' of countries during the 2000s (La Porta et al., 2008). It is hard to disentangle the impact of the idea and the body of research with which it is associated from the more obvious and direct influence of the World Bank and the other global financial institutions, including the IMF and regional development banks, in pressing for 'structural' reforms, which included additional protections for shareholders and creditors. Nonetheless, legal origins theory undoubtedly had an impact beyond the academy, with its novel mode of production of metrics for benchmarking laws and regulations proving highly attractive to policy makers and researchers alike.

The academic reception of the work is instructive for the tenuous connection it reveals between social science research and its practical application. As replications and extensions of the original studies were attempted, most of the initial findings of the field were rejected (see Deakin & Pistor, 2012). It appeared that common law systems did not enjoy faster growth than countries with a civil law origin (Klerman et al., 2011). And that while there were systematic differences across countries in the content of laws regulating labour and capital, these were not consistently correlated with the economic consequences, which had been claimed for them (on shareholder rights, see Deakin, Sarkar, & Siems, 2018; on labour laws, Adams et al., 2019). Even the foundational legal origin claim that legal rules and institutions were the driving force behind economic development was significantly qualified once time-series evidence became available: laws were just as likely to be endogenous to national industrial and social contexts, or the result of political and economic shocks (Deakin & Sarkar, 2011; Deakin, Sarkar, & Siems, 2018). These modifications to the research programme of legal origins theory were largely accepted, and in some cases actively taken up, by those who were responsible for the field's early development (La Porta et al., 2008; Klerman et al., 2011). Legal origins theory was, after all, a hypothesis awaiting empirical verification or, as it turned out, falsification, rather than an assumed truth. However, the refinement of the field's core claims had little impact on policy makers who, with World Bank support, largely continued to follow the template of shareholder- and investor-centric structural reforms with which the theory was associated.

If there is an enduring legacy of the legal origins debate, it lies in the identification of relatively autonomous, state-centred legal systems as among the factors shaping long-run economic and social development, albeit according to a non-linear, 'co-evolutionary' dynamic, which is not easily modelled or predicted. Whatever the impacts of specific laws might be in particular contexts, law as a generic mode of governance has had a close connection to the rise of market economies (Deakin et al., 2016; Hodgson, 2015). In this respect, Karl Polanyi's observation retains its force: "not human beings and natural resources only but the organisation of capitalistic production itself [has] to be sheltered from the devastating effects of a self-regulating market" (Polanyi, 1944, p. 132).

Polanyi's (1944) idea of the 'double movement' implies that capitalism undergoes cycles of embedding and dis-embedding, with periodic crises triggering a regulatory response. However, even in periods of relative dis-embedding when protective regulations are withdrawn or their scope confined, capitalism remains an 'instituted economic process' (Harvey & Geras, 2018), in which the legal system, along with other manifestations of state power including the fiscal regime, shapes the operation of markets. As Harvey (2018) suggests, Britain's experience of industrialisation was one in which "the historical and political development of legal, fiscal and welfare instruments, along with changes in economic organisation, co-constituted the exchange between labour and capital in a complex process of institutional change" (p. 98). From this point of view, Britain's relatively early industrialisation was due in part to the institution of the Poor Laws, which provided a measure of protection against labour market risks from the time of the late Middle Ages. While administration of the Poor Law was largely decentralised, its operation was governed by national legislation which gave effect to the policy goals of the central state, which included the development of rural and urban labour markets through a mix of wage regulation, controls over migration and the provision of publicly funded poor relief (Deakin & Wilkinson, 2005). Although coercive for most of its history, the English poor law was also more extensive than similar systems on the European mainland: it had reached a point by the middle of the eighteenth century when per capita expenditure on poor relief targeted at the unemployed and elderly was several times that of other Western European states (Solar, 1995). In the twentieth century, it was the fiscal organisation of wage labour through income taxation and social insurance which made it possible for the centralised state to provide public goods, in the form of education, health and welfare systems, without which the market economy itself "did not and could not have developed" (Harvey, 2018, p. 27).

3 Institutions and Inequality

If legal and other formal institutional processes play a central role in constituting and shaping capitalism, what is their connection to inequality? We know from the empirical research conducted over the past decade (see in particular Atkinson, 2015; Milanovic, 2016; Palma, 2011, 2019a,

2019b; Piketty, 2014, 2019; Saez & Zucman, 2019) that income and wealth inequalities in the industrialised world peaked in the second decade of the twentieth century. And then began to revive from the early 1970s, in the USA, and from the 1980s, in Western Europe. Piketty's (2014) explanation for this is that there is an inherent tendency in a capitalist system for the rate of return on capital to exceed the growth rate of the economy. The decline in inequality in the middle decades of the twentieth century was the result of the destruction of rentier wealth brought about by the two world wars. From the final quarter of the twentieth century, returns to capital increased exponentially even as the economy was slowing, as a result of reduced population growth and limited improvements in productivity.

Piketty (2014) does not exactly claim that rising inequality under capitalism is unavoidable. Indeed, any such claim would plainly be inconsistent with the long-term trend from the 1910s to the 1970s. Piketty (op. cit.) ascribes a role to policies when he suggests that "the reduction of inequality that took place in most developed countries between 1910 and 1950 was above all a consequence of war *and of policies adopted to cope with the shocks of war*" (p. 20; emphasis added). He adds, however, "there is no natural spontaneous process to prevent destabilising, inegalitarian forces from prevailing permanently" (Piketty, op. cit., p. 21). In particular, he rejects the argument that "ever more fully guaranteed property rights, ever freer markets, and ever 'purer and more perfect' competition are enough to ensure a just, prosperous and harmonious society" (p. 30). This last suggestion is certainly consistent with the historical record: belief in the self-organising properties of the market went hand in hand with rising wealth and income disparities in the 'first globalisation', which ended in 1914, just as it has more recently. However, how exactly was inequality addressed in the intervening period?

Prior to the relatively recent rediscovery of inequality as an issue for the social sciences, it was generally believed that economic development had led to a convergence of wealth and incomes over time since the beginning of the modern industrial era, and would continue to do so. Kuznets (1955) observed in the 1950s that developed economies displayed lower levels of income inequality, whether from the point of view of earnings or household incomes, than developing ones. The dynamics of the transition from a subsistence economy to one based on industrial modes of production were seen as providing the explanation for this empirical result. In Lewis's (1954) 'structural transformation' model, developing economies initially enjoy a comparative advantage in being able to tap into a pool of low-cost labour during the transition period. In this period, income inequality increases as workers lose access to the land and employment is not yet stabilised. As wage labour becomes normalised, however, a 'Lewisian turning point' is reached when labour market institutions such as social insurance and collective bargaining can start to emerge. Similarly, the 'Kuznets curve' describes a process of rising inequality giving way to a more egalitarian distribution of incomes over time.

In the models proposed by Kuznets (1955) and Lewis (1954), the main drivers of economic development are technological change and the spread of knowledge. Nevertheless, they also both acknowledged the role played by politics and ideology as preconditions for the adoption of egalitarian social legislation. One way of understanding structural adjustment theory is that capitalism creates the conditions for the emergence of extensive labour market institutions, involving risk sharing and income pooling on a national level; but does not guarantee that this will happen. The political process is sufficiently autonomous from the economy for the advanced welfare state of the middle decades of the twentieth century to be only one possible outcome among many. Factors internal to the political system affecting the extent to which working-class movements are able to articulate a distinctive set of policies and positions, such as the degree to which, and speed with which, a given country adopts universal suffrage, are important. In addition, democratic representation within the framework of a rule of law state can be expected to play a role in helping to select in more egalitarian outcomes.

Why exactly should we expect labour market institutions such as collective bargaining and social insurance to lead to the convergence of incomes? In a purely static model in which the labour market was in equilibrium as a result of the interaction of supply and demand, no such effect could be expected: in this world, such institutions would take on the character of the 'distortions' and 'inefficiencies' identified in the World Bank's 2007 *Doing Business Report* (World Bank, 2007). In practice, labour is not priced solely by reference to supply and demand: labour markets are structured both spatially and temporally (Harvey & Geras, 2018). The identification of a labour market as 'national' in character is a function of a given state's capacity to exercise a monopoly of force within a bounded territorial space. Similarly, the inter-temporal aspect of labour contracting takes on a different dimension according to the presence of a legal system, which lends the power of the state to the monitoring and enforcement of agreements: 'private' law is still a law created and enforced by the state. Conventions of quality, which serve to coordinate complex exchange relations, may well operate at a social or inter-personal level but nevertheless find expression in, and derive stability from, formal legal institutions and mechanisms. Suffice to say that in these and numerous other ways, the legal system is an independent variable altering the allocation of power and distribution of risk between labour and capital, and between different groups in the workforce. Within the limits posed by the nature of existing technologies and resource endowments, there is considerable scope for labour to be contracted in ways which are more or less egalitarian in their results, depending on choices articulated through the political process and embedded in legal rules and mechanisms.

The history of labour law in the UK is a case in point. From the beginnings of industrialisation in the eighteenth century through to the early decades of the twentieth, the labour market was governed by punitive laws, which criminalised the formation and operation of trade unions (see Deakin & Wilkinson, 2005). Breach of the service contract on the part of the worker was a crime punishable by imprisonment or fine. These restraints were gradually lifted, beginning in the final quarter of the nineteenth century, through legislation, which lagged the extension of the franchise by around a decade. The removal of legal controls permitted trade unions to form on a nationwide basis for most industrial sectors, so that union membership and coverage of collective bargaining rose together. While this process was not uniform, as there were reversals in times of high unemployment, it culminated in 1945 in the formation of a national industrial relations system in which the wages and working conditions of over 80% of the labour force were regulated collectively. In addition, this was a system in which the principal mode of delivery of labour market governance were sector-level collective agreements, which achieved a high degree of wage compression along with industry-wide floors to conditions of employment.

The pattern of decriminalisation followed by legal support for collectivisation was the same in other industrialising systems during this period, but, importantly, with variations across countries. In France, for example, the degree to which the employment relationship was standardised through law and then regulated through a single classification system, which tied wage rates to occupational categories, exceeded in scale and scope the processes by which wage labour was similarly 'instituted' in Britain during the twentieth century. The effect was that while in the UK 'we have multiple institutions of price, in public and private sectors, firm-specific price systems, spot prices, sector price hierarchies, international labour market prices, and so on', in France by contrast "within the salariat, we have one national salarial grid across industries, related directly to established criteria of qualification" (Harvey & Geras, 2018. p. 49). The effect is not just to impart a greater degree of institutional stability to the French labour market, but also, through standardisation, to embed common quality standards and professional norms across a single national, territorially bounded labour market. To this day, the French system of industrial relations remains more highly institutionalised than its UK counterpart, more resistant to the disembedding effects of selective deregulatory policies, and more egalitarian in its outcomes.

A contrasting case at the other extreme is the USA (Tomlins, 1985). The USA enacted national-level laws supporting collective bargaining over wages and conditions later than other industrialised states, in the 1930s. The legislation of this period, however, stopped short of establishing effective mechanisms for sectoral or multi-employer bargaining, leaving unions to organise at plant level. The result was a decentralised collective bargaining system from the beginning, which only became further fragmented over time. Specific legal factors played a role in shaping the limited territorial and sectoral reach of US collective bargaining. The Supreme Court struck down legislation intended to promote sectoral agreements in the 1930s, mobilising to this end the provisions of the US Constitution prioritising the protection of private property over social regulation, and this measure not subsequently revived even when more modest legislative initiatives overcame the constitutional block. Then in the post-war period, the USA's federal structure allowed regulatory competition to develop between 'right to work' states in the south and west of the country and the more heavily regulated and industrialised states of the north. In time, this led to capital flight and to the erosion of such collective bargaining as remained in the private sector. The USA never achieved the degree of wage compression that became the norm in Europe in the post-1945 period, and continues to have one of the most unequal earnings distributions of the first wave of industrialised countries.

If trade union organisation, collective bargaining, and collective labour laws together act as significant determinants of the way labour is priced in different ways and at different times, in particular national-territorial and sectoral-industrial contexts, then a further source of variation is the system of social reproduction of labour, broadly conceived to include social security, education, and health, and correlatively, the organisation of taxation and public finance, through which these collective goods are supplied. These institutions serve to constitute and reproduce the fundamental commodity of a capitalist system, labour power (Harvey & Geras, 2018, p. 37). Prior to, or in the absence of, a centralised state, these pre-market functions were performed by households or communities. With the rise of the welfare state, governments undertook the task of providing them as collectively financed public goods. The degree to which the state assumed the responsibility for providing collective goods directly, as opposed to devolving it to private actors, differed across national systems, along with the scope to use the welfare state to achieve redistributive goals. Universalism in social security, eliminating targeting and means-testing, coupled with progressive taxation and solidaristic forms of social insurance, helped to bring about highly egalitarian distributions of wealth and income in certain industrialised states, particularly the Nordic systems, in the middle decades of the twentieth century (Esping-Andersen, 1990).

The British variant of the welfare state, while proving to be less stable and enduring than its Nordic counterparts, nevertheless achieved similar results for a period following its high point after 1945. At the end of the nineteenth century, the pioneering social surveys of Booth and Rowntree estimated that anywhere between 10% and 30% of urban households had incomes insufficient to meet their physical subsistence needs. At this point, only 3% of the urban population was in receipt of poor relief, and, for the unemployed, refusing work was effectively criminalised. The poor law, and with it the disciplinary institution of the workhouse, continued in force in some parts of the country until the 1940s. However, its effects were at first mitigated and then circumvented through the institution of a comprehensive, state-organised social security system, which provided universal access to health and education, and organised a single nation-wide, cross-sectoral social insurance regime. This included an unemployment compensation system embedding the principle of the right to refuse to work for wages below the 'going rate' set by collective bargaining. In 1950, the Rowntree poverty survey recorded a 'primary poverty' rate of below 2% of households in the city of York; the corresponding figure had been 18% in 1936. At this point, joblessness had been effectively abolished as the cause of poverty, with no single household being recorded as in poverty by virtue of unemployment (Deakin & Wilkinson, 2005).

Just as the implementation of the egalitarian policies of the mid-twentieth century entailed the interlocking of various legal, regulatory, and administrative measures, so their reversal from the 1980s onwards was achieved by policies which delinked these previously related mechanisms and created new complementarities; those fostered the return of inequality. The replacement of universalism with means-testing in social security, the reintroduction and intensification of sanctions for refusing work, and the removal of state support for sectoral collective bargaining together operated to remove the floor of rights to wages and conditions which had previously operated to compress wages and earnings. Deakin and Wilkinson (1991) chart this process as it unfolded during the 1980s. The removal of wage controls in conjunction with various 'activation' policies in the sphere of social security law brought about a widening of the inter-decile range for earnings and an increase in the proportion of low-paid jobs in the economy. In this period, the UK went from having one of the most egalitarian wage and employment structures in the industrialised world to having one of the most polarised and unequal. Alongside these labour market shifts, the downgrading of the principle of progressivity in taxation left a greater share of post-tax income in the hands of the wealthy. Meanwhile the encouragement of private provision and market-mimicking mechanisms in the delivery of health and education introduced elements of pricing into the provision of what had previously been public goods, differentially disadvantaging lower income groups. These changes were all initiated by conscious policy choices and were implemented through specific legislative and administrative initiatives.

Much of the originality of Piketty's work lies in his use of tax data to chart changes in wealth distribution over time. While trends in earnings and income inequalities were well understood prior to the appearance of *Capital in the Twenty-First Century* in 2014, the evidence it presented on the growing concentration of wealth opened up a new dimension to the debate. According to Piketty, the position of rentier-based wealth within capitalism is crucial to understanding inequality dynamics. While most of the households in the top 10% by wealth owe their position to the earnings of very highly paid professionals and managers, those in the top 1% are there by virtue of access to income from their ownership of capital (Piketty, 2014, 2019).

Piketty's (2014, 2019) work demonstrates the need to widen analysis of the institutional causes of inequality beyond a focus on wages and employment. The erosion of collective bargaining and the welfare state in many countries since the late 1970s does not directly account for the hyper-inequalities in the top 1% and even 0.1% that Piketty identifies. Returns to capital have increased for a variety of reasons including changes to the way in which dividends and other capital gains are taxed, and to the pushing back of inheritance taxes and taxes on accumulated wealth more generally. Corporate governance reforms strengthening the claims of shareholders as a class and their ability to exercise control over managers in the context of publicly listed companies have also played a role.

These changes in tax and corporate law are complementary to the changes in the laws governing wages and employment, which have allowed earnings inequalities to rise. The trend towards the strengthening of shareholder protection rights is a global one, affecting countries at all levels of development since the 1990s (Deakin et al., 2018). Table 8.1 and Figs. 8.1 and 8.2 explain and illustrate these trends. Figure 8.1 shows how shareholder rights have been strengthened between 1990 and 2013 in a range of developed and developing countries, using a 'leximetric' coding methodology. It associates a higher score on a 0–1 scale with an increased degree of legally mandated shareholder protection (for

Table 8.1 Variables on shareholder protection: definition and coding algorithms

Definition	Algorithm
1. Powers of the general meeting for de facto changes	If the sale of more than 50% of the company's assets requires approval of the general meeting it equals 1; if the sale of more than 80% of the assets requires approval it equals 0.5; otherwise 0
2. Agenda setting power	Equals 1 if shareholders who hold 1% or less of the capital can put an item on the agenda; equals 0.75 if there is a hurdle of more than 1% but not more than 3%; equals 0.5 if there is a hurdle of more than 3% but not more than 5%; equals 0.25 if there is a hurdle of more than 5% but not more than 10%; equals 0 otherwise
3. Anticipation of shareholder decision facilitated	Equals 1 if (1) postal voting is possible or (2) proxy solicitation with two-way voting proxy form has to be provided by the company (i.e., the directors or managers); equals 0.5 if (1) postal voting is possible if provided in the articles or allowed by the directors, or (2) the company has to provide a two-way proxy form but not proxy solicitation; equals 0 otherwise
4. Prohibition of multiple voting rights (super voting rights)	Equals 1 if there is a prohibition of multiple voting rights; equals 2/3 if only companies which already have multiple voting rights can keep them; equals 1/3 if state approval is necessary; equals 0 otherwise
5. Independent board members	Equals 1 if at least half of the board members must be independent; equals 0.5 if 25% of them must be independent; equals 0 otherwise
6. Feasibility of director's dismissal	Equals 0 if good reason is required for the dismissal of directors; equals 0.25 if directors can always be dismissed but are always compensated for dismissal without good reason; equals 0.5 if directors are not always compensated for dismissal without good reason but they could have concluded a non-fixed-term contract with the company; equals 0.75 if in cases of dismissal without good reason directors are only compensated if compensation is specifically contractually agreed; equals 1 if there are no special requirements for dismissal and no compensation has to be paid Note: If there is a statutory limit on the amount of compensation, this can lead to a higher score

(continued)

Table 8.1 (continued)

Definition	Algorithm
7. Private enforcement of directors duties (derivative suit)	Equals 0 if this is typically excluded (e.g., because of strict subsidiarity requirement, hurdle which is at least 20%); equals 0.5 if there are some restrictions (e.g., certain percentage of share capital; demand requirement); equals 1 if private enforcement of directors duties is readily possible
8. Shareholder action against resolutions of the general meeting	Equals 1 if every shareholder can file a claim against a resolution by the general meeting; equals 0.5 if there is a threshold of 10% voting rights; equals 0 if this kind of shareholder action does not exist
9. Mandatory bid	Equals 1 if there is a mandatory public bid for the entirety of shares in case of purchase of 30% or 1/3 of the shares; equals 0.5 if the mandatory bid is triggered at a higher percentage (such as 40 or 50%); further, it equals 0.5 if there is a mandatory bid but the bidder is only required to buy part of the shares; equals 0 if there is no mandatory bid at all
10. Disclosure of major share ownership	Equals 1 if shareholders who acquire at least 3% of the company's capital have to disclose it; equals 0.75 if this concerns 5% of the capital; equals 0.5 if this concerns 10%; equals 0.25 if this concerns 25%; equals 0 otherwise

Source: Deakin, S., Armour, J., & Siems, M. (2017). CBR Leximetric Datasets [updated] [Dataset]. https://doi.org/10.17863/CAM.9130

discussion of the coding method, see Deakin et al., 2018; the indicators are set out in Table 8.1). As Fig. 8.1 shows, there has been considerable convergence around a significantly higher degree of shareholder protection over this period. Figure 8.2 presents the same data in a different way, by charting the scale of the increase in particular types of legal rule. This Figure shows that the largest changes were made in two particular variables, those relating to board independence and the 'mandatory bid' rule in hostile takeover bids. These two indicators are strongly associated with changes in corporate governance practice which seek to 'align' managers' interests with those of shareholders, and which have led to loss of managerial autonomy in deciding how to respond to takeover bids and activist hedge fund interventions of the kind which, in practice, involve the prioritisation of the shareholder interest.

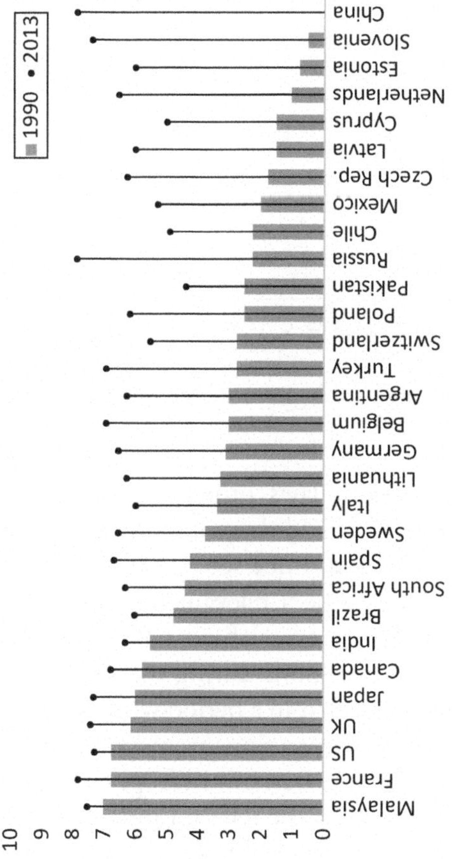

Fig. 8.1 Shareholder protection in 30 countries, 1990 and 2013. (Source: Katelouzou & Siems, 2015)

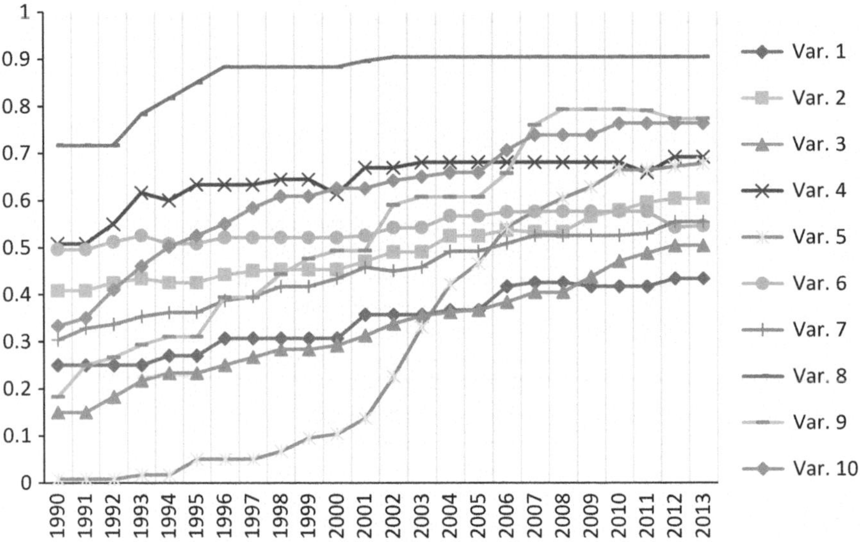

Fig. 8.2 Shareholder protection in 30 countries, 1990–2013, scores for individual variables (see Table 8.1). (Source: Katelouzou & Siems, 2015)

During the same period, laws protecting worker rights, including employment protection laws and those underpinning collective bargaining and the right to strike, did not see overall declines, suggesting that labour law did not cease to be a relevant instrument of labour market regulation in this period. However, labour rights, which were strengthening in many countries and regions during the 1970s, were largely static from the 1990s onwards, so that in a period when shareholder rights were being strengthened, labour protections were weakening in relative terms (for further detail, see Adams, Bastani, Bishop, & Deakin, 2017; Adams et al., 2019). Table 8.2 sets out the relevant indicators and coding definitions. The trends can be seen in Figs. 8.3 and 8.4, which chart time series in employment protection laws in selected regions and countries from the 1970s to 2013. European Union countries generally maintained a high level of employment protection laws throughout the 2000s, with a small decline after the global financial crisis of 2008–9, which nevertheless did not see a wholesale reversal of the gains made in previous decades. Among developing countries, there has been a tendency for employment

Table 8.2 Variables on employment protection: definition and coding algorithms

Definition	Algorithm
1. The law, as opposed to the contracting parties, determines the legal status of the worker	Equals 0 if the parties are free to stipulate that the relationship is one of self-employment as opposed to employee status; 0.5 if the law allows the issue of status to be determined by the nature of the contract made by the parties (as in the case of the English common law 'mutuality of obligation' test); and 1 if the law mandates employee status on the parties if certain specified criteria are met (such as form of payment, duration of hiring, etc.)
2. The cost of dismissing part-time workers is equal in proportionate terms to the cost of dismissing full-time workers	Equals 1 if as a matter of law part-time workers enjoy proportionate rights to full-time workers in respect of dismissal protection (notice periods, severance pay and unjust dismissal protection). Equals 0 otherwise. Scope for gradation between 0 and 1 to reflect changes in the strength of the law
3. Fixed-term contracts are allowed only for work of limited duration	Equals 1 if the law imposes a substantive constraint on the conclusion of a fixed-term contract, by, for example, allowing temporary hirings only for jobs which are temporary by nature, training, seasonal work, replacement of workers on maternity or sick leave, or other specified reasons. Equals 0 otherwise. Scope for gradation between 0 and 1 to reflect changes in the strength of the law
4. Maximum duration of fixed-term contracts	Measures the maximum cumulative duration of fixed-term contracts permitted by law before the employment is deemed to be permanent. The score is normalised from 0 to 1, with higher values indicating a lower permitted duration. The score equals 1 if the maximum limit is less than 1 year and 0 if it is 10 years or more or if there is no legal limit
5. Legally mandated notice period	Measures the length of notice, in weeks, that has to be given to a worker with 3 years' employment. Normalise the score so that 0 weeks = 0 and 12 weeks = 1

(*continued*)

Table 8.2 (continued)

Definition	Algorithm
6. Legally mandated redundancy compensation	Measures the amount of redundancy compensation payable to a worker made redundant after 3 years of employment, measured in weeks of pay. Normalise the score so that 0 weeks = 0 and 12 weeks = 1
7. Minimum qualifying period of service for normal case of unjust dismissal	Measures the period of service required before a worker qualifies for general protection against unjust dismissal. Normalise the score so that 3 years or more = 0, 0 months = 1
8. Law imposes procedural constraints on dismissal	Equals 1 if a dismissal is necessarily unjust if the employer fails to follow procedural requirements prior to dismissal. Equals 0.67 if failure to follow procedural requirements will normally lead to a finding of unjust dismissal. Equals 0.33 if failure to follow procedural requirement is just one factor taken into account in unjust dismissal cases. Equals 0 if there are no procedural requirements for dismissal. Scope for gradations between 0 and 1 to reflect changes in the strength of the law
9. Law imposes substantive constraints on dismissal	Equals 1 if dismissal is only permissible for serious misconduct or fault of the employee. Equals 0.67 if dismissal is lawful according to a wider range of legitimate reasons (misconduct, lack of capability, redundancy, etc.). Equals 0.33 if dismissal is permissible if it is 'just' or 'fair' as defined by case law. Equals 0 if employment is at will (i.e., no cause dismissal is normally permissible). Scope for gradations between 0 and 1 to reflect changes in the strength of the law
10. Reinstatement normal remedy for unfair dismissal	Equals 1 if reinstatement is the normal remedy for unjust dismissal and is regularly enforced. Equals 0.67 if reinstatement and compensation are, de jure and de facto, alternative remedies. Equals 0.33 if compensation is the normal remedy. Equals 0 if no remedy is available as of right. Scope for further gradations between 0 and 1 to reflect changes in the strength of the law

(*continued*)

Table 8.2 (continued)

Definition	Algorithm
11. Notification of dismissal	Equals 1 if by law or binding collective agreement the employer has to obtain the permission of a state body or third party prior to an individual or collective dismissal. Equals 0.67 if a state body or third party has to be notified prior to the dismissal. Equals 0.33 if the employer has to give the worker written reasons for the dismissal. Equals 0 if an oral statement of dismissal to the worker suffices. Scope for further gradations between 0 and 1 to reflect changes in the strength of the law
12. Redundancy selection	Equals 1 if by law or binding collective agreement the employer must follow priority rules based on seniority, marital status, number or dependants, and so on, prior to dismissing for redundancy. Equals 0 otherwise. Scope for further gradations between 0 and 1 to reflect changes in the strength of the law
13. Priority in re-employment	Equals 1 if by law or binding collective agreement the employer must follow priority rules relating to the re-employment of former workers. Equals 0 otherwise. Scope for further gradations between 0 and 1 to reflect changes in the strength of the law
14. Codetermination: board membership	Equals 1 if the law gives unions and/or workers to right to nominate board-level directors in companies of a certain size. Equals 0 otherwise. Scope for further gradations between 0 and 1 to reflect changes in the strength of the law

(*continued*)

Table 8.2 (continued)

Definition	Algorithm
15. Codetermination and information/ consultation of workers	Equals 1 if the works councils or enterprise committees have legal powers of co-decision making. Equals 0.67 if works councils or enterprise committees must be provided by law under certain conditions but do not have the power of co-decision making. Equals 0.5 if works councils or enterprise committees may be required by law unless the employer can point to alternative or pre-existing alternative arrangements. Equals 0.33 if the law provides for information and consultation of workers or worker representatives on certain matters but where there is no obligation to maintain a works council or enterprise committee as a standing body. Equals 0 otherwise. Scope for further gradations between 0 and 1 to reflect changes in the strength of the law

Source: Deakin, S., Armour, J., & Siems, M. (2017). CBR Leximetric Datasets [updated] [Dataset]. https://doi.org/10.17863/CAM.9130

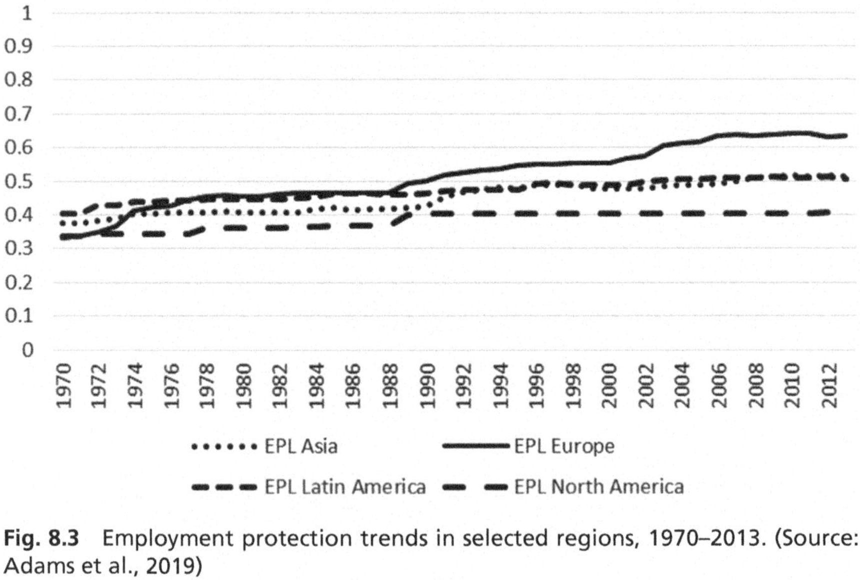

Fig. 8.3 Employment protection trends in selected regions, 1970–2013. (Source: Adams et al., 2019)

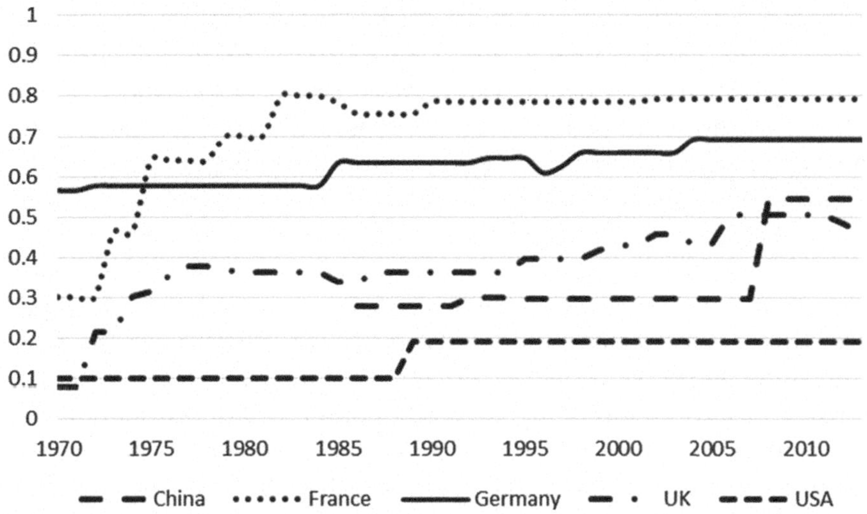

Fig. 8.4 Employment protection trends in selected countries, 1970–2013 (China from 1986). (Source: Adams et al., 2019)

protection laws to strengthen from a relatively weak base, with China being such a case. These trends in labour laws must be put in the context of significant declines in the coverage and effectiveness of multi-employer collective bargaining over the same period (Visser, 2013).

The strengthening of shareholder rights during a period when worker protections were mostly static (in the case of labour law) or declining (in the case of multi-employer collective bargaining) is connected to increases in the capital share of national income and corresponding declines in the labour share, which became pronounced during the 2000s. In the middle decades of the twentieth century the labour share was stable at around 65% of national income in most industrialised countries; since 1990 it has fallen by 5% in the UK, France, Germany, Canada, and Japan and over 10% in the USA, Korea, Spain and Italy. Sjöberg (2009) demonstrates that a link exists between shareholder rights and the capital share, while Adams et al. (2019) show that changes in labour laws have an impact on the labour share. Ferguson, Power, Stevenson, and Collinson (2017) identify correlations between the degree of legal protection accorded to shareholders and health inequalities as evidenced by, among other things, child mortality rates. Palma (2019a, 2019b) discusses the extent to which the widening gap between labour output and wages in OECD countries, in particular the USA, is attributable to changes permitting shareholders to extract higher returns (including the lifting of the legal ban on share buy-backs in the early 1980s) at the same time as institutional protections for wage bargaining were being weakened.

Addressing the situation of the top 1% and 0.1% will inevitably require changes to laws governing capital in a broad sense to include both corporate governance and taxation, as Piketty (2014, 2019) has argued for some time. However, if the negative effects of inequality are to be countered, a focus on the very highest reaches of the wealth distribution will be insufficient. Epidemiological evidence links inequality of income and status to measures of social well-being, which includes infant mortality, obesity, mental illness, educational performance, teenage motherhood, and homicide; it is relative inequalities throughout the income distribution which matter here (Wilkinson & Pickett, 2008). If this research has one overriding message it is that "everything else being equal, it is better to live in a more equal society", even for "the richer part of society", since "people compare themselves to those who are closer to them – and the more unequal the society, the greater distance between people, even among those with the highest incomes" (Baumard, 2016, p. 1137).

High inequality generating insecurity at every level of society is the result of a combination of measures affecting returns to labour and capital, and thus the consequence of the laws which together institute capitalist markets and forms of production in this broad sense. As Harvey and Geras insist (2018), "the laws of the market are just that: politically instituted as much as economic. And what can be done politically can be undone" (p. 139). However, to see why this is such a challenge means understanding how inequality has come to undermine the fabric of the state itself.

4 The 'Malign Spirit' of Contemporary Capitalism: Regulatory Competition, Tax Avoidance and the Erosion of the Rule of Law

What Gomez (2019) has called the 'malign spirit' of capitalism locates its current dysfunctions in an over-financialised economy, in which speculation overtakes production as the dominant mode of 'rational' behaviour. This phenomenon has an institutional dimension, in which law as a mode of governance is turned against itself, and 'opting out' through regulatory arbitrage and avoidance is normalised.

One particularly striking manifestation of this trend is the exponential increase since the 1980s in the use of tax havens to conceal private and corporate wealth and to shield it from taxation (Shaxson, 2011). Zucman (2015) calculates that the percentage of financial wealth held offshore is 4% of the total in the USA and 10% of the total in Europe. The corresponding figure is 22% in Latin America, 30% in Africa, 52% in Russia and 57% in the Gulf countries. Since overall inequalities are closely correlated with the relative income shares of the top 10% of earners, it is highly likely that tax evasion is playing a significant role in perpetuating the extreme inequalities associated with Latin America, parts of sub-Saharan Africa (including post-Apartheid South Africa) and the Gulf states (Palma, 2011).

Tax havens can only operate as repositories of capital if capital-exporting states recognise them as such. Specifically, the court of the exporting ('onshore') state must recognise as valid the attribution of profits or income to the importing ('offshore') state if the latter's fiscal advantage is to be legally effective. In the USA and the UK, a series of regulatory changes was made in the early 1980s to facilitate this form of 'mutual recognition'. British governments actively encouraged the development of the tax haven status of its dependencies and Crown territories, and US governments condoned the use of third countries, in particular Panama, for the same ends. The Panama Papers leak threw a bright light on the scale and sophistication of legal and financial expertise, which has developed over time to service the growing demand for tax planning. Today, tax haven status is no longer exclusively 'offshore'. Within the European Union, the member states actively pursuing fiscal policies designed to attract and retain inward investments include sizable industrial economies such as the Netherlands and Ireland.

Similar processes affect the operation of labour laws. As laws setting minimum labour standards on such matters as wages, hours of work and termination of employment were extended in most industrialised countries throughout the course of the twentieth century, they were almost invariably given mandatory territorial effect, meaning that the 'applicable' laws of an employment contract would be those of the state where the work was carried out. However, just as in tax law it has become increasingly possible over time to attribute income earned in one jurisdiction to another for the purposes of accessing a more favourable tax rate, so in employment law there has been an expansion of the situations in which work done in the territory of one legal system can be understood legally to be governed by the rules of another. This is particularly the case when workers are assigned or 'posted' by their employer to work in a third country. Within the European Union, 'host' states have had limited power to impose local labour laws and collectively agreed terms and conditions on workers posted from another member state following the ruling of the European Court of Justice in the *Laval* case (2007).

The 'deterritorialisation' of rules of labour law and corporate governance is in part the result of competition between states to attract capital by the downgrading of regulatory standards, but is also the result of the growing influence of international economic law as a mode of governance. International economic law has a history going back to the foundation of GATT and the EEC in the immediate post-1945 years. But it has risen in importance in more recent decades as a result of the foundation of the World Trade Organization (WTO) in 1995, the negotiation of a growing number of bilateral free trade agreements (FTAs), and the deepening of the EU's internal market. The default position of international economic law is that domestic regulations governing trade and business constitute 'non-tariff barriers to trade'. And so, as interferences, they need to be justified as legitimate (in the sense of aiming at a legitimate economic or social policy goals) and proportionate (in the sense of achieving that goal while interfering as little as possible with the cross-border flows of resources). By its structure, then, international economic law assumes a core feature of neoclassical, general-equilibrium models of the economy: the market is a self-adjusting economic order, which is in a state of equilibrium prior to any regulatory intervention.

A further feature of international economic law is that it does not treat capital and labour symmetrically. This is exhibited, for example, in the widespread practice of inserting procedures for investor-state dispute settlement (ISDS) into FTAs. These allow companies from outside the host state to challenge regulations such as laws on labour and environment, on the grounds that they deter potential investments or harm those already made. Complaints of this kind are generally heard in specialist tribunals outside the regular court system of the host state. They can result in significant liabilities for states. By contrast, few if any legal options are available under the terms of FTAs for workers or governments to challenge instances of firms taking advantage of regulatory divergences, such as relocations to regimes with weak or incompletely enforced labour laws, or the cross-border movement of goods produced in breach of labour standards. These outcomes are not inevitable: it would have been possible and remains possible for the future, to design an international economic law regime which treats capital flight and social dumping as true 'distortions' of trade.

Along with the deterritorialisation of law, there comes also its commodification: law itself is increasingly seen as a product, to be 'purchased' by corporations and hyper-rich households, whose freedom to move across borders gives them the option choosing from among a number of regulatory and fiscal options for the protection of their wealth (Supiot, 2017). The post-enlightenment concept of equality under the rule of law finds little place in this conception of a stratified legal system. The hollowing out of the legal system and the erosion of the public-private divide have the additional effect of undermining trust in the state as an impartial arbiter. This can be seen in the correlations identified in field experiments between rising inequality and growing distrust of the state (Herrmann, Thöni, & Gächter, 2008). As inequality increases, it also undermines the state's ability to respond to it through the provision of collective goods and an impartial rule of law.

5 New Wage and Employment Policies: Feasibility and Policy Delivery

From the analysis so far, it can be seen that the task of framing new wage and employment policies to address inequality is not confined to issues of substantive law; it extends to an analysis of the institutions and mechanisms through which these policies could feasibly be delivered. Discussions in the relevant inequality literature along the lines of 'what can we do about it?' have devoted relatively little attention to the issue of policy delivery. Piketty's analysis is a case in point. He concludes his *Capital in the Twenty-First Century* (2014) with a series of proposals for tax reform, at the core of which is a proposal for a global wealth tax, which, he accepts, is 'utopian'. In *Capital et idéologie* (2019), the focus of his analysis is again on taxation, which would achieve a 'socialisation' of property by breaking up concentrations of wealth and so permitting the more effective circulation of capital, and on the need to address educational inequalities. Addressing the issue of international cooperation, he proposes the creation of 'transnational assemblies', which would be charged with the task of administering global public goods on the basis of 'global fiscal justice'. The discussion remains somewhat abstract, as he does not explore the features of existing international organisations, beyond noting the tendency for the EU's internal market laws to prioritise the free movement of capital. There is no substantive discussion of the International Labour Organization (ILO), which is perhaps a missed opportunity in view of the latter's distinctive tripartite decision-making structure.

Atkinson's *Inequality: What Can Be Done?* (2015) takes a broader view than Piketty in terms of the range of measures needed to inequalities and, in particular, has more to say about wages and employment. Atkinson (op. cit.) makes a case for the success of mid-twentieth-century institutions of the social state, including statutory minimum wages, sector-level collective bargaining, solidaristic social insurance, and progressive taxation, in creating the conditions for the convergence of wealth and incomes in the economies of the global north during this period. His 15 proposals for reform are a mix of targets ("the government should adopt an explicit target for preventing and reducing unemployment"), capital reallocations ("there should be a capital endowment (minimum inheritance) paid to all at adulthood"), fiscal adjustments ("receipts of inheritance and gifts inter vivos should be taxed under a progressive lifetime capital receipts tax"), and general aims ("public policy should aim at a proper balance of power among stakeholders, and to this end should… ensure a legal framework that allows trade unions to represent workers on level terms") (Atkinson, 2015, pp. 236–237). Atkinson (op. cit.) points to historical antecedents in arguing for the ability of nation states to enact such changes and to agree between them the basis for international cooperation to prevent defection from common standards, although he proceeds by way of examples rather than any more systematic analysis of the capacity of states to address collective action problems.

Milanovic's *Global Inequality* (2016) assumes that globalisation will continue in more or less its current form and that it will, as a result, constrain the scope for policy to address inequalities. Broadly following Piketty in arguing that declines in inequality in the middle decades of the twentieth century were brought about by "increased taxation and social transfers, hyperinflation, nationalisation of property, and wars", he doubts that these conditions can be repeated, since "globalisation makes increased taxation of the most significant contributor to inequality – namely capital income – very difficult, and without a fully concerted action from most countries, which does not seem even remotely possible today, highly improbable" (Milanovic, 2016, p. 217). He argues instead for governments to take steps to equalise endowments by making capital ownership and access to education more generally available. In relation to labour, his principal suggestion is that the promotion of 'orderly migration' would lower global poverty and inequality. He proposes the "redefinition of citizenship" to allow for migrant workers to be granted "an intermediate level of citizenship that would be less valuable (because, for example, it might involve higher taxation, lower access to social services, or an obligation to return to work in one's country of origin at periodic intervals)" (p. 231). He seems unaware that this already describes the situation of many migrants working in the countries of the global north under the terms of restricted visa schemes, or of posted workers inside the EU. He at least mentions the ILO, albeit as an entity with "little power" which "deals mostly with national labour rules" (p. 230), overlooking the coordinating role played by ILO conventions on, among other things, the rights of migrant workers.

Milanovic (2016) effectively closes down the discussion by taking the current nature of globalisation more or less for granted. Atkinson (2015), by contrast, sets out a detailed programme of reform and appeals to history to justify its feasibility, but in doing so neglects the argument that the middle decades of the twentieth century were a one-off. The proposals he makes also speak, for the most part, to the condition of economies in the global north. Piketty's (2019) latest work situates the current debates not just in a global context, but in a much longer historical span than Atkinson's (2015); thereby enabling him to make the case that it is capitalism itself which is exceptional, and will pass. His call for a participative socialism, which can be constructed through the coordination of national and transnational modes of governance, is perhaps no less utopian than his earlier proposals for global fiscal reform.

Much of the discussion of policy reforms in the literature on inequality has a programmatic quality, which neglects the issue of how feasible major structural breaks in policy making are likely to be in practice. Less noticed are policy developments actually underway, which in various ways have sought to renew or modernise labour market institutions. They include measures to stabilise the coverage of employment and tax laws in the face of new forms of casual labour associated with the 'gig economy', equalise the treatment of different so-called flexible forms of work, reinforce minimum wage floors, strengthen public enforcement of labour standards, and integrate labour rights into the rules governing international trade and capital flows. Each of these will now be briefly considered.

5.1 Stabilising the Employment Relationship

The 'end of work' or, in a variation on this theme, the demise of the 'standard employment relationship' has been regularly predicted since at least the early 1980s, without showing any evidence of coming to pass. Most recently, the claim has been revived in the context of the rise of the 'gig economy'. The literature on this issue is by now very extensive, but not entirely productive as it mostly proceeds on the basis that the form in which labour is contracted is technologically determined. In practice, wage labour is at least partially constituted through social norms and institutions and has historically been stabilised by legal interventions of various kinds (Harvey & Geras, 2018). In some countries, policy makers have condoned the proliferation of casual and informal forms of work as part of an effort to promote 'flexibility' or even on occasion 'innovation' (to which any real link seems tenuous). However, states also have an interest in maintaining the employment relationship as the predominant mode of labour contracting for reasons of fiscal stability, given the importance of income tax and social insurance contributions for public finances. Stable employment is associated with other positive externalities including investment in education and training and the maintenance of demand for locally produced goods and services. For these various reasons, while technological change might be expected to put pressure on the employment model by opening up new possibilities for disintermediation in supply chains and the associated offloading of risks, there are countervailing pressures on states to preserve the employment model. The rise of the platform economy does not, in itself, close off all policy options (Prassl, 2018).

Conflicting pressures are evident, for example, in the US context, where technology companies have successfully lobbied for state laws establishing a presumption that platform workers, in particular drivers working for Uber and similar ride-hailing apps, are self-employed. However, they have met resistance from unions and civil society organisations, leading to the adoption in some states of the 'ABC' test of employment status (Deakin, 2020). This effectively establishes the reverse presumption, namely that there is an employment relationship between the platform and the driver, where elements of control are present. A law to this effect was adopted in California in 2019 and was then the focus of concerted efforts, which eventually proved successful, by technology companies to have the measure reversed through a state-wide ballot. The issue is commercially sensitive for Uber as, according to documents accompanying its US stock market listing in 2018, its business model would come under pressure if it had to assume the normal responsibilities of an employer, such as paying the minimum wage. In Europe, a parallel process is taking place, mostly in the context of litigation. The tendency so far is for courts to rule that platform work can give rise to an employment contract or a close equivalent, although there is some variability of approach.

5.2 Trends in the Regulation of Precarious and Informal Work

As with the 'end of work' debate, the rise of precarious work is often presented as an inevitability, but the evidence on this point is equivocal; trends in self-employment appear to be largely cyclical. The incidence of so-called non-standard forms of work, such as part-time work, fixed-term employment, and temporary agency work, is linked to, and largely determined by, the regulatory framework in place, in a given country. There is considerable cross-country variation in the extent of such 'non-standard' work and in the degree to which it is inherently 'precarious' or low-paid.

Policy with respect to the non-standard forms of work has also fluctuated over time. From the 1980s through to the early 2000s, the promotion of fixed-term and agency work was seen as an appropriate response to concerns over flexibility of labour in a number of countries, particularly in Western Europe. Sentiment began to shift when it became clear that removing protective controls over these forms of work was not having a positive impact on employment growth, and might instead be creating new 'rigidities' by embedding a 'dualist' approach to regulation. In recognition of this problem, the OECD, whose 1994 *Jobs Report* had done much to initiate the earlier trend towards selective deregulation, shifted its position and began to argue for the alignment of the legal treatment of the 'non-standard' forms of employment with the rules governing the 'standard' contract.

The OECD's change of heart was consistent with the policy adopted by the EU in social policy directives adopted from the late 1990s, and as these were implemented in the member states over the course of the 2000s, there was a discernible augmentation of labour law protections relating to part-time, fixed-term, and agency work. Again, conflicting pressures were in play as some member states took the opportunity presented by the Eurozone area financial crisis after 2009 to implement reductions in the protections accorded to 'core' workers, for example by replacing reinstatement with compensation as the principal remedy for unjustified dismissal. However, the impact of these 'structural' reforms on employment protection law proved, in the end, to be relatively marginal (see Adams et al., 2019).

The message for policy makers is that the employment contract, as an evolved practice and legally recognised institution in the economies of the global north, is probably more stable than has been thought. This is important since many policies, which are in principle capable of mitigating or reversing inequality trends, such as minimum wages and the delivery of public goods financed from income taxation and social security contributions, depend for their operation on the continuing economic and technological relevance of the employment model. Conversely, policies which either actively undermine the employment model or implicitly condone its decline pose problems for these types of response to inequality.

In developing and emerging markets, the issues are somewhat distinct, in the sense that the employment contract has yet to achieve there the level of normalisation which can be observed in the case of the global north; rather, the persistence of informality in labour markets appears to constrain the adoption of egalitarian wage and employment policies. Labour market informality, however, is a complex phenomenon and takes a number of forms, some of which are themselves amenable to policy interventions. There appears to have been a significant reduction in the extent of the informal labour market in Brazil in the early and mid-2000s, as a result of a combination of circumstances: on one hand, a sustained period of economic growth, ending only with the onset of the global financial crisis in 2008; on the other, targeted institutional reforms including the promotion of sectoral collective bargaining and a social assistance programme, the *bolsa familia* (Fraile, 2009). China has also seen a fall in informality rates at the same time as its employment laws were being strengthened, in particular following the passage of the Labour Contracts Act in 2007 (Cooney, Biddulph, Li, & Zhu, 2013). The much slower trend in the reduction of informal work in India is attributable at least in part to institutional factors (Deakin, Marshall, & Pinto, 2019).

5.3 Minimum Wages and Sectoral Collective Bargaining

The minimum wage is another area in which there have been significant policy reversals. Consistently with the neoclassical economic critique of wage regulation, the federal minimum wage was allowed to stagnate in the USA during the 1980s and 1990s, and state laws did little to compensate. In Britain, wage fixing in selected sectors was removed in the mid-1990s, leaving virtually no floor of any kind in place for a number of years. However, a national minimum wage was reintroduced with effect from 1999, and was subsequently raised above general wage inflation with no observed disemployment effect. Beginning in the early 2000s, community-based campaigns for a 'living wage' became widespread in both the USA and Britain, and these were reflected in a proliferation of legislative initiatives in US states and cities, and in the adoption in the UK of a statutory version of the living wage in 2016.

The revival of the minimum wage as an instrument of labour market regulation in the USA and Britain reflects, in part, the weakness of sectoral collective bargaining in those countries, as well as the perceived need to raise the wage floor in order to reduce public expenditure on tax credits targeted on the low paid (the US earned income tax credit, and its UK equivalents, family credits of various kinds and, latterly, universal credit). In Germany it was, similarly, concern over the decline in effectiveness of sectoral collective bargaining which prompted the introduction of a statutory minimum wage in 2016, although sectoral collective agreements remain in force to a greater extent than in the USA or the UK. In Germany, as in France since the 1950s, the statutory minimum wage takes effect below legally binding sectoral collective agreements, creating strong pressure for wage compression. In the Nordic systems, while there is no statutory minimum wage, sectoral agreements set a relatively high wage floor, to the point where the introduction of statutory wage fixing is generally seen as unnecessary.

Nor is the minimum wage by any means confined to Europe and North America. Minimum wages are set at state (regional) level in Brazil and in most Chinese cities. South Africa has a system of legally enforceable minimum wage rates based on sectoral collective bargaining. India, with no national minimum and incomplete coverage at state and city level, is something of an outlier in this respect.

The prevalence of the minimum wage as an instrument of labour market regulation in countries at various different stages of development, along with the growing body of evidence, based on practical experience, that it does not entail the negative effects presupposed by equilibrium-based economic models, together suggest that it should be at the core of measures to address inequality. However, for the full potential of minimum wage laws to be captured, they should be combined with higher level, sectoral wage floors, supported by legal extension mechanisms, thereby taking wages and employment conditions more generally out of competition at an industry level.

5.4 Public Enforcement of Labour Laws

In principle, a variety of means exist to enforce labour laws, including inspection, civil actions, criminal fines, and the selective use of public procurement systems. As labour laws came under pressure from statutory deregulatory initiatives in many countries from the early 1980s, enforcement regimes were also weakened. The USA is one of the clearest cases of this trend, with even those employment rights supposedly guaranteed by federal legislation being removed from the remit of the general courts and subsumed within employer-led private arbitration. The power of the agencies designed to promote labour standards and collective bargaining, most notably the National Labor Relations Board, has been whittled away over several decades by hostile judicial interpretations and by the politicisation of the appointments process.

For labour laws to operate in such a way as to rebalance the distribution of power in the employment relationship, effective public enforcement is essential; but such enforcement itself is a collective good, which depends on adequate resourcing of dispute resolution processes and on the maintenance of low-cost access to justice. In Britain, the imposition of employment tribunal fees in 2013 was nullified in a UK Supreme Court ruling in 2017 on precisely this ground: a striking contrast to the active support shown by its US counterpart to the privatisation of labour dispute resolution.

The issue of access to justice is a major one in middle-income countries. South Africa adopted a public labour arbitration system based on low-cost access for claimants in the 1990s, and China followed suit shortly after the passage of the Labour Contracts Act, in 2008. Both of these two national systems now processes hundreds of thousands of employment claims every year, and so by volume alone, outrank their counterparts in the global north.

5.5 Labour Rights and International Trade: The Evolving Role of the ILO

The ILO was a product of, and reaction to, the 'first globalisation', which was abruptly ended with the outbreak of the First World War. In the middle decades of the twentieth century, the ILO was one of the institutions to give practical effect to the idea that for international trade to be sustainable, there had to be a common agreement between states on social and labour standards. In the period of the 'second globalisation', which began with the fall of the Berlin Wall, that idea came under pressure, with international labour standards increasingly described as an impediment to competition and trade. However, recent developments in the interaction of trade law and ILO standard-setting indicate ways in which the Organization's role is changing in conjunction with an increasing focus on labour issues in trade agreements. Partly as a result of EU pressure to make a new FTA conditional upon compliance with ILO standards, Vietnam has recently agreed to align its domestic labour laws with the ILO's freedom of association conventions. This is a potentially significant development in the context of former state-socialist countries, which, until now, have rejected the relevance of free trade unions and autonomous collective bargaining for their developmental model.

FTAs between developed nations regularly contain clauses stipulating compliance with ILO conventions. Until recently this has appeared to be little more than a façade, but the newly agreed US-Mexico-Canada Trade Agreement, which will replace NAFTA, goes further towards recognising a degree of conditionality between collective bargaining rights and trade, by requiring Mexico to enact new freedom of association laws as a condition of retaining access to US markets. Compliance with the EU's *social acquis* is also a condition of trade access for neighbouring states under recent FTAs, such as the association agreement with Ukraine in which entered into force in 2017.

5.6 Labour Market Measures During the COVID-19 Crisis

If there were signs prior to the COVID-19 crisis of a push back against neoliberal wage and employment policies in a number of countries and regions, as well as globally, the crisis has propelled labour market measures to the forefront of attention. Within days of lockdowns beginning to counter the spread of virus, states in certain regions, with Western Europe leading the way, announced wage subsidy and short-time working schemes aimed at mitigating the impact of the crisis on employment and consumption. Such schemes are not entirely new. In the UK, government paid wages directly to employers to avoid large-scale redundancies in manufacturing and heavy industry in the crisis of the late 1970s and early 1980s. The last of these measures, the Temporary Short-Time Working Compensation Scheme, closed only in 1984, and legal powers to reopen it were retained until 1990, throughout the period in office of the supposedly anti-interventionist Thatcher administration. The German *Kurzarbeit* scheme, revived in 2020, had previously been tried out in the recession following the global financial crisis of 2008–9. These precedents notwithstanding, the response of Western governments, including the UK through its emergency Coronavirus Job Retention Scheme, potentially dwarfs what came before in terms of the scale of the financing involved, although whether current schemes will turn out to have this effect depends on the length of time for which they have to be maintained. It needs to be remembered that such measures are designed, by their nature, to be temporary, and can be unwound almost as quickly as they are set up. The same point applies to the suspension of the Eurozone's balanced budget rules, announced at the end of March 2020:

it is possible that these norms will return, conceivably in an even stricter form, as the crisis abates.

A more long-lasting break with neoliberal policies is only like to come about if the medium-term effect of the COVID crisis requires a more sustained policy response. This will be the case, for example, if policy makers perceive a need to reintroduce a variant of demand management in order to avert a slump. Fiscal and macroeconomic policies of the kind, which sought to maintain effective consumption during the middle decades of the twentieth century made a good fit with the extension of multi-employer collective bargaining and solidaristic forms of social insurance in the same period (Deakin & Wilkinson, 2005: chapter 4). Indeed, there is a case for regarding labour market regulations of these kinds, which stabilise the employment relationship and put a floor under wages, as essential, if demand-orientated macroeconomic and fiscal measures are to have their desired effect of supporting consumption. If policies of labour market 'flexibilisation' remain in place, it is likely that fiscal interventions will disproportionately benefit rentier interests. Not only would such an outcome reinforce existing wealth and income inequalities, it would also under-deliver on the goal of maintaining consumption, given the higher marginal propensity to consume of lower income, non-rentier groups.

To say that a policy of continuing to prioritise shareholder and creditor rights over those of labour would be self-defeating in the circumstances of the COVID crisis does not mean that it will not be adopted. However, from the point of view of the practical feasibility of bringing about a policy shift, COVID-19 provides states with the kind of opportunity to reregulate capital which generally only happens during wartime. During the two world wars of the twentieth century, the normal working of financial markets was essentially in abeyance, and governments assumed powers of direct management over most of the industrial economy. The COVID crisis has not yet reached that stage, but within a few weeks of its beginning, it had become practically infeasible for dividend payments and share buy-backs to continue as before. Financial speculation by no means ceased, and it will be interesting to see whether regulators have the appetite to restrict the trading strategies of hedge funds in future. This will be a good test of whether theories of the informational efficiency of capital markets continue to have the sway they held even at the height of the 2008–9 crisis.

For those who have been critical of the neoliberal policy turn of recent decades, the COVID crisis is ample justification for renewed investment in public goods and for a redrawing of the public-private divide, which is better able to protect the sphere of the state from that of the market. Without effective international cooperation to build social standards into the structure of global trade, however, little will be achieved. It follows that wage and employment policies will have to address not just the substance of regulation, but also modes of governance in a wider sense: setting limits on capital mobility and the scope of the 'mutual recognition' principle in so far as it is simply an open door to tax avoidance and regulatory arbitrage. This will require thinking the role of law as a mode of transnational governance, in ways that address its tendency to reinforce the power of capital at the expense of social interests and public goods (Pistor, 2019).

6 Summary and Conclusions

This chapter has sought to review and synthesise the literature linking trends in inequality to the way that labour and capital markets are constituted and governed. It has sought to show that widening disparities of wealth and income since the 1980s can be attributed at least in part to institutional changes which have, broadly speaking, weakened labour, while strengthening capital. The removal of legal support for sectoral wage setting and for collective bargaining more generally is one such factor; another is the strengthening of shareholder rights through reforms to company law and corporate governance. These legal and institutional changes are behind some of the more significant indicators of growing inequality in developed countries, such as the widening gap between wages and labour output in the USA, and the rise in the capital share, and corresponding fall in the labour share, which has been experienced across the OECD since the 1990s. The chapter has also reviewed the contribution of legal and institutional factors to the growing use of tax havens to conceal financial wealth, and specifically has highlighted changes in the legal and fiscal regimes of 'onshore' states as a critical factor in the success of their 'offshore' counterparts.

The argument that 'institutions matter' opens up a space for policy reforms that might otherwise be closed off by an over-naturalised understanding of inequality, that is, one which understands inequality as inherent in capitalism to the point of being irremediable. This is not to say that institutions are entirely malleable. There are path-dependent aspects to legal and other institutions, which make them difficult to reform, and obstacles to constructing coalitions of the kind needed to overcome collective action problems. A closer look at recent trends in institutional reform suggests, however, that there are many contexts in which egalitarian and solidaristic policies are currently being implemented. The revival of the minimum wage as an instrument of labour market policy is a case in point. Once the need for a statutory wage floor is accepted, it becomes more straightforward to argue for the revival of sectoral collective bargaining. Similarly, the negative experience of 'dualism' in employment protection has led to a reappraisal of the importance of dismissal laws in promoting investment in human capital. The promotion of wage and employment stability is also becoming integral to efforts to push back against the erosion of the tax base. It is possible then to envisage scenarios in which complementary policy changes in labour, company, and fiscal law interact to promote egalitarian wage and employment policies, a re-embedding to match the dis-embedding which began in the early 1980s.

Structural breaks in policy making generally require a crisis to trigger them. The 2008–9 financial crisis failed to catalyse the necessary changes, and whether the COVID-19 crisis will prove to be any more transformational remains to be seen. The early weeks of the crisis saw far-reaching developments in wage and employment policy, as states put in place economy-wide wage subsidy and short-time working schemes to shore up employment, while suspending the operation of balanced budget rules. Far-reaching as these developments were, they were not exactly unprecedented. Similar wage and employment subsidy schemes had operated, if not quite on the same scale, in the 1970s and 1980s, and during the global financial crisis. Moreover, it is in the nature of such measures that they can be quickly unwound. Having said that, such is the shock administered by the COVID-19 crisis that there is likely to be a continuing need for fiscal measures to underpin demand. Under those circumstances, there will be a pressing need for solidaristic wage and social security policies, and a much-strengthened role of the state in putting a floor of rights under the operation of the labour market.

Yet if the COVID-19 crisis is to be the catalyst for lasting change, it will be necessary to address not simply the substance of economic governance, but its mode. In the long period of neoliberal policy hegemony, the legal system became an instrument of regulatory arbitrage and avoidance, amplifying shifts in the balance of power between capital and labour, and undermining state capacity. A recalibration of the role of law, aimed at promoting investment in national and global public goods, is long overdue.

References

Adams, Z., Bastani, P., Bishop, L., & Deakin, S. (2017). The CBR-LRI Dataset: Methods, Properties and Potential of Leximetric Coding of Labour Laws. *International Journal of Comparative Labour Law and Industrial Relations, 33*, 59–91.

Adams, Z., Bishop, L., Deakin, S., Fenwick, C., Martinsson-Garzelli, S., & Rusconi, G. (2019). The Economic Significance of Laws Relating to Employment Protection and Different Forms of Employment: Analysis of a Panel of 117 Countries, 1990–2013. *International Labour Review, 158*, 1–35.

Atkinson, A. (2015). *Inequality: What Can be Done?* Cambridge, MA: Harvard University Press.

Baumard, N. (2016). Evolutionary Psychology and Public Policy. In D. Buss (Ed.), *The Handbook of Evolutionary Psychology Volume 2: Integrations* (2nd ed., p. 1137). Chichester, UK: Wiley.

Botero, J., Djankov, S., La Porta, R., Lopez-de-Silanes, F., & Shleifer, A. (2004). The Regulation of Labor. *Quarterly Journal of Economics, 119*, 1339–1382.

Coase, R. H. (1960). The Problem of Social Cost. *Journal of Law and Economics, 3*, 1–44.

Coase, R. H. (1988). *The Firm, the Market and the Law*. Chicago: Chicago University Press.

Cooney, S., Biddulph, S., Li, K., & Zhu, Y. (2013). *Law and Fair Work in China*. London: Routledge.

Deakin, S. (2020). 'Decoding Employment Status', Under Review. *King's Law Journal, 31*(2), 180–193.

Deakin, S., Gindis, D., Hodgson, G., Huang, K., & Pistor, K. (2016). Legal Institutionalism: Capitalism and the Constitutive Role of Law. *Journal of Comparative Economics, 45*, 188–200.

Deakin, S., Marshall, S., & Pinto, S. (2019). Labour Laws and Informality: Comparing India and China. In D. Ashiagbor (Ed.), *Reimagining Labour Law for Development: Informal Work in the Global North and South*. Oxford, UK: Hart.

Deakin, S., & Pistor, K. (Eds.) (2012). *Legal Origin Theory Cheltenham*. UK: Edward Elgar.

Deakin, S., & Sarkar, P. (2011). Indian Labour Law and its Impact on Unemployment, 1973–2006: A Leximetric Study. *Indian Journal of Labour Economics, 53*, 607–629.

Deakin, S., Sarkar, P., & Siems, M. (2018). Is there a Relationship Between Shareholder Protection and Stock Market Development? *Journal of Law, Finance and Accounting, 3*, 115–146.

Deakin, S., & Wilkinson, F. (1991). Labour Law, Social Security and Economic Inequality. *Cambridge Journal of Economics, 15*, 125–148.

Deakin, S., & Wilkinson, F. (2005). *The Law of the Labour Market: Industrialization, Employment, and Legal Evolution*. Oxford, UK: Oxford University Press.

Esping-Andersen, G. (1990). *The Three Worlds of Welfare Capitalism*. Oxford, UK: Polity.

Ferguson, J., Power, D., Stevenson, L., & Collinson, D. (2017). Shareholder Protection, Income Inequality and Social Health: A Proposed Research Agenda. *Accounting Forum, 41*, 253–265.

Fraile, L. (2009). Lessons from Latin America's Neo-liberal Experiment: An Overview of Labour and Social Policies Since the 1980s. *International Labour Review, 148*, 215–233.

Gomez, P. Y. (2019). *L'Ésprit malin du capitalism*. Paris: Desclée de Brouwer.

Harvey, M. (2018). Making People Work for Wages: Instituting the Capital-Labour Exchange in the United Kingdom. In M. Harvey & N. Geras (Eds.), *Inequality and Democratic Egalitarianism: 'Marx's Political Economy and Beyond' and Other Essays*. Manchester, UK: Manchester University Press.

Harvey, M., & Geras, N. (2018). Marx's Political Economy and Beyond. In M. Harvey & N. Geras (Eds.), *Inequality and Democratic Egalitarianism: 'Marx's Political Economy and Beyond' and Other Essays*. Manchester, UK: Manchester University Press.

Hayek, F. (1982). *Law, Legislation and Liberty*. London: Routledge.

Herrmann, B., Thöni, C., & Gächter, S. (2008). Anti-Social Punishment Across Societies. *Science, 319*, 1362–1367.

Hodgson, G. (2015). *Conceptualising Capitalism*. Chicago: Chicago University Press.

Katelouzou, D., & Siems, M. (2015). Disappearing Paradigms in Shareholder Protection: Leximetric Evidence for 30 Countries, 1990–2013. *Journal of Corporate Law Studies, 15*, 127–160.

Klerman, M., Mahoney, P., Spamann, H., & Weinstein, M. (2011). Legal Origin or Colonial History? *Journal of Legal Analysis, 3*, 379–409.

Kuznets, S. (1955). Economic Growth and Income Inequality. *American Economic Review, 65*, 1–28.

La Porta, R., Lopez-de-Silanes, F., & Shleifer, A. (2008). The Economic Consequences of Legal Origins. *Journal of Economic Literature, 46*, 285–333.

La Porta, R., Lopez-de-Silanes, F., Shleifer, A., & Vishny, R. (1996). Law and Finance. *Journal of Political Economy, 106*, 1113–1155.

Lewis, A. (1954). Economic Development with Unlimited Supplies of Labour. *Manchester School, 22*, 139–191.

Milanovic, B. (2016). *Global Inequality: A New Approach for the Age of Globalization*. Cambridge, MA: Harvard University Press.

Palma, J. G. (2011). Homogeneous Middles vs. Heterogeneous Tails, and the End of the "Inverted-U": It's All About the Share of the Rich. *Development and Change, 42*, 87–153.

Palma, J. G. (2019a). *Why Is Inequality So Unequal Across the World? Part 1. The Diversity of Inequality in Disposable Income: Multiplicity of Fundamentals, or Complex Interactions Between Political Settlements and Market Failures?* (Cambridge Working Papers in Economics CWPE1999). http://www.econ.cam.ac.uk/research-files/repec/cam/pdf/cwpe1999.pdf

Palma, J. G. (2019b). *Why Is Inequality So Unequal Across the World? Part 2: Why Is Inequality So Unequal Across the World? Part 2: The Diversity of Inequality in 'Market' Income – And the Increasing Asymmetry Between the Distribution of Income Before and After Taxes and Transferences* (Cambridge Working Papers in Economics CWPE19100). http://www.econ.cam.ac.uk/researchfiles/repec/cam/pdf/cwpe19100.pdf

Piketty, T. (2014). *Capital in the Twenty-First Century*. Cambridge, MA: Harvard University Press.

Piketty, T. (2019). *Capital et idéologie*. Paris: Seuil.

Pistor, K. (2019). *The Code of Capital: How the Law Creates Wealth and Inequality*. Princeton, NJ: Princeton University Press.

Polanyi, K. (1944). *The Great Transformation*. New York: Farrar and Rinehart.

Prassl, J. (2018). *Humans as a Service: The Promise and Perils of Work in the Gig Economy*. Oxford, UK: Oxford University Press.

Roe, M. (1996). Chaos and Evolution in Law and Economics. *Harvard Law Review, 109*, 641–668.

Saez, E., & Zucman, G. (2019). *The Triumph of Injustice. How the Rich Dodge Taxes and How to Make Them Pay*. New York: Norton.

Shaxson, N. (2011). *Treasure Islands. Tax Havens and the Men Who Stole the World*. London: Vintage.

Sjöberg, O. (2009). Corporate Governance and Earnings Inequality in the OECD Countries 1979–2000. *European Sociological Review, 25*, 519–533.

Solar, P. (1995). Poor Relief and English Economic Development before the Industrial Revolution. *Economic History Review (NS), 42*, 1–22.

Supiot, A. (2017). *Governance by Numbers: The Making of a Legal Model of Allegiance*. Oxford, UK: Hart.

Tomlins, C. (1985). *The State and the Unions: Labor Relations, Law, and the Organized Labor Movement in America, 1880–1960*. Cambridge, UK/New York: Cambridge University Press.

Visser, J. (2013). *Wage Bargaining Institutions: From Crisis to Crisis* (Economic Paper 488). European Commission, Directorate General for Economic and Financial Affairs.

Wilkinson, R., & Pickett, K. (2008). *The Spirit Level*. London: Penguin.

World Bank. (2007). *Doing Business 2008. Comparing Regulations in 178 Countries*. Washington, DC: World Bank.

Zucman, G. (2015). *The Hidden Wealth of Nations*. Chicago: Chicago University Press.

Index[1]

A

Abatement/mitigation, 187, 194–195
Atkinson, A., 95, 96, 287, 303, 304, 306, 351, 372–374

B

Bank of England (BoE), 3, 6n3, 7, 14–16, 20, 21, 24–27, 28n18, 30, 32, 33, 163, 164
Bank of International Settlements (BIS), 2, 14, 15, 30
Basel III/Basel IV package, 8–10

C

Canada, 8, 62, 154, 238, 323, 367
Capital flows and growth, 90
Capitalism, 35, 43–81, 164, 166, 227n1, 237, 271–280, 283–286, 304, 346–353, 358, 369–371, 374, 384
Carbon emissions, 186, 191, 196, 211
Carbon price, 186, 187, 196–197, 218
Central and Eastern European Countries (CEECs), 115–122
Central Bank, 2, 8, 10, 15, 17, 18, 20, 20n13, 22n15, 22n16, 25, 27–35, 30n19, 78, 79, 90, 180, 215
China, 11–14, 17, 17–18n9, 18, 22, 22n15, 25, 50, 62, 63, 208, 215, 231, 237, 367, 377, 380
Clean technologies, 196, 198, 202, 207–210

[1] Note: Page numbers followed by 'n' refer to notes.

P. Arestis, M. Sawyer (eds.), *Economic Policies for a Post-Neoliberal World*, International Papers in Political Economy, https://doi.org/10.1007/978-3-030-56735-4

Climate change, 45, 46, 54, 56–62, 64–70, 79, 80, 180, 183, 185, 186, 191, 193, 194, 206, 210, 215, 233, 234, 239, 240, 246, 248, 252, 259, 263
Collective bargaining, 327, 347, 353–358, 362, 367, 372, 377–384
Commodification, 281, 282, 371
Communism, 43, 46, 47, 49–51
Control, 1, 3, 5, 30, 30n19, 31, 54, 63, 75, 77, 93, 142, 235, 237, 239–243, 245, 251, 255, 256, 269–272, 274–276, 278–280, 282, 284, 293, 297–306, 309, 312, 351, 354, 357, 358, 375, 376
Cooperative ownership, 228, 249
Coronavirus syndrome, 2, 14, 17, 18, 18n9, 20, 20n13, 21, 23, 26, 27, 31, 35
Costa Rica, 253, 256
Cost-benefit analysis, 5
CO2 emissions, 57–59, 70, 187, 200, 208, 212n25, 241
Counter-cyclical capital buffer (CCyB), 28–30, 28n18
COVID-19 pandemic, v, 46, 71–79, 90

D

Damage function, 187, 192–194
Democracy, 48, 50, 51, 62, 63, 68, 69, 225–263, 274, 276, 277, 284, 307, 311, 345
Denmark, 228, 240, 248, 249, 251, 252, 271, 286n4, 287, 291n8, 294, 296n11, 299, 300, 303, 303n18, 304, 308–310
DICE integrated assessment model (IAM), 186
Discount rate, 187–191
Dodd-Frank Act, 3–6, 10
Downsize-and-distribute, 150
Dworkin, R., 272, 273, 275, 279

E

Ecosystem services, 181–183, 202
Emerging markets, 90, 134, 141, 377
Employment policies, 296, 372–384
Energy sector, 228, 229, 232, 234, 238–240, 245, 254, 263
Environmental degradation, 180–197, 218
Esping-Andersen, G., 281, 282, 356
EU-Canada Comprehensive and Economic Trade Agreement (CETA), 111
Euro Area, 17n9, 18, 19, 19n10, 19n11, 22, 23, 25, 29, 30n20, 32, 33, 162
European Commission (EC), 7, 100, 118, 198, 199, 202–204, 206, 212, 215, 216, 232, 246, 247, 299, 299n16
European Union (EU), 18n9, 19n12, 20, 21, 63, 86, 94–96, 100, 104, 111, 113–122, 139, 145, 158, 198–200, 202–205, 208, 212, 212n25, 214, 227, 228, 243–248, 245n9, 250, 252, 254, 259, 362, 370, 372, 373, 376, 380, 381
EU single market, 231, 239

Externality, 54, 65, 101, 102, 180, 184, 185, 196, 202, 210, 348, 375

F

Federal Reserve Board, 5
Finance, 25, 46, 60, 76, 77, 79, 108, 143, 146, 150, 151, 163, 166, 180, 192, 196, 207, 209–217, 236, 236n7, 242, 271, 280, 288–297, 300, 311, 323, 346, 349, 356, 375
Financial deregulation, 226
Financial instability, 11–17, 24, 33
Financialisation, 92, 93, 226
Financial markets, 17n9, 26, 53, 72, 140, 152, 163, 190, 218, 231, 382
Financial stability, 1–35, 215, 252n11
Fiscal policy, 2, 11, 17, 19–21, 22n15, 23, 25, 26, 31, 33–35, 33n23, 71, 72, 79, 370
Foreign direct investment, 55, 142
Fossil fuels, 58, 59, 63, 183, 195, 198, 200, 201, 203, 204, 206–208, 210, 211, 217, 239, 245, 248, 254
France, 19, 24, 62, 103, 117, 136, 137, 146, 165, 207, 239, 262, 286n4, 323, 327, 331, 336, 355, 367, 378
Free movement, 86–89, 97–101, 108–116, 118–121, 372
Friedman, M., 48, 49, 51, 53, 55
Fuel poverty, 207, 233
Future of capitalism, 43–81

G

Germany, 9, 13, 19, 19n10, 19n12, 24, 62, 117–120, 136, 137, 146, 147, 205, 233, 239, 240, 249, 256, 282, 283, 323, 367, 378
Global Financial Crisis (GFC), 1–4, 3n1, 6, 8, 10–19, 20n13, 21, 24, 26, 27, 32–34, 34n24, 56, 71, 80, 89–92, 134, 136, 138, 139, 141, 142, 146, 148, 149, 156, 157, 163, 166, 225, 345, 362, 381, 384
Globalisation, 92, 94, 106, 123, 153, 161, 226, 271, 291, 305, 309, 310, 373, 374
Global warming, 57–60, 62, 66–69, 180, 183, 186–188, 196, 197, 203, 212, 218, 232
Greenhouse gases (GHGs), 58, 59, 61, 62, 64, 181, 183, 185, 187, 191–194, 198–203
Green New Deal, 70, 80, 216, 217
Growth, 4, 5, 11, 12, 15–27, 17n9, 19n10, 34, 49, 51, 55, 75, 86, 89–93, 123, 134–144, 146–150, 152–165, 167, 168, 186, 191, 192, 194, 195, 198, 200, 201, 208, 218, 227, 231, 235, 249, 256, 258, 286, 296, 346, 350, 352, 376, 377

H

Harvey, M., 351, 354–356, 368, 375
Hayek, F., 47, 48, 51, 55, 253, 260, 261, 348, 349
Household debt, 13

Human capital, 115, 143, 158, 160, 162, 167, 181, 384
Human development, 271–280, 307, 313–315
Human development approach (HDA), 270
Hungary, 119, 204, 237, 262, 323

I

Inclusive growth, 27
Inequality, 14, 27, 44, 54–57, 81, 87, 89–97, 133–168, 231, 252, 259, 261, 274n1, 277, 277n3, 283–285, 288, 289, 293–296, 306, 345–347, 351–369, 371–374, 377, 379, 382–384
Inequality of income, 53, 57, 86, 123, 134, 368
Inequality of wealth, 53, 57, 134
Informal work, 376–377
Institutionalist political economy, 270, 281
Intangible assets, 162, 226n1
Integrated assessment models (IAMs), 186, 191–195, 201
Interest rates, 10, 12–14, 12n6, 20, 22n15, 23–25, 27, 33, 75, 140, 145, 147, 152, 157, 163, 164, 188, 202, 213, 241
Intergovernmental Panel on Climate Change (IPCC), 57–59, 182, 187, 195, 200, 202, 203, 211, 212
International economic law, 346, 370, 371
International Labour Organization (ILO), 114, 204, 298, 327, 372–374, 380–381
International migration, 97, 100
International Monetary Fund (IMF), 1, 3, 7–9, 11, 13–15, 17, 17n9, 18, 20–27, 31n22, 33–35, 34n25, 48, 55, 74, 75, 90, 91, 140, 141, 156, 227, 230–232, 237, 349
Investment, 4, 6, 6n3, 21, 22, 22n14, 27, 54, 55, 59, 70, 79–81, 92, 106, 112, 115, 134, 135, 137, 139–152, 155–158, 162–167, 186, 189, 190, 192, 197, 199, 201, 202, 206, 207, 209–215, 214n27, 218, 226, 227, 231–233, 235, 236, 241, 244, 246, 251, 256, 257, 283, 286, 289, 296, 304, 347, 370, 371, 375, 383–385
Investment banking, 6, 10, 31
Italy, 19, 62, 231, 286n4, 299, 323, 327, 331, 367

J

Japan, 8, 13, 15n7, 62, 63, 77, 319, 323, 327, 331, 367

K

Keynes, J. M., 47–49, 71, 77, 78, 165
Kuznets curve, 353

L

Labour laws, 347–350, 354, 356, 362, 367, 370, 371, 376, 379–380
Liikanen Report, 7

M

Macroprudential policies, 3, 27, 28, 33
Mainstream economics, 65, 71, 186–187, 217, 218, 228, 247, 252, 253, 256
Market failure, 65, 66, 70, 144, 164–166, 180
MERCOSUR, 111
Microprudential policies, 3
Milanovic, B., 43, 352, 373, 374
Minimum wages, 152, 153, 276n2, 347, 372, 374, 375, 377–379, 384
Minsky, H., 17, 24–26
Mobility of capital, 85
Mobility of labour, 86, 100, 101, 112, 114
Modern Monetary Theory (MMT), 77–79
Monetary policy, 1, 11, 17, 19, 19n11, 20, 22n15, 23, 25, 26, 28–33, 30n19, 31n22, 72, 146, 147, 157
Mont Pelerin Society, 47
Municipalism, 228, 254

N

Natural capital, 181–183
Neo-classical economics, 108
Neoliberal economics, 46, 48, 71, 76, 179, 180, 184, 188, 259
Neoliberalism, 34, 35, 45–52, 55, 56, 70–79, 81, 85, 87–89, 99, 184, 231, 232, 237, 260, 262
Neoliberal policy hegemony, 239, 385
Net-zero greenhouse gas emissions, 198–200
Non-standard work, 376
Nordhaus, W., 61, 62, 69, 186–188, 186n8, 191–196
North, D., 277, 281
Norway, 57, 114, 161, 257, 286n4, 303n18, 323, 327, 331
Nuclear power, 234
Nussbaum, M., 271, 277, 279

O

OECD, 90, 93, 106, 143, 145–147, 152, 156, 164, 211, 229, 237, 271, 288, 291n8, 296, 296n12, 299, 300, 303, 303n18, 304, 316–319, 323, 327, 331, 336, 368, 376, 383

P

Paris Agreement, 59–63, 179, 180, 183, 187, 212n25, 214
Piketty, T., 227n1, 286, 299, 352, 358, 368, 372–374
Polanyi, K., 350
Populism, 45, 64, 227, 231
Post-Keynesian economics, 180
Precarious work, 376
Private Finance Initiative (PFI), 236, 236n7
Privatisation, 46, 48, 52, 53, 184, 226–239, 252, 253, 259, 261–263, 380
Productivity, 14, 21, 55, 89, 99, 104, 105, 107, 133–168, 252, 286, 352

Public debt, 74–76, 78, 286
Public goods, 61, 62, 65, 66, 107, 109, 113, 347, 351, 356, 358, 372, 377, 383, 385
Public ownership, 48, 225–263
Public sector development, 270, 271, 280–288, 290, 306
Public services, 48, 87, 108–109, 120, 123, 163, 237, 252, 262, 289, 295, 306

Q

Quantitative easing, 10, 152, 157, 163

R

Rail industry, 227
Rail privatisation, 232
Rawls, J., 272, 274–275, 277
Reagan, R., 48, 51, 52
Remunicipalisation, 228, 236–241
Rent seeking, 233, 259
Retail banking, 6, 10, 31
Retain-and-reinvest, 150
Risk-weighted assets (RWA), 7, 9, 9n4

S

Schumpeter, J., 55
Schumpeterian economics, 180
Sectoral collective bargaining, 357, 377–379, 384
Sen, A., 271, 277, 279, 280, 306
Shadow banking, 4, 9, 11, 28
Shareholder value, 44, 53, 54, 56, 235
Short termism, 140, 147, 157, 226
Skills, 86, 88, 95, 98, 99, 99n3, 103–105, 117, 121, 122, 148, 150, 152, 158–160, 162, 164, 167, 181, 205, 233, 254, 281–283, 309
Socio-cultural concerns, 88
Sovereign wealth funds, 227, 236, 257
Stakeholder capitalism, 45, 54, 70
State intervention, 165, 185, 228, 230, 260
Superstar firms, 142, 156, 159, 160, 165
Sweden, 119, 233, 286, 286n4, 294, 294n9, 299, 300, 303n18, 323
Systems of well-being, 284, 304–311
Systems varieties literature (SVL), 270, 281, 312

T

Taxation systems, 105
Tax avoidance, 369–371, 383
Tax havens, 161, 369, 370, 383
Temporary nationalisations, 227
Thatcher, M., 48, 51, 52, 81, 229, 262, 381
Third Way, 237, 239
Time, 3n1, 5, 12, 15, 16, 21, 24, 26, 28, 48, 50, 56, 57, 59, 63–65, 68, 71, 72, 74–76, 79, 80, 87–92, 94, 97, 104, 108, 110, 113, 115–118, 120, 134, 138, 141, 146–148, 153, 160, 163, 164, 167, 183, 184, 186–191,

193, 195, 196, 201, 203, 206, 209–211, 213, 214, 217, 225, 226, 226n1, 231, 236, 237, 241, 245, 246, 249, 250, 253, 257, 258, 262, 270, 271, 275–278, 280, 282, 285, 287–289, 291, 296–306, 296n11, 296n13, 309, 312, 332–336, 347, 349, 351–356, 358, 362, 368–370, 376, 377, 381
Trade unions, 46, 48, 52, 120, 152, 153, 160–162, 354, 356, 373, 380
Trickle-down economics, 53

U

Uncertainty, 18, 19n10, 19n11, 20, 21, 25, 26, 26n17, 44, 67–69, 74, 102, 115, 139–141, 147, 148, 180, 183, 187, 194–197, 208–210, 214, 217, 218, 261, 262, 281
Unconventional monetary policy, 147, 157
United Kingdom (UK), v, 2, 6–7, 10, 13, 14, 16, 20, 21, 25, 27, 30, 30n21, 51, 52, 62, 68, 79, 80, 86, 89, 91–97, 99, 103, 105n4, 107, 115, 116, 118–121, 123–125, 133, 135–139, 141–143, 145–153, 155, 157–163, 191n14, 205, 205n22, 207, 214, 216, 227, 229, 230, 232–235, 234n5, 236n7, 239, 243, 251–253, 252n11, 256, 262, 263, 271, 285–287, 286n4, 289, 289n6, 291, 294, 294n10, 296, 296n11, 296n12, 297, 297n14, 297n15, 299, 299n16, 300, 303, 303n18, 303n19, 304, 308–312, 308n22, 323, 351, 354, 355, 357, 367, 369, 378, 379, 381
United States-Mexico-Canada Agreement, 111
United States of America (USA), 4–6, 11–13, 15–18, 15n7, 17–18n9, 20, 22, 22n14, 23, 25, 32, 44, 45, 47, 50–53, 55, 57, 62–64, 67, 71, 78, 80, 94, 95, 106, 108, 111, 118, 135–137, 140–143, 146, 147, 151, 153–155, 159, 162, 164, 179, 216, 217, 238, 239, 248, 283, 285, 286, 288, 289, 291, 296, 303n19, 323, 352, 355, 356, 367–369, 375, 378–381, 383
Universal Basic Income (UBI), 271, 304–312
Universal Basic Services (UBS), 306, 310

V

van Parijs, P., 271, 272, 274
Varieties of Capitalism (VoC), 281–283
Vickers Report, 6–7
Volker Rule, 4

W

Wage policies, 345–385
Wage share of income, 92
Washington Consensus, 226
Welfare-As-Freedom (WAF), 269–336
Welfare states, 48, 97, 108, 123, 270–272, 274, 287, 307, 309, 310, 313–315, 353, 356, 358
Welfare State Varieties (WSV), 270, 281, 282
Welfare systems, 106–107, 269, 281, 282, 351
Well-being, 88, 134, 158, 162, 181, 182, 188, 269, 270, 276, 283, 301, 302, 304–311, 368
World Bank, 34n25, 35, 48, 55, 75, 193, 230, 231, 237, 347, 349, 350, 353
World Trade Organization (WTO), 49, 109, 110, 370

Y

Yield curve, 12, 12n6, 13, 20, 30n19, 71

Z

Zombie firms, 143, 145–147, 156, 167

The manufacturer's authorised representative in the EU is Springer Nature Customer Service Centre GmbH, Europaplatz 3, 69115 Heidelberg, Germany. If you have any concerns regarding our products, please contact ProductSafety@springernature.com

Printed and bound by CPI Group (UK) Ltd, Croydon, CR0 4YY

30/09/2026

02225696-0006